# FAST CASTLE

## EXCAVATIONS 1971–86

**KEITH L MITCHELL, K ROBIN MURDOCH & JOHN R WARD**

with

**HUGH P DINWOODIE & HUGH G ROBERTSON**

**FOREWORD by DAVID H CALDWELL**

Contributions by

Stuart W Allan, Lin P D Barnetson, Trevor Cowie, Valerie E Dean, Geoffrey Egan, Thea Gabra-Sanders, Dennis B Gallagher, George Haggarty, Ywonne Hallén, David Heppel, Nicholas McQ Holmes, Fraser Hunter, Sarah Jennings, Mary Kennaway, Graeme Lawson, Diane Mitchell, Jackie Moran, Frances Pritchard, Nigel A Ruckley, Bill Russell, Michael L Ryder, Clare Thomas and Paul Wilthew

Illustrations

Valerie E Dean, K Robin Murdoch and Marion O'Neil
with Trevor Cowie, Dennis B Gallagher, Diane Mitchell, Eric Robertson, David Simon, Clare Thomas, John Wallender and John R Ward

**EDINBURGH ARCHAEOLOGICAL FIELD SOCIETY**

EDINBURGH 2001

This report is published with the aid of a generous grant in the form of a
Glenfiddich Living Scotland Award

---

Illustration of the report has been assisted by a
generous grant from the Society of Antiquaries of Scotland.

---

Copyright 2001 Edinburgh Archaeological Field Society

All rights reserved. No part of this publication may be reproduced in any form by any means,
electronic, mechanical, photocopying, recording or otherwise without the prior permission
of the Edinburgh Archaeological Field Society.

**ISBN 0 9513156 2 5**

Digitally printed by Transcolour (Scotland) Ltd, Edinburgh
Tel. 0131-316-4500

## CONTENTS

|  |  | Page |
|---|---|---|
|  | List of Black and White Illustrations | v |
|  | List of Colour Plates | vii |
|  | Charts and Tables | ix |
|  | Acknowledgements | xi |
|  | **Foreword**<br>Dr David H Caldwell | xv |
| 1 | Introduction | 1 |
| 2 | **History**<br>Mary Kennaway | 6 |
| 3 | **Geology**<br>Nigel A Ruckley | 7 |
| 4 | The Excavations | 13 |
|  | 4.1 **The Lower Courtyard** | 13 |
|  | 4.1.1 The Outer Lower Courtyard: Keith L Mitchell & K Robin Murdoch | 18 |
|  | 4.1.2 The Inner Lower Courtyard: John R Ward | 22 |
|  | 4.2 **The Kitchen:** K Robin Murdoch | 29 |
|  | 4.3 **The Well:** John R Ward | 35 |
| 5 | The Finds | 45 |
|  | 5.1 **Numismatica** (Coins & Jetons): Nicholas McQ Holmes | 45 |
|  | 5.2 **Ceramics:** Valerie E Dean & Hugh G Robertson; Trevor Cowie; Sarah Jennings & George Haggarty | 51 |
|  | 5.3 **Glass & Window Lead:** K Robin Murdoch | 81 |
|  | 5.4 **Pipe-clay Figurines**: Thea Gabra-Sanders | 88 |
|  | 5.5 **Enamelled Gold Button:** Keith L Mitchell & Hugh P Dinwoodie | 89 |
|  | 5.6 **Copper Alloy:** Fraser Hunter; Thea Gabra-Sanders; Keith L Mitchell & Hugh P Dinwoodie | 90 |
|  | 5.7 **Lead:** Keith L Mitchell & Hugh P Dinwoodie | 96 |
|  | 5.8 **Pewter**: Keith L Mitchell & Hugh P Dinwoodie | 97 |

|  |  |  | Page |
|---|---|---|---|
| | 5.9 | **Iron:** Hugh P Dinwoodie & Keith L Mitchell | 99 |
| | 5.10 | **Ordnance:** Stuart W Allan | 109 |
| | 5.11 | **Musical Relics:** Graeme Lawson | 114 |
| | 5.12 | **Amber, Jet, & Opal:** Jackie Moran; Fraser Hunter & Bill Russell; Diane Mitchell | 117 |
| | 5.13 | **Textiles (and associated objects):** Thea Gabra-Sanders & Michael L Ryder: Frances Pritchard, Geoffrey Egan | 125 |
| | 5.14 | **Leather:** Clare Thomas | 138 |
| | 5.15 | **Wood:** Keith L Mitchell & Hugh P Dinwoodie | 143 |
| | 5.16 | **Worked Bone:** Ywonne Hallén (with addendum by Fraser Hunter) | 147 |
| | 5.17 | **Faunal Remains:** Lin P D Barnetson | 152 |
| | 5.18 | **Other Organic Material:** Keith L Mitchell & Hugh P Dinwoodie | 167 |
| | 5.19 | **Clay Tobacco Pipes:** Dennis B Gallagher | 167 |
| | 5.20 | **Shells:** Keith L Mitchell & Hugh P Dinwoodie; David Heppell | 169 |
| | 5.21 | **Stone:** Fraser Hunter, Alan Saville, K Robin Murdoch; Keith L Mitchell & Hugh P Dinwoodie | 169 |
| | 5.22 | **Coal, Charcoal, & Cinder:** Keith L Mitchell & Hugh P Dinwoodie | 176 |
| | 5.23 | **Slag:** Keith L Mitchell & Hugh P Dinwoodie | 177 |
| 6 | **Discussion** | | 178 |
| 7 | **Appendices** | | 183 |
| | 7.1 | **The Gold Button:** Keith L Mitchell & Hugh P Dinwoodie; Diane Mitchell, K Robin Murdoch, Paul Wilthew | 183 |
| | 7.2 | **Water Supply to Coastal Castles:** Nigel A Ruckley | 195 |
| | 7.3 | **The Caves:** Hugh P Dinwoodie, Keith L Mitchell & K Robin Murdoch | 200 |
| | 7.4 | **The Crane:** Hugh P Dinwoodie, Keith L Mitchell & K Robin Murdoch | 202 |
| 8 | **Glossary** | | 205 |
| 9 | **References** | | 208 |

## LIST OF BLACK AND WHITE ILLUSTRATIONS

| | | | Page |
|---|---|---|---|
| 1 | Map of East Scotland | | 2 |
| 2 | Map of East Lothian and Berwickshire coast | | 2 |
| 3 | Map of Fast Castle and environs | | 2 |
| 4 | Fast Castle: c1820s | | 4 |
| 5 | Fast Castle in the 1970s | | 4 |
| 6 | Fast Castle: 1549 plan | | 5 |
| 7 | Plan of existing ruins | | 14 |
| 8 | Lower Courtyard: Excavation areas | | 15 |
| 9 | Plan of Lower Courtyard and Kitchen | | 16 |
| 10 | Courtyard: | Room 1 | 19 |
| 11 | | Outer rampart | 19 |
| 12 | | S part (area 1) | 19 |
| 13 | | W-E section | 21 |
| 14 | Quarry pit: | Quarry access | 24 |
| 15 | | Roofing tiles | 24 |
| 16 | | Excavation completed | 24 |
| 17 | | Enclosure wall | 24 |
| 18 | | Recess | 24 |
| 19 | | E-W section | 26 |
| 20 | | S-N section | 27 |
| 21 | Kitchen: | Main hearth and SE corner | 30 |
| 22 | | S wall with drain | 30 |
| 23 | | Plan | 31 |
| 24 | | S-N section through doorway | 31 |
| 25 | | W-E section | 33 |
| 26 | | Elevation of N wall and doorway | 33 |
| 27 | | Drain | 33 |
| 28 | Well: | Plan | 37 |
| 29 | | Section | 37 |
| 30 | | Well-head | 39 |
| 31 | Coin | James IV half plack | 46 |
| 32 | Pottery: | Iron age | 55 |
| 33 | | Scottish, Medieval and later, Groups C, D, E | 68 |
| 34 | | Scottish, Medieval and later, Group E | 69 |
| 35 | | Scottish, Medieval and later, Groups F, G | 70 |
| 36 | | Imported wares | 75 |
| 37 | Ceramic tiles | | 79 |
| 38 | Glass and Window lead | | 82 |
| 39 | Pipeclay: | Madonna & child; figurine legs | 88 |

| | | Page |
|---|---|---|
| 40 | Enamelled gold button | 89 |
| 41-43 | Copper Alloy | 90-1, 94 |
| 44 | Lead weight | 96 |
| 45 | Pilgrim's badge | 97 |
| 46-51 | Iron | 103-4, 106-8 |
| 52-54 | Ordnance | 109, 111-12 |
| 55 | Jew's harp | 114 |
| 56 | Music wire | 115 |
| 57 | Jet and Amber | 118 |
| 58-60 | Opal | 123-4 |
| 61-63 | Wool cloth | 125-6 |
| 64-65 | Silk braid | 128 |
| 66 | Spindlewhorls | 136 |
| 67 | Lead cloth seal | 137 |
| 68-69 | Leather | 138-9 |
| 70-73 | Wood | 143-6 |
| 74-77 | Worked bone | 147-9, 152 |
| 78 | Bone pathology | 154 |
| 79 | Bone trauma | 155 |
| 80 | Clay pipes | 168 |
| 81-85 | Stone | 170-1, 173-4 |
| 86-96 | Appendix 7.1: Gold Button | 183-4, 187-9, 192 |
| 97 | Appendix 7.3: Cave | 201 |
| 98 | End of Excavation | 204 |

## LIST OF COLOUR PLATES

|  |  | Page |
|---|---|---|
| I | Fast Castle: view from Telegraph Hill | 9 |
| II | Fast Castle: aerial view | 9 |
| III | Fast Castle: the present ruins | 10 |
| IV | Reconstruction of the castle by David Simon | 10 |
| V-VI | Quarry pit, during excavation | 11 |
| VII | Kitchen entrance | 12 |
| VIII | Well, and adjacent wall foundation | 12 |
| IX | Gold button | 41 |
| X-XII | Scottish medieval and later pottery | 42-3 |
| XIII | Opal | 44 |
| XIV | Iron grille | 44 |
| XV-XVI | Wood | 44 |

Front cover: Aerial view of Fast Castle from the north-east (by courtesy of Denis Harding)

Rear cover: Entrance to the castle from the landward (EAFS)

## CHARTS

| | | Page |
|---|---|---|
| Chart 1 | Ceramics: all fabrics: Sherd, Weight and Vessel Percentages | 51 |
| Chart 2 | Ceramics: all fabrics: Percentages by Period: Period II | 54 |
| Chart 3 | Ceramics: all fabrics: Percentages by Period: Period II-III | 54 |
| Chart 4 | Ceramics: all fabrics: Percentages by Period: Period III | 54 |
| Chart 5 | Ceramics: all fabrics: Percentages by Period: Period III-IV | 54 |
| Chart 6 | Ceramics: all fabrics: Percentages by Period: Period IV | 54 |
| Chart 7 | Ceramics: all fabrics: Percentages by Period: Unstratified deposits | 54 |
| Chart 8 | Ceramics: all fabrics: Percentages by Period: The well | 54 |
| Chart 9 | Scottish medieval and later Pottery: Sherd, Weight and Vessel Percentages | 56 |
| Chart 10 | Distribution of fibre diameters | 133 |
| Chart 11 | Changes in fibre diameter distribution during fleece evolution | 133 |
| Chart 12 | Sheep Calcanea, all periods: Greatest length in mm | 165 |
| Chart 13 | Sheep Horncores, all periods: Base circumference in mm | 165 |
| Chart 14 | Cattle Astragali, all periods: Lateral length in mm | 165 |
| Chart 15 | Sheep Tibiae, Period II: Distal breadth in mm | 165 |
| Chart 16 | Sheep Tibiae, Period III: Distal breadth in mm | 165 |
| Chart 17 | Sheep Tibiae, Period IV: Distal breadth in mm | 165 |

## TABLES

| | | |
|---|---|---|
| Table 1 | Ceramics: distribution of fabrics | 52-3 |
| Table 2 | Glass composition | 84 |
| Table 3 | Window lead | 87 |
| Table 4 | Nail length | 100 |
| Table 5 | Gunshot | 110 |
| Table 6 | Medieval jet & related materials in Scotland | 120 |
| Table 7 | Jet: elements detected in XRF analyses | 121 |
| Table 8 | Catalogue of wool cloth fragments, all woven in tabby weave from single ply yarn | 127 |
| Table 9 | The kinds of wool in relation to the cloth samples | 130 |
| Table 10 | Textiles: fibre diameters in microns | 132 |
| Table 11 | Percentage of different fleece types found | 134 |
| Table 12 | Spindle whorls: catalogue, with description and dimensions | 136 |
| Table 13 | Leather: hair follicle analysis | 141 |
| Table 14 | Faunal remains: range of species and number of fragments | 164 |
| Table 15 | Faunal remains: sheep, MNI and epiphyseal fusion | 166 |
| Table 16 | Faunal remains: cattle, MNI and epiphyseal fusion | 166 |
| Table 17 | Faunal remains: sheep mandibles with *in situ* dentition | 167 |
| Table 18 | Context analysis of clay tobacco pipe fragments | 168 |
| Table 19 | Iron Age and Roman finds from Fast Castle | 178 |
| Table 20 | Gold button: results of the SEM and XRF studies | 194 |

# ACKNOWLEDGEMENTS

Generous financial support is gratefully acknowledged from two principal sources, William Grant & Sons Ltd, and the Society of Antiquaries of Scotland.

The Edinburgh Archaeological Field Society received a Glenfiddich Living Scotland Award in 1995. The award was made to assist towards costs involved in publishing the Fast Castle Excavation Report.

The Glenfiddich Living Scotland Awards scheme was established in 1985 by William Grant & Sons Ltd, one of the last independent, family owned and managed, whisky companies in Scotland, to promote and conserve Scotland's history, heritage, traditions and countryside. Since its formation many projects, covering almost every part of Scotland, have been assisted by a Glenfiddich Living Scotland Award.

\* \* \* \* \* \* \* \*

The Edinburgh Archaeological Field Society also received grants from the Society of Antiquaries of Scotland, in 1993 and 1994, to assist in costs involved in the preparation of illustrations.

The Society of Antiquaries of Scotland, founded in 1780, is the second oldest antiquarian society in Britain. In line with its main purpose '...*the Study of the Antiquities and History of Scotland, more particularly by means of archaeological research...*', the Society grant-aids all aspects of archaeological and historical research from its Research Funds, which include monies from the Dorothy Marshall and Angus Graham bequests.

Further information on the various grants and necessary application forms are obtainable from: The Director, The Society of Antiquaries of Scotland, Royal Museum of Scotland, Chambers Street, Edinburgh EH1 1JF.

\* \* \* \* \* \* \* \*

The Edinburgh Archaeological Field Society received a grant from the Pasold Research Fund towards prior publication of the textile report, which is reproduced here with minor alterations

\* \* \* \* \* \* \* \*

Donations were also received from the Atomic Energy Authority, Torness; Berwickshire District Council; and from anonymous sources. All grants and donations are gratefully acknowledged

\* \* \* \* \* \* \* \*

The Society is deeply grateful to the landowners, Mr Frank Usher, of Dunglass estate, and Mr Tom Dykes, of Redheugh Farm, without whose generous co-operation the excavation could not have been completed. As the site was scheduled in 1976 by the Historic Buildings and Monuments Commission, we are indebted to them for supporting the continuing excavation. Very considerable thanks also go to the staff of the National Museums of Scotland, in particular David Caldwell and Jackie Moran, without whose friendly help and encouragement the post-excavation work would have been significantly delayed. Thanks are due for the conservation work on the Fast Castle finds over many years, by Tom Bryce and his staff at the National Museums of Scotland, and also the photographic department. Members of the Museum staff, gave freely of their time and expertise, in advice and in preparation of specialist reports. Particular thanks are due to Dorothy Laing and her colleagues at the former Society of Antiquaries of Scotland Library in Queen Street.

## DIRECTION

The excavation from 1971 was directed by Keith Mitchell and Eric Robertson until 1973 when Keith moved to leading Historical Research (completed in 1992). Between 1982 and 1986 Keith Mitchell, Robin Murdoch, and John Ward shared the responsibility of supervision. The post-excavation work from 1986 until 1998 has been directed by Keith Mitchell. The editorial team for the Excavation Report, under the direction of John Ward, was: Hugh Dinwoodie, Keith Mitchell, Robin Murdoch, and Hugh Robertson.

## PARTICIPANTS

Thanks are due to over 200 people who contributed, at some time or other, to the excavation, historical research, and post-excavation work relating to this site. Any attempt to list all who took part will inevitably contain errors and omissions, for which apologies are offered. Nevertheless, it is felt that the attempt should be made, as this work could not have been completed without them.

### Excavation

D & G Adams, Helen Aitken, Mary Alexander, Peter Allen, Alister Anderson, R Beveridge, Irene Bramwell, J Brown, Kevin Brown, J Brownlee, W J Buchan, Lawrence Buckley, William Buckley, Janice Burns, David Burrows, Patricia Cairney, David Caldwell, Ralph Caldwell, Ruth Caldwell, Robin Callander, Shirley Cameron, B Campbell, Elaine Campbell, R Campbell, Maurice Carmichael, Jackie Clark, D Cowell, R Craig, Mike Curtis, C Cuthbert, John Cuthbert, N Cuthbert, Valerie Dean, A G Dickinson, Mrs Dickinson, Mrs Dickson, N Dickson, Stephen Dickson, R Dundas, L Dunning, C Durie, Bill Ellen, Dorothy Ellen, E Ellet, Maureen Erasmusson, Bill Fernie, W Fietz, Caroline Friend, Gillian Friend, Dennis B Gallagher, E E Gardiner (Gee), Margaret Gardiner, M Gerry, Sheila Glendinning, William Gowans, Mrs Gowland, Ian Graham, Kirsty Grant, A Gray, Eric Greenhill, John Griffen, George Haggarty, Val Hanlon, L Haywood, N Higgs, Stuart Holliday, Charlie Hoy, Miss D Hunter, George Hunter, Janice James, H Jordan, C Kelly, M Kird, John Laxton, David Lowson, S Lowson, Ian MacDonald, Margaret Macdonald, R MacDonald, I MacDowall, D M McGregor, Vannan McKellar, William MacLean, Archie McLellan, C MacRae, G Marshall, Esmeralda Mead, Margaret R Meikle, Martin Millar, Martin Milne, Michele Mingo, David Mitchell, Diane Mitchell, Fiona Mitchell, Helen Mitchell, Robin Muir, Maureen Murdoch, Neil Murdoch, Anne Murray, John Murray, Richard Newmark, Norman Nicholas, Keith Otto, Leslie Oxbrow, Louise C Parker, Denise Percival, Kay Porche, Theresa Powell, Peter Raison, Ian Ramsay, James Reid, Jane Reid, J Riddell, Craig Robertson, Dan Robertson, David Robertson, Graeme Robertson, Hugh Robertson, S Robinson, A Rolland, Bill Russell, Stewart Russell, David Simon, Mr Small, Janet Small, Michael Small, Neil Small, Elizabeth Smith, G Smith, Jane Smith, Leslie Smith, David Stanger, Alison Stewart, M Stewart, Mrs Stirling, James Stobie, May Strachan, Jill Strobridge, A Swan, Lockhart Taylor, T Thomson, N Thorpe, J Tome, J Torrie, Roddy Tulloch, Trevor Turner, J Waddell, Colin Wallace, Philip Wallace, D Ward, Elizabeth Ward, J Wardell, F Watt, Wendy Watt, D Webster, Moira White, S Williamson, Fiona Wilson, A Wolff, Gillian Wood, Joan Wood, Neil Young and W Young. Also, from 16th Battalion RAOC: Capt. Richard Powell, Lt. Adrian Ashby-Smith, L/Cpl Alan Cotterill, L/Cpl Kevin Roberts, Pte Marian Arlett WRAC, Pte Hilary Atherton WRAC, Pte Maureen Sammons WRAC, Pte Sam Sampson, Pte Colin Smith and Pte Kevin Taylor.

### Historical Research

Helen Aitken, Bill Baptie, Sid Boyd, David Caldwell, Maurice Carmichael, Eleanor Connolly, June Davidson, Valerie Dean, Chris Dallman, Jennifer Dunbar, Dorothy Ellen, E E Gardiner (Gee), Mary Kennaway, Helen Mitchell, Chris Paxton, Duncan Paxton, Dan Robertson, Hugh G Robertson, David Simon, Denis Smith, Jill Strobridge, John Ward and Donald Whitehead.

### Post-Excavation

Stuart Allan, Brian Bleakley, June Davidson, Hugh Dinwoodie, Chris Dallman, Valerie Dean, Sandra Fordyce, Colin Govier, Sophie Hague, Lindsay Hamilton, Dave Jones, Robert McClelland, Ian MacLean, Jennie MacKay, Clare Nicol, Hugh Robertson, Bill Russell and John Scott.

### Contributors and Advisers

Stuart Allan, Allan Armstrong, Lin Barnetson, Brett Beddoe-Stephens, Petra van Boheemen, Tom Bryce, Charles Burnett, David Caldwell, David Chamberlain, John Cherry, Mark Collard, Trevor Cowie, George Dalgleish, Valerie Dean, Hugh Dinwoodie, Geoffrey Egan, Thea Gabra-Sanders, Dennis Gallagher, George Haggarty, Yvonne Hallén, David Heppel, Nicholas Holmes, Fraser Hunter, Sarah Jennings, Mary Kennaway, Graeme Lawson, Rosalind Marshall, Diane Mitchell, Keith Mitchell, Lisa Monnas, Jackie Moran, Robin Murdoch, Marion O'Neil, Nigel Ruckley, Michael Ryder, Theo Skinner, Mike Spearman, Brian Spencer, Sheana Stephen, Clare Thomas, John Wallace, Tam Ward and Paul Wilthew.

EAFS also wishes to acknowledge the willing assistance given by British Geological Survey, Historic Scotland, Meteorological Office Climatological Service (Scotland), and the Royal Commission on Ancient and Historical Monuments in Scotland.

**Illustrations**

Illustrations are acknowledged as follows

Denis Harding; Cover and Plate II

Marion O'Neill; Illus 41, 43-52, 54-57, 66, 71-72, 74-75, 77, 81-86

Valerie Dean; Illus 33-35, 37

Robin Murdoch; Illus 1-3, 8-9, 13, 19-20, 23-26, 38, 70

John Ward; Illus 28-29

David Simon; Illus 53, 73, Plate IV

Trevor Cowie; Illus 32

Denis Gallagher; Illus 80

Clare Thomas; Illus 68-69

John Wallender; Illus 36

Photographic Department of the National Museums of Scotland; Illus 31, 39-40, 42, 61-65, 67, 76, 78-79, 87, Plates IX-XIII

EAFS photographic archive; Illus 5, 10-12, 14-18, 21-22, 27, 30, 97-98, Plates I, III, V-VIII, XIV-XVI

Illus 7 is reproduced by courtesy of the Royal Commission on Ancient and Historic Monuments of Scotland, with minor amendments and additions by Robin Murdoch

Illus 6 is reproduced by courtesy of the Duke of Rutland

Scanning facilities were provided by Valerie Dean, Lamond Laing, Keith Mitchell, Robin Murdoch and Alan Wills

Desk-top publication was carried out by Lamond Laing and Robin Murdoch, to whom the Society is much indebted.

DISPOSAL OF FINDS AND DOCUMENTS

The finds, with a full register of published material, have been deposited in the Royal Museum of Scotland, Chambers Street, Edinburgh. The complete archive, including unpublished material, site records, catalogues and specialist reports and documents, will be deposited at the National Monuments Record for Scotland, (RCAHMS), John Sinclair House, Bernard Terrace, Edinburgh

# FOREWORD

## Dr David H Caldwell

Fast Castle is one of the most remarkable castles in Scotland. Anyone who has visited it is unlikely to forget in a hurry that feeling of awe engendered by its isolation, its precarious setting on a sheer-sided rock jutting into the North Sea, and its rugged, romantic beauty. The excavations which are the subject of this book are themselves a remarkable achievement, the outcome of considerable effort by a dedicated band of amateurs over a great number of years. The excavators may have been amateurs but the results are certainly not amateurish.

My knowledge of the work at Fast Castle goes back to the early 1970s when I joined the staff of the National Museums of Antiquities of Scotland. Eric Robertson was a regular visitor, bringing in finds from the dig for identification and conservation. We soon became friends, and through Eric I was introduced to the other main players, Robin Murdoch and Keith Mitchell. I eventually made the trip down to the excavations where I could not but be impressed by the dedication and care of the team, Sunday after Sunday. The work was soon to be of added interest to me as I started excavating the neighbouring Eyemouth Fort, also occupied by an English garrison in the late 1540s.

Professional archaeologists are expected to publish their excavations speedily, preferably within months rather than years. This amateur society, however, has taken fifteen years since digging stopped to produce this monograph. I have never doubted that the work would be done and that it would be of a professional standard. I have witnessed much of the effort that has gone into it, week after week of the whole period since 1986 as a small band, including Hugh Robertson and Hugh Dinwoodie, committed every Thursday to come to the Museum and work on the finds. Under the leadership of Keith Mitchell the attention to detail has been meticulous. No question – as I soon learnt the hard way! – was left unasked in an endeavour to produce the best possible answers. It is clear to me that the long haul has been well worthwhile, that much more has been achieved than would have been possible by a rush into print. There will be many professionals who will envy the team's generous time-scale, the added scope for reflection, allowed for in the preparation of this book.

The Edinburgh Archaeological Field Society is fortunate that the archaeological site in which they have invested so much has been shown to be well worth the effort. The following pages do not just contain much of interest about Fast Castle itself, but also information about important assemblages of well stratified and dated medieval finds. The publication of these will have a considerable bearing on our understanding of medieval Scotland and the interpretation of finds from other sites.

The excavation of Fast Castle shows what amateurs can achieve for the advancement of archaeology in Scotland. The Edinburgh Archaeological Field Society has now broadened out its field of interests, undertaking fieldwork and research elsewhere in Scotland, and several of its members have become much valued archaeological practitioners and specialists. I hope others will draw inspiration from this solid achievement.

# FAST CASTLE EXCAVATIONS

## 1971-86

### KEITH L MITCHELL, K ROBIN MURDOCH, & JOHN R WARD

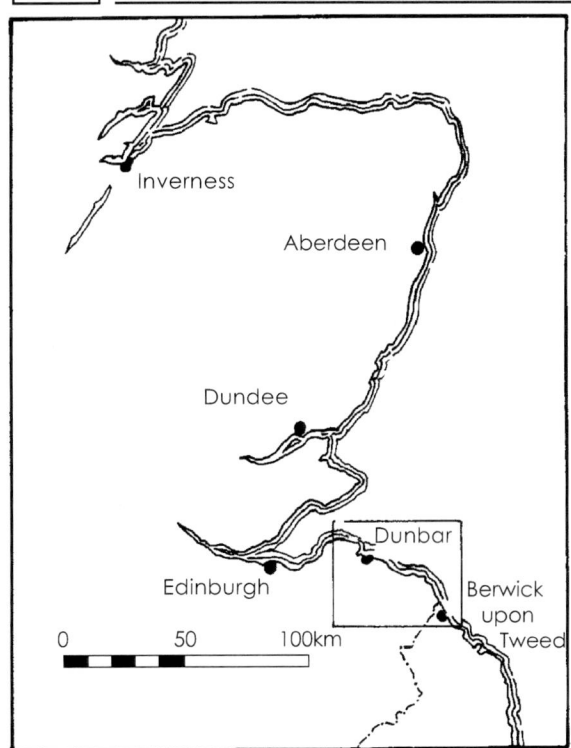

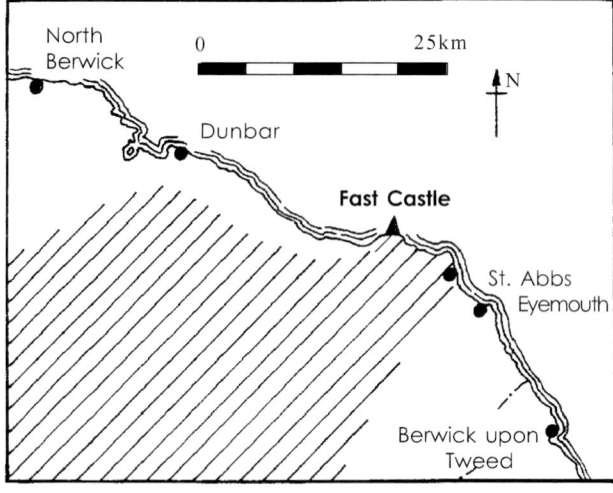

**Illus 2** East Lothian and Berwickshire coast, Lammermuir Hills shaded

**Illus 1** East Scotland

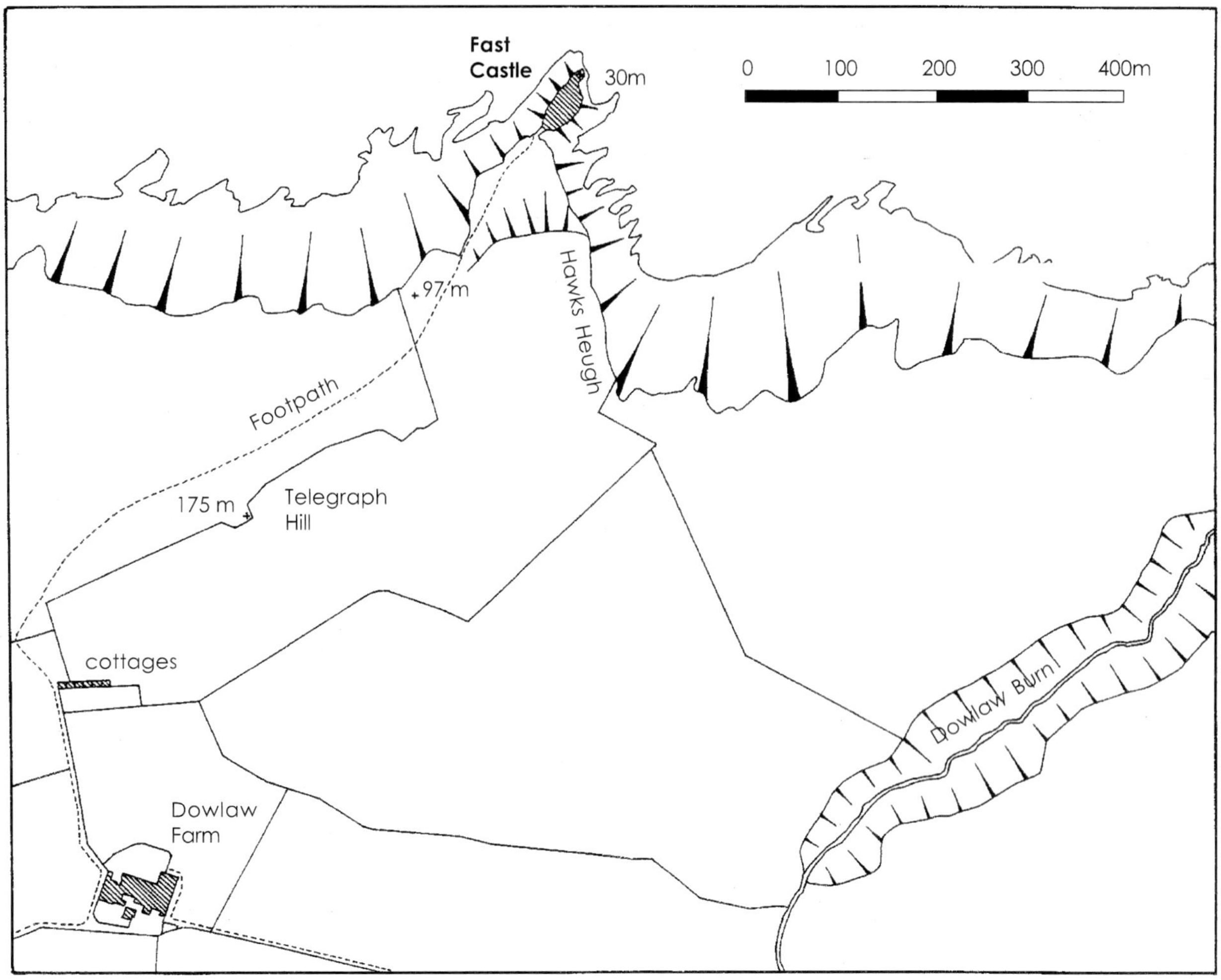

**Illus 3** Fast Castle and its environs, spot heights shown (based on O.S. 1:2500 map, 1908 edition)

# 1 INTRODUCTION

The ruins of Fast Castle, Coldingham parish, Berwickshire (NGR NT 861 710), lie on a rock peninsula jutting out into the North Sea, 64km (40 miles) E of Edinburgh and 20km (13 miles) NW of Berwick-upon-Tweed (Plate I; illus 2). The promontory marks the northern edge of the Lammermuir Hills on the southern flank of Scotland's central lowlands. The castle's remains cover an area of about 1000 square metres, bounded on three sides by cliffs that range from 30m at the seaward extremity to between 45m and 50m near the entrance (Plate III; illus 3, 5 and rear cover) which today is little more than a metre wide. It is probable that the entrance, now represented by a modern causeway, was quarried in order to create a more formidable defensive feature. Two caves penetrate the promontory from the E. The cliffs SW of the castle reach to over 120m in height, towards a prominent ridge known as Hawks Heugh, which dominates a relatively level triangular 'mainland' area adjacent to the entrance, part of which may have represented an outer ward of the castle (Plate II).

Exactly when Fast Castle was first built is still not known. Evidence from the excavations indicates that there was Iron Age activity on the site. Scattered documentary references to it in official records begin appearing from the early 15th century (Kennaway 1992, 14-30). The site's strategic importance was probably enhanced by the fact that in the medieval period it was less than 2km from the main road which ran N from England to Edinburgh, through Coldingham and Cockburnspath. Historical evidence becomes more abundant by the 1480s, when the castle was controlled by Sir Patrick Home, a member of a prominent local landowning family. In 1532, Fast Castle passed by marriage to the Logans of Restalrig, near Edinburgh, who owned the property until 1602 (Kennaway 1992, 71). English forces briefly held the castle in 1548-9, and during their occupation a plan of the buildings was drawn up under the direction of Henry, second Earl of Rutland, as Lord Warden of the East and Middle Marches. This plan, one of a series which also included fortifications at Broughty, Eyemouth, Lauder and Roxburgh, and one of the earliest for any Scottish residence, identifies the Hall, the Brewhouse, and two courtyards (illus 6). In the E courtyard a crane is drawn, located at the edge of the cliff above the cave entrance, for communication with vessels in the sea inlet below. Upstanding visible remains survive of the entrance way, the N curtain wall, the Hall, and the structure immediately adjacent to the E, identified by excavation as the Kitchen. The range of five rooms to the N is still visible as a series of grass-covered depressions, sloping downwards to the NE. The Hall, Kitchen, Brewhouse, and Upper Courtyard to the N all stood at about the same level. Before being excavated the area corresponding to the E courtyard lay 6m below the level of the Kitchen and Brewhouse sites, at the foot of a nearly vertical rock face or cliff, which had been created by quarrying at an early stage of the development of the present castle. This E area is therefore termed the Lower Courtyard. A putative reconstruction of the castle by David Simon is shown in Plate IV.

In 1594 Sir Robert Logan, then Fast Castle's owner, made a contract to search there for treasure with the mathematician John Napier of Merchiston. This episode helped to lay the basis for the rumours of buried treasure subsequently attached to the site. Both documentary and archaeological evidence indicate that the castle went out of regular occupation in the early 17th century; however, in 1651 when it was surrendered to Cromwell's troops, it was still considered 'strong, though of little importance'. In 1703 it was described as ruinous (Mitchell 1988, 42; Adair 1703). The remains were featured as a notable antiquity by a number of late 18th-century and early 19th-century illustrators (illus 4). Fast Castle was supposedly the inspiration for the fortress Wolf's Crag in Sir Walter Scott's *The Bride of Lammermoor* (1819).

During 1969-70, Fast Castle became the subject both of historical research and small-scale treasure-hunting activities. These projects were undertaken by Fred Douglas, and were described in his book, *Gold at Wolf's Crag*, published in 1971. Initially the activities lacked archaeological rigour, but in 1970 some of the volunteers attempted to remedy the situation, with Mr Douglas's consent, by expanding the previous year's diggings into a more systematic amateur archaeological investigation.

A society was formed in 1971 with the sole purpose of continuing excavation at Fast Castle. Originally the East of Scotland Archaeological Association (ESAA), in 1975 the name was changed to the Edinburgh Archaeological Field Society (EAFS), which more closely reflected the geographical base and designation as a local group. By this time the interests and activities of the Society had expanded beyond the limits of Fast Castle. The site was scheduled as a historic monument in 1976, but the Society was permitted to continue the excavation of the areas selected until completion in 1986. Post-excavation work lasted until 1998, culminating in the production of this report.

**Illus 4** Fast Castle: a romanticised view, painted by the Rev John Thomson of Duddingston, c1820.

**Illus 5** The castle in the 1970s; excavated area to the right of surviving walls

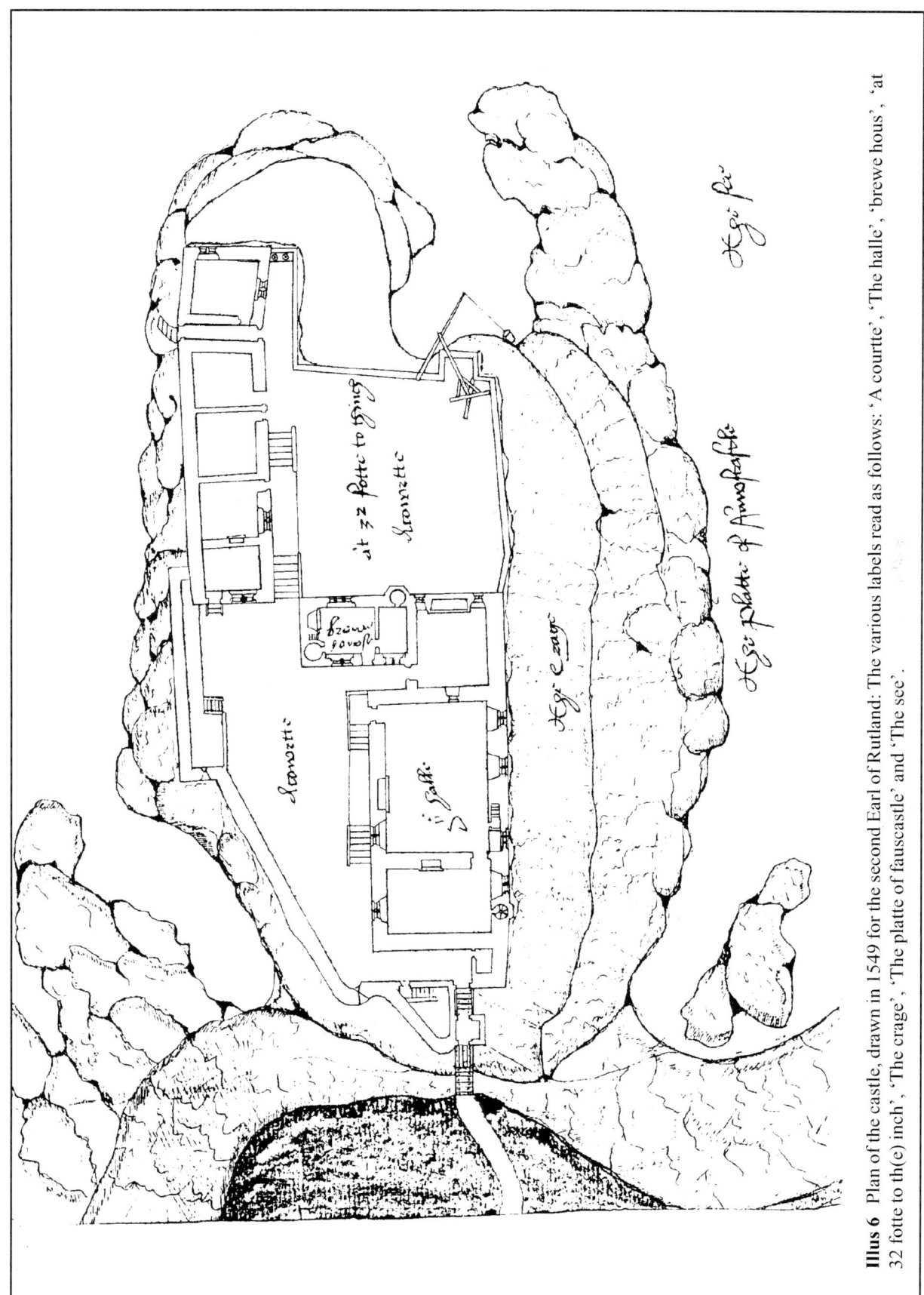

**Illus 6** Plan of the castle, drawn in 1549 for the second Earl of Rutland: The various labels read as follows: 'A courtte', 'The halle', 'brewe hous', 'at 32 fotte to th(e) inch', 'The crage', 'The platte of fauscastle' and 'The see'.

# 3 HISTORY

Mary Kennaway

The site of Fast Castle is likely to have been occupied in the Iron Age, when there were settlements of the Votadini tribe in the neighbourhood. However, the castle itself probably dates from the fourteenth century. It was almost certainly a government fortress in a strategic position, ideal for the detection of illicit activities, such as smuggling, or the possibility of attack on more accessible parts of the coast. At various times it was held by both Scottish and English forces.

The first official reference to Fast Castle was in 1404 when William Clifford was the English governor. He was succeeded by John of Lancaster, the third son of Henry IV. In 1410 Patrick Dunbar, the fourth son of the Earl of March, took Fast Castle in a daring surprise attack and captured the English captain, Thomas Holden. Considering the almost impregnable position of the castle, this must have been a prodigious feat.

Fast Castle figured in an alleged incident in 1429, when the Scottish ambassador was taking two thousand merks to the king of England and was robbed by Sir David Home of Wedderburn and William Drax, prior of Coldingham. The booty was reputedly taken to Fast Castle. Given the characters of these two men, it is not an unlikely tale and there are grounds for supposing that the money may have been part of the ransom of James I due to Henry VI. At this time, the Lumsden family were associated with Fast Castle and it later passed from them to the Homes who were one of the wealthiest and most powerful families in the kingdom.

Patrick Home, the fourth son of the first Lord Home, held Fast Castle from about 1488 until his death in 1508. He and his wife, Isobel, were hosts to Margaret Tudor in 1503, when she spent one night at Fast Castle on her way north to marry James IV. Unfortunately, we have no details of her reception or a description of the interior of the castle, but we do know that when she left next day 'they schott much Ordonnounce, and had varey good Chere, and soe that every man was content'. Patrick was succeeded by his son, Cuthbert, who was killed at Flodden in 1513. After Cuthbert's death Alexander, the third Lord Home, took charge of Fast Castle, possibly in his capacity as warden of the East and Middle Marches. Because of his opposition to the Duke of Albany, governor of Scotland, and the general unrest in the Borders, he was ordered by the duke in 1515 to surrender his castles at Home and Fast. Albany got both, but Alexander retook Home Castle and virtually demolished it. Fast Castle may well have suffered some damage at the same time, but to what extent is unknown. Contemporary records show that it certainly remained habitable. Elizabeth, the eldest daughter and heir to Cuthbert, married Sir Robert Logan, fifth Baron of Restalrig (near Edinburgh) in 1532, and so the castle passed to the Logan family, in whose hands it was held until the end of the century.

In 1547 during the second stage of the 'Rough Wooing', Sir Robert Logan, the sixth Baron of Restalrig, was appointed to have charge of the beacon to be lit at Dowlaw close to Fast Castle to alert the lieges in the event of attack by the English. In the following year the castle was in English hands and in 1549 the Earl of Rutland was responsible for the garrisons in the Borders including Fast Castle. He had a plan drawn of the castle which gives us a very good idea of the lay-out and is one of the earliest plans of a Scottish castle (illus 6). It provides evidence of a crane above the cave entrance, indicating comparatively easy access to supplies by sea.

The castle was won back for the Scots in the winter of 1549-1550 in a remarkable exploit, possibly led by Alexander, fifth Lord Home. He later married the widow of Sir Robert Logan, the sixth baron, and so a Home once more had some influence at Fast Castle. Alexander Home gave hospitality and sanctuary to the Catholic earls in the north of England who rebelled against Elizabeth in the Northern Rising of 1569. For this, Elizabeth sent the Earl of Sussex with an army and her expressed hope that Fast Castle would be taken and it was indeed surrendered in 1570.

By 1573 it was again in Scottish hands and three years later the son of Lady Home, by her marriage to Sir Robert Logan, came into his inheritance as Sir Robert Logan, the seventh Baron of Restalrig. He was notorious for his intrigues, lawlessness and association with Francis Stewart, the Earl of Bothwell. With the latter and John Napier of Merchiston, both of whom were interested in witchcraft and the occult, Logan was said to have engaged in a bizarre search by supernatural means for treasure which was alleged to be hidden at Fast Castle. We do not know if any treasure was found, but the contract which Napier drew up and signed along with Logan survived them. The most momentous event of Logan's time at Fast Castle must be the Gowrie conspiracy in 1600. There are strong indications that he may have been involved, but nothing has been proved. He sold all his lands and George Home of Spott, now the Earl of Dunbar, acquired Fast Castle and so the Homes were again in possession. Logan died in 1606, but his bones were tried for treason in a macabre trial in 1609 and his estate was forfeited.

On the death of the Earl of Dunbar in 1611, Fast Castle passed to his daughters and then to Sir John Arnott, by whose son, James, it was sold to Alexander, the sixth Lord Home and first Earl of Home. In 1642, the third Earl of Home sold the castle to Sir Patrick Hepburn of Waughton.

The last noteworthy event in its history occurred in 1651 when the castle surrendered to Cromwell who, after his victory over the Scots at the battle of Dunbar in the previous year, took most of the strongholds in the Borders.

Sir Alexander Waughton, a descendant of Sir Patrick Hepburn, sold Fast Castle in 1682 to John Hall, a wealthy Edinburgh merchant and Baronet of Dunglass. By 1703 it was in ruins, but it remained in the Hall family until sold in 1919 by the ninth baronet, changing hands again in 1979.

Although there are historical references to Cromwellian ccupation, the archaeological evidence indicates that the castle had been abandoned as a permanently inhabited site some decades earlier.

A comprehensive history, in two parts, with references, is contained in Kennaway (1992) and Mitchell (1988).

## 2 GEOLOGY

Nigel A Ruckley

The geology of the area immediately surrounding the castle can be divided into two parts: the underlying rocks (solid geology) and the overlying superficial sands and clays (drift geology) (Greig 1988).

SOLID GEOLOGY

The coastal exposures around Fast Castle are famous for their highly contorted sequence of greywackes and finer grained siltstones and mudstones of Silurian Llandoverian (Gala Group) age. The intense folding of these rocks and their ability to change their fold-profile dramatically within a short distance is classically demonstrated immediately on the foreshore NW of the castle (NT 8600 7104). Here, an antiform with a complex hinge incorporating at least five folds alters in shape from a distinct w-shaped structure into a slightly distorted fold in the space of less than 100m (Greig 1988, 11; McAdam, Clarkson & Stone (ed) 1992, 23-30). Greywackes were deposited by underwater turbidity currents in beds usually up to 2m thick. Each bed is formed from an individual flow and often exhibits grading where coarser material has formed the base of the flow.

Sedimentary structures such as ripple marks on the upper surfaces of beds and sole marks on basal beds have, along with the graded bedding, been an essential tool in the recognition of the correct way up (ie the deposition) of individual horizons within the intensely folded strata.

The medium to coarse grade greywackes consist mainly of quartz grains with varying amounts of feldspar, micas and clasts of generally well-rounded fragments of igneous, sedimentary and metamorphic rocks. All the rocks have been subjected to a low level of regional metamorphism.

DRIFT GEOLOGY

During the Quaternary period Scotland was subjected several times to glaciation. Traces abound of the last glaciation, the Devensian, which affect the area along with features produced by the wasting away of the massive ice sheets that once extended over the Lammermuir Hills and offshore onto the shallow North Sea (Greig 1988, 56-63).

The glacial erosion in the coastal area was enhanced by the SE-moving ice sheets when they were obstructed by combined contact of the Southern Uplands ice sheet and the North Sea ice sheets to the E. Classic ice-moulded topography in the Fast Castle/St Abbs area includes crag and tail structures (cf Edinburgh Castle, NT 252 735), over deepened valleys and glacial striae on exposed rock surfaces.

The northerly decay of the ice sheets, which must have been at one time close to the present coast, produced glacial meltwater channels cut into the rock and earlier superficial deposits. Underground streams in glaciers have left sinuous ridges of sand and gravel on today's land surface. Larger expanses of fluvioglacial gravels were deposited close to the decaying ice front and traces of these gravels are visible along the coastal zone from the cliffs S of Pease Bay to St Abbs.

Greig (1988, 57) describes a 3m thick deposit of poorly stratified fluvial gravel with a very sparse sandy matrix at the cliff top (NT 8603 7097) SW of Fast Castle, resting on what was tentatively described as boulder clay.

Gravel deposits, including eskers and delta-like spreads of gravel occur N of Haud Yauds. The eskers are thought to have been formed by englacial meltwater streams flowing SE. S of the Hirst Rocks, between the 122 and 152m contours, broad terrace-like spreads of gravel as well as delta-like features have been identified as meltwater deposits, formed when the general height of the ice fell towards the N, thus allowing glacial meltwater streams to flow N depositing their load. Near the cliff tops, mound-like deposits of gravels are thought to have originated as ice-contact deposits.

Boulder clay has been traced on the cliffs N of Redheugh where gravel deposits up to 4.5m thick have been proved at the base of the boulder clay. A good example can be seen S of the mouth of the Hazeldean Burn (NT 8211 7050) (Greig 1988, 56).

Evidence from numerous deposits of boulder clay and gravel lenses from Pease Bay in the N to Burnmouth indicate that penecontemporaneous reworking of the initial deposits (ie soon after formation) by meltwater was a regular occurrence.

When these glacial sands and gravel occupy a natural hollow, water will percolate through and form a shallow aquifer and it is from just such a pocket of glacial gravels, augmented by natural run-off from the cliffs, that Fast Castle's Well obtains its water supply (see Appendix 7.2).

**Plate I** View from Telegraph Hill (EAFS)

**Plate II** Aerial view from N (Denis Harding)

**Plate III** The present ruins (EAFS)

**Plate IV** Reconstruction (David Simon)

# The Excavations

**Plate V** Excavation in the Quarry pit, pit 2 in left foreground, view from the E (EAFS)

**Plate VI** Excavation in the Quarry pit, view from the NW (EAFS)

**Plate VII**  Kitchen entrance, view from the S (EAFS)

**Plate VIII**  Well-head with possible Iron Age wall beyond, view from the N (EAFS)

# 4 THE EXCAVATIONS

Keith L Mitchell, K Robin Murdoch, & John R Ward

The excavations by EAFS at Fast Castle, originally expected to take two years, in fact lasted for sixteen (1971-86), and covered the Lower Courtyard, Kitchen, and Well (illus 7). Work on the Lower Courtyard continued throughout 1971-85. Excavation of the Kitchen took place in the years 1973-5 and 1985-6, and of the Well in 1975-7 and 1986. The remainder of the castle was not excavated, but accompanying fieldwork included exploration of the two caves that penetrate the Fast Castle promontory (Appendix 7.3).

EAFS activities at the castle were undertaken by volunteers, mainly from the Society's membership, generally working the majority of Sundays over annual excavation seasons that lasted from April to September. A team of army volunteers explored the caves in July 1976. Week-long excavations took place occasionally between the years 1971 and 1981.

**Note:** Some inconsistency exists with compass bearings between the previously published histories and this excavation report. During site work, and when the histories were written, the long axis of the crag was regarded as N-S although, in reality, it is nearer E-W. See Illus 7 for the true orientation.

## 4.1 THE LOWER COURTYARD

The Lower Courtyard occupies an area 18m E-W by 18m N-S on the E side, narrowing to 14.5m on the W (illus 7-9). Most of this area lies about 6m below the level of the Kitchen, Brewhouse and Hall. Evidently this configuration had been created by quarrying into the bedrock during the late 15th century. Resource limitations, and the extremely restricted space available for locating spoil heaps, made it necessary to investigate the Lower Courtyard by successive Areas, rather than as a whole. Areas 1, 2, 3 and 7, termed the Outer Lower Courtyard, were excavated in 1971-4. Excavation of Areas 4, 5, 6 and 8, the Inner Lower Courtyard, continued from 1973 to 1985 (illus 8).

Work here was unexpectedly long, because Areas 4 and 5, and part of Area 6, proved to cover a substantial hole cut several metres deeper than the rest of the Lower Courtyard into the natural bedrock. It was concluded that this feature had been created through quarrying, probably to supply building stone for the castle. The feature will subsequently be referred to as the Quarry pit. Excavation removed most of the fill from this Quarry. Investigation of Areas 6 and 8 began during the 1973 season, and was completed in 1974, except for the N part of the Quarry covered by Area 6. Work in Areas 4 and 5 began in 1974 and proceeded until 1985, together with the 'Quarry part' of Area 6.

During the seasons 1974-8 work continued in the Quarry pit. A walled enclosure was found at its W end. Behind and adjacent to this, a large reference baulk was left, but in 1979, it was decided for safety reasons to begin removing material from this baulk. This work also uncovered a recess extending into the rock face beneath the Brewhouse. The lower levels within and adjacent to the Recess, W of a wall running parallel to the rock face, included waterlogged deposits, yielding substantial quantities of organic material and many artefacts. From 1979-81, work concentrated on excavating most of the Enclosure to the W of the wall. Some organic deposits were left undisturbed *in situ* at the back of the Recess as a resource for future investigators. The rest of the Quarry, to the E of the wall, was then excavated to bedrock between 1981 and 1985. Prior to excavation, most of the outer part of the Lower Courtyard was covered with grass, and much of the inner part with nettles. The outer part sloped gently downwards from S to N with the angle of slope becoming more pronounced in the NE corner. The inner part lay between two masses of bedrock and had assumed a concave profile.

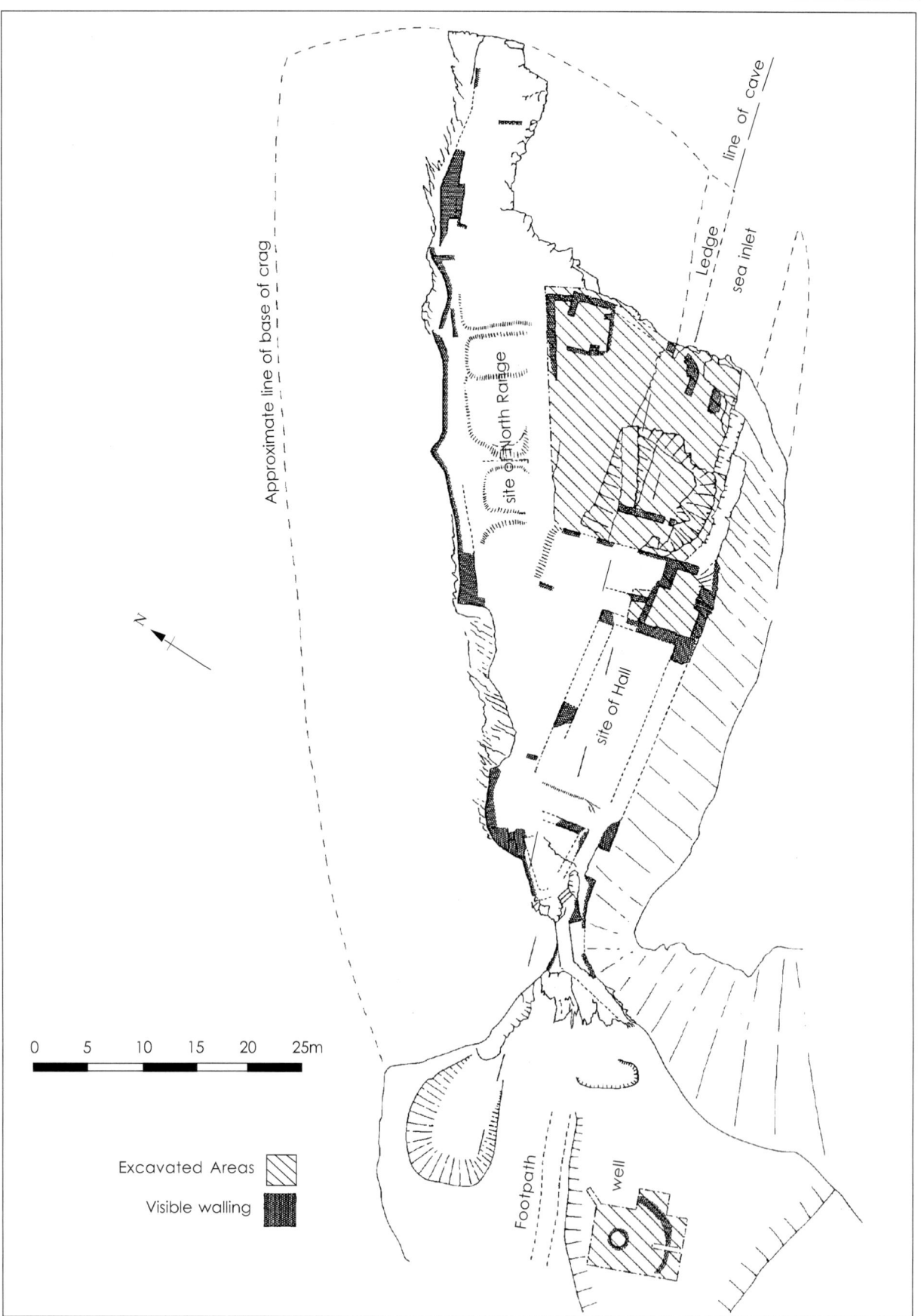

**Illus 7** Plan of existing ruins, based on RCAHMS survey of 1976

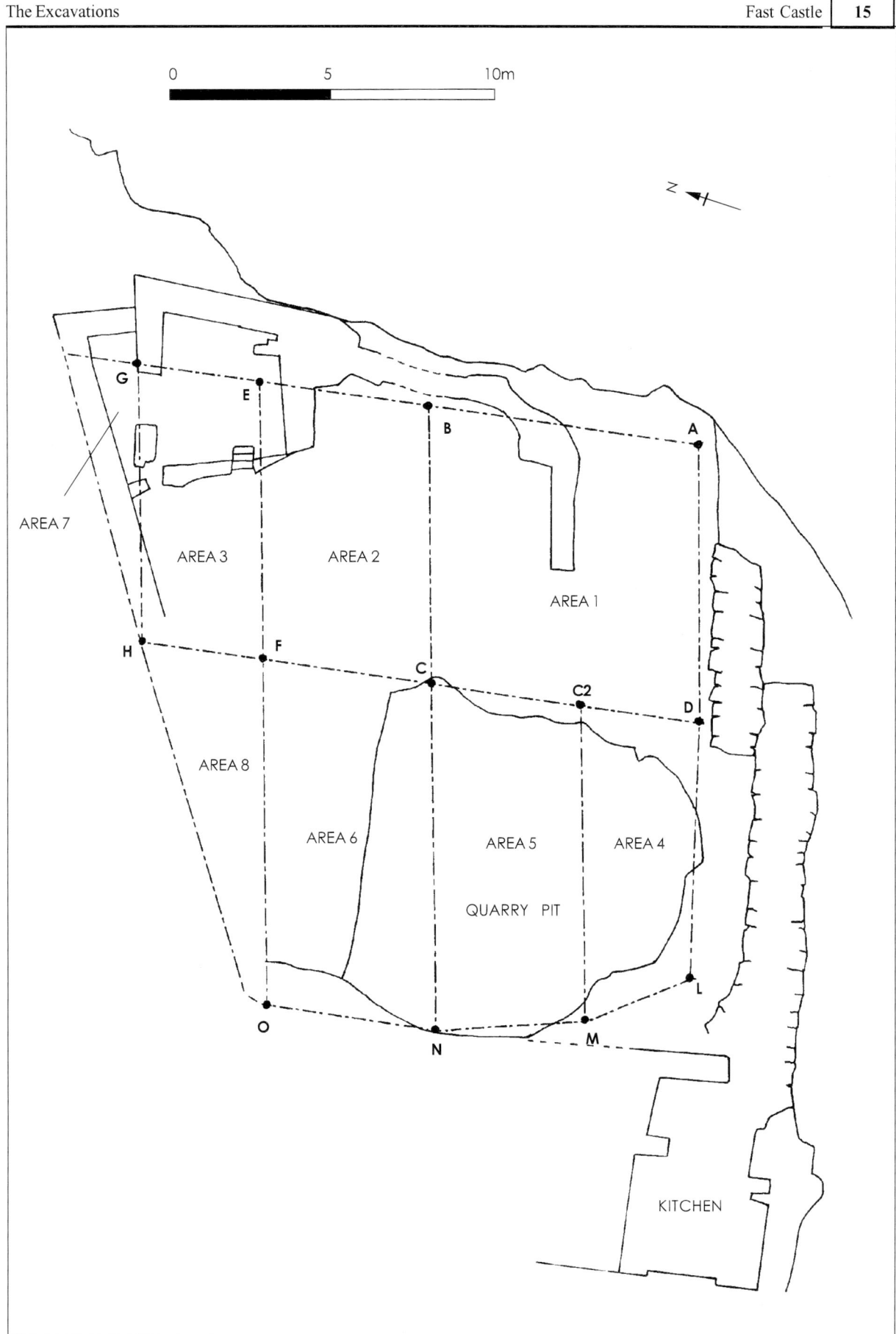

**Illus 8** Lower Courtyard: excavation area and reference peg locations

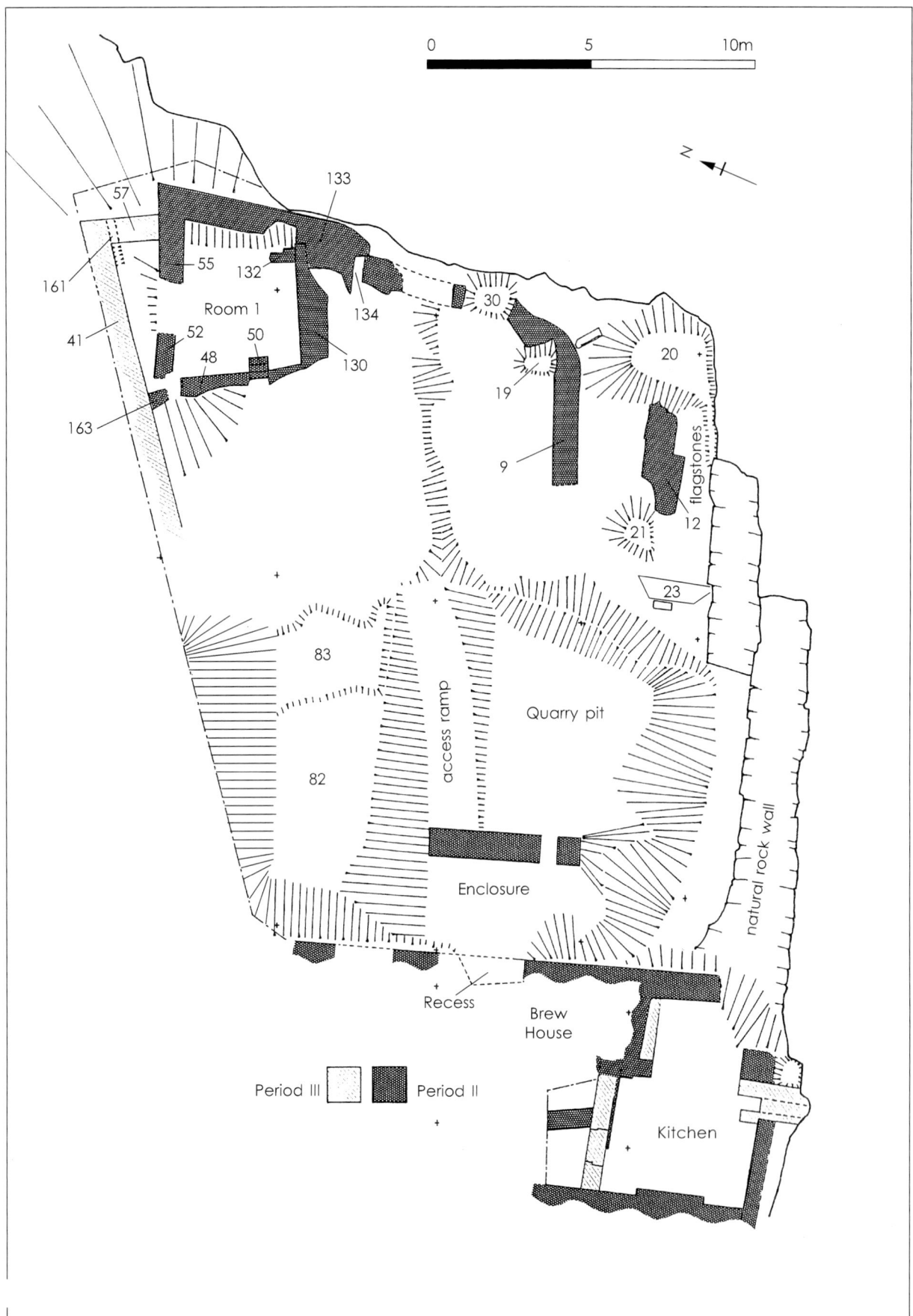

**Illus 9** Plan of Lower Courtyard and Kitchen, figures shown are feature numbers

At the S end of the Outer Lower Courtyard the bedrock had been left unquarried to create a natural wall at least 2m high and upwards of 1.5m thick. As local rock strata is tilted at 60 degrees to the horizontal and splits readily along shear planes between the layers of sedimentary rock, it had been relatively easy to create this barrier. The wall ran approximately W-E for 14.5m starting at the brewhouse cliff and ending 4m W of the SE corner of the Outer Lower Courtyard. A remnant of constructed wall survived on top of the 'natural' wall at its W end.

The Outer Lower Courtyard measured approximately 9m E-W and stepped down slightly from S to N forming three platforms, which although distinct, only varied about 1.0m in overall level. The highest of these platforms was at the S end, adjacent to the natural wall.

Immediately W of the highest platform, an irregular area, of maximum dimensions 10m N-S by 10m E-W, had been quarried to a greater degree. This Quarry pit had an average depth of 4-5m and a maximum of 6.2m with respect to the adjacent platform. N of the Quarry, and overlooking it, a ledge, feature (F)82, 8.5m E-W and 2.5m N-S had been cut. At the E end of this ledge was a small slightly raised bedrock shelf (F83). During the excavations, the Quarry pit and the adjoining ledge and shelf were described as the Inner Lower Courtyard, and were distinguished from the Outer Lower Courtyard. However, the discussion of dating and phasing that concludes this section treats the Lower Courtyard as a whole, except where indicated.

On the basis of the excavations, the development of the Lower Courtyard and Kitchen has been divided into four Periods, two of which are subdivided.

**PERIOD I** Occupation prior to the second half of the 15th century.

**PERIOD II** Late 15th-century structure, late 15th- to very early 16th-century occupation: Courtyard and Kitchen.

    PERIOD II.1    Late 15th-century structure, late 15th- to very early 16th- century occupation: Quarry pit only.
    PERIOD II.2    Fill and levelling deposits, superimposed on Period II.1 structures: Quarry pit only.

**PERIOD III** Early 16th century to early 17th century.

    PERIOD III.1    Early 16th-century reworking of the Lower Courtyard which covered many of the 15th-century structures, plus rework of the Kitchen at about the same time. This probably corresponds to the open courtyard indicated by the 1549 plan.
    PERIOD III.2    Subsequent structures and deposits: early 16th to early 17th century.

**PERIOD IV** Post-abandonment collapse and accumulation: early 17th to 20th century.

### 4.1.1 OUTER LOWER COURTYARD
Related features 1 - 60, 121 - 134, 161 - 165

PERIOD II

A small room (Room 1) was built in the NE corner of the Outer Lower Courtyard. It measured approximately 4m E-W by 3m N-S internally (illus 9).

The lowest, most northerly, platform (F46) in the Outer Lower Courtyard had been quarried, to form the floor of Room 1, about 0.5m below the level of the area to its S and W. The N side of Room 1 appeared to be the limit of the quarried area of the Outer Lower Courtyard with the ground level dropping steadily from this point N. Wall foundations, revetted against the step down of the bedrock, survived on the W and S sides of the Room as F48 and F130 respectively. Built with clay-bonded greywacke rubble, these walls retained traces of lime rendering or plaster. A flight of three steps (F50) (illus 10) gave access to the interior of the Room through its W wall. The E and N walls of the Room had been almost completely demolished.

Two fairly insubstantial fragments of wall, F58 and F132, may be the surviving remnants of the E wall of Room 1, although the fact that F132 was butt-joined to F130 may indicate that it was slightly later and possibly a partition.

A short section of wall (F52) and the return (F55) of the outer rampart may represent the remains of the N wall of Room 1. The outer rampart at this point was built in clay-bonded greywacke rubble and was so ruinous that separate phases of building (if they existed) could not be identified.

The quarried bedrock floor (F46) of Room 1 was covered with a heavy red clay (F59) which butted against the walls F48 and F130, and also F52 and F55, indicating that the latter two, if not contemporary, were definitely not later than the Room (illus 9,13). The clay (F59) was overlaid by a yellow silty clay (F56) which ended abruptly in line with the N edge of the platform (F46). A Crux Pellit coin attributable to the late 15th century was found in F56.

Just W of the W end of F52, a fragment of possible wall foundation (F163), 0.6m long and 0.4m wide, extended NW from Room 1 and disappeared below the later Courtyard boundary wall (F41). F163 was sealed below the clay (F59) and is therefore likely to predate Room 1.

To the S and W of Room 1 archaeological deposits were generally thin, containing no significant features, other than a levelling deposit (F122), a red clay, and F128, red clay with rubble, in bedrock channels. A Crux Pellit coin of late 15th-century date was recovered from F122, just above bedrock. There was also evidence of a shallow pit, possibly a later robber trench, in this area.

At the E side of Room 1, the outer rampart (Illus 11) reached a width of 1.5m, stepping rapidly back to 0.6m S of a drain (F134), which had been let through the rampart S of the Room. Again, due to the type of building material and the robbed out appearance of the rampart, it was not possible to identify separate phases, although the haphazard arrangement E of Room 1 did suggest more than one. S of the drain (F134), part of the outer rampart was missing altogether and it resumed after a break of 2m adjacent to, and on the N side of, a raised part of bedrock (F30).

The overall level of the bedrock stepped up again, 4m S of Room 1, creating the highest platform of the Outer Lower Courtyard; an area approximately 9m N-S by 9m E-W, bounded on its S side by the natural bedrock wall (illus 12).

**Illus 10** Outer Courtyard: Room 1, entrance steps, Period II floor and Period III levelling

**Illus 11** Outer Courtyard: outer rampart and drain outlet

**Illus 12** Outer Courtyard: Area 1, Period II

The raised bedrock feature (F30), along with three others (F19, F20 and F21) on the highest platform, appeared to have been deliberately left during the quarrying phase at the start of Period II. The largest of these features (F20) formed a low natural perimeter in the SE corner of the Courtyard. No evidence of constructed rampart was found on top of F20. The other two raised bedrock features (F19 and F21) had been left projecting 0.5m above the surrounding area. Part of the S face of F21 and the W face of F19 had been cut, to form almost vertical flat faces, the latter against the grain of the rock.

Between the bedrock outcrops (F30 and F20) lay a gap (F26), possibly partly natural but also with evidence of deliberate quarrying. This gap, 2m wide, had a flat base level with the rest of the platform floor, and deliberately angled sides. Within the gap lay a sandstone lintel.

Starting within the gap, against the S side of F30, a stone feature (F9) was uncovered, which skirted the E side of the outcrop (F19) and then turned abruptly W to run into the Courtyard a distance of 4.5m. It had originally run slightly further but the W end had been robbed out. An 'ecclesiastical issue' copper farthing, attributable to the late 15th century, was recovered from this disturbed area. However, the coin was recovered from a cleft in the bedrock, which may mean that it had not been dislodged from its original context.

The structure (F9) was 0.8m wide, built from clay-bonded greywacke and survived to a maximum height of 0.25m. It may have had the effect of partitioning off an area about 4m square in the SE corner of the Outer Lower Courtyard, although other possible functions include part of a crane or gun platform.

Three patches of charcoal and ash (F15, F16, and F25) were found directly on bedrock and probably represented small fires made during the construction phase (Period II). The largest patch (F16) extended below F9.

The quarried bedrock to the N of F9 had been levelled with small stone and clay deposits, F2 and F3. To the S of F9 an area of red sandstone and greywacke flagstones (F12), 3.2m E-W and a maximum of 1.3m N-S, had been laid, just W of the largest bedrock outcrop (F20). These flags were sitting on a layer of slightly smaller flat stones (F22), which in turn lay on bedrock. The lower stone feature was interpreted as foundations for F12 rather than an earlier phase. Two Crux Pellit coins attributable to the late 15th century were found below F12. An area of fairly large boulders in clay (F11) lay between the flags (F12) and F9. 1.9m W of the flags (F12) and overlooking what originally would have been the drop into the Quarry pit, was a small group of greywacke flagstones (F23), almost certainly part of a walkway, aligned N-S and bounded on their W side by a single red sandstone block (F18). The most southerly flagstone of F23 abutted the base of the natural bedrock wall.

Period II could not easily be separated into Periods II.1 and II.2 in the Outer Lower Courtyard, nor in the Kitchen, owing to the thin depth of deposits above the bedrock. Period II.1 and II.2 deposits are only differentiated in the Quarry pit.


PERIOD III

Room 1 was abandoned, its walls demolished to foundation level and covered with a levelling deposit of greywacke rubble, clay, mortar and rendering (F49), much of it derived from the reduced walling. This in turn was covered with a lighter soil/clay mix (F42) which brought at least the S end of the Room up to a level with the surrounding Courtyard (illus 13).

A long section of wall (F41) was built immediately N of the site of Room 1 after its abandonment (illus 9).

# The Excavations

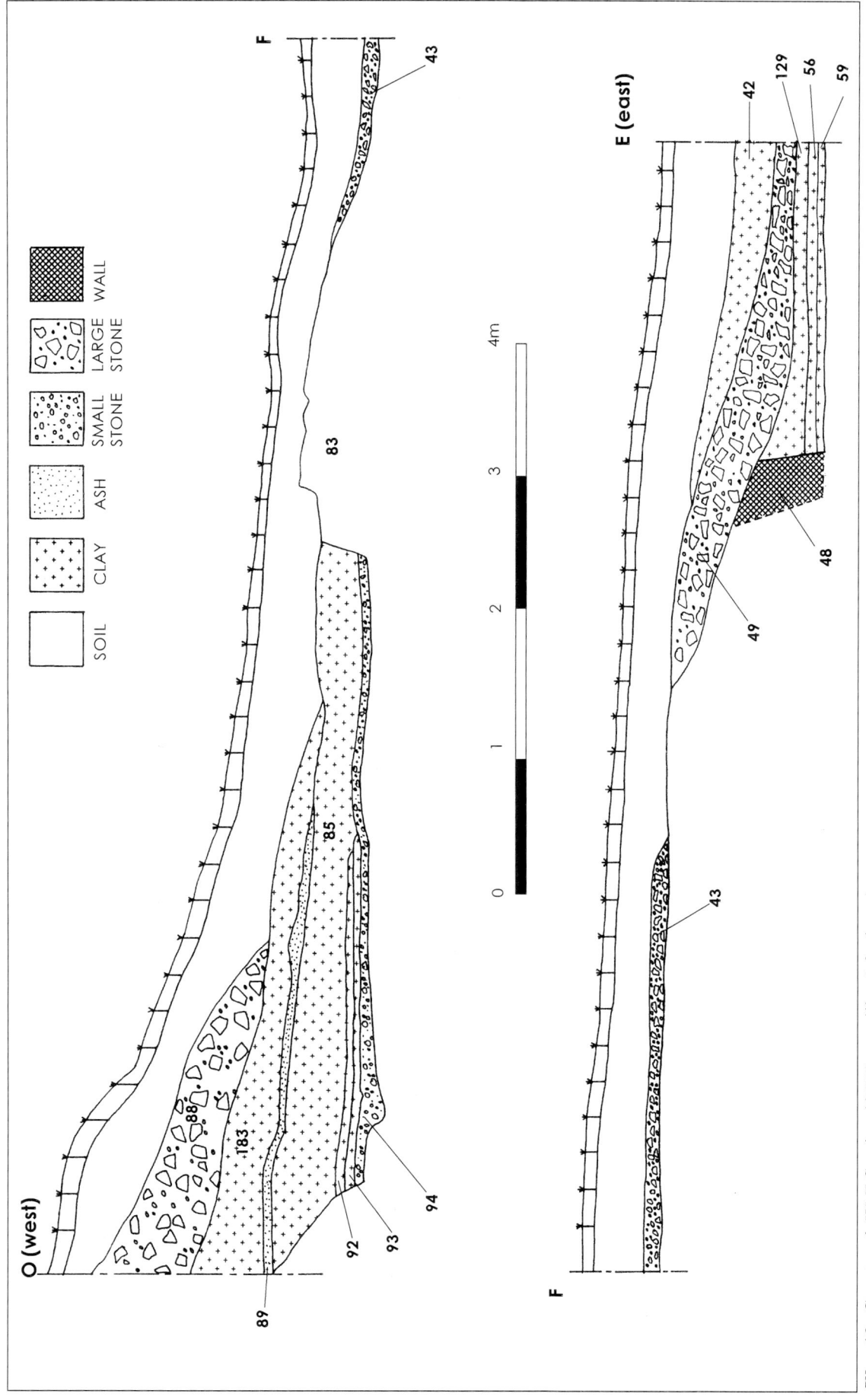

Fast Castle

**Illus 13** Courtyard: W-E Section (OFE); see illus 8 for location

The ground level, on which F41 had been built, sloped down quite abruptly from SW to NE indicating that the extreme NW corner of the Outer Lower Courtyard had not been levelled up to any great extent. F41 was clay-bonded and substantial tumble from it (F45) lay against part of its S face. The N side of F41 was not excavated. At its E end the F41 wall turned S. This portion (F57) butted against the N face of F55, but is much later. A drain (F161) had been let through F57 at its junction with F41 probably explaining the reason why that corner was left sloping away. The wall (F57) was sitting on a thick deposit of red clay. It is likely that the outer rampart to the E of Room 1 was refurbished after the demolition of the Room but it was not possible to define exactly how. On the highest platform further clay levelling deposits (F5, F6, and F8) overlay the flagstones F12 and F23. The wall (F9) appears to have continued in use in Period III.1 since these levelling clays abutted its S face. A very thin layer of red clay (F14), covering an approximately rectangular area, 4m E-W by 2.2m N-S, overlay the wall (F9) and the disturbance at its W end. This was interpreted as the site of a probable temporary timber structure either dating to very late in the occupation of the castle or post-dating it altogether.

Some of the topsoil in the Courtyard appeared to have been laid deliberately or had accumulated during periods of inactivity before the end of the 16th century. Scottish and English coins from that era were found in the topsoil.

### 4.1.2 INNER LOWER COURTYARD

This section describes the excavation of Areas 4, 5, 6, and 8, and the short extensions of Areas 4, 5, and 6 to the W, between the western boundaries of these areas and the base of the Brewhouse cliff (illus 8). Area 8 and the 'non-Quarry' part of Area 6 is considered first, where there was shallow stratigraphy, closely resembling that of the Outer Courtyard. Then follows an account of the more substantial Quarry pit excavations.

**Areas 6 (north part) & 8**
Related features 81 - 95, 181 - 188.

PERIOD II.1

Bedrock was encountered immediately below the turf line along the N side of Area 8. From here the bedrock slopes down at a 60 degree angle into Area 6, where it forms a relatively level shelf (F82) 2.5m wide along the N edge of the Quarry. At the E end of the shelf there is a small platform (F83), standing about 0.3m higher than the rest. A similar bedrock configuration appears in Area 1. The lower section of bedrock to the W was covered to a depth of 0.3-0.75m by successive layers (proceeding upwards from bedrock) of small greywacke chippings (F94), red clay with loam (F93), and yellow clay (F92) (illus 13). F92 was thought to be an occupation level, similar to F56 recorded in Areas 2 and 3. On top of F92 a Crux Pellit coin of the later 15th century was found.

PERIOD II.2 - PERIOD III.2

A layer of red clay with greywacke chippings (F85) was added, creating a fairly uniform common level with the higher area of bedrock to the E (illus 13), and representing a second occupation surface. This clay and bedrock floor was covered with layers of loam, clay, and greywacke stones (F89, F183, F88), at their deepest (1.5m) to the S. These layers, partly collapsed building material, included fragments of roofing tiles, and traces of charcoal, ash and mortar. They yielded three rectangular dressed sandstone blocks, found loose, possibly displaced steps from the staircase recorded in the 1549 plan as leading down from the Hall area past the N range of rooms (illus 6). In the N part of Area 8 the edge of two sandstone steps with traces of mortar were uncovered *in situ*, resting on bedrock.

**Quarry Pit - Areas 4, 5 & south part of 6,**
Related features 86, 95 - 109, 201 - 209, 401 - 403.

PERIOD II.1

The Quarry's maximum depth of 6.2m, measured from the Outer Lower Courtyard bedrock platform, was reached close to the NE corner. From this point the Quarry bottom is irregularly stepped upwards, at a general angle of about 25 degrees towards the SW and 10 degrees towards the W, with an average depth of about 4m overall. The Quarry is roughly 10m by 10m in area, and a minimum of 500 cubic metres in capacity. Stone cutting had presumably been undertaken along and down the natural faultlines that run approximately E-W. The process had left the Quarry with its N side as a 55 degree slope, quite smooth-surfaced except for some crude access steps (Plate V; illus 14), and a buttress to the S supporting a wall (Plate VI).

About 70 per cent of the Quarry bottom had been covered to a maximum depth of 1.6m at the NE corner with a stone/clay/soil mixture (F402-3), the stones, typically 100 to 300mm but exceptionally to 1m, predominating (illus 19). On this fill a clay-bonded greywacke stone wall was constructed, 0.8m-1m high, 0.5m thick, and cut by an entrance way (illus 9, 17). This wall and its rubble/clay/soil foundations were left in place by the excavators. The top of the wall had slumped, with the upper courses projecting into the entrance way, probably through subsidence of the rubble foundations between the bedrock at either end. The wall, including the entrance, runs for 5m, parallel to, and at a distance of 3m from, the Brewhouse cliff face, between a bedrock outcrop to the S and the Quarry's N side. In the cliff face to the W of the wall two recesses have been cut, the largest, to the right, about 3m wide and penetrating 1.4m into the cliff (illus 18). The small recess to the left is about 1m wide and penetrates about 1m into the cliff. The area between the wall and the cliff face, including the recesses, is about 15 square metres. This area is referred to as the Enclosure. There are no traces in the cliff face of any sockets to receive roof beams, so the wall was probably built to form an open arrangement, not as part of a roofed structure. The local rock is unsuitable for cutting joist holes; there could have been a cruck frame instead. The entrance to the Enclosure was 0.7-0.8m wide. Contemporary with the wall to the E and W was a 0.4m-1m layer of small stones, red clay and ash (F107, F109), interpreted as an occupation surface or floor level. The floor's extension to the E over the rubble fill included several sheeps' skulls. In the Enclosure to the W of the wall the floor was rather lower than to the E, and separated from the Quarry bedrock base (rising upwards from the E) by only 50-100mm of greywacke chippings.

PERIOD II.2

Overlying the floor, both inside and outside the Enclosure, were several layers of material (F104, F103, F100, F99, F97a&b). These layers comprised, in varying proportions, clay, loam, ash, and organic material (wood, twigs, roots, peat, straw, textiles, leather). Most of the organic material was found within the Enclosure. From the mixed and often indeterminate character of the layers, their steeply sloping tip lines when they approached the Quarry edge (illus19, 20), and from the finds evidence, it seems clear that these features constitute fill, deposited over a short period of time. Apart from covering the F107/109 floor they also buried the wall to a depth of 0.7-0.8m. F99 and F100 included some broken stone roofing tiles.

PERIOD III.1

Superimposed on F97a&b, an ash layer, was F86, a 0.2-0.4m layer of red clay and greywacke chippings, extending over the whole Quarry area in a roughly saucer-shaped configuration, caused by settlement of deposits below, and whose centre lay about 1.4m below its rim to the E. The hard-packed composition and quite uniform thickness of F86, together with the finds evidence, indicate that it was an occupation floor laid over the fill. F86 sloped upwards at a 30 degree angle over the E Quarry edge, giving access to and from the Outer Lower Courtyard, where it continued into Areas 2 and 3 as F122. It continued onto the Area 6

**Illus 14** Quarry access 'steps'

**Illus 15** Roofing tiles on Period III floor

**Illus 16** Quarry pit : Excavation completed; note access 'steps' to left

**Illus 17** Enclosure wall and entrance

**Illus 18** Recess

platform as F85. Two parallel alignments of small stones, 0.8m apart, running E-W, were observed embedded in the surface of F86. Their significance is unknown. A number of stone roofing tiles appear to have been laid out deliberately on F86 in the SW corner of Area 5.(illus 15).

PERIOD III.2-IV

The layers superimposed on F86 (illus 19), proceeding in sequence upwards, included firstly F207 and F209, mixtures of loam, clay and ash, with the laid-out roofing tiles already mentioned. These layers were probably a build-up of occupation material. Then came F206, ash with clay inclusions. F204, loam and greywacke rubble with cut red sandstone pieces, was found only to the W of the Quarry area, spread in a band 1.5-2.0m wide along the base of the Brewhouse cliff. F204 probably represents collapse from the buildings above the Lower Courtyard as they became ruinous. F202, extending into the Outer Lower Courtyard as Layer 2, comprised loam and stone. Although F206, 204 and 202 represented mainly collapse, finds recovered from these features suggest that some of this material had apparently been laid down while the castle was still in occupation.

These upper layers were cut through by five pits (numbered 1,3,4,5 and 6). Three of the pits (1, 5 and 6) appear in the E-W section (illus 19). They were 0.5m-1.4m deep and reached down only to the F86 floor. Another pit (4) was located at the base of the Brewhouse cliff, immediately adjacent to the Enclosure recess. Pit 4 reached 2.5m deep to the bedrock base of the recess.

At the time of the excavation the lowest part of the disturbance (Pit 4) was recorded as the separate Pit 3, but there now seems to be no clear basis for maintaining this distinction. Pits 1, 4, 5 and 6 were filled with stone, clay and loam mixtures. Pit 2 (Plate V), created in Period III.2, was rectangular in shape, about 2.5m long on a N-S alignment, 0.7m-1m wide, and 0.8m deep. Its contents comprised loam, clay, ash, stone, and pieces of roofing tiles.

DISCUSSION

The Lower Courtyard excavations identified distinct stages in Fast Castle's development. Period II is represented by the floor and Enclosure wall at the base of the Quarry pit, by the lower level of flooring (F92) on the bedrock shelf in Area 6, by Room 1, and by the associated walls in Areas 1 and 2. Late in Period II, or more probably in Period III.1, Room 1 was demolished, the Quarry pit filled, and the surface levelled with deposits of red clay and greywacke chippings (F85, F86, F122). This levelling process created the Period III.1 open courtyard arrangement which corresponded to the 1549 plan.

It has been possible to reconstruct, partially, several items of pottery by joining sherds recovered from different features in the Quarry pit. Most of the joined pottery comes from the layers between the floor levels F86 and F107/F109. Few reconstructions cross either of the postulated floors, confirming the interpretation already advanced: that the Quarry area had at least two distinct occupational phases, separated by intervening fill. This fill must have been deposited over a short period. It is not clear from the immediate archaeological evidence whether the lower floor and wall were laid down immediately after the Quarry had ceased to function as such, or after some interval had elapsed. However, from the way in which both ends of the wall rest on bedrock projections, and from the form of the recesses, it might be inferred that the later stages of quarrying were deliberately planned to accommodate the Enclosure as eventually created.

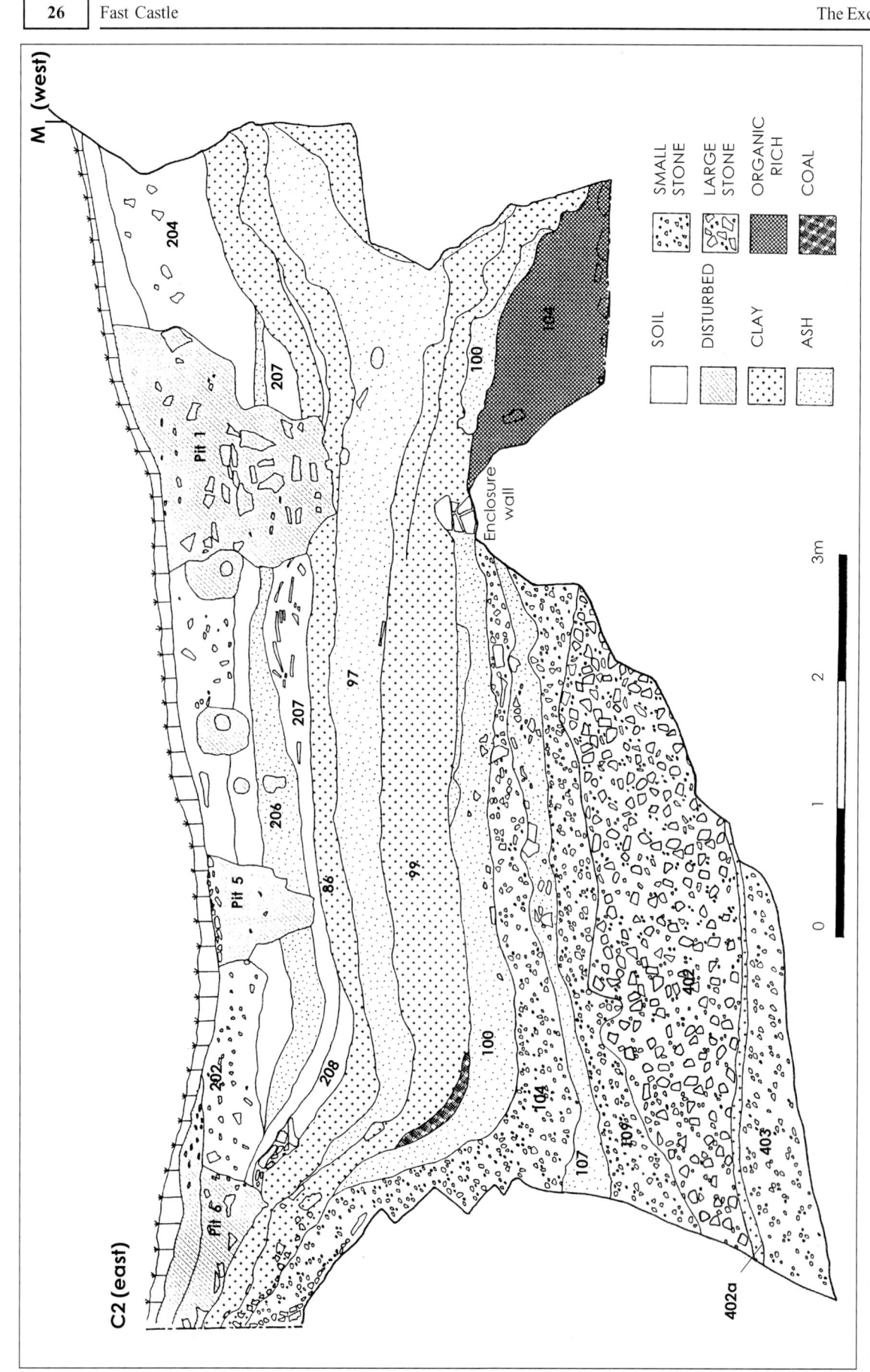

**Illus 19** Quarry pit: E-W section (C2-M); see illus 8.

# The Excavations

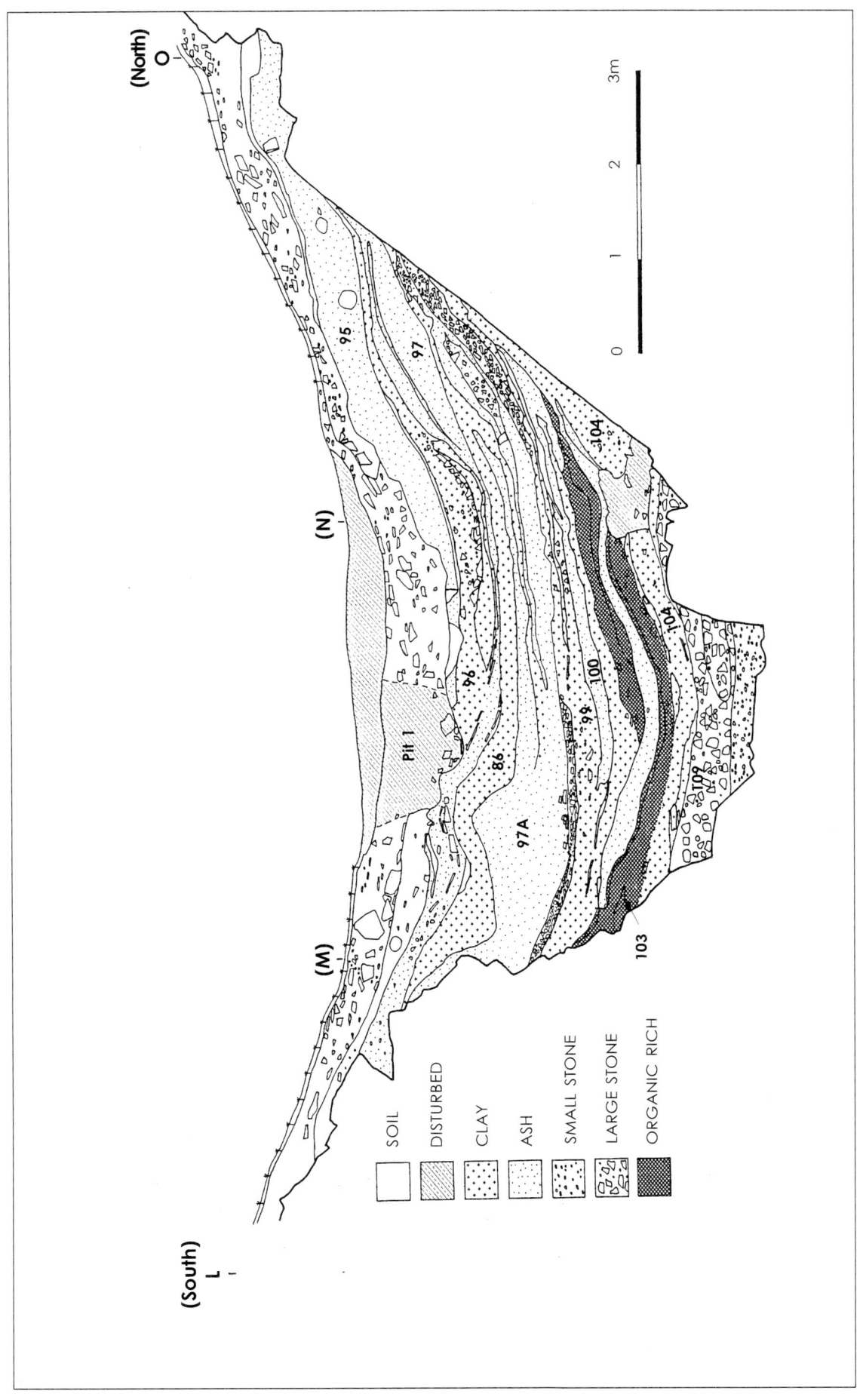

Fast Castle | 27

**Illus 20** Quarry pit: S-N section (L [M] [N] O): This section was located slightly E of the reference posts

The absence of any evidence for the Enclosure being roofed suggests that the structure served as a pen holding animals for consumption by the castle's occupants. The numerous animal bones and sheeps' skulls found embedded in the floor material to the E suggest that this may have been a butchery area. The abundance of floor-level leather, textile and wood finds suggests that the area might also have been used for working those materials.

Most of the organic materials from the Quarry and all of F103a-c, the most organically rich layers, were found within the Enclosure. Comparatively little came from outside the Enclosure to the E. This distribution is explicable in two ways, which can be taken as complementary rather than mutually exclusive. First, organic matter may originally have been quite evenly distributed over the lower floor level, as occupational deposits and/or fill, and become more heavily waterlogged and better preserved within the Enclosure, where the depth of loose stones immediately above bedrock was much less than at the Quarry's E end. Second, when the Enclosure was in use, particularly large amounts of organic matter may have built up there through the penning of animals, and/or through midden deposits.

To what dates should the Periods be assigned? Almost certainly Period II.2 was superimposed on Period II.1 in the later 15th century, or very early in the 16th century. Datable finds from the Quarry fill between the upper and lower floors include three Crux Pellit coins (nos 4, 9a, and 12), a German jeton (no 32), a pewter pilgrim's badge (illus 45), and a pipe-clay Madonna and Child figurine (illus 39). All these items have been attributed to the period c1450-1513, with a concentration in the 1480s and 1490s (see finds reports).

For Period II.1 matters are less clear-cut. The lower Quarry pit floor and its base yielded no coins or other readily datable finds. Two later 15th-century Crux Pellit coins were found close to the bedrock in Area 1, and another Crux Pellit coin was similarly located in Area 6. This might be taken to show that the final stage of quarrying was completed throughout the Lower Courtyard during the late 15th century. However, such an inference would not be safe, because in Area 1 and much of Area 6 the deposits overlying bedrock were much thinner than elsewhere in the Lower Courtyard. Crux Pellit coins were found on the floor of Room 1, and on the Period II.1 occupation level (F92) in Area 6, but it is uncertain how long these features had been in place before the coins' deposit. As noted in the Coins and Jetons report, while Fast Castle did not yield any coins earlier than the mid-15th century, their absence is not normally considered to prove lack of prior occupation on Scottish sites, because the low value billon and copper currency likely to be associated with frequent coin loss only became common from about that time. The Room 1 floor overlay a wall fragment which possibly represented the trace of some previous construction phase.

On the other hand, the Ceramics report emphasises the small quantity of wares from even the lowest Quarry pit levels which can be attributed to any period before the 15th century. Therefore the balance of probabilities must be that the oldest Lower Courtyard archaeological deposits did not pre-date the 15th century. This, of course, does not rule out the possibility of earlier medieval occupation, all traces of which had been eliminated by late-medieval quarrying and rebuilding.

As noticed already, no evidence was found for any major structures on the Period III.1 floor. However, there does seem to have been a relatively deep build-up of occupational material, at least in the area covering the filled Quarry pit. The pit would have sunk over time, even more so as it included large quantities of decomposing organic material. Further layers were added, possibly for levelling.

While 16th-century coins were abundant in the Period III features, the Coins and Jetons report notes that the complete absence of post-1600 coinage makes it almost certain that the castle passed out of occupation during the early 17th century: a point confirmed by the pottery and historical evidence.

Pit 2 produced items which were all probably attributable to the 16th century: a brass thimble, and pieces of vessel glass and pottery. But from the finds evidence, including several pieces of modern bottle glass, the other pits (pits 1, 4, 5, 6) were apparently created by random digging and treasure hunts after occupation at the castle had ceased. The exceptional depth of Pit 4 against the Brewhouse cliff, dug during treasure hunting, perhaps reflected hopes that a subterranean room or passage way was to be found there, cut into the bedrock.

## 4.2 KITCHEN
Related features 301 - 330

The Kitchen, so designated during the excavation, lies immediately E of the Hall on the S side of the crag, with the E wall of the room overlooking the Lower Courtyard and the S wall running along the edge of the main crag (Illus 7). The Brewhouse lay immediately N of the Kitchen; turf was removed from part of this area, but it was not excavated further.

Designated Area 9 during the excavations, the Kitchen consisted of a slightly irregular main area approximately 4.5m N-S by 3.6m E-W, with a smaller rectangular extension, 2.9m N-S by 2.4m E-W, opening off its E side (illus 21-23). Ash deposits identified this eastern extension as a large hearth (F300), obviously far too big to be a source of room heating, leading to the interpretation of the room as a kitchen. Its position with respect to the Hall and Brewhouse supported this interpretation. Most of the surviving construction was executed in the local angular greywacke rock with only limited use of pink and red sandstone, reflecting the general practice elsewhere on site. Illus 23 indicates the Period II and Period III layouts.

As with the Lower Courtyard, there was evidence of quarrying to obtain a reasonably level area on which to build. It is likely that abrupt deepening of the bedrock in the SE corner and in the centre N of the room reflects the original contours of the crag. The SE corner of the room had in fact disappeared taking with it some of the material used to bring that corner up to a uniform level with the rest of the room. Part of the natural bedrock was used to form a base course for the S wall of the room, mirroring use of bedrock as a natural boundary on the S side of the Lower Courtyard. The Kitchen's archaeological phasing apparently corresponds to that of the Lower Courtyard.

PERIOD II

The large hearth (F300), 2m E-W by up to 2.9m N-S occupied at least the N side, if not all of the E end of the room; collapse of the SE corner of the room had removed part of the hearth. No trace of an E-W dividing wall was found, but it is possible that the hearth may not have extended to the full width of the room; the 1549 plan implies windows at each side of the hearth. Where the bedrock dropped rapidly away in the SE corner of the room, remnants of rubble (F323) survived, but this is likely to have been infill to bring that corner up to a uniform level.

Above F323, and extending over the entire surviving E end of the room, was a bright red deposit (F318), with mainly heat-shattered stone contained within it. This appeared to be the original working surface of the hearth, the stone element surviving in better condition as F327, near its N wall. Heat penetration, as revealed by the gradual change from bright red to dark brown, was at least 150mm; the dark brown F319 phased into bedrock fill. A Crux Pellit coin, attributable to the late 15th century, was found in F319, indicating that the major quarrying activity in the Kitchen was probably contemporary with that in the Lower Courtyard.

During Period II the N wall of the large hearth, and also of the room, was F325, which survived to a height of about 1m (illus 23). Butted to the W end of F325 and projecting at least 0.6m southwards was a wall

**Illus 21** Kitchen: Main hearth and collapsed SE corner

**Illus 22** Kitchen: South wall with drain

The Excavations | Fast Castle | 31

**Illus 23** Kitchen: Plan

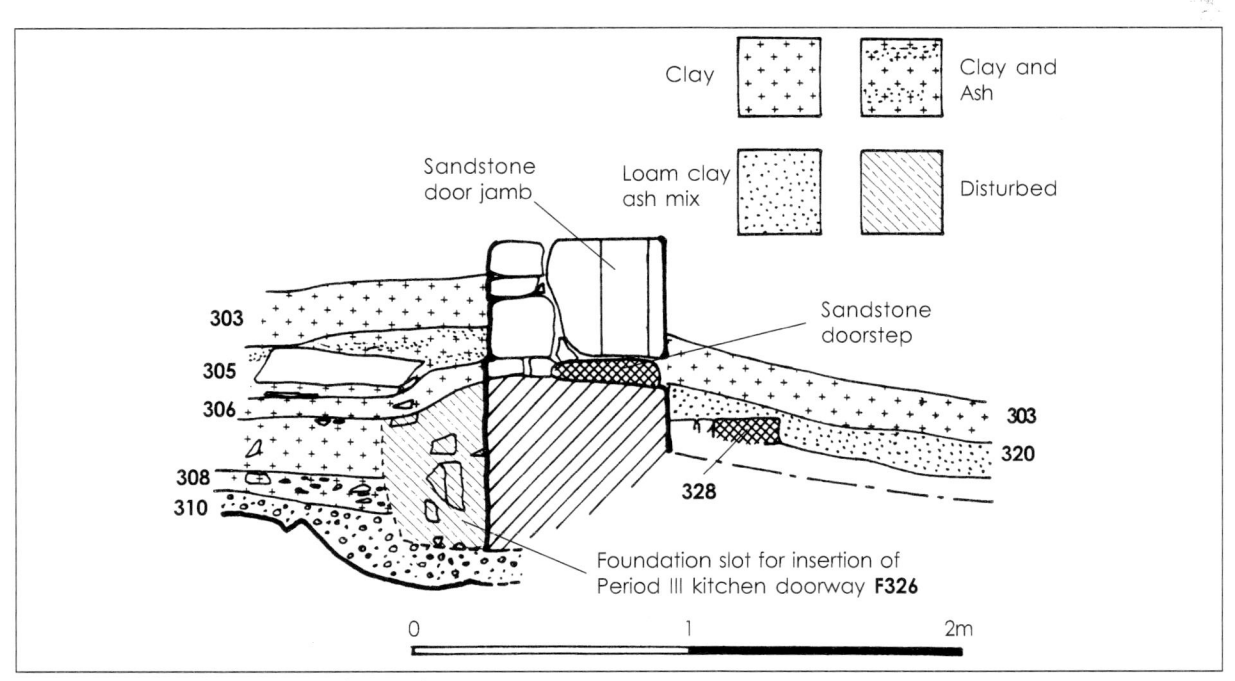

**Illus 24** S-N section through kitchen doorway

foundation (F341), which in effect partially separated the hearth (F300) from the rest of the Kitchen. A single sandstone block (F342) aligned N-S lay 0.2m E of F341. The E face of F342 was the limit of the bright red clay (F318), suggesting that it was the surviving remnant of a kerb which once bounded the W side of the hearth. A jamb (F343), constructed mainly from sandstone, had been built directly on top of F341 butting against F325 and was probably also a Period II feature. It is likely that the Period II doorway to the kitchen was situated just W of F325, slightly N of where it was to be placed later in Period III.

In the centre of the room lay a second, much smaller hearth (F316), 0.7m wide (E-W), open on its N side. The foundations of this hearth were observed to lie on a hard clay (F308), which in turn abutted F322, a low wall-like feature running N-S. F322 lay NW of the hearth (F316). F322 therefore predated F316 but since the hard clay (F308) is interpreted as the earliest floor, then the hearth (F316), built directly on it, is also regarded as Period II. Bedrock fill (F309 & F310) lay directly below F308. A dark ash (F307) 100 to 110mm thick, interpreted as the detritus from the first occupational use of the room, abutted the hearth (F316), and covered the floor (F308).

Unlike the main hearth (F300), the clay floor within and below F316 was not significantly heat reddened which implies the use of a grate to raise the fire above floor level. There was evidence that F308, the Period II clay floor and crude flagging within its matrix, extended over the entire area S and W of the hearth (F316), but this area was never completely excavated.

PERIOD III

Because of the limited stratigraphy and a lack of diagnostic finds, subsequent changes to the Kitchen are grouped together in this section.

The small hearth (F316) appears to have retained a function throughout the life of the room. A thick deposit of charcoal was found within the hearth at a contemporary level with the Period II ash (F307), which in turn had been covered by an upper clay floor (F306), varying in thickness from a few mm to c200mm. A deposit of charcoal, within the confines of the hearth, sitting on F306 indicated that the hearth had been reused. An upper layer of grey ash, typically 50-60mm thick, had covered virtually the entire area of the kitchen above F306 level. This grey ash (F305) was interpreted as either a last occupation-use deposit or a possible destruction level, perhaps partly both (illus 24, 25).

A finely-made stone-capped drain (F317), 2.3m long and 0.4m wide, constructed mainly in sandstone, had been let through the S wall of the room with its base course sitting on the Period II (F307) ash (illus 27).

Crude flagging in sandstone and greywacke had been used to level the L-shaped area, which ran from the drain, down the S side of the hearth (F316) and then N along the W side. The kerb of the hearth and the low wall (F322), standing at a maximum surviving height of 0.25m, looked as if they may have been truncated at this stage to give a uniform level with the flagging. Probes below the flagging indicated the presence of the Period II ash (F307).

The Excavations　　　　　　　　　　　　　　　　　　　　　　　　　　　　　　　　　Fast Castle　　33

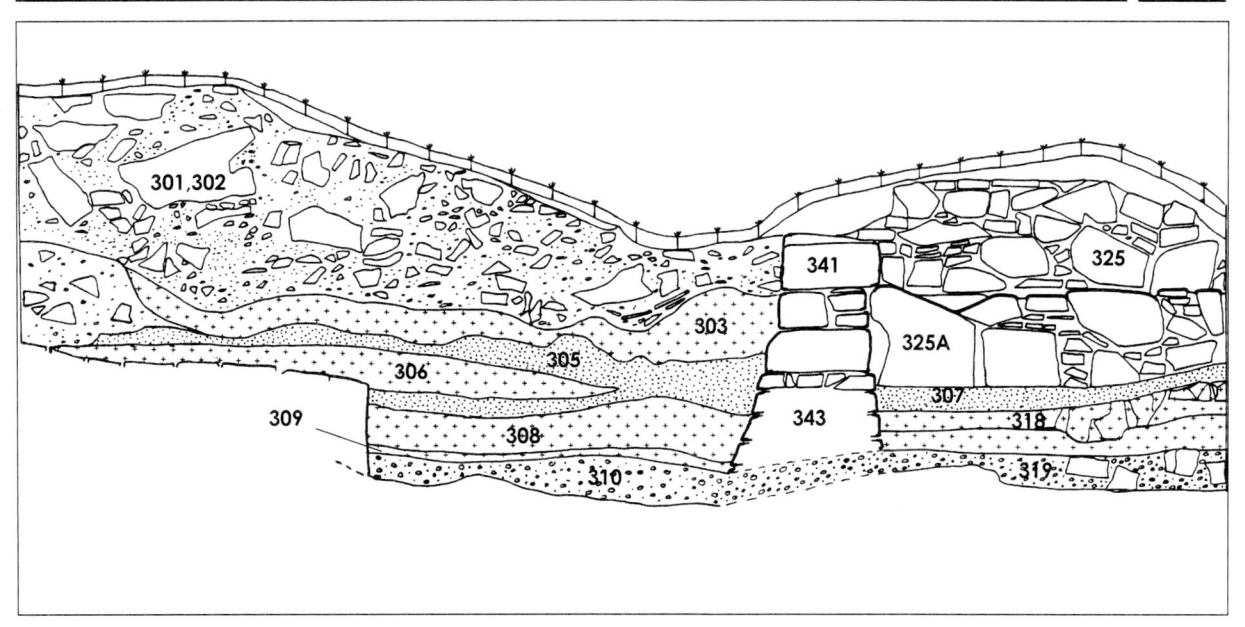

**Illus 25** Kitchen: West - East section; Period III features removed to east of F343, scale as Illus 26

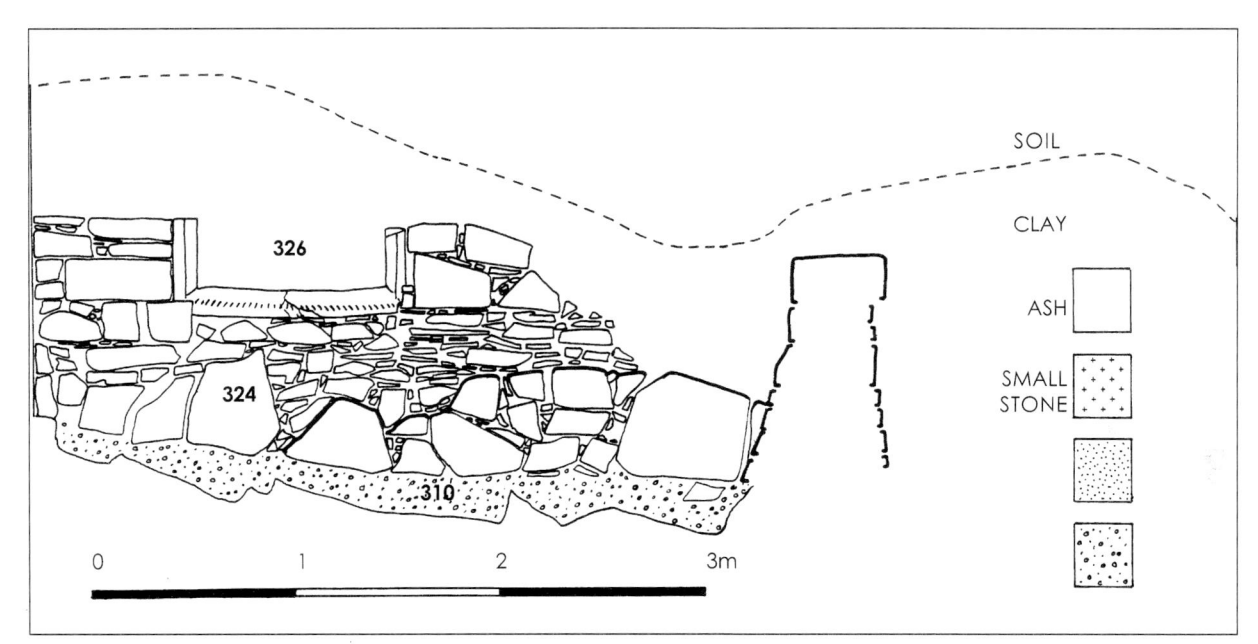

**Illus 26** West - East section removed revealing elevation of N wall and kitchen doorway

**Illus 27** Drain in south wall of Kitchen

From the open N side of the hearth (F316), the upper clay floor (F306) sloped gradually upwards as it approached F324, the N wall of the main area of the Kitchen. Clearance of rubble and accumulation deposits from the top of F324 had revealed the presence of a doorway (F326), 0.95m wide, giving access to a passage running N, adjacent and parallel to the E wall of the Hall. The clay floor (F306) had been deliberately sloped to access this doorway and the upper ash (F305) butted the threshold step, the surface of which was also slightly blackened. Excavation of the features against the wall (F324), adjacent to the doorway (F 326), revealed that deposits below F306 appeared to be mixed or disturbed (Pl.VII). This, coupled with differences in construction and alignment, between the upper and lower courses of F324, indicated that the doorway (F326) was an insertion. The upper part of F324, associated with the doorway, clearly abutted the E wall of the Hall; the relationship of the lower courses was not so obvious.

A layer of silty clay (F303), averaging 150mm thick, and interpreted as accumulation, had covered all of the W half of the room just below the rubble collapse (F301-302), which had a combined thickness of just over 1m adjacent to the Hall. F303 had lain directly on top of the threshold step of the doorway (F326), indicating that the doorway had been in use until the abandonment of the castle.

The N side of the main hearth (F300) had also undergone some change during Period III. An inner wall (F325a), built against F325, was added from the E side of the jamb (F343) to the E wall of the room, a distance of 1.8m. F325a was sitting directly on top of the Period II ash, F307, and did not show the same heat discolouration as either the E wall of the room or the original N wall of the hearth (F325). It looked as if F325a had been added as a repair, since the original F325 had apparently suffered damage behind it.

Excavation to the N of the doorway (F326) revealed a passageway (F329), heading N between the E wall of the Hall and what is presumed to be the W wall of the Brewhouse. A maximum of 1.2m length of passageway (F329) was partially excavated, though not to bedrock. The passage width reduced from 1.8m to 1.5m over this short distance because the Brewhouse wall was at an oblique angle to that of the Hall, which formed its W boundary.

A path made up of mostly angular greywacke rock set in red clay (F330), ran N-S along the E side of the passageway, approximately half its width. The W half of the passageway contained, on a level with the path surface, a red brown clay (F332), with virtually no stone content. Adjacent to the doorway (F326), on its N side, a red sandstone riser slab (F328) had been set into the surface of the path (F330). Neither F330 or F332 were excavated and they are interpreted as Period III features, probably contemporary with the insertion of the doorway (F326). On top of F332 lay a deposit of black clay, loam and ash mix (F320), which may be contemporary with the most recent ash feature in the Kitchen itself (F305). The silty clay accumulation (F303) extended directly over F320 and F330.

## DISCUSSION

Because the Kitchen at Fast Castle is physically separated from the Lower Courtyard, relationships between the structures were not directly comparable. In addition to this, the number of stratified diagnostic finds in the Kitchen was small. However, two good datable items were recovered from reliable contexts representing *termini ante* and *post quem* for the occupation of the room. These finds were a Crux Pellit coin (late 15th century) in the bedrock fill (F319) below the large primary hearth and a clay pipe bowl of mid 17th- century date in the lowest part of the post-abandonment accumulation (F303). This indicated that the span of time for the occupation of the Kitchen matched that of the Lower Courtyard.

Although this evidence may be regarded as slight, the method of construction of the Kitchen, and the fact that the original build appeared to have been followed by only one major modification, closely reflected the situation in the Lower Courtyard.

The roughly levelled area, the platform for the Kitchen, immediately E of the Hall, appears to have been quarried at the same time as the Lower Courtyard, ie in Period II in the late 15th century. First built in Period II, the Kitchen occupied approximately the same area throughout its useful life. The original configuration comprised the following:

> A large cooking hearth (F300) occupying most, if not all of the E end of the room. Towards the centre of the room lay a second, smaller, hearth (F316) one of whose possible functions was to provide a source of ignition for the main hearth. There was evidence to indicate that some sort of structure, possibly a bread oven, had existed in the NW corner of the room at this time, with which the small hearth may also have had some connection. During Period II the entrance to the Kitchen appears to have been through the N wall (F324) just W of where the room narrows.

In Period III, several modifications were made to the Kitchen:

> Most of the floor of the room, excluding the area of the main hearth, was levelled by the deposition of clay (F306) to the E and N of the small central hearth (F316) and by crude flagging (F311) to its W and S. The small central hearth continued in use in Period III. The structure in the NW corner of the room was removed at this point and the 'new' floor sealed the Period II ash deposits.

> A drain (F317) was let through the S wall of the room with its flagstone base clearly resting on the top of the Period II ash (F 307/314). The original entrance to the Kitchen was blocked and a new one (F326) inserted, still in the N wall, but W of the original position and adjacent to the wall of the Hall. This entrance position coincides with that shown on the 1549 plan (illus 6, 25-26).

> The inner N wall (F325) of the main hearth was refaced by the addition of a new skin of masonry (F325a). Examination of the original wall behind the new facing indicated damage which presumably was the reason for its addition. The new facing had no apparent heat damage, when compared with older exposed walling in the hearth, and there are two likely explanations: either the room had altered function, or more probably, the facing was added very late in Period III.2 towards the end of the occupation of the castle.

## 4.3 THE WELL

The site of the Well was visible before excavation as a circular depression, 3m in diameter, located on the relatively level area immediately to the SW of the promontory where the Castle is built (illus 7). To the E and N of this area cliffs reach down to the sea, and inland, to the S, the ground rises abruptly to form Hawks Heugh. Smaller-scale surface features include a truncated bank or causeway, running to within 3m of the Well on its NW side, and followed by the line of the path to the castle. A less pronounced bank runs from the E side of the Well to the foot of the slope at the S. Thus the Well lies towards the S side of a roughly triangular area bounded by these two banks and the hillside. The earliest plan of the castle drawn in 1549 does not indicate any method of water supply to the inner ward of the castle, or cover the location of the Well on the landward approach to the castle. An excavation (Craw 1924) is recorded as having uncovered at least part of the Well-head. Subsequently some inaccurate remarks on the Well were published, apparently derived loosely from this excavation (Russell 1938, 47).

In 1975-7, an area 3m by 6m (area ABCD in illus 28), including half of the Well-head, was excavated to the water table. Also a drainage ditch, 0.5m by 1.5m, was dug leading from the N corner of the main excavation area. This slightly lowered the water table, but not enough to allow work to continue. In 1986 the excavation was extended to include all the Well-head and its immediate surroundings. At the same time the Well was siphoned and baled, so that it could be completely excavated.

Work in the Well area identified three phases, but because they have not been related to the Lower Courtyard and Kitchen Periods, they are given the separate designations Phase 1W, Phase 2W, and Phase 3W.

PHASE 1W

This comprises a curving, clay-bonded stone wall, 7.5m long, lying at the S and E sides of the excavated area. A shelf had been cut into the upward-sloping natural to provide the wall with a level base. The wall as found stands 0.3-0.5m high, and was left in place by the excavators (Plate VIII; illus 28-29). It is constructed with a base of greywacke boulders, on average 0.4m long and 0.2m high, topped by two or three courses of smaller greywacke stones. Although there are a number of gaps in the upper courses, in some cases corresponding to stones found lying at its base, the impression formed was that the wall remains more or less complete, as originally built. From the wall's limited thickness in the upper courses, there seems little likelihood that it could ever have reached a much greater height. No traces were found of any post holes indicating a supplementary fence or palisade. The wall was backed to the S and E by a fill of stones and dark soil. The rear edge of the fill was marked in places by rather tenuous and fragmentary alignments of greywacke stones. Behind the wall and its fill, the natural slopes upward, covered by a 0.25m layer of small stones and sandy soil. This layer, accumulated by downwash from the hillside after the wall's construction, was topped at the site's SE corner by a level of red clay up to 0.1m deep.

The wall may have been constructed in association with the Well, providing a revetment holding back soil from slipping down the hillslope that lies to the S. However, it is also possible that the wall constituted part of an Iron Age round house base. First, there is a marked resemblance in form. Second, the wall seems unnecessarily elaborate as a revetment, because the slope here is not very steep. Third, fourteen sherds of Iron Age pottery, from at least two separate vessels, were found lying close together N of the wall close to its base (see below, Ceramics report). Although the pottery lay in an occupation level which might be interpreted as an extension of the floor associated with the Well-head, its disposition would suggest that the sherds had not been redeposited. Perhaps they were buried soon after breakage.

PHASES 2W, 3W

All the area round the Well-head was excavated to the water table, reached at an average depth of about 1.3m below the present turf line (Plate VIII; illus 29). Also, in a small area towards the NW corner of the site the excavation was continued down a further 0.5m, after the water table had been lowered by siphoning. The material removed comprised greywacke rubble, mostly from 50-150mm in diameter, but with a number of larger boulders, as much as 0.7m in diameter. Some of the stones showed marks of burning. The upper levels of rubble were loose and almost completely soil-free; further down, where most of the large boulders were located, the greywacke was embedded in considerable amounts of red soil or clay.

At about the same level as the top of the Well shaft, all this material was covered by a large 50-100mm layer of greywacke stones, mixed with red soil and clay, and fragments of broken sandstone, probably a floor or walking surface giving access to the Well (Phase 2W). This was overlaid in turn by a 0.4-0.6m layer of soil-free greywacke stones, on the whole very similar in size to those beneath the presumed floor, but with only one much larger boulder, 0.7m in diameter, found about the middle of the site close to the Well-head. The upper greywacke rubble was topped by a 50-100mm stone/soil/ clay layer (without broken sandstone), apparently a second, higher floor (Phase 3W). The N corner was filled by dark wet loam with a few greywacke stones, the two floors and two stone layers having been cut through at least to the lowest level reached here by the excavation. Immediately to the S and W of this corner the stones in the upper layer were somewhat larger and more loosely packed than average. Probably they include material from the N cut. The topsoil included a scattering of greywacke rubble with a few dressed sandstone fragments, concentrated at the N and W sides of the site, possibly from earlier excavations of the Well-head. To the E and S, 1.2-2m from the

**Illus 28** Plan, Well and wall

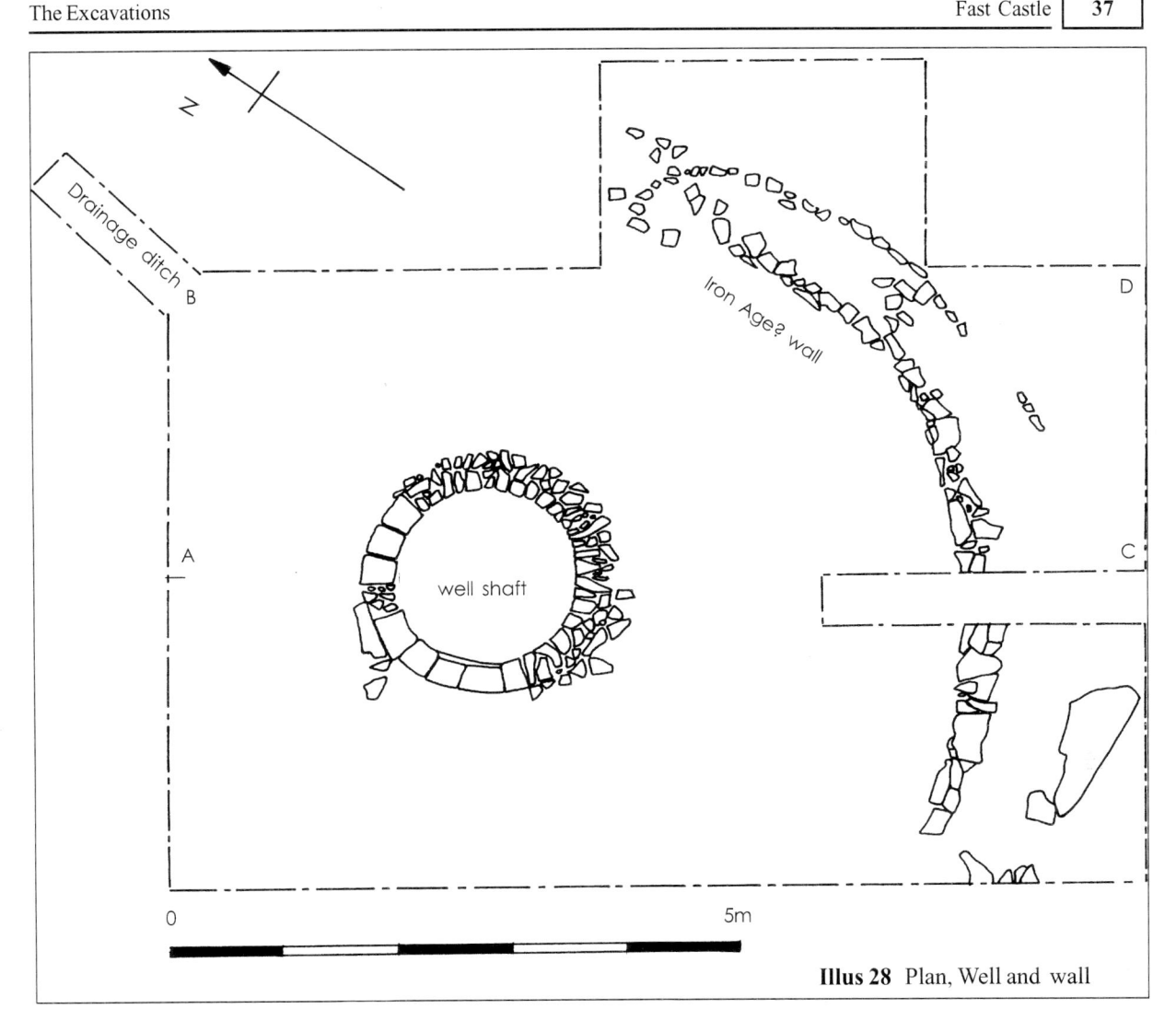

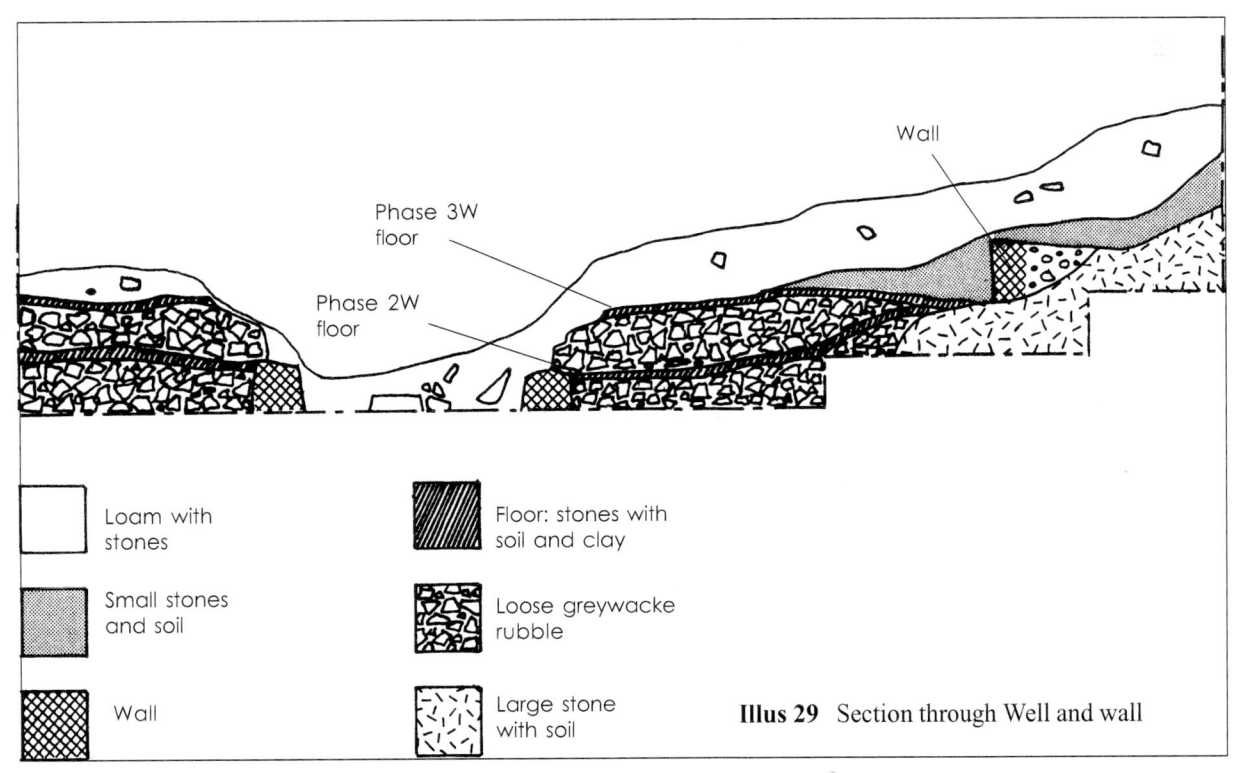

**Illus 29** Section through Well and wall

Well-head, the greywacke rubble was terminated by a mixture of flat stones and gritty soil, natural glacial till, sloping up towards the hill side. At the edge of the greywacke rubble the two floors joined together and became indistinguishable.

The Well lining, 0.3-0.4m thick, is constructed of greywacke rubble, to size 50-400mm, wedged firmly together, clay-bonded to the water line, and forming a circle 1.65m in diameter at its top inside edge. This structure was left intact by the excavators. The surface of the stones facing towards the interior of the Well shaft is a smooth face, while on the outer side the stones protrude into the lower floor and greywacke rubble. At its N and W sides the lining was topped with eight coping stones of dressed sandstone, the rest having been removed pre-1969 (illus 28, 30). The water table was reached 0.27m below the edge of the existing Well-head. After draining, the Well shaft was excavated, but it proved impractical to section its contents. As a safety precaution, when the excavation reached 1.8m in depth the part of the shaft which had been exposed to that point was lined with corrugated steel sheeting, held by a timber framework and ribs of reinforced concrete with steel bars. This shoring was left in place after the excavation had been completed. The base to the Well, greywacke bedrock sloping downwards from S to N at a 45 degree angle, was reached 3.78m below the shaft's top. The original paved floor had been cut through at an earlier date, as demonstrated by broken remnants of stone projecting from the Well side, at 3.27m depth. The internal diameter of the Well shaft at this point is 1.42m. Between the projecting stones and the bedrock base there was what appeared to be some of the original bedding material for the paved floor, comprising 0.1-0.2m stones, small stone chippings, and red clay. The fill removed from the Well shaft included greywacke rubble and silt. There was also a certain amount of organic material, most abundant in the upper levels, including in excess of 300 pieces of branch or twig, nearly half of which was identified as silver birch and hawthorn.

## DISCUSSION

The only datable medieval or early modern period finds were made in the topsoil. They comprised a large iron key of 16th-century type, and a James IV billon penny. A few undatable finds were made in stratified locations on the floors adjacent to the Well shaft. These included: from the lower floor, an iron nailhead and a fragment of bone; from the upper floor, a small iron nailhead or bootstud, and two small pieces of green-glazed pottery. Finds from the Well shaft included: the neck of a modern glass bottle, one small and very abraded sherd of pottery, a 45mm diameter lead disk, two stone roofing tiles, twelve dressed stones, most of them broken, and five pieces of worked wood, one of which may have been part of a ladder. The bottle neck was found at a depth of 0.4m from the top of the Well lining. Three of the dressed stones were curved in shape, cut from red sandstone, with the same radius as the Well-head. The length of these pieces ranged from 0.27m to 0.56m, their height from 0.15m to 0.26m, and their thickness, between inner and outer curve, from 0.19m to 0.2m. They were found at a depth of about 2m. The lead disk and the five pieces of worked wood came from a depth of c3m, being the only artefacts found in the Well's lower levels, even though all excavated material from below 2.5m was sieved through 10mm square mesh.

The Well shaft had two phases. The first, Phase 2W, associated with the lower floor, is represented by the surviving structure, which remains almost complete, except for its coping stones, and a semi-circular scoop, 0.25m deep, missing from the rubble lining fabric at the NW. In the Well's second phase, Phase 3W, the top of the Well shaft was raised by c0.4m, together with the addition of a further layer of surrounding greywacke rubble and the upper floor. The only identifiable remains of the extra Well fabric are the three pieces of curved stonework found in the shaft. On each piece one inside curved edge is rounded in section, so apparently they were coping stones. Presumably the Well-head was raised in order to increase shaft capacity; perhaps the removal of the Well's paved floor had the same purpose.

**Illus 30** Well-head

The material excavated from the Well shaft, mainly medium-sized rubble, with a few large stones, was clearly placed there by deliberate filling. The roofing tiles, and broken pieces of dressed red sandstone, similar to material found in the main castle buildings, may have resulted from the castle passing out of use. However, so few artefacts were recovered from the Well shaft, in particular from its lower levels, as to preclude any firm judgement on the circumstances under which it ceased to function as a water supply. The paucity of finds might be due to post-occupation excavations (although the 1924 diggers do not seem to have gone very deep), or to the fact that, while in use, the Well was regularly cleaned out. This has been the practice in modern times with such shallow wells or cisterns. The absence of closely-datable, stratified finds makes it impossible to relate the Well area's phasing to the Periods of the Lower Courtyard and Kitchen.

Because the united floor level associated with the Well-head came so close to the putative Iron Age wall, probably this wall had been exposed when the well was in use, helping to define the access area.

The subsequent cut found at the N corner of the site was probably intended to reach the water table again, perhaps as provision for livestock. From this corner a slight surface depression runs from the excavated area down the slope in a N direction. The depression is marked in dry weather by a line of greener, lusher grass. A painting of Fast Castle and its approaches, made about 1820 by the Rev John Thomson (illus 4), shows a hollow aligned from N to S, at a point corresponding to the present depression (Lang 1902, 154). Apparently the Well shaft was built for most of its depth in a bed of loose stones that filled a depression in the greywacke bedrock, perhaps a quarry used to supply building material for the castle. This would create a sump or reservoir for water running from the hill slope at the S, with the banks to the E and NW serving as retaining barriers (illus 7). Excavation indicates that the E bank at least is mainly natural. The fire blackening found on many of the large greywacke stones may result from attempts to break them up and increase the amount of water that the reservoir could hold. From observation of siphoning during drainage, it is estimated that the present water capacity of the Well to its maximum depth, and its surrounding aquifer, is about 23,000 litres, with eighty per cent of the containment space lying around the shaft's upper 2m. However, if the soil and clay found among the lower rubble levels result from the long-term accumulation of sediment, then the Well's capacity may in the past have been greater, perhaps about 27,000 litres. After being drained out to a depth of 1.8m, the water level did not rise significantly during five weeks of dry weather in June-July 1986. It was also found that light showers had little or no effect in raising the water level, but heavier rainfall (10-20mm) filled the Well within a few days. The Well is therefore not fed by regular springs. Nevertheless, it is estimated that it would usually have been able to deliver at least 450 litres of water per day, which should have been enough for the castle's normal number of occupants with their livestock. However, during extreme drought the Well may not have been sufficient to meet the needs of an enlarged garrison or population at the castle. (The local average annual rainfall is 694mm, or 58mm per month, but from February to June the monthly average is only 47mm). Fast Castle's water supply is considered further in Appendix 7.2.

The Finds — Fast Castle — 41

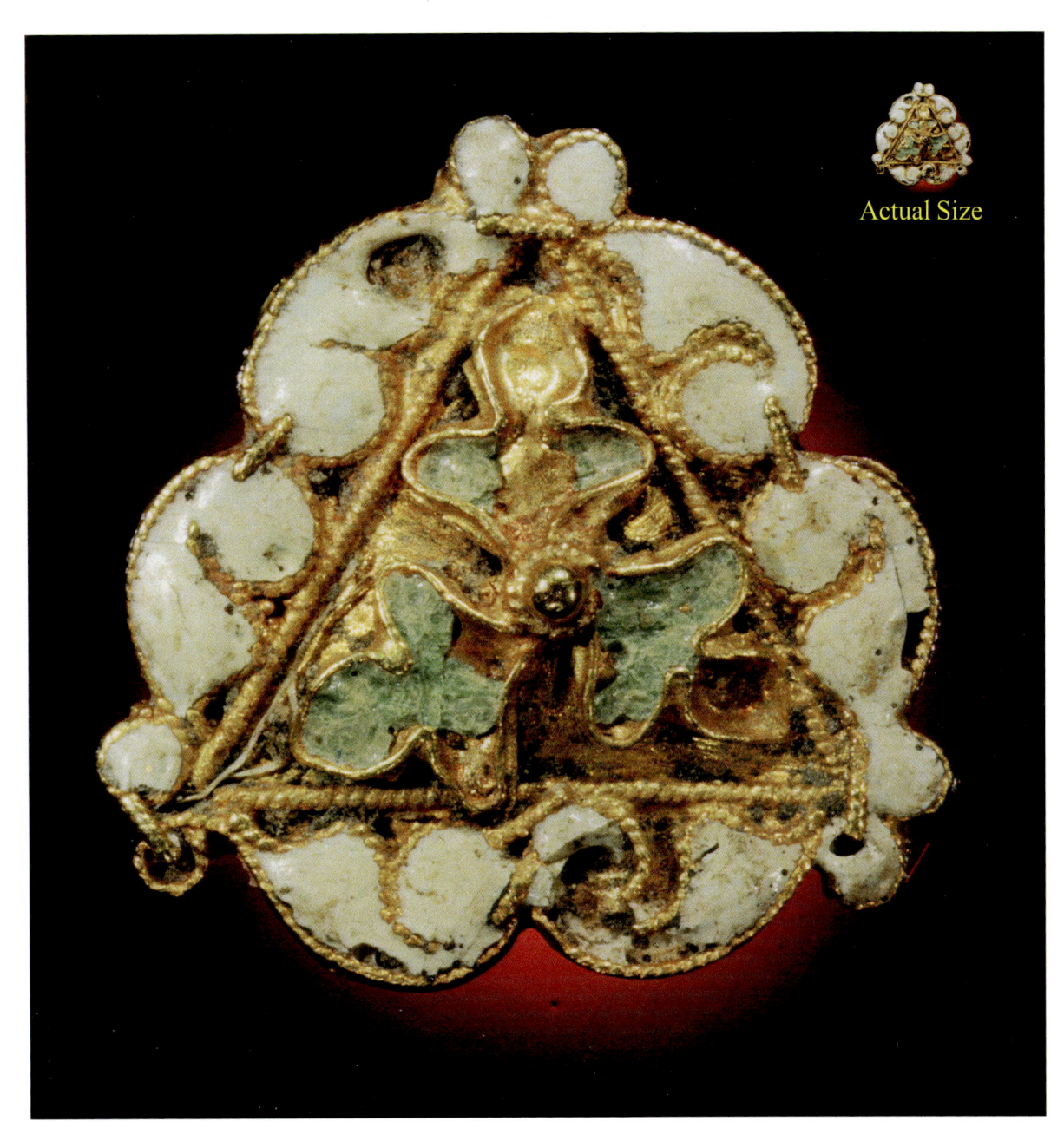

**Plate IX** Enamelled gold button; Scale 9:1 (NMS)

Actual Size

**Plate X** Scottish Medieval and later pottery
Group D; Red Ware; Urinal (NMS)

**Plate XI** Scottish Medieval and later pottery; Group E; Reduced Gritty Ware, 34.55 and 34.57 (NMS).

**Plate XII** Scottish Medieval and later pottery: Clockwise from left; 1 & 2: Group E, Reduced Gritty Ware, 34.54 and 34.43; 3: Group F, Partially Reduced Gritty Ware, 35.59; 4: Group J, Imported Ware, 36.21 (NMS)

**Plate XIII** Opal fragments
(NMS)

**Plate XIV** Iron 'grille', Cat No 65
(EAFS)

**Plate XV** Wooden beam end with iron attachment
Scale 1:10 (EAFS)

**Plate XVI** as Plate XV, reverse side
Scale 1:8 (EAFS)

# 5 FINDS

## 5.1 NUMISMATICA (Coins and Jetons)

Nicholas McQ Holmes

The items examined comprised 34 coins, two jetons, and seven complete or fragmentary blank discs of copper alloy. The date range represented by the identifiable pieces covers the period from the second half of the 15th century to the late 16th century. All the coins are of comparatively low tariff, with the Scottish pieces all being of billon or copper. The three English coins, although of silver, are also of fairly small denominations for the 16th century. English low-value coins continued to be struck in silver until the 17th century.

**Archaeological Significance**

Most of the numismatic finds came from the Lower Courtyard. A consideration of the stratigraphic distribution of datable items may have some value in dating the deposition of the material excavated from this area.

OUTER LOWER COURTYARD (Areas 1, 2, 3, and 7)

The most deeply stratified coins in this area were five Scottish copper CRUX PELLIT issues, generally accepted as belonging within the second half of the 15th century (nos 5-8, & 11). The suggested attribution of these coins to an ecclesiastical mint owned by Bishop Kennedy of St Andrews has been challenged (Murray 1977, 121), and their dating to within Kennedy's episcopate (c1452-80) is therefore also open to doubt, but it is fairly certain that at least some of these coins belong within this period, and quite possibly all of them. All five of these CRUX PELLITS were found not far above bedrock, implying a *terminus post quem* of c1450 for the earliest deposits in this area. An 'ecclesiastical issue' copper farthing (no 13) from F13a, just above bedrock, also belongs to the latter part of the 15th century.

A CRUX PELLIT coin (no 6) from F6 was accompanied by a forgery of a billon bawbee of Mary (no 21). The earlier coin must clearly have been redeposited. The forgery would have been identified and rejected fairly rapidly, and appears to display comparatively little evidence of wear. Single CRUX PELLIT coins in F56 (no 11) and F122 (no 5) also tend to support a mid to late 15th century date for these deposits.

Topsoil (Layer 2) in the Outer Lower Courtyard contained five coins and one jeton definitely minted during the second half of the 16th century (nos 2, 3, 22, 23, 27 & 33), and nothing demonstrably later. In the case of such a wide-spread deposit it is dangerous to draw too many conclusions, but if Layer 2 represents a single and homogeneous deposit, the *terminus post quem* for its formation must be at least 1583, the earliest date of issue for the James VI billon plack (no 27), and probably somewhat later. The absence of common 17th-century issues such as turners of Charles I strongly suggests, but does not prove, that deposition had been completed before c1632.

INNER LOWER COURTYARD (Areas 4, 5, 6 and 8)

Somewhat more complicated stratigraphy in this area renders dating of individual features rather more hazardous, but the overall picture appears to be similar to that in the Outer Lower Courtyard. The most deeply stratified coins were two further CRUX PELLIT issues, one of them fragmentary (nos 9a & 12) from F104a and a fragment of a plack (no 19) in F83. Unfortunately the latter is not attributable more closely than to James III-V. Between the horizons represented by F104 (earlier) and F86 (later) belong four items dating from the later 15th century: two further CRUX PELLIT coins (no 10 in F92, no 4 in F99a), a fragmentary plack of James IV (no 14 in F102) and a late 15th-century jeton (no 32 in F103b).

Stratified and identifiable items from F86 and above it are all of 16th-century date, the earliest being a half-plack and two pennies of James IV (nos 15, 16a, & 17). The half-plack was found in topsoil (Layer 2) and had been redeposited. Later issues comprised an early penny and a fragmentary lion/hardhead of Mary (nos 20 & 24), a plack of James VI (no 26) and an English groat of Henry VIII (no 1). The stratigraphic distribution of these 16th-century coins was not directly related to their chronology, but the absence of any 17th-century or later items again points to a cessation of activity in the area by c1632, if not earlier.

The overall picture presented by all the numismatic finds from the Lower Courtyard is thus generally consistent. The absence of any coins earlier than the middle of the 15th century is not normally regarded as conclusive evidence of lack of earlier activity on Scottish sites, since it was only at that time, when the advent of billon and copper 'small change' placed money in any quantity within the reach of poorer people, that casual coin losses became commonplace. However, at Fast Castle there were few 'coinless' deposits below those in which CRUX PELLIT issues were found, (except in the Quarry, below F104), and the number of these coins which were recovered strongly suggests that they are to be seen as associated with the earliest archaeologically recorded activity in this area of the castle.

With the exception of a few obviously redeposited items, a steady pattern of coin loss from mid-15th to late 16th century is apparent from the stratified finds, with a concentration of the latest items in the highest levels. This latter aspect, together with a total absence of any numismatic material minted later than 1600, points clearly towards a cessation of activity on the site at around that time, although the relative scarcity of late James VI and early Charles I coppers, compared with those of the 1632 and later issues, must result in the exercise of caution in putting so precise a date on this. The absence of any of the ubiquitous 'Stirling turners', issued in huge numbers from 1632, however, is almost certainly conclusive evidence of abandonment by that date.

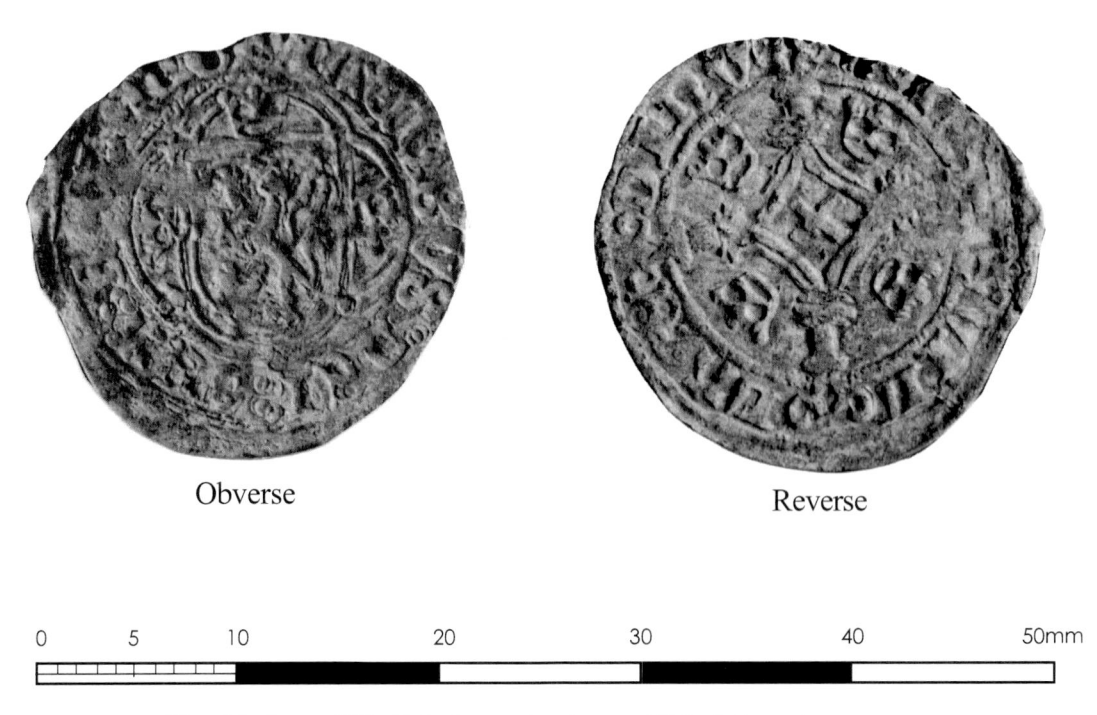

**Illus 31** James IV half plack; previously unpublished die variety

## Numismatic Significance

The presence of ten examples of the Scottish copper CRUX PELLIT issue (nos 4-12) at Fast Castle provides further evidence that these coins were in common use in the later 15th century. By contrast, only one example of the roughly contemporary copper farthings was recovered (no 13). The CRUX PELLIT coins comprise five specimens of type Ia, two of IIa, two of III, and one uncertain. These proportions are unusual, since type III coins are normally the most common amongst finds from excavations. Since there is no evidence for the relative dating of the various types, however, it is impossible to say whether this has any significance. The one copper farthing is of one of the so-called 'ecclesiastical' issues, a description for which the justification is open to considerable doubt.

Later coins provide a fair cross-section of the base metal coinage which circulated in Scotland in the 16th century, with billon issues of James IV, Mary, and James VI. The most interesting individual piece is a rare half-plack of James IV (no 15, illus 31). It belongs to type IIa, as listed by Stewart (1967), but it displays several variations from previously recorded examples. The obverse and reverse initial marks, of a cross pattée and a crown respectively, are recorded on placks of type IIa, but not previously on halves. The single stop on the reverse comprises four pellets arranged in the form of a cross. Burns (1887, 215-6) mentions a third variety of half-plack illustrated by Cardonnel (1786, 35 & Pl.I, no 4, attributed to James II) 'having the words represented as divided by four points disposed as crosses'. These stops are on the obverse of the coin illustrated by Cardonnel, and Burns regarded them as mistaken readings of five-pointed stars, on the grounds that the initial mark was a slender cross fleurie, as found on placks with words divided by five-pointed stars. The Fast Castle example has an obverse initial mark of a cross pattée, however, so this argument is not valid despite the indistinct nature of the reverse stop.

Other items worthy of note are examples of two rare issues - the early penny of Mary (no 20) and the half-hardhead of James VI (no 29) - and the forgery of a bawbee of Mary (no 21). The latter may have been made on the continent, perhaps in Flanders, which was the source of widespread forgeries of various small denomination Scottish coins in the 16th century.

The two jetons were both made in Nuremberg, Germany, the earlier being a close copy of a contemporary French type struck for use in the Dauphiné (no 32). The obverse type of these jetons was, in turn, copied from that of the gold Ecus, for the Dauphiné, of Louis XI (1461-83). The French jetons were probably struck both during Louis XI's reign and for some time afterwards, into the early 16th century. The Nuremberg copies are thought to belong to the 1480s and 1490s, and can usually be distinguished from the French issues by the presence of one or two issue letters at the end of the obverse and reverse legends. Unfortunately the piece from Fast Castle does not display these, but there is space for extra letters at the end of the obverse legend, where the actual reading is not legible. Both legends also contain minor spelling errors - ENTENDE for ENTENDES, and MESCOMPTE for MESCOMPTES - each representing a grammatical error. This suggests that the dies were prepared by someone unfamiliar with the French language. This jeton was found with a round piece of leather cut to the same size. The purpose of this is uncertain.

The later jeton is an issue of Hans Krauwinckel I, probably dating from the period 1580-6, and is of a very common type (no 33). This Krauwinckel was the uncle of Hans II, who was the most prolific of all the Nuremberg jeton-makers.

The most puzzling of this group of finds are a collection of plain copper alloy discs. Apart from no 34, all the complete examples are of similar diameter, averaging 20mm or slightly over. One (no 40) has traces of a silver wash on both surfaces, and since there has been surface corrosion on all these pieces, it may be that others were at one time coated in a similar way. One disc (no 36) has an arc cut from the edge, and this would have resulted if another disc of similar diameter had been cut from a sheet overlapping this one. The purpose of these items can not be firmly established. It has been suggested that they were blanks intended for use in the striking of forged coins, and circumstantial evidence might support this. All the discs came from later levels on the site, where 16th-century coins were also found. The discs are of a suitable size for use in forging billon placks or bawbees of the middle of the 16th century, and the silver wash might suggest that this was the intention. This can only be speculation, however, since no evidence was found for the striking of coins at Fast Castle, nor was there anything to prove that the discs themselves had been manufactured at this location. Other uses for the discs are equally plausible, including gaming counters or makeshift jetons for use with a counting-board.

### CATALOGUE

N = North (1975);   S = Stewart (1967)

ENGLISH COINS

**1** HENRY VIII : silver groat, 3rd coinage, Tower mint (1544-47): 1.77g : type as N.1844.
obv: lis hEnRI[C'ₓ 8]⊹G[RAˣₓ AGLˣₓ FRAˣₓ Z ]hIBˣₓ RE[Xˣₓ ]
: 2nd bust
rev: lis [POSVIˣₓ DE]Vˣₓ [A] DIVTOREˣₓ MEVˣₓ
: annulets (?) in cross-ends.
Worn and bent; part of coin missing (below bust on obverse).
FD 332. Area 5, F202 (?); Period III-IV

**2** ELIZABETH I : silver threepence, 2nd issue (1578-9) : 1.20g type as N.1998.
obv: +ELIZAB D G ANG FR ET HIB REGI
: rose behind head
rev: +POSVI|DE[ ]D|IVTORE|M[ ]V :
: date above shield, last figure illegible; plain cross initial marks.
Fairly light wear on obverse; apparently more on reverse, possibly resulting from surface corrosion.
TH 11/23.  Area 1, Layer 2; Period III-IV

**3** ELIZABETH I : silver sixpence, 2nd issue (1581): 3.00g : type as N.1997.
obv: +ELIZABETH:D'.G'.ANG⁽¹⁾.FR'.ET:HI'.REGINA
: rose behind head
rev: +POSVI|DEV'.AD|IVTORE|M.MEV' .
: date above shield; long cross initial marks.
Most of surfaces apparently fairly worn, but probably weakly struck in parts.
TH 18/1.  Area 2, Layer 2; Period III-IV

SCOTTISH COINS

**4** Copper CRUX PELLIT issue, type Ia : 1.60g : type as S.95.
obv: IAC[        ]AˣREXˣₓ

rev: [       ]ˣPELLIT[       ]
: stop may be a star or a saltire; pellets on cusps, nothing in spandrels. Moderate wear; some surface corrosion.
FK 197.  Area 5, F99a; Period II.2

**5** Copper CRUX PELLIT issue, type Ia : 0.90g : type as S.95.
obv: illegible
rev: [         ]PELLIT⍨0[       ]

: pellets on cusps; nothing in spandrels.
Moderate wear; surfaces corroded.
FC 253.  Area 2, F122/126; Period II-III.1

**6** Copper CRUX PELLIT issue, type Ia : 1.36g : type as S.95.
obv: IACOBVS[        ]GRA⁽ˣ⁾REXˣ

rev: +[     ]ˣPELLITˣOIEˣ[   ]II'
: pellets on cusps, nothing in spandrels.
Poorly struck in parts; slight wear only.
FB 557. Area 1, F6; Period II-III

**7** Copper CRUX PELLIT issue, type Ia : 1.59g : type as S.95.
obv: IACOBVS⁽ˣ⁾D[       ]BAˣREXˣₓˣ

rev: +CR[         ]OIE[     ]RIM
: pellets on cusps, nothing in spandrels.
Fairly thick flan; only slight wear, but some parts poorly struck; slight surface corrosion on reverse.
FB 1128. Area 1, F25; Period II

**8** Copper CRUX PELLIT issue, type Ia : 2.57g : type as S.95 var. (p141).
obv: IACOBVS_ DEI_GRAˣREXˣₓ

rev: +PELLITˣOIEˣC[     ]
: pellets on cusps, nothing in spandrels.
Fairly worn; some surface corrosion.
FB 1129. Area 1, F25; Period II

**9** Copper CRUX PELLIT issue, type IIa : 1.74g : type as S.97.
obv: +_IACOBVS[               ]

rev: [        ]ITːOEᵒC[        ]
: ?saltires on cusps, annulets in spandrels.
Surfaces much corroded.
FP 182.  Kitchen area, F319; Period II

**9a** Copper CRUX PELLIT issue, type IIa : 0.87g. :type as S.97.
obv: [IACO] BVS DEI GRA REX
: stops, if any, are illegible
rev: [            ]OIEːC[        ]

: symbols on cusps and in spandrels not distinguishable.
Reverse off-centre; highly corroded.
FI 2166a.   Area 5, F104a; Period II.2

**10** Copper CRUX PELLIT issue, type IIIa (orb tilted up & to left) : 1.62g.: type as S.99.
obv: [           ]S∘DEI∘GRAR[           ]

rev:  +CRVX✻PELLT✻OIE✻CRI✻
: apparently star stops; stars on cusps, nothing in spandrels.
Fairly worn; some surface corrosion.
FC 959.   Area 6, F92; Period II.1

**11** Copper CRUX PELLIT issue, type III (orb tilted upwards, but lateral direction uncertain) : 1.63g.
obv:  IACOBVSE_I_BABEX
: no stops, very small rosette
rev:  C[           ]∘OIE∘CRIM⁂
: no initial mark; annulets on cusps, nothing in spandrels.
Struck off-centre; fairly worn; some surface corrosion.
FB 1056.   Area 3, F56; Period II

**12** Fragment of a copper CRUX PELLIT issue, of uncertain type.
Only central part of coin survives, and obverse is almost entirely featureless: cross visible in centre of reverse, with part of tressure, but no other details.
Probably average wear; much surface corrosion.
FL 1.   Area 5, F104a; Period II.2

**13** 'Ecclesiastical issue' copper farthing, type III : 0.31g : type as S.101.
obv: trefoil

rev:  MO|PA|VP|ER
Probably slight to moderate wear; much surface corrosion.
FB 160.   Area 1, F13a; Period II-III

**14** Three fragments of a billon plack of JAMES IV.
obv: illegible
rev: crowns in angles of cross; plain saltire in centre
Badly corroded.
FD 1207.   Area 6, F102; Period II.2

**15** JAMES IV : billon half-plack, type IIa : 0.78g.
obv:  +IACOBVS:DEI:GRA:BEX:SCO
: initial mark cross pattée
rev:  crown VIL|LA∴E|DInV|RGh
: stop of 4 pellets in form of cross. Stewart (p146) does not list cross pattée or crown initial marks for type IIa half-placks, but they are found on IIa placks.
Light to moderate wear; some corrosion at edge.
FA 63.   Area 6, Layer 2; Period III-IV  (illus 31)

**16** JAMES IV : billon penny, 2nd issue, type IV (c1504/5-10) : type as S.134.
Large piece missing below and to left of bust; edge damaged elsewhere; some surface corrosion; probably average wear.
Unstratified.  Period II-IV

**16a** JAMES IV : billon penny, 2nd issue, type IV (c1504/5-10) : 0.52g : type as S.134.
obv:  +IA[COBVS………S]COTTORV

rev: illegible : crowns and lys in angles
Mostly worn.
FF 747.   Area 5, F86; Period III.1

**17** Billon penny, almost certainly of JAMES IV, 2nd issue, type IV : (c1504/5-10) : 0.41g.: type as S.134.
obv: illegible : no distinguishable features
rev: long cross with crowns and lys in alternate angles
Very worn, with some surface corrosion : the large size of the lys on the reverse suggests that the coin is of James IV, and not of the rare type III of the first issue of Mary (S.163). The small size of the flan suggests that the coin is of type IV of James IV's 2nd issue.
FG 1446.   Area 5, F206; Period III-IV

**18** Four fragments of a billon penny of JAMES IV, 2nd issue, uncertain type (c1500-10).
Largest fragment shows little wear on reverse, but all are dirty and corroded.
FF 1018a.   From top of Well; Phase 3W

**19** Fragment of a billon plack of JAMES III, IV, or V (c1470-1526).
FC 680.   Area 6, F83; Period II.1

**20** MARY : billon penny, 1st issue, type 1a (c1547-50) : 0.54g : type as S.162.
Moderate wear : some corrosion on reverse.
FD 145.   Area 5, F202; Period III-IV

**21** Forgery of a billon bawbee of MARY, early type (c1542-54) : 2.04g : type as S.154.
Very base alloy; bent; surface corroded; degree of wear uncertain, but possibly not very great.
FA 343.   Area 1, F6; Period II-III

**22** MARY : billon plack, 1st period (1557) : 1.42g : type as S.157.
Moderate wear; some surface corrosion.
TH 19/1.   Area 2, Layer 2; Period III-IV

**23** MARY : billon lion/hardhead, 1st period (1555-8) : 0.80g : type as S.160. Countermarked with heart and star in 1572.
Fairly worn.
FA 258.   Area 3, Layer 2; Period III-IV

**24** Two fragments of a billon lion/hardhead of FRANCIS & MARY (1559-60) : type as S.161.
Surfaces corroded; traces of silvering on reverse.
FG 1518.   Area 5, F206; Period III-IV

**25** JAMES VI : billon plack, type 2 (1583-90) : 1.59g : type as S. page 153.
Fairly worn.
FI 305a.   Area 5, F97(?); Period III

**26** JAMES VI : billon plack, type 3 (1583-90) : 1.02g : type as S.192.
Large flan; worn and bent.
FE 852a.   Area 5, F206; Period III-IV

**27** JAMES VI : billon plack, type 3 (1583-90) : 1.83g : type as S.192.

Moderate wear; coin has turned over during striking and been struck twice, so that part of obverse legend appears on reverse and vice versa.
TH 3/10. Area 1, Layer 2; Period III-IV

**28** JAMES VI : billon hardhead, 2nd issue (Nov 1588) : 1.42g : type as S.200.
Much corroded; probably average wear.
FG 2945. Area 5, F209; Period III.2

**29** JAMES VI : billon half-hardhead (Nov 1588) : 0.58g : type as S.201.
Slight to moderate wear, with some surface pitting; corroded at edge.
FB 363. Area 1, F13; Period II-III

**30** Illegible and highly corroded billon or copper disc, of maximum diameter c21mm.
No details survive; possibly burnt.
FI 960d. Area 4 or 5, F202; Period III-IV

**30a** Illegible and highly corroded billon or copper disc, of diameter 18mm: 15th-17th century.
No details survive.
FD 450. Area 5, F86; Period III.1

**31** Almost entirely illegible coin of base billon or copper, diameter 19 x 17mm: probably 16th or 17th century.
Both surfaces are highly corroded, but there is a suggestion of a crowned FM monogram on one side. The coin may therefore be a 12-penny groat, or 'nonsunt', of Francis and Mary (1558-9), type as S.158.
FC 1046. Area 1, Layer 2; Period III-IV


JETONS

**32** German brass jeton of Nuremberg : diameter 30mm : 1.69g : probably 1480s-1490s.
obv: +GETTES:EnTEnDE:AV:COmPT[ ]
: a field of France-modern and Dauphiné quarterly, within a granulated inner circle.
rev: crown GARDES:VOVS:DE:mESCOmPTE
: a field of France-ancient within a granulated inner circle. Cf. Mitchiner (1988), 345-6, nos 1035-8.
Slight wear; corroded.
FH 3179. Area 5, F103b; Period II.2

**33** German brass jeton of Hans Krauwinckel I, Nuremberg : diameter 25mm : 1.69g : probably c1580-6.
obv: -¦-HANS-¦-KRAVWINCKEL-¦-GOTESS
: 3 open crowns and 3 lys arranged alternately around a rose, within plain inner circle.
rev: -¦-RECHEN-¦-PFENNIG-¦-NVRENBER
: Reichsapfel in double tressure of 3 curves and 3 angles alternately: symbols in spandrels: plain inner circle. Type as Mitchiner (1988), 432, nos 1486-9.
Very little wear; pierced, and with 2 chips missing from edge.
FD 24. Area 2, Layer 2?; Period III-IV

BLANK COPPER ALLOY DISCS

**34** 17.5 x 16.5mm : 0.92g.
FC 254. Area 5, Layer 2; Period III-IV

**35** 20mm : 1.23g.
TH 4/2. Area 1, probably Layer 2; Period III-IV

**36** Incomplete disc, of diameter 20mm, with arc cut from edge as if another disc had been cut from a sheet overlapping this one; also an irregular hole and a crack : 1.55g.
FB 319. Area 1, Layer 2; Period III-IV

**37** 21 x 20mm : 1.23g.
TH 3/11. Area 1, Layer 2 ? Period III-IV

**38** Broken segment of a disc of diameter c20mm.
FE 852. Area 5, F204; Period III-IV

**39** 20.5mm : 1.30g.
TH 12/4. Area 1, Layer 2; Period III-IV

**40** 22 x 19mm : 2.10g : traces of silver wash on both surfaces
TH 12/11. Area 1, Layer 2; Period III-IV

## 5.2 CERAMICS

Valerie E Dean; Trevor Cowie; George Haggarty & Sarah Jennings; Hugh G Robertson

This is an interesting assemblage of some 1697 sherds, with a total weight of 33.315kg, representing a minimum count of 268 vessels. Iron Age material (Fabric group A) accounts for 0.8 per cent of the total sherd assemblage and the Roman (Fabric group B) for less than 0.1 per cent. The Scottish medieval and later pottery (Fabric groups C-H) comprises 86.3 per cent and the imported medieval pottery (Fabric group J) accounts for a further 10.5 per cent (Chart 1). The post-occupation and modern (Fabric groups K-L) sherds account for 2.4 per cent. The miscellaneous ceramics (Fabric group M) are not included in the quantification. The bulk of the pottery comes from the Quarry pit at Fast Castle, other sherds being from the Outer Lower Courtyard and the Kitchen. Some material comes from the area around the Well, situated a short distance from the castle promontory. Table 1 shows the distribution of the fabrics within these areas.

The importance of this assemblage is that as most of it emanates from the Quarry pit, later used as a midden, deposits can be dated to the period between the last quarter of the 15th century and the early to mid 17th century. In the relatively short time span of about 150 years, the collection provides a useful stratified example of the pottery used in a fortified house of the period. However, consideration must be given to later disturbances by visitors, including treasure hunters. These could well date from as early as 1594 until more recent times and could account for some of the very late ceramic material. Charts 2-8 show fabric quantification related to the phasing of the site.

Reports on the different fabric groups are as follows:

| | | | |
|---|---|---|---|
| **A** | **Iron Age pottery** | **J** | **Imported medieval pottery** |
| **B** | **Roman pottery** | **K-L** | **Post-occupation and modern pottery** |
| **C-H** | **Scottish medieval and later pottery** | **M** | **Miscellaneous ceramics** |

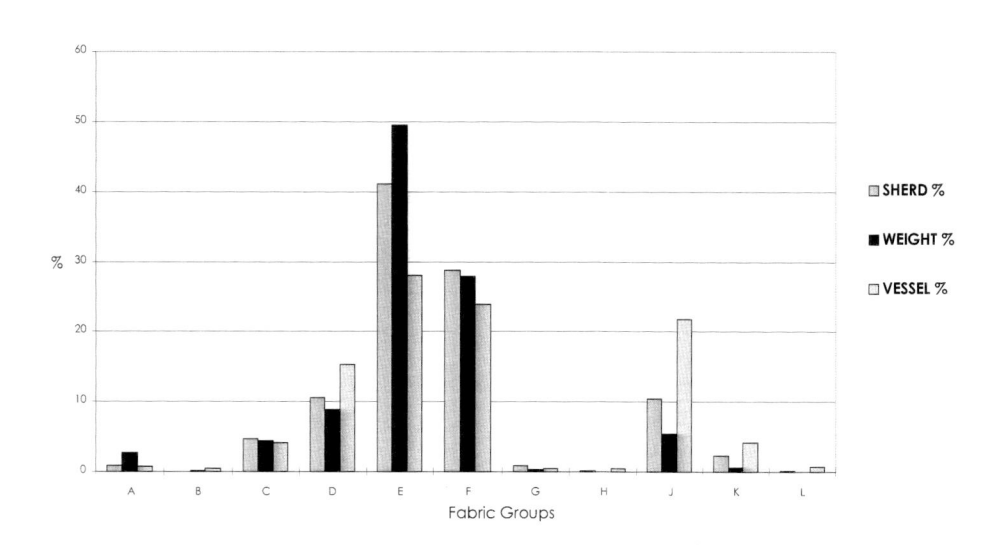

**Chart 1**
Ceramics: all fabrics: Sherd, Weight and Vessel Percentages

## QUARRY PIT

| FEATURE | A | B | C | D | E | F | G | H | J | K | L | Totals across | Sub-totals | PERIOD |
|---|---|---|---|---|---|---|---|---|---|---|---|---|---|---|
| pit 3 | | | | | 2 | 1 | | | 1 | | | 4 | | IV |
| pit 6 | | | | | | | | | | 1 | | 1 | 5 | IV |
| 202 | | | 1 | 4 | 11 | 21 | 2 | | 2 | 11 | | 52 | | III-IV |
| 204 | | | | 2 | 3 | 7 | | | 3 | 1 | | 16 | | III-IV |
| 206 | | | | 5 | 9 | 15 | | | | 1 | | 30 | 98 | III-IV |
| pit 2 | | | | 1 | 5 | 4 | | | 1 | | | 11 | | III |
| 95 | | | | | | 1 | | | 1 | | | 2 | | III.2 |
| 207 | | | | 1 | 4 | 1 | | | | | | 6 | | III.2 |
| 209 | | | | | | 2 | | | 1 | | | 3 | | III.2 |
| 96 | | | | 4 | 2 | 2 | | | | | | 8 | | III.2 |
| 97 | | | | 4 | 13 | 16 | | | 3 | | | 36 | | III.2 |
| 86 | | | | 16 | 31 | 50 | | 1 | 10 | | | 108 | 174 | III.1 |
| 97a | | | | 10 | 19 | 31 | | | 1 | | | 61 | | II.2 |
| 97a/b | | | | 3 | 33 | 7 | | | 1 | | | 44 | | II.2 |
| 99 | | 1 | 1 | 3 | 48 | 10 | | | 3 | 1 | | 67 | | II.2 |
| 97b | | | | 4 | 22 | 15 | | | 2 | | | 43 | | II.2 |
| 99(1) | | | | | 10 | 4 | | | | | | 14 | | II.2 |
| 99a | | | 1 | | 3 | 9 | | | | | | 13 | | II.2 |
| 99a/b | | | | | 4 | 5 | | | 1 | | | 10 | | II.2 |
| 97c | | | | | 2 | 3 | | | | | | 5 | | II.2 |
| 102 | | | 1 | 2 | 1 | 3 | | | | | | 7 | | II.2 |
| 100 | | | | 2 | 12 | 5 | | | 3 | | | 22 | | II.2 |
| 100a | | | | 2 | 12 | | | | 2 | | | 16 | | II.2 |
| 103 | | | 5 | 11 | 56 | 32 | | | 39 | | | 143 | | II.2 |
| 104 | | | 5 | 38 | 159 | 39 | | | 31 | | | 272 | 717 | II.2 |
| 105 | | | | 1 | | | | | | | | 1 | | II.1 |
| 106 | | | | 2 | 11 | 4 | | | | | | 17 | | II.1 |
| 107 | | | | | | 1 | | | | | | 1 | | II.1 |
| 108 | | | | 1 | | 1 | | | | | | 2 | | II.1 |
| 109 | | | 13 | 3 | 67 | 33 | | | 12 | | | 128 | | II.1 |
| 401 | | | | | 1 | 2 | | | | | | 3 | | II.1 |
| 402 | | | 4 | 11 | 4 | 4 | | | 1 | | | 24 | | II.1 |
| 403 | | | | 8 | 3 | 5 | | | 3 | | | 19 | 195 | II.1 |
| Sub-total | 0 | 1 | 31 | 138 | 547 | 333 | 2 | 1 | 121 | 15 | 0 | 1189 | 1189 | |

## QUARRY LEDGE

| FEATURE | A | B | C | D | E | F | G | H | J | K | L | Totals across | Sub-totals | PERIOD |
|---|---|---|---|---|---|---|---|---|---|---|---|---|---|---|
| 81 | | | | | 1 | 5 | | | 3 | | | 9 | 9 | III-IV |
| 88 | | | | | | 1 | | | | | | 1 | | III.2 |
| 85 | | | 1 | 1 | 1 | 6 | | | 2 | | | 11 | 12 | III.1 |
| 98 | | | 2 | 1 | 2 | 1 | | | 1 | | | 7 | | II |
| 92 | | | | | 1 | | | | 3 | | | 4 | | II.1 |
| 93 | | | 1 | 2 | 3 | 3 | | 1 | 1 | | | 11 | | II.1 |
| 83 | | | | | | 2 | | | | | | 2 | 24 | II.1 |
| Sub-total | 0 | 0 | 4 | 4 | 8 | 18 | 0 | 1 | 10 | 0 | 0 | 45 | 45 | |

**Table 1**
Ceramics: distribution of fabrics

## OUTER LOWER COURTYARD

| FEATURE | A | B | C | D | E | F | G | H | J | K | L | Totals across | Sub-totals | PERIOD |
|---|---|---|---|---|---|---|---|---|---|---|---|---|---|---|
| L2 | | | 15 | 18 | 34 | 51 | 6 | | 28 | 2 | 1 | 155 | 155 | III-IV |
| 49 | | | 1 | | 1 | | | | 1 | | | 3 | | III |
| 122 | | | 1 | | 2 | 1 | | | | | | 4 | | III.1 |
| 124 | | | | | | | | | 1 | | | 1 | 8 | III.1 |
| L3 | | | 2 | 1 | 11 | 7 | | | | | | 21 | | II-III |
| 1 | | | | 1 | | | | | | | | 1 | | II-III |
| 2 | | | | | 1 | 4 | | | | | | 5 | | II-III |
| 13 | | | 2 | 1 | 8 | 10 | | | 2 | 2 | | 25 | 52 | II-III |
| 8 | | | | | | 2 | | | | | | 2 | | II.1 |
| 3 | | | | | 1 | 1 | 1 | | 1 | | | 4 | | II.1 |
| 22 | | | 1 | | | | | | | | | 1 | | II.1 |
| 5 | | | 1 | | 1 | | | | | | | 2 | | II.1 |
| 23 | | | | | 1 | | | | | | | 1 | | II.1 |
| 24 | | | | | | 6 | | | | | | 6 | | II.1 |
| 56 | | | | | 2 | | | | 1 | | | 3 | | II.1 |
| 59 | | | | 3 | 1 | 2 | | | 1 | | | 7 | | II.1 |
| 162 | | | | | | 1 | | | | | | 1 | 27 | II.1 |
| Sub-total | 0 | 0 | 23 | 24 | 62 | 86 | 7 | 0 | 35 | 4 | 1 | 242 | 242 | |

## KITCHEN

| FEATURE | A | B | C | D | E | F | G | H | J | K | L | Totals across | Sub-totals | PERIOD |
|---|---|---|---|---|---|---|---|---|---|---|---|---|---|---|
| 301 | | | | | | | | | | | 1 | 1 | | IV |
| 303 | | | | | 3 | 2 | | | | | | 5 | 6 | IV |
| 305 | | | | | 1 | | | | | | | 1 | | III.2 |
| 306 | | | 6 | | | | | | | | | 6 | | III |
| 311 | | | | | | 1 | | | | | | 1 | | III |
| 313 | | | | | 1 | | | | | | | 1 | 9 | III |
| Sub-total | 0 | 0 | 6 | 0 | 5 | 3 | 0 | 0 | 0 | 0 | 1 | 15 | 15 | |

## BREWHOUSE

| FEATURE | A | B | C | D | E | F | G | H | J | K | L | Totals across | Sub-totals | PERIOD |
|---|---|---|---|---|---|---|---|---|---|---|---|---|---|---|
| 330 | | | | | | | | | | 4 | | 4 | 4 | IV |
| Total | | | | | | | | | | 4 | | 4 | 4 | |

## WELL

| FEATURE | A | B | C | D | E | F | G | H | J | K | L | Totals across | Sub-totals | PERIOD |
|---|---|---|---|---|---|---|---|---|---|---|---|---|---|---|
| Well | 14 | | | | | 2 | | | | | | 16 | 16 | WELL |
| Sub-total | 14 | 0 | 0 | 0 | 0 | 2 | 0 | 0 | 0 | 0 | 0 | 16 | 16 | |

## TREASURE HUNT and UNSTRATIFIED

| FEATURE | A | B | C | D | E | F | G | H | J | K | L | Totals across | Sub-totals | PERIOD |
|---|---|---|---|---|---|---|---|---|---|---|---|---|---|---|
| TH | | | 14 | 1 | 23 | 15 | 3 | | 4 | 1 | | 61 | 61 | U/S |
| U/S | | | 2 | 14 | 53 | 32 | 2 | | 8 | 14 | | 125 | 125 | U/S |
| Sub-total | 0 | 0 | 16 | 15 | 76 | 47 | 5 | | 12 | 15 | 0 | 186 | 186 | |
| TOTALS | 14 | 1 | 80 | 181 | 698 | 489 | 14 | 2 | 178 | 38 | 2 | | 1697 | |

**Table 1** (continued)

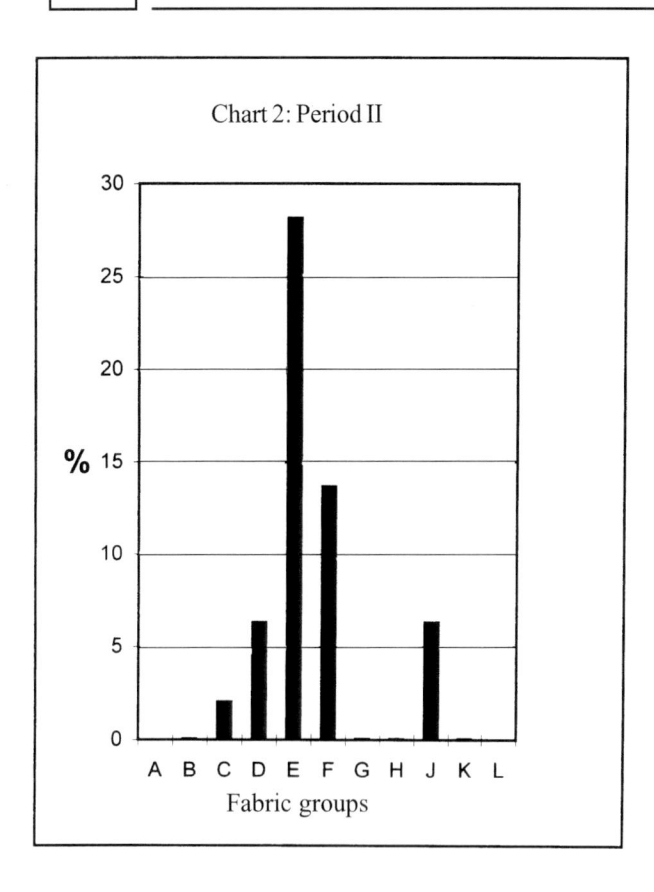

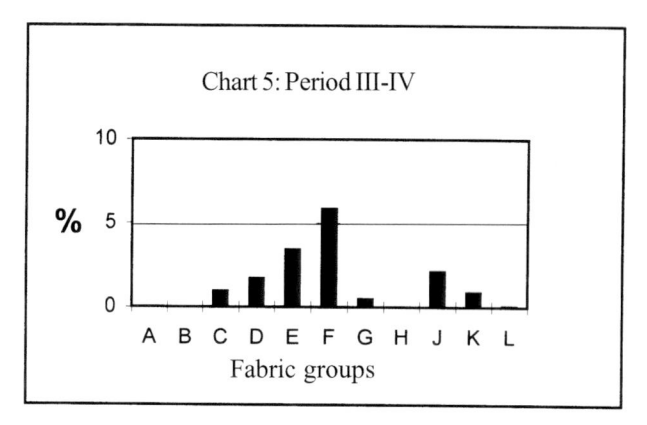

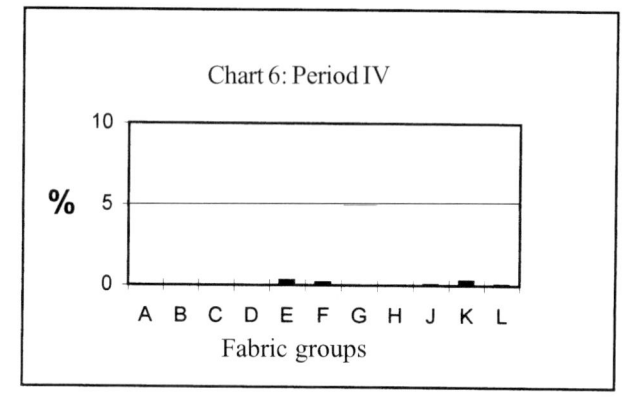

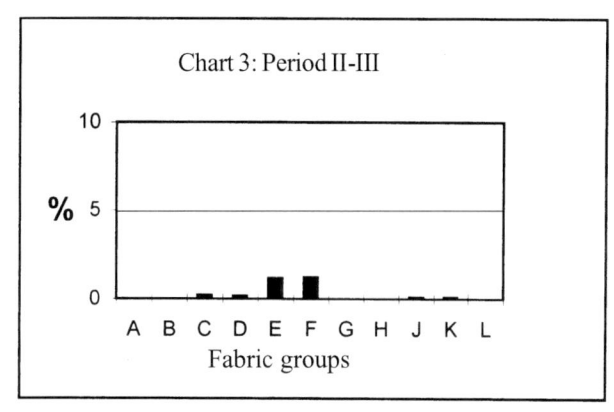

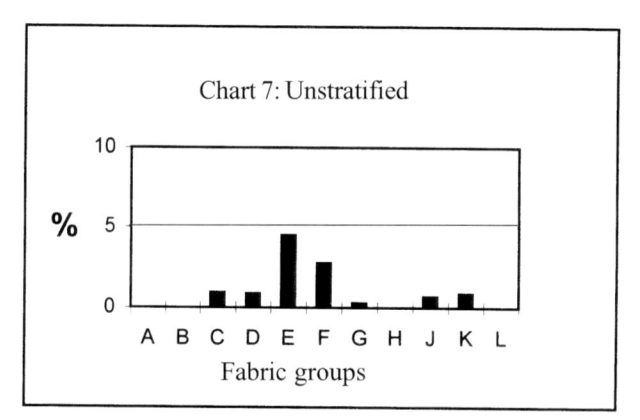

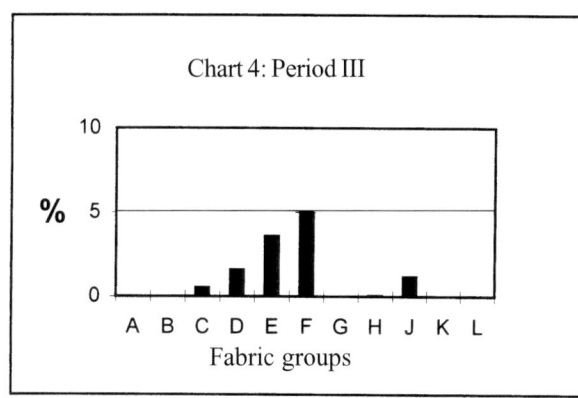

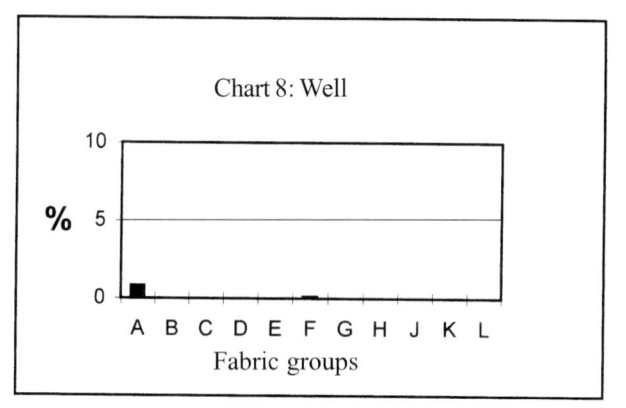

**Charts 2-8** Ceramics: all fabrics: percentages by Period

## A  Iron Age Pottery

Trevor Cowie

This small group of pottery comprises portions of two plain vessels in a coarse though compact and comparatively hard, well-fired fabric. Each appears to have been constructed using a similar manufacturing technique involving the building up of the pot using rings mortised into each other using a tongue-and-groove technique. While the original profiles are uncertain, the surviving portions suggest heavy bucket-shaped vessels, the bodies of which would probably have tapered slightly to meet proportionately broad flat bases.

The forms and fabric of this group invite comparison with Iron Age ceramics from a number of sites in SE Scotland. Other sites in Berwickshire which have produced similar pottery include Earn's Heugh (Childe & Forde 1932, 179-181) and Marygold Hill Plantation (National Museums of Scotland cat no: HH 559). Close parallels are also to be found among the pottery from East Lothian sites such as Craig's Quarry, Dirleton (Piggott & Piggott 1952, 195, Fig 7.2; Piggott 1958, 76 and fig 7), North Berwick Law (NMS cat no: HR 746), Ghegan Rock, Seacliff (Laidlay 1870; NMS cat nos: HD 103, HD 105) and Traprain Law (Curle 1915, 155-57). Analysis of the relatively well-dated assemblage of finds from Broxmouth Hill led Cool to suggest that this general class of pottery (her Type II) might range in date from the 2nd century BC through to the 1st century AD (Cool 1982, 99).

### CATALOGUE

1  Part of the upper portion of a large coarse bucket-shaped vessel with a flattened and inbent rim, represented by eight joining sherds and three small slivers (illus 32.1); a further two detached sherds may be from the lower part of the vessel; coarse well-gritted fabric with hard fine clay matrix containing inclusions up to 15mm across; ring-built construction technique extremely clear, several of the sherds having broken along tongue-and-groove type joints; ridges on surfaces left by the thumbs/fingertips of the potter; dark grey reduced core with orange exterior; one area of surface soot-blackened.
   Dimensions: estimated diameter of rim: 240mm; surviving height: 210mm.
   Well: floor to N of Wall. Phase: 1W.

2  Rim sherd (illus 32.2) from vessel of broadly similar form to 1, but rim more rounded, and lacking the pronounced in-turn; surface of rim uneven; coarse well-gritted fabric with compact hard fine clay matrix; ring built, with clear joints visible in section; surface slightly dimpled/ridged by thumb/fingertipping during manufacture.
   Dimensions: estimated diameter of rim: 230mm; surviving height: 70mm.
   Well: floor to N of Wall. Phase: 1W.

Both the above were found near the Well, on the landward side of the castle; from the 'united' floor level near base of wall to SSE of well head (illus 7)

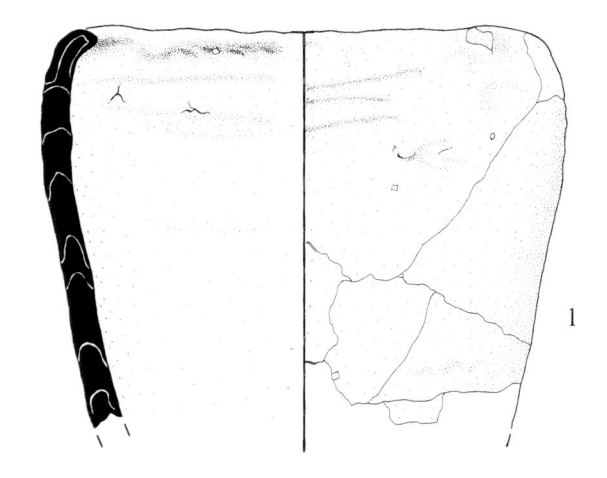

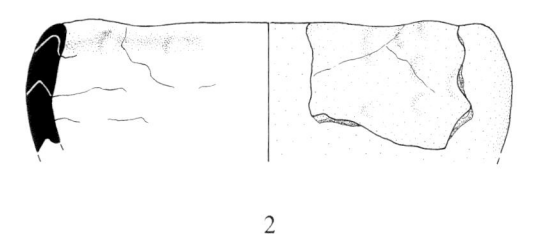

**Illus 32**
Pottery: Iron Age. Scale 1:4

## B  Roman Pottery

### Valerie E Dean

This single sherd has been identified as from a south Spanish amphora, probably Dressel 20 (olive oil amphora), and dated to the first to third centuries AD (Colin Wallace, pers comm). This is a common form which was widely distributed in Roman sites in southern Scotland (Fitzpatrick 1992, 179-83). The nearest known site to Fast Castle is the marching camp at Norham, Northumberland, some 25 km to the south-east. However, Roman finds have come from native sites, such as Traprain Law in East Lothian.

## C-H  Scottish Medieval and Later Pottery

### Valerie E Dean & Hugh Robertson

This section covers the 1464 sherds of the Scottish medieval pottery (Types C-H). The bulk of the material is probably Scottish, of local manufacture but, given the proximity of the Border, the presence of unidentified English material is likely. Wherever possible, sources or parallels are given.

METHODOLOGY

Analysis of the assemblage and establishment of the type series was undertaken initially by Hugh Robertson and continued by Valerie Dean. Detailed fabric descriptions are based on the method outlined by Orton, Tyers & Vince (1993). Colour descriptions and classifications are taken from the *Munsell Soil Color Charts*.

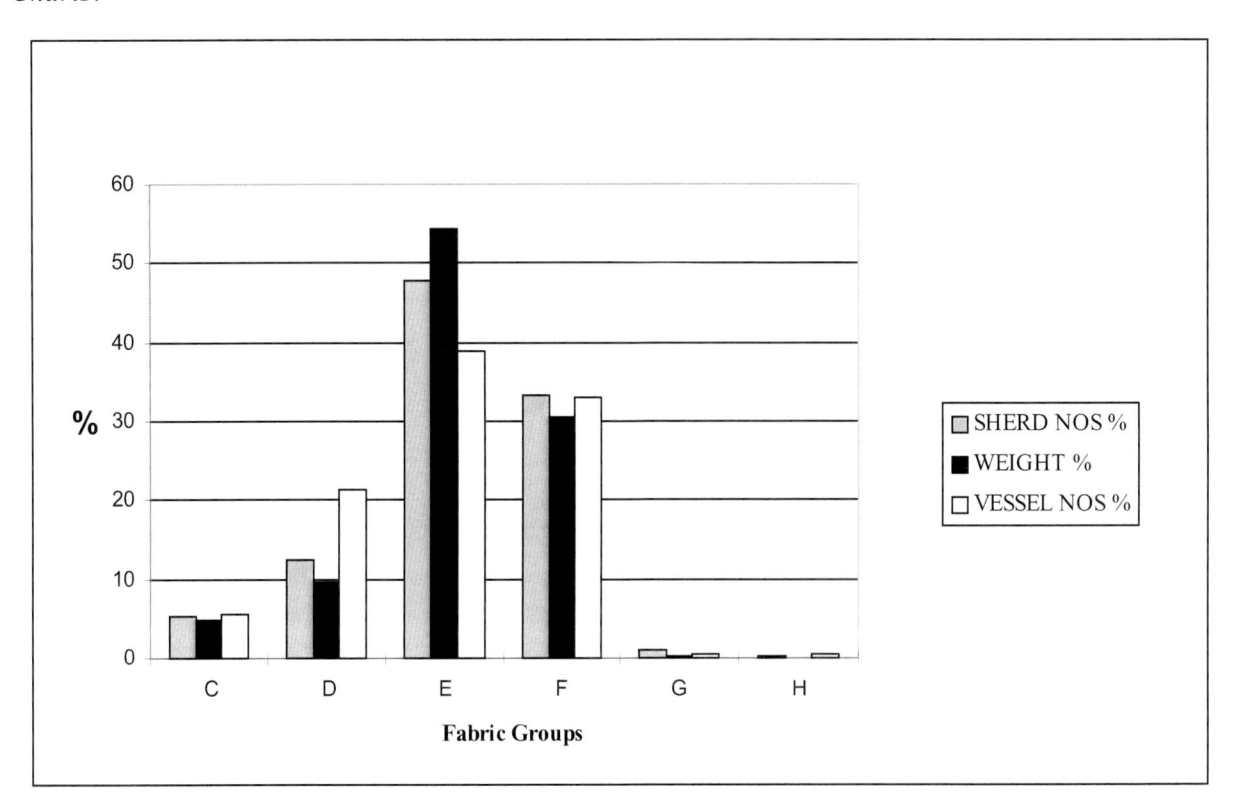

**Chart 9**  Scottish Medieval and later Pottery: sherd, weight and vessel percentages

The work was carried out by visual examination, with a binocular microscope at x20 where appropriate. Without thin sectioning and geological analysis, detailed identification of inclusions was not practicable. Differentiation between natural inclusions in the clay matrix and added temper has not been made.

The Scottish pottery covered by this report has been divided into six main groups (C-H) on the basis of fabric analysis. These have then been split into fabric types which range from approximately the 12th to the 17th century. It is hoped that some of these categories will fit into Scottish fabric groups in general.

Quantification is given by sherd, weight and minimum vessel percentages in each group (Chart 9) but may be distorted by the number of large jugs reconstructed from up to 41 joining sherds. Figures for the vessels are based on reconstructed vessels and rims, where present, otherwise on estimates. Weights and sherd figures may give a better idea of the relative quantities. Many sherds may well be from one vessel, but cannot be so attributed with confidence when they lie within different contexts. All vessels are wheelmade unless otherwise stated.

There are several near-complete profiles, due to the fortuitous containment of the fragments within the discrete area of the Quarry pit. Nineteen vessels have been significantly reconstructed, and numerous sherd joins have been made.

## C Light Gritty Ware

A range of fabrics, varying in colour from white to light buff and grey. Most of these may well be of local origin, possibly from the kiln site at Colstoun (Brooks 1981, 364-403). However, similarities have been noted in type C.1 to material from Bernard Street, Leith (NMS reference collection), and from Dundonald Castle, Ayrshire (Franklin, forthcoming). Types C.4, C.5 and C.8 resemble sherds from Coldingham Priory (NMS reference collection). Type C.6 compares with fabric 2.5 from The Hirsel, Coldstream (Dean, forthcoming) and contains the only unglazed sherd in this category.

Light gritty fabrics are widespread throughout eastern Scotland, at the town of Eyemouth (Crowdy 1986, 39-49), and in north-eastern England, at Lindisfarne (Bown 1985, 51-9) and Berwick (Moorhouse 1982, 113-21). However, the name East Coast White Gritty seems inappropriate since the fabric is sometimes not white, as at Colstoun (Brooks 1981, 365-6), and sometimes found inland, as at Kelso (Cox *et al* 1985, 381-98) and Jedburgh abbeys (Haggarty & Will 1995, 98-105). It is also found in Ayrshire at Dundonald Castle and at Ayr (NMS reference collection) and elsewhere in south-west Scotland (Cheer 1995, 83-6). Unfortunately, Colstoun material is difficult to date with any degree of accuracy, but light gritty fabrics span the period from the 12th to early 15th centuries.

TYPE C.1

A hard fabric, 5-10mm thick, with fine texture, slightly rough surfaces and a rough fracture. Outer surfaces are light reddish brown (5YR 6/4) to light brown (7.5YR 6/4), cores vary from pinkish white (5YR 8/2) to light grey (5YR 7/1) and light reddish brown (5YR 6/3), and inner surfaces are pinkish white (5YR 8/2) to pinkish grey (7.5YR 7/2). The 5% inclusions are sparse to moderate amounts of poorly-sorted, medium to coarse, sub-angular, translucent quartz; sparse, poorly-sorted, fine to coarse, sub-round haematite; and a moderate amount of fine mica. The quality and coverage of the external glaze varies considerably, and is olive brown (2.5Y 4/4) to pale olive (5Y 6/4).

Forms: Jugs, jars? (illus 33.1)

## TYPE C.2

A hard fabric, 5-8mm thick, with a fine, crumbly texture, smooth or slightly rough surfaces and a slightly rough fracture. Outer surfaces are light brown (7.5YR 6/4) to grey (10YR 5/1), cores are white (10YR 8/2) to light grey (10YR 7/1), and interiors range from very pale brown (10YR 8/3) to light grey (10YR 7/1) and grey (10YR 5/1). The 5-10% inclusions comprise a moderate amount of fairly-sorted, fine to medium, sub-angular, translucent quartz; sparse, poorly-sorted, very fine to coarse, sub-round haematite; and a moderate amount of fine mica. The quality and coverage of the external glaze varies considerably, and colours vary from very dark brown (10YR 2/2) to olive brown (2.5Y 4/4) and olive (5Y 4/3).

Forms:    Cooking pot or jar; jugs? (not illustrated)

## TYPE C.4

One sherd of a hard fabric, 4mm thick, with a hackly texture, slightly rough surfaces and a rough fracture. The inner surface is pinkish grey (7.5YR 6/2) with a grey (7.5YR 6/0) core. The 15% inclusions comprise abundant, poorly-sorted, medium to coarse, sub-round, translucent quartz; sparse, poorly-sorted, medium, sub-angular haematite; sparse, poorly-sorted, medium to coarse, sub-round rock; and sparse, fine mica. The pimply external glaze is olive (5Y 5/4).

Forms:    Indeterminate (not illustrated)

## TYPE C.5

A hard fabric, 5-10mm thick, with an irregular, crumbly texture, smooth surfaces and a slightly rough fracture. Some grass tempering is visible, and the clay matrix can be streaky. The outer surfaces are light reddish brown (5YR 6/4), cores are light grey (5YR 7/1) and the interiors are light grey (10YR 7/1). The 5% inclusions are a moderate amount of fairly-sorted, fine to medium, sub-round, translucent quartz; a moderate amount of poorly-sorted, fine to coarse, sub-angular haematite; and abundant, fine mica. Glaze covers most of the exterior, and is even and glossy; it is olive (5Y 5/6-4/4)

Forms:    Jug? (not illustrated)

## TYPE C.6

One sherd of a hard fabric, 10mm thick, with an irregular texture, slightly rough surfaces and rough fracture. The exterior and core are pink (7.5YR 6/4 and 7/4 respectively) and the interior is pinkish grey (7.5YR 6/2). The 15% inclusions are abundant, poorly-sorted, coarse to very coarse, sub-angular, translucent quartz; a moderate amount of poorly-sorted, coarse to very coarse, sub-round rock; and sparse, fine mica. It is unglazed.

Forms:    Industrial vessel? (not illustrated)

TYPE C.8

One sherd of a hard fabric, 5 mm thick, with a fine, crumbly texture. The sherd is abraded, but may have had a smooth surface and a clean fracture. The core is white (10YR 8/2). The 5-10% inclusions are a moderate amount of fairly-sorted, fine to medium, sub-angular, translucent quartz; sparse, poorly-sorted, medium to coarse, flattish rock and haematite; and sparse, well-sorted, very fine mica. Both surfaces are covered with a bubbly, pitted glaze, possibly over-fired; it is black (2.5Y 2/0) with a purple, metallic appearance.

Forms:     Indeterminate (not illustrated)

**D   Red Ware**

A range of light red fabrics, most of which resemble Group E in spite of their being completely oxidised. Glaze can be external and/or internal, usually a glossy yellowish brown; this noticeably resembles sherds from Coldingham Abbey (NMS reference collection). A number of sherds of this fabric show some similarity to pottery from the north of England, as indicated by Jennings elsewhere in this report, and to material from Berwick-upon-Tweed (Anne Jenner, pers comm). However, sub-group D.3 has similarities to material excavated in 1994 at Burgess Street, Leith (Mark Collard, pers comm).

Many burghs and towns produced their own redwares, such as Perth (MacAskill 1987, 89-120) and Aberdeen (Murray 1982, 116-76), especially from the late 12th to the 15th centuries.

TYPE D.1

A medium to hard fabric, 3-11mm thick, with an irregular, crumbly texture, smooth surfaces and a slightly rough fracture. The outer surface of this oxidised fabric varies from reddish brown (2.5YR 5/4) to pink (7.5YR 7/4); inner surfaces range from pink (5YR 7/4) to reddish yellow (5YR 6/6) and pinkish grey (7.5YR 7/2), and the core ranges from pinkish grey (5YR 7/2) to pink (5YR 7/4 and 7.5YR 7/4). The 10% inclusions comprise a moderate amount of poorly-sorted, fine to medium and occasionally coarse, sub-round, translucent quartz; sparse, well-sorted, medium to coarse, sub-round haematite; and a moderate amount of fine mica. Glaze can be internal or external, and varies in extent and quality. It ranges from yellowish red (5 YR 5/6) to strong brown (7.5 YR 5/6) and yellowish brown (10 YR 5/4).

Plate X; illus 33.3, 33.7-9, 33.11-14, 33.16-19

Forms:
A urinal (Plate X, illus 33.17), with a range of incised and stabbed decoration, including irregular wavy lines, a fleur de lys and stylised flower, the last similar to decoration on vessels from St Andrews cathedral (Cruden 1958, fig 53) and Stenhouse kiln site (NMS collection); the orifice is on the upper shoulder, like those from Melrose Abbey (Cruden 1955, figs 24-26) and Glenluce Abbey (Cruden 1951, fig 9) which are dated to the 14th century. The capacity of the urinal would have been 4 litres. Jugs, one with a gridiron impression on its long narrow neck (illus 33.8), jars and a cooking pot. A shallow drug jar (illus 33.14) is similar in form to one from Hyndford House, Lanark (Dean, unpublished) dated to the 16th or 17th centuries.

TYPE D.2

A hard fabric, 4-8mm thick, with a fine texture, smooth surfaces and a slightly rough fracture. The outer surfaces of this oxidised fabric are reddish brown (5YR 5/4) to reddish yellow (7.5YR 6/6), inner surfaces are light brown (7.5YR 6/4) and the core is pink (5YR 7/4) to light brown (7.5YR 6/4). The 5-10% inclusions comprise a moderate amount of well-sorted, fine to medium, sub-round, translucent and occasionally white quartz; a moderate amount of well-sorted, fine to medium, sub-round haematite; and a moderate amount of fine mica. Glaze can be external and/or internal, even or patchy, and glossy; a few sherds are unglazed. The colour varies from yellowish red (5YR 5/6) to strong brown (7.5YR 5/6), brownish yellow (10YR 6/8) and reddish brown (10YR 5/6).

Illus 33.5, 33.10, 33.15

Forms:     Jugs (illus 33.5); a bowl?; a drinking vessel? (illus 33.15)


TYPE D.3

The hard fabrics of this rather mixed group of sherds are 4-8mm thick, with an irregular, crumbly texture, smooth surfaces and slightly rough to rough fractures. The outer surfaces are red (2.5YR 5/6) to yellowish red (5YR 5/6), the cores are light red (2.5YR 6/8) to yellowish red (5YR 5/6), and internal surfaces are light red (2.5YR 6/6) to reddish yellow (5YR 6/6). The 15% inclusions are a moderate amount of poorly-sorted, fine to coarse, sub-round, translucent and occasionally white quartz; sparse, poorly-sorted, fine to coarse, sub-round haematite; sparse, poorly-sorted, fine to coarse, sub-angular rock; and a moderate amount of fine mica. Some sherds are unglazed, and others are glazed externally; coverage and quality are very varied. Colour ranges from red (2.5YR 4/6) to yellowish red (5YR 5/8) and dark yellowish brown (10YR 4/6).

Forms:     Jugs (illus 33.4)


TYPE D.4

A hard fabric, 4-10mm thick, with a fine texture, smooth surfaces and a slightly rough fracture. The outer surfaces and cores are light brown (7.5YR 6/4) and the interiors are pinkish grey (7.5YR 7/2) to light brown (7.5YR 6/4). Inclusions are less than 5% and comprise sparse, poorly-sorted, fine to coarse, sub-round, translucent and white quartz; sparse, poorly-sorted, fine to coarse, sub-round haematite; and sparse, fine mica. The external glaze is thin and pitted, and is yellowish brown (10YR 5/4).

Illus 33.2, 33.6, 33.20

Forms:
Jugs, one with a combed decoration on the shoulder, below a cordon (illus 33.2). A drug jar (illus 33.6) of a form widely found in southern Scotland; these are dated to the late 15th to 16th centuries at Glenluce Abbey (Cruden 1951, figs 13, 14) and to the 16th and 17th centuries at Linlithgow Palace (Laing 1971, fig 5.18) and at the kiln site at Throsk (Caldwell & Dean 1992, fig 8.39). There is a twisted, ribbed rod handle (illus 33.20) of the 13th- to 14th- century form as found at Berwick (Moorhouse 1982, fig 16.38) and Colstoun (Brooks 1981, fig 3.44).

## E Reduced Gritty Ware

The bulk of this fabric is most likely of local origin, and closely resembles material from nearby Eyemouth Fort (Franklin, 1998), where deposits can be closely dated to 1547-1559, and to sherds from neighbouring Coldingham Priory (NMS reference collection). Reduced wares occur widely in Scotland, and at Bothwell Castle they were originally dated to the 13th and 14th centuries although later research found that 'the pottair of Bothuile' was supplying the castle in the early 16th century (Caldwell & Dean 1992, 7). The fact that they are found at Fast Castle in deposits which can be dated to possibly as late as the middle of the 17th century suggests that the use of reduced wares continued over a considerable period.

The significant feature of this group is that the fabric is mainly thick and heavy, and of a sandwich appearance in profile, apparently resulting from uneven firing or cooling. In some cases, there is a pronounced outer margin, lighter in colour, taking up as much as a third of the thickness although, in other cases, it is paper-thin. The glaze is almost universally of the darker shades of green, although with odd patches of brown. The internal surface is seldom glazed. There is very little decoration.

The fabrics of types E.1 and E.2 are very similar, the principal difference being the greater amount of inclusions in the finer vessels of type E.2. The sherds of type E.5 are of particular interest in that they may be unique in the combining of two completely different fabrics in the one vessel.

## TYPE E.1

This hard fabric, 4-14mm thick, has an irregular, crumbly texture, and slightly rough fractures. Surfaces are usually smooth, but are sometimes pitted or slightly pimply. It is generally completely reduced, but occasionally may have an oxidised inner surface. In section, sherds have a sandwich appearance, with a sharp external margin up to 3mm thick; this is a light grey where below the glaze. Where unglazed, the outer surface is reddish brown (5YR 5/4) to pinkish grey (7.5YR 6/2) and the core is grey (10YR 5/1) to very dark grey (2.5Y 3/0). Interiors are also grey to very dark grey, with the exception of the oxidised surfaces which are pink (5YR 7/3) to light reddish brown (5YR 6/4). The 10% inclusions comprise a moderate amount of well-sorted, fine to medium, sub-round, translucent and white quartz; sparse haematite of very varied size and shape, with grains up to 3mm; very sparse, fairly-sorted, fine, sub-round rock; and a moderate amount of very fine mica. The glaze is usually external and covers most of the vessel, but occasionally it occurs on both surfaces; it is olive (5Y 5/4-4/4) and varies considerably in quality. Decoration is almost completely absent, with occasional shoulder cordons or a single wavy line around the body.

Plate XI.1-2, XII.1-2, illus 33.22-23, 33.30, 33.36-37, 34.40-43, 34.47, 34.50-51, 34.53-57

Forms:
Principally large, ovoid, thick-walled jugs, with some knife-trimming on the lower body (Plate XII.1/ illus 34.54; Plate XI.1/illus 34.55; Plate XI.2/illus 34.57) and some smaller jugs (illus 34.56). The shoulder of one of these (illus 34.57) shows a shatter mark, suggesting the point of impact of a blow; its original capacity is estimated at approximately 13 litres and when full its total weight would have been about 20 kg. Two vessels have bases with thumbed decoration (illus 33.36, 33.37). Strap handles may be plain (Plate XII.1/illus 34.54) or thumbed down their length (illus 33.22) like some from Colstoun (Brooks, 1981, fig 3.36) and the 15th-century handle in Linlithgow Palace Museum (Laing 1971, fig 4.12). There is a large bowl (illus 34.40) and a drinking vessel? (illus 34.50). A fine rim (illus 33.30) may belong to an oil lamp like that in fabric E.5 (illus 33.31).

TYPE E.2

A very hard, finely-potted fabric, 2-10mm thick, with a fine or irregular texture, smooth surface and clean or slightly rough fracture. It is completely reduced, with very thin external margins on some sherds. Where unglazed, the outer surface is reddish brown (5YR 5/4) to pinkish grey (7.5YR 6/2), interiors are grey (10YR 6/1) to very dark grey (2.5Y 3/0) and the cores are grey (10YR 5/1) to very dark grey (2.5Y 3/0). Inclusions can be 15-20%, very similar to type E.1, but finer. The olive (5Y 5/4-4/4) glaze is usually external, but can cover both surfaces; it is generally even and shiny.

Illus 33.21, 33.24-29, 33.32-35, 33.38, 34.44, 34.46, 34.48-49, 34.52

Forms:
Finely made, thin-walled jugs, some large, with knife-trimming on the lower body (illus 33.38); bowls; drinking vessels? (illus 33.35, 34.49). Part of a hand-formed condiment or sweetmeat dish (illus 33.34) resembling vessels of the 13th to 14th century from York and London (McCarthy & Brooks 1988, nos 688, 1161). An inkwell or phial (illus 33.32); inkwells have been identified as probably being of 15th-century date at Coldingham Priory (Laing 1974, fig 1.11) and at Melrose Abbey (Cruden 1955, fig 34) where one was dated to the 13th-14th centuries.

There is a variety of decoration, inluding applied thumbed cordons which can be accompanied by an applied rosette (illus 33.29); cordons have been noted on vessels of the late 13th century at Coldingham Priory (Laing 1974, fig 6) at Jedburgh Abbey (Cruden 1958, figs 22, 25). Rosettes appear on a sherd from 15th-century deposits at the High Street, Edinburgh (Thoms 1978, fig 19.128) and on Perth local fabric in deposits possibly of the 16th century at Canal Street (Scott & Blanchard 1984, fig 10.15). Stabbed designs occur, sometimes combined with a single wavy line (illus 33.24, 33.25, 33.26, 33.27); similar decoration has been noted at Deer Abbey, Aberdeenshire (Cruden 1958, fig 48), Bothwell Castle (Cruden 1954, fig 3), Coldingham Priory (Laing 1974, figs 1.2, 1.13) and Stenhouse kiln site (NMS reference collection), and dates range from 13th to early 16th centuries. A ribbed rod handle has slashed decoration (illus 33.21).

TYPE E.3

One sherd of a hard fabric, 6mm thick, with a fine, irregular texture, slightly rough surface and fracture. The inner surface and core are dark grey (2.5Y 4/0). The 10% inclusions are a moderate amount of fairly-sorted, fine to medium, sub-angular, translucent quartz; a moderate amount of fairly-sorted, medium, sub-angular, white rock; and a moderate amount of very fine mica. The external glaze is even and slightly matt in appearance; it varies from light yellowish brown (2.5Y 6/4) to light olive brown (2.5Y 5/4)

Forms:     Jug? (not illustrated)

TYPE E.4

Three sherds of a hard, coarse fabric, 3-7mm thick, with a hackly texture, slightly rough surface and rough fracture. The internal surface is dark grey (7.5YR 4/0) with a grey (7.5YR 5/0) to dark grey (7.5YR 4/0) core. The 20% inclusions comprise abundant, poorly-sorted, medium to very coarse, sub-angular, translucent and white quartz; sparse, poorly-sorted, medium to coarse, sub-round haematite; sparse, poorly-sorted, coarse to very coarse, sub-round rock; and a moderate amount of fine mica. Glaze can be external only or on both surfaces, and is usually abraded. It varies from olive brown (2.5Y 4/4) to olive (5Y 4/4).

Illus 34.39, 34.45

Forms:     Jugs; a large bowl (illus 34.39)

## TYPE E.5

An unusual combination of two hard fabrics, 3-10mm thick, each with slightly rough feel and fracture; the sherds have broken along the line of the fabric join. This combination of fabrics may well be unique. It is wheel made although the union of the two fabrics has been hand-smoothed. The upper fabric has a laminated texture and a white (5YR 8/1) core. Its 5% inclusions comprise sparse, fairly-sorted, fine, sub-round, translucent quartz; sparse, fairly-sorted, very fine, sub-round haematite; and abundant, poorly-sorted, fine to medium mica. The lower fabric has an irregular texture and a grey (5YR 6/1) core. Its 15% inclusions comprise abundant, poorly-sorted, medium to coarse, sub-angular, translucent and white quartz; sparse, poorly-sorted, coarse to very coarse, sub-round haematite; and sparse, fairly-sorted, fine mica. Both surfaces covered with an even, shiny, olive yellow (2.5Y 6/6-6/8) glaze.

Illus 33.31

Forms:
Possibly an oil lamp (illus 33.31), but the form of the lower part can not be ascertained. It may be in imitation of lamps with tapering rims from the early 15th-century kiln site of Utrecht (Bruijn 1979, illus 33, 34). A lamp has also been found at Tynemouth Priory (Edwards 1967, fig 9.26) of possible 13th-century date, and another at Castle Street, Inverness in a midden of late 13th- to 14th-century date (MacAskill 1983, fig 18.8).

## F Partially-Reduced Gritty Ware

This seems to be a partially reduced version of Group E; otherwise the characteristics are similar. This may be explained by the method of stacking vessels in the kiln. Jugs frequently bear the impression of a rim on their base, indicative of having been stood upon another jug. This would have had the effect of excluding oxygen, thus causing reduction of the fabric. It would not have been possible to do this with vessels whose rim diameter was greater than that of their base, thus accounting for the fact that these are usually of an oxidised character.

## TYPE F.1

A hard fabric, 3-10mm thick, with an irregular, crumbly texture, surfaces which are generally smooth but occasionally pitted or pimply, and a slightly rough fracture. It is variably fired and the inner surfaces are oxidised; margins can be very thin or thick and blurred. There are considerable variations in the fabric colours, outer surfaces varying from light reddish brown (2.5YR 6/4) to weak red (2.5YR 5/2), with a grey (7/5YR 6/0-5/0) core; inner surfaces are reddish yellow (5YR 6/6) to light brown (7.5YR 6/4). The 15% inclusions are abundant, fairly-sorted, fine to medium, sub-round, translucent quartz; occasional, well-sorted, fine, sub-round haematite; occasional, fairly-sorted, medium, sub-round rock; and sparse, fine mica. The glaze is usually external, but may be internal only. It is light olive brown (2.5Y 5/4) to olive (5Y 4/4), and varies considerably in quality and coverage.

Illus 35.58, 35.62-68, 35.70, 35.72-85

Forms:
Mostly jugs of varied sizes, with knife-trimming on the lower body (illus 35.76, 35.77) and one with a thumbed base. One jug (illus 35.77) would have had an estimated capacity of 12 litres. There are the rims of two face-mask jugs. The first of these (illus 35.63) has an eye impressed into the beard at the point where it meets the rim; it has the appearance of a Grimston-type jug, of which there are many copies in Scotland, eg Deer Abbey, Aberdeenshire (Cruden 1958, fig 30). The second (illus 35.64) has a similar facial expression and prominent nose to two from Tantallon Castle (Laing & Robertson 1973, fig 3.3; Caldwell 1991a, figs 9.149, 9.150) of possible 14th century date, and to one from Colstoun (Brooks 1981, fig 4.54). However, this one does not form part of a spout; the sherd is not large enough to determine whether it continued down into a handle. There are cooking pots (illus 35.83). A globular, flat-bottomed vessel (illus 35.85) is similar in form to jugs of late 12th- to 15th-century date from Kelso Abbey (Cox *et al* 1985, fig 19.26), Jedburgh Abbey (Cruden 1958, fig 7) and Perth (MacAskill 1987, fig 46.48); a small globular jug, containing a hoard of coins dated to no later than 1322, was found at Ednam, Kelso (Dean 1997, 43). There is a bowl (illus 35.84); a drug jar (illus 35.65) whose form resembles that of a jar from the kiln site at Throsk (Caldwell & Dean 1992, fig 8.39). There is a portion of a watering pot or censer (illus 35.75); it does not appear to be a colander since such a vessel would be expected to have larger holes in its base to allow free drainage; watering pots have been noted at Coldingham Abbey (Laing 1974, fig 2.16), perhaps dated to the 15th century, and in early 16th- to 17th- or 18th-century deposits at Norwich (Jennings 1981, fig 80.1351). Decoration on vessels is sparse, and comprises single, broad wavy lines between ridges on jug shoulders (illus 35.70, 35.72). A short, extended strap handle (illus 35.68) may be from a pipkin or pan, as in 16th-century examples from Bristol (Good 1987, figs 23.157, 25.188).

TYPE F.2

A hard fabric, 3-7mm thick, with a fine texture, smooth surfaces and a clean fracture. Firing is variable; inner surfaces are oxidised, and margins are very thin or thick and blurred. Outer surfaces are weak red (2.5YR 5/2), interiors vary from reddish yellow (5YR 6/6) to very pale brown (10YR 7/3) with a grey (7.5 YR 6/0-5/0) core. The 5% inclusions are sparse, well-sorted, fine, sub-round, translucent quartz; sparse, poorly-sorted, medium to very coarse, haematite; very sparse, fairly-sorted, fine, sub-round rock; and sparse, very fine mica. Glaze is external, dark brown (7.5YR 3/2) to olive (5Y 4/4), and varies considerably in quality and coverage.

Plate XII.3/illus 35.59

Forms:
Jugs, small and medium (Plate XII.3/ illus 35.59). One vessel (illus 35.59) has a cordoned shoulder. There is a grooved strap handle similar to those from the 13th- to 14th-century kiln site at Colstoun (Brooks 1981, figs 3.29, 3.31) and Jedburgh Abbey (Haggarty & Will 1995, fig 84.75) in 14th- to late 15th-century deposits.

TYPE F.3

A hard fabric, 8-10mm thick, with an irregular, crumbly texture, smooth surfaces and slightly rough fracture. The outer surface is weak red (2.5YR 5.2) where unglazed, with a grey (5YR 6/0) core and pink (7.5YR 7/4) nner surface. The 10-15% inclusions are abundant, fairly-sorted, fine to medium and occasionally coarse, sub-round, translucent quartz; a moderate amount of poorly-sorted, fine to coarse, sub-round haematite; sparse, fairly-sorted, fine, sub-angular rock; and sparse, fine mica. The external glaze is pale olive (5Y 6/4) to olive (5Y 4/4), and is patchy and pitted.

Illus 35.60-61, 35.69, 35.71

Forms:
Jugs? There is a thumbed strap handle (illus 35.69) like that in fabric type E.1 (illus 33.22)

TYPE F.4

One sherd of a hard fabric, 5-7 mm thick, with an irregular, crumbly texture, smooth surfaces and a rough fracture. The outer surface is reddish brown (5YR 5/4) with a light reddish brown (5YR 6/3) core. The 20% inclusions are abundant, poorly-sorted, medium to very coarse, sub-round, translucent quartz; a moderate amount of poorly sorted, medium to coarse, sub-angular rock; and a moderate amount of fine mica. The abraded, external glaze is a mottled reddish brown (10YR 5/4).

Forms:    Cooking pot? (not illustrated)

## G    Proto-stoneware?

A very hard fabric, 4-7mm thick, with a fine texture, slightly rough surfaces and a clean break. The inner surface is reddish brown (5YR 5/3) with a dark grey core (7.5YR 4/0). The 10% inclusions comprise a moderate amount of fairly-sorted, medium, sub-round, translucent quartz; a sparse amount of fairly-sorted, fine to medium and occasionally very coarse, sub-round haematite; and a moderate amount of fine mica. The external glaze is mottled and varies from weak red (2.5YR 4/2) to olive brown (2.5Y 4/4); it is very thin, burned and abraded, suggesting that in fact this may be an over-fired vessel.

Illus 35.86

Forms:
Jug, probably 15th- to 16th-century (illus 35.86). It has a similar rim form and neck ridge to a jug in fabric type C.1 (illus 33.1) although the ridge is more pronounced. This is a feature of jugs from the Colstoun kiln site (Brooks 1981, fig 2.1-12) and of a post-medieval jug from Lesmahagow Priory (Hall 1982, fig 18.22).

## H    Cistercian ware

Cistercian ware is generally considered to be English, but a Scottish source cannot be discounted. Two small sherds have been identified, but the vessel form was not ascertainable. Probably late 15th- to 16th-century.

Forms:    Indeterminate. (not illustrated)

## DISCUSSION

Within the Scottish pottery groups C to H, there is very little light gritty ware (group C) present: it comprises only 5.5 per cent of the this assemblage. This would suggest that the fabric, dated to the 12th to 15th centuries, was no longer in fashion and had been superseded by the red and reduced gritty wares (groups D-F) which comprise 93 per cent of the assemblage, and which were in widespread use in Scotland from the 13th to 17th centuries. These are well distributed throughout the fill of the Quarry pit, indicating that their deposition occurred over a relatively short timespan. Two vessels (illus 33.14, 34.54) in fabrics D and E, which came from the lowest levels of Period II, could hardly be given a date earlier than the 15th century, suggesting a date around then for the initial deposition. This would agree with the evidence from coins, none of which pre-date the second half of the 15th century. Also, Scarborough ware is conspicuous by its absence, and this may reinforce the above view on the infilling of the Quarry pit.

It is interesting that much of the fabric shows a resemblance to sherds from the 16th-century Eyemouth Fort. However, there is a disparity in the forms present. At Eyemouth, the bulk of the identified vessels are cooking pots, whereas at Fast Castle these are few and far between, with jugs predominating. This could perhaps reflect the different form of occupancy, with the gentry at the fortified house of Fast Castle perhaps favouring imported vessels and metal cooking pots. This suggestion may be borne out by the range of unusual forms in the assemblage: the condiment dish and the possible oil lamps, inkwell and watering-pot.

The fabric noted as being similar to that from Coldingham Priory (group D) is like a finer version of that from the kiln site at Colstoun, with similar inclusions; this was also noted by Laing (1974, 242). It is tempting to hint that there may be a continuation of the Colstoun tradition producing this material, perhaps in the Coldingham area. The possibility that fabrics E and F were also locally made is suggested by similarities to material from such nearby sites as Eyemouth, Tantallon Castle and Coldingham Priory. Fabrics E and F display a number of characteristics of the earlier Colstoun vessels, such as grooved, twisted and thumbed handles and ridged jug necks, which may reinforce this suggestion. Such handles may have been developed to give a better grip when lifted.

One important result of the reconstruction of the pots is that it has enabled different strata within the Quarry pit to be judged as contemporaneous. Conversely, what is of particular importance is that dating evidence from other sources, documentary and artefactual, is giving a period of usage for the pottery assemblage.

## ACKNOWLEDGEMENTS

The authors' appreciation is due to David Caldwell for his unstinting advice and support, and to Mark Collard, George Dalgleish, Julie Franklin, Anne Jenner and Colin Wallace for giving the benefit of their knowledge. Access to the National Museums of Scotland's medieval pottery reference collection was particularly appreciated. The pottery was drawn by Valerie Dean.

# CATALOGUE OF ILLUSTRATED POTTERY

| Illus | Fabric | Vessel Type |
|---|---|---|
| 33.1 | C.1 | Jug. Rim and shoulder. Incised decoration. Mottled exterior glaze. Period III-IV |
| 33.2 | D.4 | Jug. Shoulder. Incised decoration. Degraded external glaze. Period III-IV |
| 33.3 | D.1 | Jug. Rim and neck. Shiny external glaze. Period II.2 |
| 33.4 | D.3 | Jug. Rim, neck and part of narrow strap handle. Glazed exterior. Period II.2 |
| 33.5 | D.2 | Jug. Rim, with grooved rod handle. Very abraded external glaze. Period II.1 |
| 33.6 | D.4 | Small drug jar. Rim and upper body. Glazed internally and outside rim. Period III-IV |
| 33.7 | D.1 | Small jug? Rim. Glazed exterior. Period II.2 |
| 33.8 | D.1 | Jug. Rim and neck with portion of stamped gridiron. Shiny glaze externally and inside rim. Period II.1 |
| 33.9 | D.1 | Jug. Rim. Shiny external glaze. Period III-IV |
| 33.10 | D.2 | Jug. Rim and neck. Glazed exterior. Period II.1 |
| 33.11 | D.1 | Small jug? Rim. Shiny external glaze. Period III-IV |
| 33.12 | D.1 | Jug. Rim and neck. Glazed exterior. Period II.1 |
| 33.13 | D.1 | Jug. Rim. Glazed exterior. Period II.2 |
| 33.14 | D.1 | Small drug jar. Base has traces of wire marks. Glazed interior. Period II.1 |
| 33.15 | D.2 | Drinking vessel? Lower body and base. Glazed exterior and interior. Period II |
| 33.16 | D.1 | Jar or jug. Rim. Glazed exterior. Period II.2 |
| 33.17 | D.1 | Urinal. Incised and stabbed decoration. Glazed exterior. Period II (Plate X) |
| 33.18 | D.1 | Ribbed rod handle. Glazed. Period II.2 |
| 33.19 | D.1 | Grooved rod handle. Glazed. Period II.1 |
| 33.20 | D.4 | Twisted, ribbed rod handle. Degraded glaze. Period III.1 |
| 33.21 | E.2 | Ribbed rod handle. Slashed decoration. Glazed. Period II.2 |
| 33.22 | E.1 | Strap handle. Thumbed decoration. Shiny glaze. Period II.2 |
| 33.23 | E.1 | Very broad strap handle. Degraded glaze. Period II |
| 33.24 | E.2 | Jug. Body sherd with stabbed decoration. Glazed exterior. Period II |
| 33.25 | E.2 | Jug? Body sherd, with stabbed foliage decoration. Glazed exterior. Period II.2 |
| 33.26 | E.2 | Jug? Body sherd, with incised decoration. Glazed exterior. Period II.1 |
| 33.27 | E.2 | Jug? Body sherd, with incised and stabbed decoration. Glazed exterior. Period II.2 |
| 33.28 | E.2 | Jug? Body sherd, with incised and stabbed decoration. External glaze. Possible same vessel as illus 33.27. Period II.2 |
| 33.29 | E.2 | Jug. Body sherd. Applied cordon with impressed fingernail decoration above an applied rosette with eight deeply impressed petals, showing fingernail marks. Shiny external glaze. Unstratified |
| 33.30 | E.1 | Oil lamp? Rim. Shiny glaze, exterior and interior. Period II.2 |
| 33.31 | E.5 | Oil lamp? Glazed exterior and interior. Period II |
| 33.32 | E.2 | Phial or inkwell. Glazed exterior and interior. Period III-IV |
| 33.33 | E.2 | Pierced lug handle. Glazed exterior. Unstrat. |
| 33.34 | E.2 | Condiment or sweetmeat dish. Central portion. Glazed exterior and interior. Unstrat. |
| 33.35 | E.2 | Drinking vessel? Lower body and base. Glazed exterior and interior. Period II |
| 33.36 | E.1 | Jug. Base. Thumbed decoration. External glaze. Unstratified. |
| 33.37 | E.1 | Jug. Lower body and base. Thumbed decoration. External glaze. Period II.1 |
| 33.38 | E.2 | Jug. Base, with large dent. Irregular scored decoration on upper body. Glazed exterior. Period II |
| 34.39 | E.4 | Large bowl? Rim. Glazed exterior and inside rim. Period II.2 |
| 34.40 | E.1 | Large bowl. Rim of large bowl. Flaking internal glaze. Period II.1 |
| 34.41 | E.1 | Jar or jug. Rim. Glazed exterior. Period II.1 |
| 34.42 | E.1 | Jug. Rim. External glaze, perhaps overfired. Period II.1 |

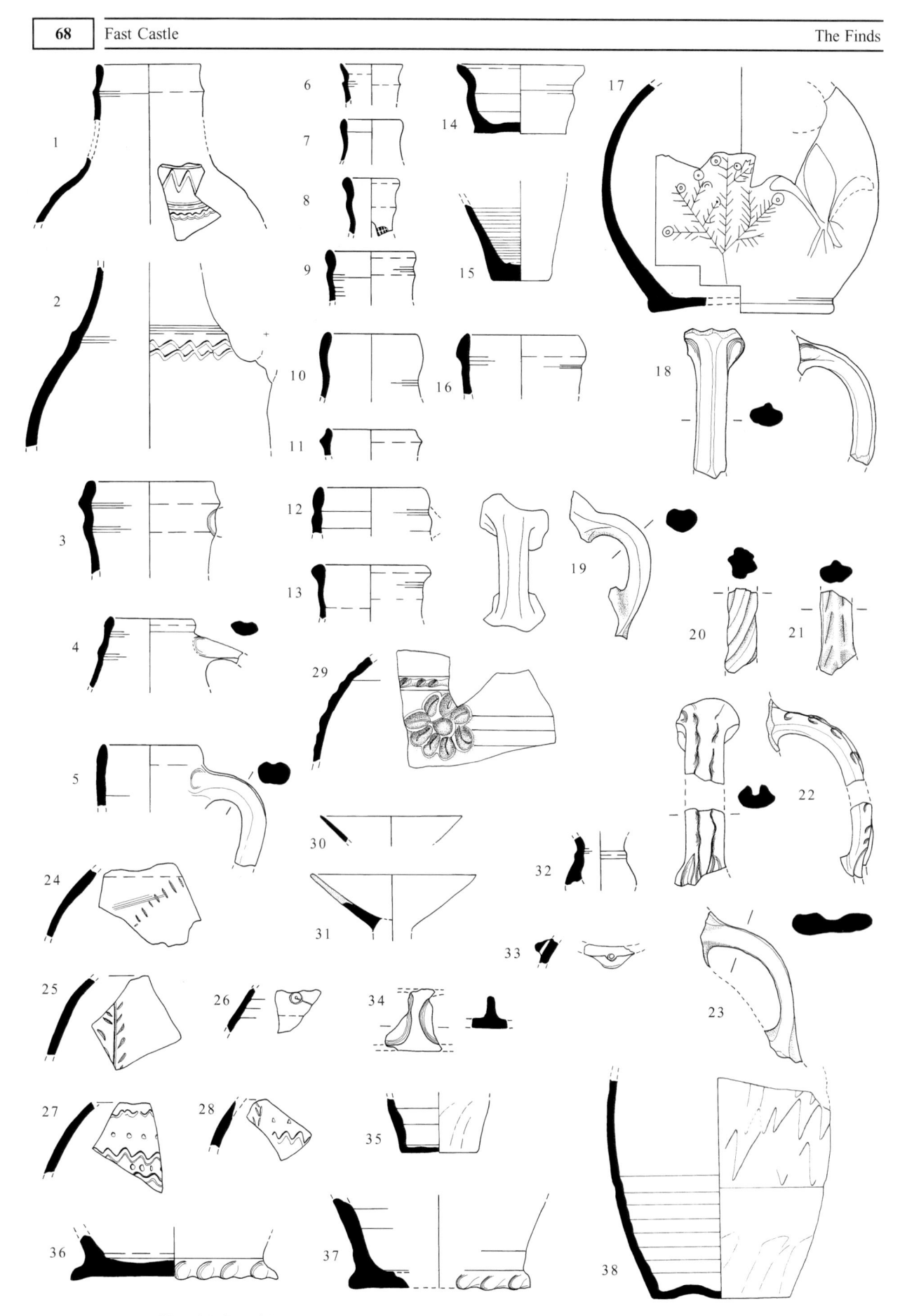

**Illus 33** Scottish Medieval and later Pottery: Groups C, D and E. Scale 1:4

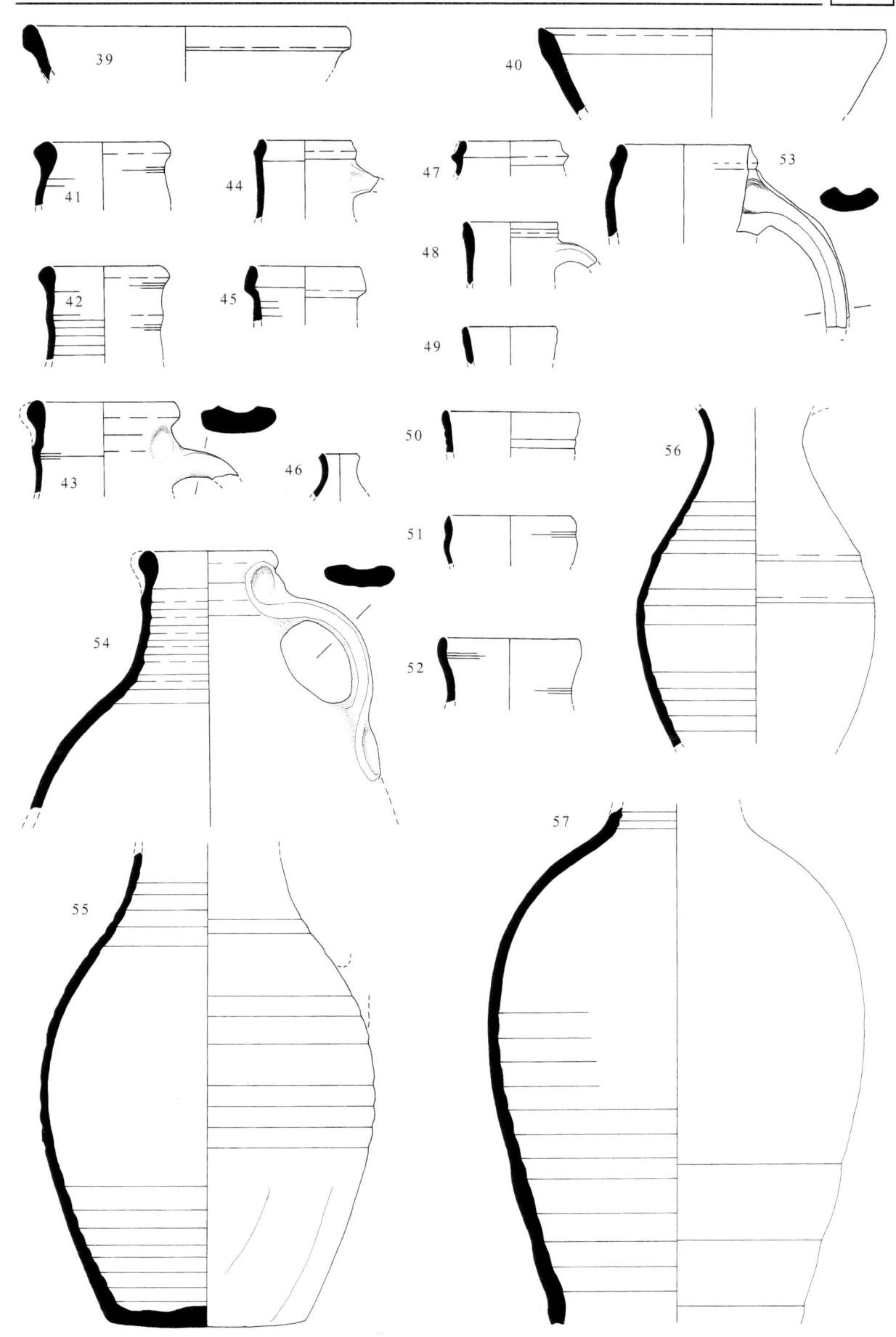

**Illus 34** Scottish Medieval and later Pottery, Group E. Scale 1:4

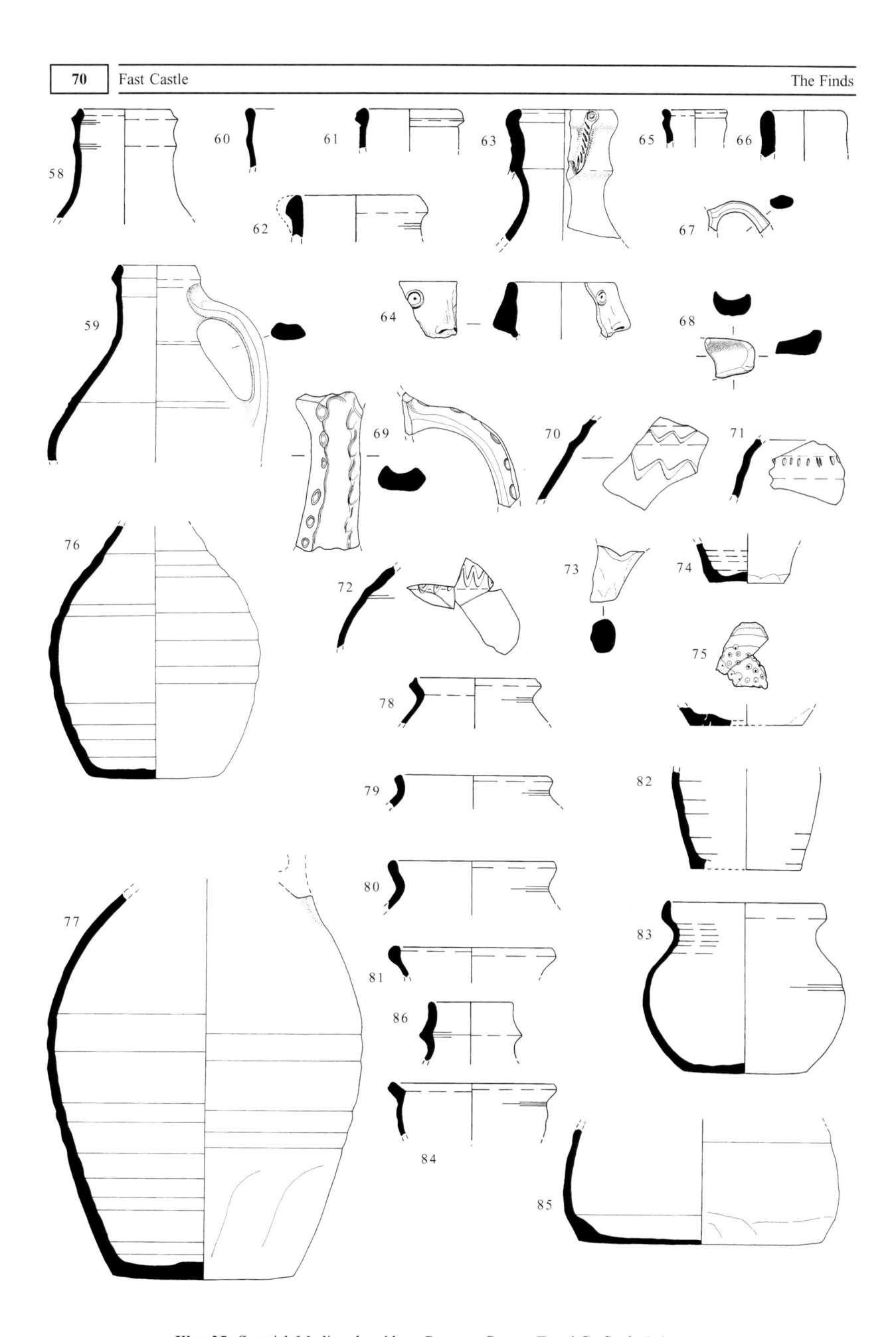

**Illus 35** Scottish Medieval and later Pottery: Groups F and G. Scale 1:4

| | | |
|---|---|---|
| 34.43 | E.1 | Jug. Rim and part of broad strap handle. Glazed exterior. Period II.1 (Plate XII.2) |
| 34.44 | E.2 | Jug. Rim and portion of rod handle. External shiny glaze. Possible waster, as glaze runs over broken end of handle. Unstrat. |
| 34.45 | E.4 | Jug. Rim. Glazed exterior. Period III-IV |
| 34.46 | E.2 | Small vessel. Rim and neck. Glazed exterior. Period II-III |
| 34.47 | E.1 | Jug? Rim. Glazed exterior. Period II.2 |
| 34.48 | E.2 | Jug? Rim and part of narrow strap handle. Glazed exterior. Period III-IV |
| 34.49 | E.2 | Drinking vessel? Rim. Glazed exterior and interior. Period II.1 |
| 34.50 | E.1 | Drinking vessel? Rim. Shiny glaze, exterior and interior. Period III.1 |
| 34.51 | E.1 | Thin-walled vessel. Rim. Shiny glaze, exterior and interior. Unstrat |
| 34.52 | E.2 | Wide-necked jar? Glazed exterior and interior. Period II.2 |
| 34.53 | E.1 | Jug. Rim and strap handle. Glazed exterior. Period II.2 |
| 34.54 | E.1 | Jug. Rim, shoulder and broad strap handle. Glazed exterior. Period II.1, Unstrat (Plate XII.1) |
| 34.55 | E.1 | Large jug. Glazed exterior. Period II.2 (Pl. XI.1) |
| 34.56 | E.1 | Jug. Glazed exterior. Period II.2, III.1, Unstrat |
| 34.57 | E.1 | Large jug. Glazed exterior. Period II, Unstrat (Plate XI.2) |
| 35.58 | F.1 | Jug. Rim and neck. Glazed exterior. Period II.2, III.1 |
| 35.59 | F.2 | Jug. Rim, neck, shoulder and strap handle. Glazed exterior. Period III-IV (Plate XII.3) |
| 35.60 | F.3 | Jug? Rim. Glazed exterior. Well |
| 35.61 | F.3 | Jug? Rim. Patchy glaze on exterior and inside rim. Period II.2 |
| 35.62 | F.1 | Jug. Rim. Glazed exterior. Period II.1 |
| 35.63 | F.1 | Anthropomorphic jug. Rim. Applied beard with stabbed decoration and impressed eye. Glazed exterior. Period II.1 |
| 35.64 | F.1 | Anthropomorphic jug. Rim. Applied nose and eye with stamped ring and dot; trace of upper lip. Shiny exterior glaze. Period II.2 |
| 35.65 | F.1 | Drug jar. Rim. Glazed exterior and interior. Unstrat |
| 35.66 | F.1 | Industrial vessel? Rim. Unglazed. Period III.IV |
| 35.67 | F.1 | Ribbed rod handle. Glazed exterior and interior. Unstrat |
| 35.68 | F.1 | Extended strap handle. Glazed both surfaces. Period II.2 |
| 35.69 | F.3 | Strap handle. Thumbed decoration. Shiny glaze. Period II.2 |
| 35.70 | F.1 | Jug. Shoulder sherd. Incised decoration. Glazed exterior. Unstrat |
| 35.71 | F.3 | Jug? Body sherd. Fingernail-impressed decoration Period II.2 |
| 35.72 | F.1 | Jug. Shoulder sherd. Incised decoration. Glazed exterior. Period II-IV |
| 35.73 | F.1 | Pipkin? Foot. Unglazed. Period II.1 |
| 35.74 | F.1 | Small jug? Base and lower body. Shiny patchy, external glaze. Period II.1 |
| 35.75 | F.1 | Watering-pot or censer. Base. Random, stabbed holes some failing to penetrate to the interior. Glazed exterior. Period II.1, III-IV |
| 35.76 | F.1 | Jug. Glazed exterior. Period II.2, Unstrat |
| 35.77 | F.1 | Large jug. Glazed exterior. Period III-IV |
| 35.78 | F.1 | Cooking pot or jar. Rim. Interior glazed, with runs on exterior. Period IV |
| 35.79 | F.1 | Cooking pot or jar. Rim. Patchy exterior glaze. Some sooting on exterior. Period II.1 |
| 35.80 | F.1 | Cooking pot or jar. Rim. Patchy interior glaze. Period II.2 |
| 35.81 | F.1 | Cooking pot or jar. Rim. Patchy interior glaze. Period III-IV |
| 35.82 | F.1 | Jug? Lower body. Glazed exterior, internal splashes. Sooted exterior. Period II.1 |
| 35.83 | F.1 | Cooking pot. Glazed interior. Period III-IV |
| 35.84 | F.1 | Small bowl. Rim. Interior partially glazed, runs on rim. Period III-IV |
| 35.85 | F.1 | Cooking pot? Glazed interior. The exterior is sooted. Period II |
| 35.86 | G.1 | Jug. Rim. Degraded exterior glaze. Period III-IV |

## J  Imported Wares

### George Haggarty & Sarah Jennings

TYPE J.1

(Adapted from Haggarty & Jennings 1994)

The imported, ie non-Scottish, pottery from the infill of the Quarry pit comes mostly from France and Germany, with only a few or individual vessels coming from the Low Countries, Italy and the Iberian Peninsula (illus 36). Most of the imported vessels are fine tablewares and, surprisingly, only one small fragment of a Low Countries Redware *grape* was recovered. Very little of the pottery from Yorkshire and East Anglia commonly found on excavations in Scottish east coast ports (Cheer 1990, 21) was identified, although there are some fragments that may have originated from East Yorkshire. Most of the imported vessels are well-known types, descriptions and definitions of which can be found in Hurst *et al* (1986); full fabric descriptions are therefore not detailed below. Details of stratigraphic location are given in the pottery archive.

It is likely that the main, and indeed the simplest, method of rubbish disposal at Fast Castle was to tip it over the side of the cliff into the sea. Therefore, the surviving pottery probably only represents a fraction of the total assemblage from the occupation of the castle. Although fragments of about fifty-five imported vessels were recovered, many were only represented by a few small sherds. It is difficult to determine the exact number of imported vessels, due to the problems of definitely attributing the many small fragments either to the same or to different vessels.

### FRANCE

Fragments of both Beauvais stonewares and lead-glazed earthenwares were found, together with several Martincamp flasks. The Beauvais stoneware comprises three vessel types: two squat *cup* or *jug* bases, one with a handle (nos 1 and 2), the base fragment from a possible *goblet* (no 3) and a *shallow drinking bowl* (no 4). The lead-glazed earthenwares seem to be represented by two different types of vessels: smaller, squatter *drinking jugs* and taller, *plain jugs*. The most complete of the drinking jugs (no 8) has a typical bright green glaze and an armorial medallion on the shoulder. A yellow-glazed jug with an identical shield to no 8, showing the Tudor coat of arms with lions and fleur-de-lis, was found at Kirkham Abbey, East Yorkshire; like the Fast Castle example, the shield forms the whole medallion without the addition of a circle (Hurst 1971, 11). There is another small sherd with a bright, thick brownish-yellow glaze, which is also likely to be from a drinking jug. The three slightly larger jugs have a much paler lemon-yellow glaze. The best preserved of these (no 11) has a pronounced cordon at the junction of the neck and shoulder and a faint groove on the shoulder, both typical features of these vessels.

All the Martincamp *flasks* recovered from the Quarry pit are of the type I or II variety. Four of the five examples have an off-white fabric, while one (no 15) has a light grey near stoneware fabric with a large patch of distinctive brownish-orange ash glaze covering the centre of one side. One sherd with identical fabric to the type I Martincamp flasks (no 19) is more likely to come from the lower wall of a *jug* or vessel of similar shape.

### GERMAN STONEWARES

The earliest of the stoneware vessels are fragments of Langerwehe/Raeren and Raeren stoneware *drinking mugs* and stonewares from the Lower Rhineland area. These come from the lowest deposits and are associated with coins of c1480. The other type of Langerwehe/Raeren vessels found in the pit are the taller *narrow-necked jugs* (no 21)(Plate XII.4), one of which also came from the bottom layers of the Quarry pit (no 26). Siegburg stonewares do not appear to be present at Fast Castle. Although impossible to tell apart from Beauvais stonewares in small fragments, all the identifiable bases have the typical attribute of the Beauvais industry of being flat. It seems unlikely, therefore, that any of the off-white to pale grey unglazed stonewares are from Siegburg *(contra* Thoms 1983, 255).

A Cologne *foliage mug* of the earlier 16th century was found in Period III.1. This has applied tendril and rose leaf decoration (no 38). No examples of mugs with oak leaves and acorns were found. Vessels with rose leaf motifs are found from c1500 onwards and are earlier than those with the oak leaf design (Hurst *et al* 1986, 208-9).

Three small fragments of one or more Cologne or Frechen *foliage band jugs* were retrieved, mainly from Period III. The surviving fragments have the typical acanthus leaf motifs and the edges of the roundels (nos 42 and 44) and one piece has part of the foliage band (no 43).

There is one example of the plain *globular jugs* with turned bases and a cordon at the junction of the neck and shoulder. This, with its shiny mid-brown wash and glaze (no 39), is paralleled by examples from the waster groups found in Maximinenstrasse, Cologne, and is not one of the Frechen examples to which this form is usually attributed. The more globular type dates to the third quarter of the 16th century, with the taller and more slender examples being slightly later (Hurst *et al* 1986, 216).

Among the unstratified sherds is one fragment of Westerwald stoneware, dating to c1700. In addition, there are several individual sherds which could not be attributed to the major stoneware industries. The suggested source for one of these (no 35) is the Hamburg/Dresden area.

LOW COUNTRIES AND BELGIUM

One rim fragment of a Low Countries Redware *'grape' (cooking pot)* was recovered from the Quarry pit, with a number of small fragments from a South Netherlands *flower* or *altar vase* (no 48). This example has a speckled overall blue tin-glaze on the outer surface (in the so-called Malling-style), with a thin, colourless lead glaze on the inner surface.

Fragments of another *flower vase* (no 49) similar in form and appearance to nos 48 and 50 were recovered from the Quarry pit. The surviving decoration, painted in blue on a white tin-glazed ground, comprises part of a central medallion with a floral motif; on one sherd the edge of a ladder decoration survives. The inner surface has a translucent milky white glaze. These sherds are slightly burnt (no 49b). A plain, straight rim fragment (no 49a) has part of a motif comprising horizontal brush strokes; although unburnt, this appears to have the same fabric and glaze and might be from the same vessel as no 49b. This is a problematical find. It might not have been made in the Low Countries, but is not likely to have been made in Italy. A possible Portuguese origin has been suggested for this vessel (J. Baart and M. Milanese pers comm). However, examples of Portuguese wares in the British Isles are extremely rare in this period, and it seems more likely that this is an unusual Low Countries product.

These tin-glazed vases are usually attributed to the Bruges or Antwerp areas; they have been found on a number of sites in England in the first half of the 16th century (Evans 1985, 35; Fig 20.75, from the 1507 fire deposits). None have so far been found in pre-1500 deposits (Hurst *et al* 1986, 199), although they are depicted in the Book of Hours painted between 1477-90 for Englebert of Nassau.

## ITALY

A *flower vase* or *jug* (no 50), similar in form to no 48, is definitely not of South Netherlands manufacture, and was made in Tuscany or Liguria towards the end of the 15th century. These sherds have thinner walls than the similar South Netherlands vessels and unlike them have a white tin glaze on both surfaces, although most of the glaze on the outer surface has been lost. One sherd with a lower handle junction has a minute piece of blue decoration on the thick, white ground.

## THE IBERIAN PENINSULA

Two small body sherds from two amphorae were recovered from the Quarry pit (nos 51, 52). The sherds are featureless and give no indication of shape, but it is likely that they are from *olive jars,* from the Seville area. Olive jars of this type are known to have been imported to London from the mid 13th century onwards (Vince 1985, 81).

Other sherds that are probably from the Iberian Peninsula include part of the body of a small, unglazed pot with a globular body, which is heavily sooted on the exterior (no 52); two sherds from the shoulder and neck of a hollow ware with a cordon and a dirty coloured tin glaze on the exterior (no 54); a small body sherd with an internal glaze (no 55).

**Note:** A further eight sherds, including two handle fragments, have since been identified as probably being part of no 54

## DISCUSSION

All the evidence from the various sources suggests a date within the last quarter of the 15th century and the first quarter of the 16th century for the deposition of the main phase of the Quarry pit fill, ie all the layers in Period II. It would seem that this filling was effected over a relatively short space of time, perhaps only 25 years, as shown by the many pottery joins between layers. This short time span is also reflected in the dating of many of the vessels found in the lower half of the pit. Stratigraphically the earliest of the imported wares are the typical Lower Rhenish and Raeren stoneware drinking jugs, which date from the third quarter of the 15th century (Gaimster 1987, 343; Hurst *et al* 1986, 184). Apart from a few later fragments from the top occupational deposit, Period III.2, the vessels in the upper part of the Quarry pit date to around the middle of the 16th century. The few later sherds could be due to the levelling up of settlement in the top of the pit, or to the extended time that this part of the site remained open, during successive seasons of excavation.

The top part of the pit, that is, all the layers in Period III may have had a shorter deposition time span than the coin evidence of c1500-1600 would suggest. Most of the glazed Beauvais earthenwares and the few Frechen wares came from this fill of the Quarry pit.

The imported assemblage from Fast Castle appears to have a different composition to other east coast groups, such as Perth (Cheer 1991, 51) and Aberdeen (Murray 1982, 122-126). The extent to which this reflects the restricted date range of the pottery, possibly only one hundred years, is difficult to tell, as few groups of the period are available for comparison in Scotland. However, the Fast Castle group does have the advantage over many urban assemblages in the absence of residual sherds.

Although Cheer, in his list of imported pottery found in Perth (Cheer 1991, 51), states that these cover the period up to c1450, the presence of Cologne/Frechen and Frechen stonewares in the list means an extended end date of some 100 years. Even allowing for the much earlier start date (c1250) for the Perth groups, detailed comparison between the imports from Fast and Perth is of limited value. At Perth, Low Countries

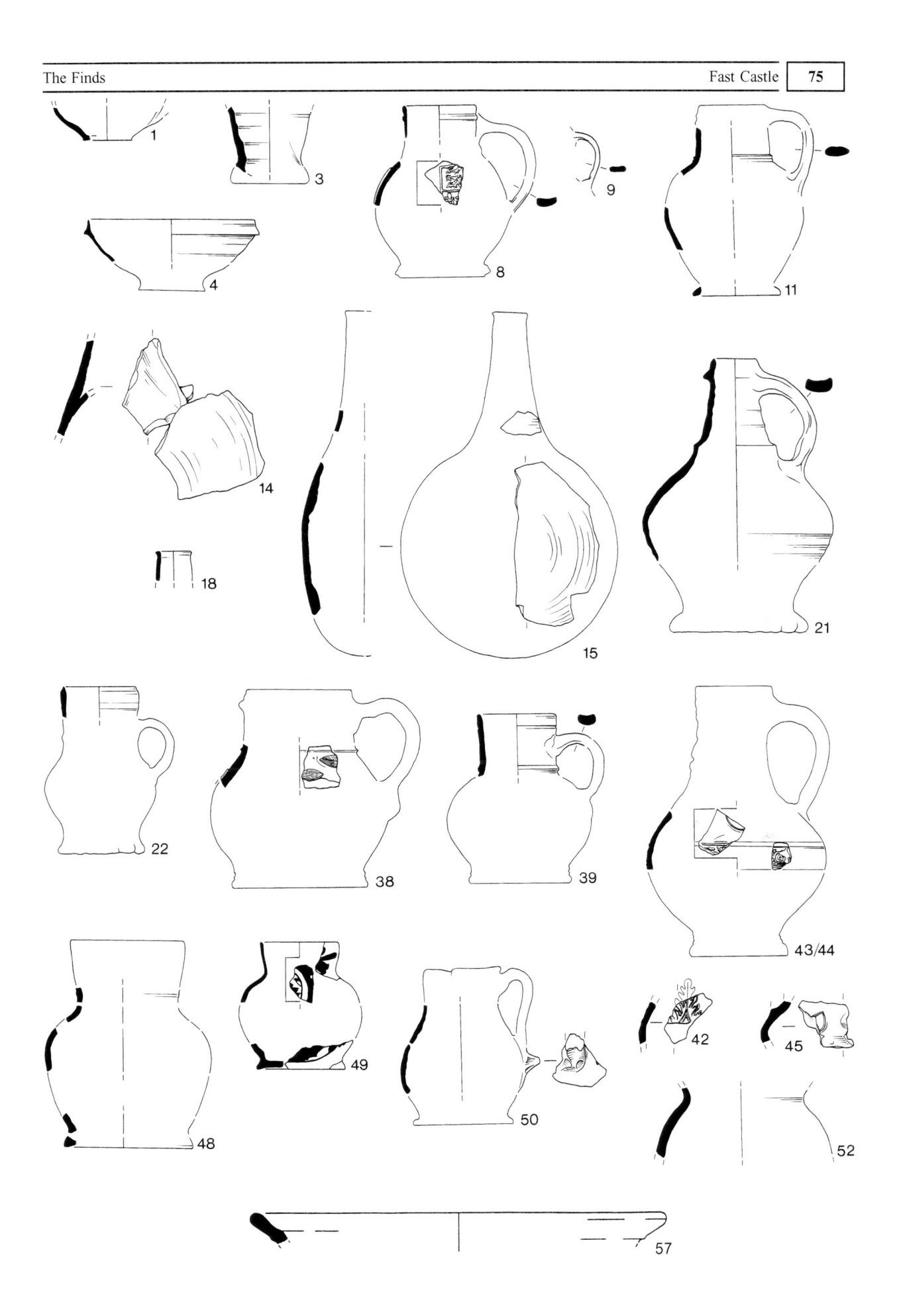

**Illus 36** Pottery: Imported wares. Scale 1:4

Redwares represent very nearly one fifth (19.1 per cent) of the 3181 sherds from both England and the Continent, whereas only one sherd was found at Fast. Siegburg stoneware forms a very small percentage of the Perth imports (0.3 per cent), but it is absent from Fast Castle. It is tempting to suggest, admittedly on rather limited evidence, that the main period for the importation of both these wares to eastern Scotland was, therefore, the second half of the 14th century and the first half of the 15th century. Their absence from Fast Castle is thus due to the later start date of that group.

## CONCLUSIONS

Fast Castle was not near a port or thriving urban centre and would, on the present limited Scottish archaeological evidence, normally be considered a poor candidate for the recovery of quality, casually-traded European pottery (Hurst *et al* 1986, 131). It is not difficult to find a reason for this. Scotland was, in economic terms, on the periphery of mainland Europe, although by the second half of the 15th century James IV and other Scottish nobles, not unmindful of their own economic interests, were trying to encourage foreign trade. For example, in 1476 James IV tried to establish a trading link with merchants from Florence (Nicholson 1978, 431-44).

The 1549 plan of Fast Castle (illus 6) shows a crane, which was used in the provisioning of the castle with sea-borne supplies. This is borne out by the archaeological evidence. Most of the earlier group of imports date to within the period when the castle was continuously occupied (1487 to 1508) as the principal residence of Sir Patrick Home. This ability to provision from passing ships along with the status of the owner probably accounts for this unique pottery assemblage

### CATALOGUE (illus 36)

Key: \* = Illustrated vessel   (S) = Stoneware
     (E) = Earthenware   U/S = Unstratified

| No | Fabric | Vessel type/Period | | | |
|---|---|---|---|---|---|
| 1* | Beauvais (S) | Cup; lower handle scar; Period II.1 | 14* | Martincamp | Flask: Type I; Period II.1 |
| 2 | Beauvais (S) | Cup; Period II.2 | 15* | Martincamp | Flask: Type II; Period II |
| 3* | Beauvais (S) | Goblet/jug; Period III-IV | 16 | Martincamp | Flask, ash glaze; Type II; Period II |
| 4* | Beauvais (S) | Bowl; Period II.1 | 17 | Martincamp | Flask; Period II.2 |
| 5 | Beauvais (S) | Sherd, small; Period III-IV | 18* | Martincamp | Flask; Period II-III |
| 6 | Beauvais (E) | Jug, yellow glaze; Period III-IV | 19 | Martincamp | Jug (not flask); Period III-1 |
| 7 | Beauvais (E) | Probably Beauvais; yellow glaze; Period III.1 | 20 | Martincamp | Flask; Period II.1 |
| 8* | Beauvais (E) | Drinking jug, green glaze; Period II.2, III-IV | 21* | Langerwehe | Narrow-necked jug; Period II.2 (Plate XII.4) |
| 9* | Beauvais (E) | Handle; Period II | 22* | Lower Rhenish | Drinking jug, rim; Period II.1 |
| 10 | Beauvais (E) | Sherd, yellow glaze; Period III-IV | 23 | Lower Rhenish | Drinking jug, rim; Period II.2 |
| 11* | Beauvais (E) | Jug, yellow glaze; Period II-IV | 24 | Raeren | Footring drinking jug; Period II.1 |
| 12 | Beauvaisis | Sherd, small; Period III-IV | 25 | Raeren | Base edge; Period II.1 |
| 13 | Martincamp/Beauvais | Sherd, ash glaze; Period II.2 | 26 | Raeren | Narrow-necked jug; Period II, III.1 |

| | | | | | |
|---|---|---|---|---|---|
| 27 | Raeren | Basal edge; Period II.2 | 42* | Cologne | Foliage band jug; Period III |
| 28 | Raeren | Body sherds; Period II.2 | 43* | Frechen | Foliage band jug; Period III-IV |
| 29 | Raeren | Small basal edge; Period III.1 | 44* | Frechen | Foliage band jug; Period III-IV |
| 30 | Raeren | Two small brown sherds; Period III.1 | 45* | Frechen | Jug, blank leaf; Period III-IV |
| 31 | Raeren | Body/base; Period III-IV | 46 | Frechen | Later type; Period III-IV |
| 32 | Raeren | Sherd; Period II.1 | 47 | Low Countries | Redware *grape* rim; Period II-III |
| 33 | Raeren | Oil-pot; Period III.1 | 48* | Low Countries | Flower vase, blue tin-glazed; Period II-IV |
| 34 | Unknown | Body sherd, stoneware; Period II.2 | 49* | Low Countries | Flower vase; Period II.2-IV |
| 35 | Hamburg/Dresden | Sherd; Period II.2 | 50* | Italian | Flower vase; Period II.2 |
| 36 | West Rhenish | Sherd, brown glaze; Period II.2 | 51 | Iberian | Olive jar; Period II.2 |
| 37 | Early Cologne | Handle, earthenware; Period II.2 | 52* | Iberian | Globular vessel, unglazed; Period II.2 |
| 38* | Cologne | Rose leaf drinking mug; Period III.1 | 53 | Iberian | Amphora; U/S |
| 39* | Cologne | Straight-necked jug; Period III.1 | 54 | Iberian | Hollow ware, tin-glazed exterior; Period II.2 |
| 40 | Cologne | Sherds, small; Period III-IV | 55 | Iberian | Sherd, glazed interior; Period III.2 |
| 41 | Cologne/Frechen | Drinking jug; Period III-IV | 56 | Chinese porcelain | Dish/plate footring; Period II.1 |

ACKNOWLEDGEMENTS

The authors are very grateful to the following for comments and advice on the imported wares from Fast Castle and for giving us the benefit of their knowledge and the latest research on ceramics in these countries - Jan Baart (the Netherlands), Pierre Ickowitz (France), Marco Milanese (Italy) and Sven Schütte (Germany). Nicholas N McQ Holmes kindly allowed us to quote from his interim numismatic report. John Wallender kindly drew the pottery.

## Imported Wares: Appendix

### Valerie E Dean & Hugh Robertson

TYPE J.3: LOW COUNTRIES WARE

The following unstratified sherd (illus 36, 57) was later identified as being Low Countries ware, probably of 17th-century date.

One sherd of a very hard fabric, 10mm thick, with a fine texture, smooth surface and rough fracture. The outer surface is reddish brown (2.5YR 5/4) with a red (2.5YR 4/8) core. The 10% inclusions comprise abundant, fairly-sorted, fine to medium and occasionally coarse, sub-round, translucent and white quartz; occasional, fairly-sorted, medium, sub-round haematite and rock; and occasional, fine mica. The interior is covered with pink (7.5YR 8/4) slip, overlain by yellow (10YR 7/8) glaze; these have a speckly appearance.

57*    Low Countries            Large dish. Rim. Glazed interior. Unstratified.

## K-L  Post-occupation and modern pottery

### Valerie E Dean & Hugh Robertson

The sherds of this group, mainly from the top layers of the excavation, are regarded as modern. They may be attributed to disturbance or contamination and may have come from earlier excavations or from visiting parties in the last two centuries.

### K  EARTHENWARE AND STONEWARE

This group covers material which most likely has been brought to the site by visitors after the castle had fallen into disuse.

TYPE K.1: RED EARTHENWARE AND SLIPWARE

A group of very mixed sherds of a very hard fabric, 3-8mm thick, with a fine texture, smooth surfaces and a clean break. The outer surfaces vary from weak red (10R 4/3) to yellowish red (5YR 4/6), the interiors are dark reddish grey (5YR 4/2) and the cores are red (2.5YR 4/6-5/6) or dark grey (5YR 4/1). The 5-10% inclusions can be sub-angular or sub-round, fairly-sorted, and comprise a moderate amount of fine to medium translucent and white quartz; sparse, fine to medium, haematite and rock; and a moderate amount of fine mica. Vessels can be glazed on the exterior only, or on both surfaces; where slip lies below the glaze, this is on the interiors. The slip is pale yellow (2.5Y 8/4), sometimes with brown streaks. The glaze varies from dark red (2.5YR 3/6), sometimes containing tiny yellow flecks, to black (5YR 2.5/1); the glaze is often abraded and flaking.

Forms: Bowls, one large. Late 18th- to 19th-century. (not illustrated)

TYPE K.2: WHITE EARTHENWARE

Sherds are 3-5mm thick, with a white (10YR 8/2) core and an all-over tin glaze.

Forms: Plates/saucers; teapot lid; cup? handle; small bowl. Decoration comprises blue-and-white transfer printing. The teapot lid is hand-painted, with a gilded line. Late 18th- to early 20th-century. (not illustrated)

TYPE K.3: MODERN STONEWARE

Two sherds of a vitrified fabric, 5-11mm thick, with a clean break. The core is white (10YR 8/2), and the all-over glaze is white (10YR 8/2) or very pale brown (10YR 7/3).

Forms: Jam jars? 19th- or early 20th-century. (not illustrated)

### L  PORCELAIN

Two sherds, 2-3mm thick. Decoration comprises hand-painted, blue-and-white patterns, internally and externally.

Forms: Cups/small bowls? Probably 19th-century. (not illustrated)

## M  Miscellaneous Ceramics

Hugh Robertson

(Initial analysis by Brian Bleakley)

TILE

Illus 37.1-3

Fifteen pieces of floor tile were recorded, three of which join. All are from the Quarry pit and therefore probably constitute discard material. All but one appear to have been deposited probably during the second half of the 15th century. All are well-fired, with a fully oxidised red fabric, coarse in texture with inclusions. There are four square corners and eleven straight edges. The edges show a distinct bevel. The thickness of the tiles ranges from 20mm to 33mm.

The pieces can be divided into five groups. Group A comprises the joined fragments and three other pieces (illus 37.1, 37.2); the fabric of all is very similar but two pieces have a thickness of 27-30mm whereas the others are uniformly of 25mm. The largest side, of one of the latter, is 86mm, and this also shows a nail-hole in one corner, a typical sign of the technique employed by the Netherlands tile-makers in the fifteenth century of using a board with protruding nails to hold the soft tiles while cutting the edges (Norton, 1994, 151). This group shows traces of dark grey glaze on the surface; the bases are rough.

Group B comprises two pieces, about 25mm in thickness, showing patches of sand on the base from the bed on which the tiles were formed, and traces of white slip and brown glaze on the surface, probably lead glaze contaminated with iron. The edges are smooth.

Group C comprises three small lumps of similar material without defined edges of any extent but showing white slip and brown glaze.

Group D comprises two pieces of coarse fabric, one 20mm in thickness and the other 30mm. Both show traces of black glaze, thought to be a lead glaze mixed with copper or brass.

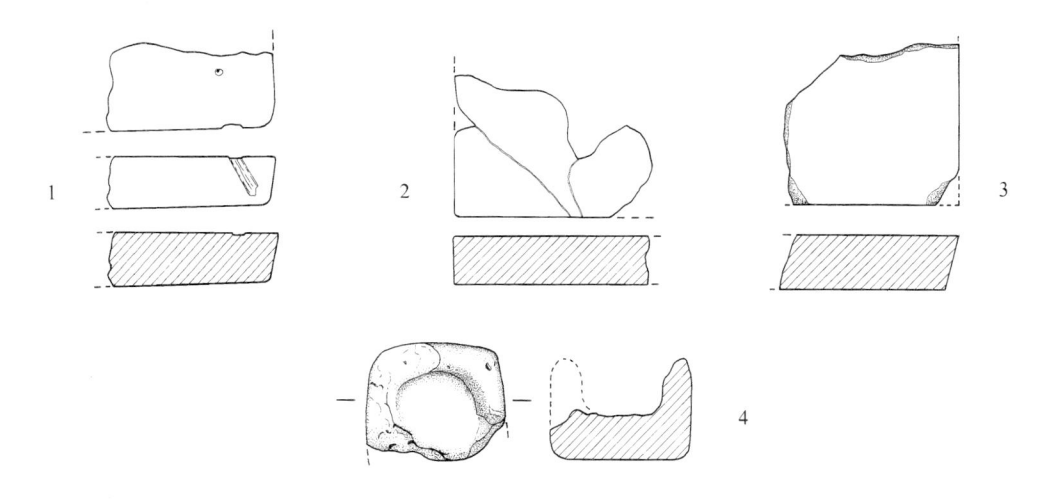

**Illus 37** Ceramic tiles. Scale 1:4

Finally, Group E comprises two substantial pieces, approximately 30mm in thickness, the base being rougher than the smooth surface. One piece shows traces of black glaze on both surface and edge. On the other (illus 37.3) the longest edge is 93mm.

The tiles appear to be similar to others recorded in Kirkwall, and also from excavations in High Street, Edinburgh (*ibid*, 171-2), having possibly been imported from the Netherlands as ballast on ships.

## MISCELLANEOUS FIRED CLAY

Illus 37.4

This includes two pieces of brick-like fabric and two of fired clay or daub. The larger brick-type piece is a rough cube, approximately 75 x 60mm, with three slightly curved sides and a large cavity in the middle (illus 37.4). The fabric is fine but soft. It is dated to the 15th century. It is difficult to guess its function, possibly part of a brick, mould, or cresset. The other piece of brick-like fabric is simply a small shapeless lump.

The larger of the two pieces of clay is a heavy shapeless lump, about 140 x 80mm, hard-fired. There is some evidence suggesting that it has been up against wood or roots when fired, perhaps during tempering. From the stratification it was deposited in the late 16th century. Conceivably it was part of a forge, kiln, or hearth; but its firing may have been accidental. The other piece is much smaller; it shows shrinkage cracks, is soft and may merely be plaster daub.

### CATALOGUE OF ILLUSTRATED ITEMS (illus 37)

1   Fragment of floor tile with thickness complete with remains of dark glaze on one side, very dark grey (2.5YR/3/0). Unglazed underside, weak red (2.5YR/5/2). 'Pin-hole' present on glazed side 4mm deep some 40mm from corner. Edge undercut. 86 x 40 x 25mm. Period III.1.

2   Fragment of floor tile, comprising three pieces which fit together. Thickness complete, with part of two straight edges. Core colour light reddish-brown (5YR/6/3). Remnants of glaze on one face very dark grey (2.5YR/3/0). Maximum dimensions: 105 x 75mm, 25mm thick. Period III.1.

3   Fragment of floor tile (or possibly hearth?) tile. Dense in weight. Two flat faces, with two straight edges, with thickness complete. Edges of faces not at right angles. Core fabric light red (2.5YR 6/6); no trace of glaze but one face of a different colour, light reddish-brown (2.5YR 6/4), and rougher in surface texture. Maximum dimensions: 81 x 93mm, 29mm thick. Period II.2.

4   Part of brick (possible mould?). Three flat sides with right angles meeting at corner. Hollow in centre. Colour uniform. Core fabric light red (2.5YR 6/6). 75 x 60mm. Period II.1.

A full catalogue of ceramic finds will be archived in the National Monuments Record of Scotland.

## 5.3 GLASS & WINDOW-LEAD

K Robin Murdoch

**VESSEL GLASS**

The vessel glass may be divided into two basic groups, the first of which derives from contexts dating from the late 15th century through to probably just after 1500. This conclusion was reached mainly through numismatic evidence, but other categories of find support the premise. Similarly, the second group of glass can be attributed to the 16th to early 17th centuries. The importance of this assemblage of glass should not be underestimated since very little glass from Scottish sites has so far been published, and even less from good datable contexts. There is, as yet, no reliable evidence of an indigenous glass manufacturing industry in the post-medieval period in Scotland before the early 17th century (Paterson 1958, 3). Therefore, it must be presumed for the moment that most, if not all, of the Fast Castle glass was imported.

PERIOD II (late 15th to early 16th century)

Thirteen shards representing a maximum of seven fine vessels plus one bottle. It was possible to establish the form or part form of four of these vessels.

VESSEL No 1 (illus 38.1) Four shards, from a probable drinking glass with an angular bucket shaped bowl, an applied cordon ring, and unusually, a strap handle. The glass has a pale amber tinge and a light primary patina. The shards have an applied white enamel plumose (featherlike) decoration.

The implied shape of the bowl and the twisted cordon ring are typical of Venetian output of the late 15th/early 16th centuries, but the style was also copied in Northern Europe. The condition of the glass in this case would slightly favour Venetian rather than North European manufacture. However, the plumose decoration is quite closely paralleled in a smooth beaker found at Dendermonde, in the Netherlands, dated to the first half of the 16th century (Henkes 1994, 53, fig 13.3). The place of manufacture of the smooth beaker is given as South Netherlands or France, but Henkes describes it as an exceptional piece, and therefore, it is just possible that it was an import to that area. Two of the shards were recovered from secure Period II.2 contexts. One shard came from the disturbed Period III Pit 2 and one (probably residual) from an early Period III context.

The vessel can therefore be attributed to Period II, late 15th to early 16th century. The practice of applying a cordon ring to the base of the bowl continued until the end of the 17th century, but the later examples tended to have knopped rather than pedestal stems (Gooder 1984, 229, fig 56).

VESSEL No 2 (illus 38.2) Three rib shards, from a ribbed beaker. The glass has a pale amber tinge and the present surfaces are matt suggesting that they are secondary. One shard still retains small patches of what appears to be dark patina. The existence and type of patination is important when considering the origins of the vessel. An amber tinge is typical of, but not exclusive to, Venetian soda glass of the late 15th - 16th centuries; a heavy dark patina is not.

This vessel is almost certainly a ribbeker from the Netherlands or Northern France and made from 'verre de fougère' or fern glass, so named because the potash fluxing alkali was derived from the ash of burnt ferns. A close parallel, found at Leiden in the Netherlands, is dated to around 1500 (Henkes 1994, 94, fig 23.2).

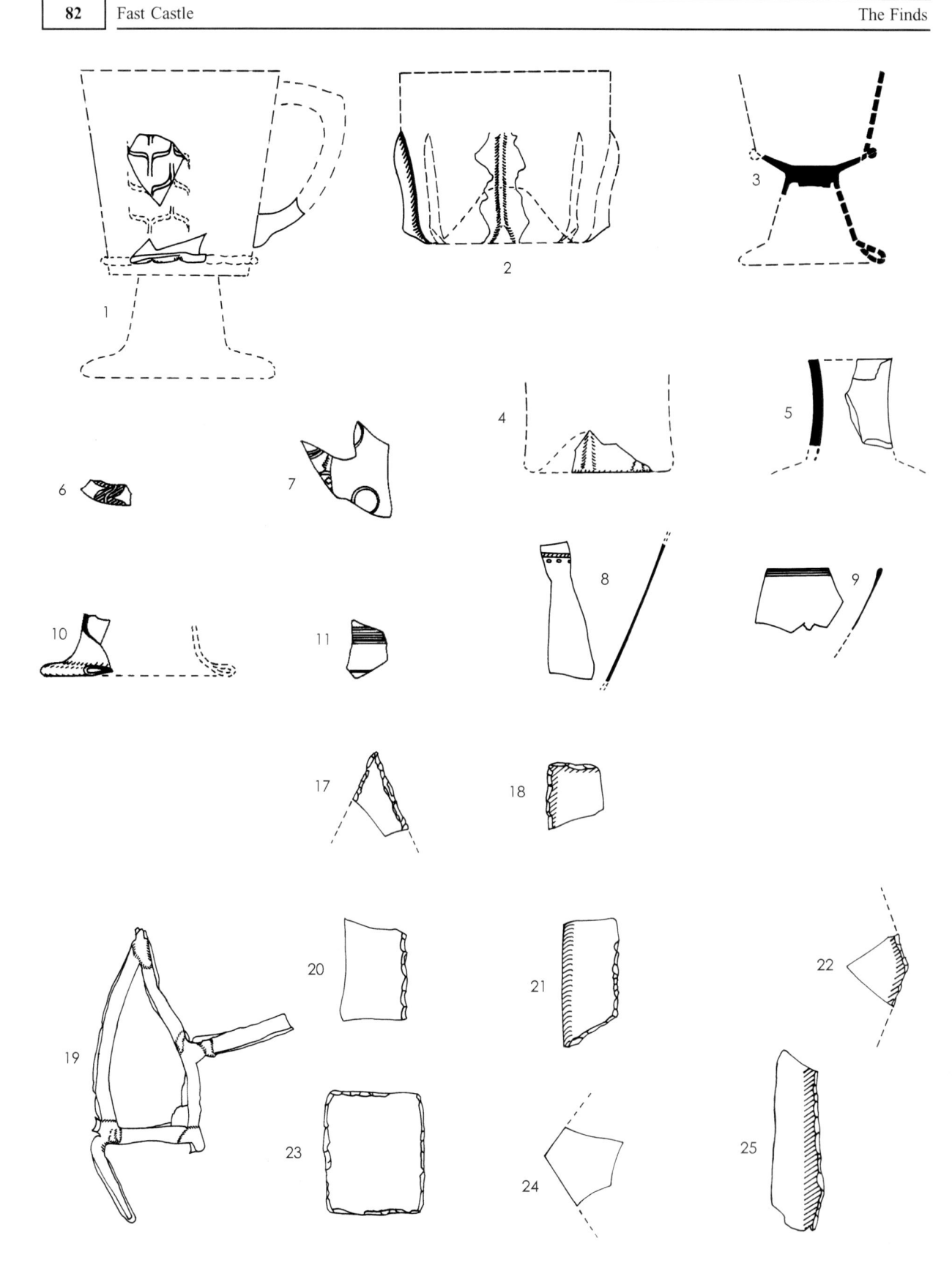

**Illus 38** Glass. Scale 1:2; Vessel and bottle glass: 1–5 Period II; 6–11 Period III.
Window glass: 17–18 Period II; 19–25 Period III.

VESSEL No 3 (illus 38.3) Part of a bowl base, with remnant of pedestal stem, just possibly part of Vessel no 1, but if not, is certainly from a vessel of very similar form, origin and date.

VESSEL No 4 (illus 38.4) A base fragment, from a small ribbed beaker or flask with a basal kick. The glass is in good condition with a pale brownish tinge and only light iridescent patina. Parts of two, fairly slight, rounded ribs are evident which are carried through the base ring into the kick. Vessel diameter has been c50-60mm. The uniformity of the ribbing and slight belling above the base indicate that the vessel has been mould blown and transferred to a pontil for finishing. The centre of the base is missing; therefore the pontil scar has not survived.

This vessel could be of German origin, possibly a form known as a Maigel beaker, late 15th century (Henkes 1994, 56, figs 14.2 and 14.3). However Dutch/N French, or even Venetian manufacture, cannot be ruled out. Maigel beakers are found extensively in the Netherlands around 1500 and could easily have infiltrated the export route to Fast Castle.

## OTHER PERIOD II FINE SHARDS

There were three other fine vessel shards, catalogue nos 12, 13 and 14 (not illus) from late 15th- to early 16th-century contexts but none carried any diagnostic or decorative feature. All are in fairly good condition with a pale brown tinge to the glass. It was not possible to suggest a place of manufacture for these shards.

## BOTTLE NECK

This item, No 5, (illus 38.5) from the deepest context within the Quarry pit, has the typical, slightly out-turned, lip of a style of bottle with a long history lasting from the 13th to the 17th centuries. The glass is pale green and has a very heavy, unstable, mottled brown patina. Potash glass from a forest glasshouse (Kenyon 1967), probably English or North European.

There is no evidence as yet of forest glasshouse activity in Scotland at the time this was made, which, from the context in which it was found, was probably not later than c1500.

## PERIOD III (early 16th to early 17th century)

Six shards representing between four and six vessels, including one possible bottle. It was possible to establish the form of one of the vessels.

VESSEL No 10 (illus 38.10) A fragment of pushed-in base, from a drinking vessel in clear glass with a faint brownish tinge. Good condition, firebright in patches with only light iridescent patina elsewhere. The foot has been c70mm diameter and the base has been pushed up, creating a wall of double thickness below the bowl.

This manufacturing technique had a long history with 4th-century Gallic examples being known. The technique became widely used in the forest glasshouses of Northern Europe and even in Venice. The style lasted until the end of the 16th century and was particularly favoured for beer and ale glasses. A mid 16th-century parallel may be seen in Wood (1982, 30). The condition of the glass in this case probably favours Venetian origin, but north European 'verre de fougère' (fern glass) cannot be ruled out.

OTHER PERIOD III FINE SHARDS

Two shards, nos 9 and 11, (illus 38.9 & 38.11) from 16th- century contexts were decorated with very thin parallel trails of white enamel, a style of decoration which is turning up on Scottish sites with some regularity. Recent examples were found at Spynie Palace, near Elgin (Lewis & Ewart, forthcoming); Niddry Castle, near Winchburgh (Murdoch 1997, 815, fig 22.1); and Liberton Tower, Edinburgh.

Two further shards, nos 6 and 8, (illus 38.6 & 38.8) carried coloured surface decoration, reminiscent of enamelled Venetian wares of the 16th and first half of the 17th centuries. No 6, however, also carried a yellow decoration which clearly had not been fired into the surface of the vessel as in the normal manner with enamel.

The presence of yet another fragment, no 7, (illus 38.7) also with an impermanent decoration, suggested that some of the decoration was cold colour painting, another, albeit much less common Venetian technique. Cold painting was also popular in Bohemia in the latter part of the 16th century (Klein & Lloyd 1991, 85)

## WINDOW GLASS

Window glass, while common in ecclesiastical buildings by the 12th century, is not believed to have been used to any great extent in secular buildings until the 15th century. It is, however, said to have been usual by the beginning of the 16th (Klein & Lloyd 1991, 48). Scotland appears to have lagged behind England and the rest of northern Europe in the manufacture of glass, and it would not be unreasonable to assume a lag in usage also. It would appear, therefore, that the late 15th-century owners of Fast Castle were probably in the forefront of secular users of glass in Scotland. The close proximity of the castle to the English border and to the trade routes to northern Europe would, of course, have been major factors.

Thanks to Effie Photos-Jones at Scottish Analytical Services for Art and Archaeology, based at Glasgow University, it was possible to have one window shard chemically analysed; catalogue number 20, a Period III shard. The table below reveals it to be a potash-lime glass. Should funding become available, it would be worthwhile analysing some of the other shards given the relatively tight context dating.

**Table 2** Glass composition of Cat no 20 from F202, Period III, percentage by weight

| Soda | Magnesia | Silica | Chloride | Tin | Potash | Lime | Titanium | Manganese | Iron | Arsenic | Sulphur |
|---|---|---|---|---|---|---|---|---|---|---|---|
| 0.49 | 1.05 | 69.62 | 0.42 | 0.67 | 6.41 | 18.03 | 0.42 | 0.84 | 1.5 | 0.14 | 0.39 |

Pending further analyses, comment is made on the possible chemical make-up of the rest of the glass based purely on physical appearance. Roughly 50% of the Period II glass has denatured to the extent that the original glass colour can not be ascertained and a further 25% has very dark or silvery patination. This is typical of potash-fluxed glass generally favoured by broad glass manufacturers at this time.

Roughly 50% of the Period III shards also look as if they are potash glass, while the rest would appear to be soda glass, generally favoured by crown glass manufacturers. However, the type of glass used by the two codes of manufacture should not be interpreted as a strict rule. While there are obvious anomalies in each group, the Period II shards average just over 2mm in thickness and those from Period III between 1.0 and 1.3mm. Typical quarry size, where it can be assessed, is very small (see catalogue no 23) (illus 38.23) and even thickened edge shards have been used (see catalogue no 21) (illus 38.21), indicating the scarcity and value of the commodity.

Broad glass is generally quite consistent in thickness, whereas crown glass can vary rapidly, even in a small shard. 20% of the Period II shards have variable thickness (however, one of these is an edge shard which could be either crown or broad); 37% of the Period III shards have variable thickness.

A particular problem with window glass, of course, is that it can have been in use for a very long time before it ends up in a destruction/ refurbishment/abandonment context. However, all of the window glass in this assemblage can be described as relatively thin, and it is thought unlikely that any of the shards are residual, or from a period earlier than the late 15th century.

All of the window shards from Fast Castle, where the colour could be ascertained, had a tinge of blue, green or slate. However, the absence of any shards with strong colouring suggests that the colour present was accidental rather than deliberate. Because of contaminants in the raw materials, and in the manufacturing crucibles, the medieval and post-medieval glassmakers had great difficulty in making colourless glass and most of what they produced was more or less tinted. Before the Reformation, many houses had feature stained glass windows, but the practice had largely died out by the end of the 16th century.

Many of the shards from the assemblage carried came shadows derived from differential weathering while in the window. Several lead cames were found confirming that the windows were typically made from small, and in many cases irregularly shaped, quarries held in position by the grooved lead cames. The cames were in two basic forms, an H-form for internal use and a C-form for the window perimeter. Lead sealing strips with remnants of iron framing were also found. The typically narrow groove width of the lead cames supports the argument that none of the finds, related to glazed windows, dates to earlier than the end of the 15th century.

A number of post-occupational shards of glass were recovered from the site. Their description, find nos and contexts are listed in archive.

## CATALOGUE (illus 38)

### VESSEL GLASS

**1** Shard, clear glass with pale amber tinge particularly in the fracture. Ogee or plumose decoration in white enamel. F97; Period III.2

Shard, clear glass with pale amber tinge and light iridescent patina. Ogee or plumose decoration in white enamel. 22 x 15mm and varies from 1.5-1.9mm thick. F99a/b; Period II.2

Shard of strap handle (probably lower end), clear glass with pale amber tinge. Handle has been applied over white enamel ogee or plumose decoration on the bowl wall. F103a/b; Period II.2

Shard, clear glass with pale amber tinge in the shatter, very light patina. Decorated with an ogee or plumose pattern in white opaque enamel which has been partially covered by the application of a gently twisted cordon. Pit 2; Period III

**2** Rib shard in very pale amber with occasional small blotches of dark patina. Some internal and external striations from manufacturing process. F103; Period II.2

Rib shard in very pale amber with light (secondary?) patina. F103; Period II.2

Rib shard 50 x 12mm in very pale amber. Maximum thickness over the rib is 5mm which reduces to a minimum of less than 0.5mm. Some light flaky patina remains on the secondary? surface. F103b; Period II.2

**3** Lower bowl in very pale amber with light iridescent patina, maximum surviving diameter 36mm. Very short, 3mm, section of plain stem topping springing of pedestal stem, 20mm diameter; pontil scar. F103a; Period II.2

**4** Base ring shard from small ribbed beaker/flask c75mm diameter with light iridescent patina. Shard thickness 0.6-1mm. F103; Period II.2

**5** Slightly flared bottle neck in pale green with heavy, mainly dark brown patina. Overall diameter of neck has been c29-30mm and the glass thickness 3.5mm. F403; Period II.1

**6** Small shard, 19 x 8 x 1.7mm, clear glass with slight amber tinge; wavy decoration in dark slate blue enamel and yellow enamel/paint. The yellow colour is impermanent suggesting poor firing or cold colour paint. F86; Period III.1

**7** Fire damaged shard, 1.2-1.3mm thick, clear glass, no apparent tinge, with part of complex enamel/paint decoration. The decoration is a yellow ground with fine line black detail on it and is not fired on to the glass; therefore, probably cold colour paint not enamel. F86; Period III.1

**8** Two shards, clear glass with slight pinkish amber tinge, slightly abraded; decorated with dark slate blue line and white dot enamel. Larger shard is 50 x 16mm and varies from 1.2-1.5mm thick. Vessel apparently had linear wall. F86; Period III.1

**9** Two conjoining rim shards from vessel c90mm diameter. The glass varies from very thin 0.6mm to 1.5mm at the rim; very pale amber tinge visible in the shatter. Three very thin parallel trails in white enamel (or lattimo) have been applied and marvered in at, and just below, the rim. The vessel apparently had a fairly linear wall, probably conical, slightly out-turned for the last 10mm below the rim. Pit 2; Period III

**10** Part pushed-in base, clear glass with pale amber tinge in the shatter. Double thickness lower wall and hollow section foot ring from vessel with pushed-in base. Diameter has been 72mm and the shard is lightly patinated. F202; Period III-IV

**11** Shard 20 x 15mm in clear thin (0.6mm) metal with light patina. The shard is decorated with 6 to 8 thin bands of white trailed enamel, marvered flat. F202; Period III-IV

**12** Shard, 1.5mm thick, clear glass with pale amber tinge and light iridescent patina. Not illus; F99/1; Period II.2

**13** Shard, 1.5-1.6mm thick, clear glass with very pale amber tinge and light patina. Not illus; F99a/b; Period II.2

**14** Shard in very thin, 0.4-0.6mm, clear glass with light flaky patina. Not illus; F103b; Period II.2

**15** Curved shard in pale greenish blue aqua, moderate to heavy patina, possible bottle shard, 27 x 17 x 1.5-3mm. Not illus; F206; Period III-IV

**16** Thin (0.9mm) wall shard from vessel in clear glass with no apparent colour tinge; surface slightly abraded with some light patina. Vessel appears to have had a conical wall. Not illus; Layer 3; Period II-III

### WINDOW GLASS

Note: Only illustrated window glass shards are included in the catalogue. Details of a further 75 shards are contained in the archive.

**17** Shard in pale bright (aqua) green with moderate dark brown patina, 30 x 14 x 1.9-2.2mm; two grozed edges at 45 deg. F99/1; Period II.2

**18** Shard in pale green with heavy stable dark brown patina, two grozed edges at right angles with came shadows, 23 x 20 x 2.1mm. Layer 3; Period II-III

**19** Section of window, which when found had a virtually complete quarry enclosed within H-section cames. The quarry was triangular 65 x 30 x 1.5-2mm thick, totally denatured. Kitchen. F303; Period IV

**20** Shard in greenish slate, good condition with only slight patina, one grozed edge, 37 x 25 x 1.5-1.6mm. F202; Period III-IV

**21** Thickened rim shard of probable crown glass, 41 x 21mm, pale green with lemon-lime coloured light to moderate patina; shard thickness 2.5-4mm. Edge parallel to rim is grozed as may be one end. Curvature at rim does suggest crown rather than broad glass although curvature is inconsistent and may be localised. F86; Period III.1

**22** Small shard in pale, slightly bluish, slate with two grozed edges at c135 deg and with came shadows; surfaces abraded. 25 x 22 x 1.2mm. Layer 2; Period III-IV

**23** Complete rectangular quarry in pale slate with light (may be secondary) patina. Four good grozed edges but no came shadows, 45 x 38 x 1.7-2.1mm. F202; Period III-IV

**24** Shard in greenish slate with light to moderate blotchy dark brown patina but also partially firebright, 28 x 26 x 1.2-1.6mm, two cut edges at 110 degrees. Kitchen. F303; Period IV

**25** Shard in greenish slate with moderate variable brown patina, one long grozed edge with came shadow, 66 x 19 x 1.3-1.5mm. Kitchen. F303; Period IV

### WINDOW LEAD (not illus, except no 17)

For measurements, and Periods, see Table 3

**1** H-form came.

**2** Strip H-form came, internal groove possibly c2mm but fragment is badly crushed.

**3** Fragment of possible sealing/packing strip, effective section is domed narrowing from 6.5, to 3.7mm with the narrow part being extremely ragged.

**4** Probable 5-way soldered junction in H-form cames, overall dimensions 57mm x 16mm. Typical flange width 4.3-5mm, height over flanges 4.6-5mm, flanges thin to 0.8mm at the edges and the internal grooves are typically 2.5mm.

**5** At least two-way soldered junction, came form similar to above.

**6** Strip, similar.

**7** Strip, heavier in section than above and form difficult to assess because of distortion. Suggestion of shallow grooving in one part 6mm wide, possibly part of outer border for glazed area.

**8** Strip, could have been raw strip for C-form came.

**9** Strip of substantial H-form came with thin mould lines on the flanges. Both ends are deliberately cut, suggesting branching.

**10** Strip H-form came, internal groove measures c2mm but piece is slightly crushed.

**11** Strip of C-form came, twisted.

**12** Strip H-form came, very thin flanges.

**13** H-form came, mould marks. Provenance insecure.

**14** Small fragment of H-form came, crushed, with thin flange and solder adhering.

**15** Small twisted strip, thin grooves suggest it may have been moulded or pressed, probable melt drip at one end.

**16** Soldered joint H-form came.

**17** Complete sub triangular enclosure in H-form came with branches for other quarries. This item when found contained a complete quarry which has since degraded leaving only a small fragment *in situ*, thickness of glass 2mm. (illus38.19).

**18** Strip, raised rounded feature one side, stepped on other, possible came.

**19** Strip, form indeterminate.

**20** Small fragment, probable fragment of C-form came.

**21** Fragment. Very deformed, but seems to consist of at least one section of H-form came with a connecting side branch.

**22** Strip of H-form came, internal groove c2.7mm, height over the flanges 4.7mm.

**23** Soldered junction of at least two H-form cames, cross junction with small extra piece to strengthen the joint. Flange width 5mm on one leg, 4.3-4.8mm on the other, internal grooves typically 2.5-2.8mm, height over flanges 4.3-5mm.

**24** Sealing strip with fragment of iron (frame?) still adhering to one side, the other side showing the rough imprint of stone contact.

**Table 3** Window Lead

| Cat | Description | Form | Len | Wid | Thk | Flange Wid | Int Groove | Flange Ht | Feature | Period |
|---|---|---|---|---|---|---|---|---|---|---|
| 1 | Came | H | 77 | | | 4.7 | 2.5 | 4 | 104 | II.2 |
| 2 | Came | H | 35 | | | 5 | 2 | | 100 | II.2 |
| 3 | Seal strip | ? | 28 | 13 | | | | | 99 | II.2 |
| 4 | 5 way junct | H | 57 | 16 | | 4.3 - 5 | 2.5 | 4.6 – 5 | 99 | II.2 |
| 5 | 2 way junct | H | 42 | 20 | | | | | 99 | II.2 |
| 6 | Strip | ? | 31 | | | | | | 99 | II.2 |
| 7 | Strip | ? | 45 | 12 | | | | | 99 | II.2 |
| 8 | Came | ? | 31 | 7 | 1 | | | | Lay 3 | II-III |
| 9 | Came | H | 60 | | | 5.3 | 2.7 – 3.1 | 7 | Lay 3 | II-III |
| 10 | Came | H | 38 | | | 5.6 | 2 | 4.5 | 86 | III.1 |
| 11 | Came | C | 107 | | | 2.5 – 3 | 2.6 | 4.7 – 5 | 86 | III.1 |
| 12 | Came | H | 60 | | | 4.3 | 2.5 | 4.1 | 86 | III.1 |
| 13 | Came | H | 125 | | | 4.6 | 3.2 | 7 | 209 | III.2 |
| 14 | Came | H | 29 | | | 4.5 | | | 209 | III.2 |
| 15 | Strip | ? | 36 | 5.5 | 1.6 | | | | 206 | III-IV |
| 16 | Joint | H | 57 | | | 5.7 | 2.5 | 4.2 | 303 | IV |
| 17* | Enclosure | H | 110 | 7.5 | | 5 | 2.4 | 5.4 | 303 | IV |
| 18 | Came | ? | 33 | 7 | 3 | | | | Lay 2 | III-IV |
| 19 | Strip | ? | 57 | 12 | 4.5 | | | | Lay 2 | III-IV |
| 20 | Came | ?C | 26 | 8 | 6 | | | | Lay 2 | III-IV |
| 21 | Came | ?H | 28 | 16 | 6 | | | | 13 | II-III |
| 22 | Came | H | 48 | | | 3.7 – 4 | 2.7 | 4.7 | Lay 2 | III-IV |
| 23 | Joint | H | 50 | | | 5 | 2.5 – 2.8 | 4.3 - 5 | Lay 2 | III-IV |
| - | do 2nd leg | H | 45 | | | 4.3 – 4.8 | | | Lay 2 | III-IV |
| 24 | Seal strip | ? | 74 | 27 | 17 | | | | Unstrat | |

Notes: * See Illus 38.19
All dimensions are in millimetres

## 5.4 PIPE-CLAY FIGURINES

Thea Gabra-Sanders

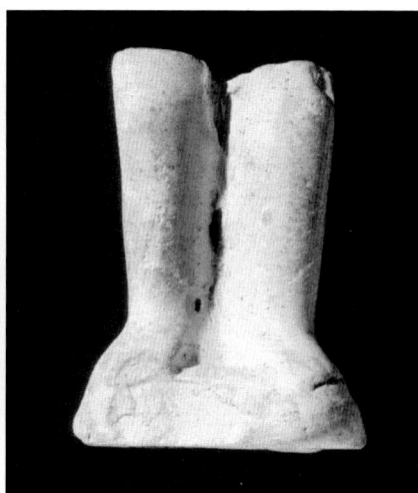

**Illus 39**
Pipe-clay figurines, Scale 3:2
Left: Madonna and Child
Above: Legs and feet

1   A pipe-clay figurine of a Madonna with Child (illus 39), broken in two halves, which dates to the late 15th century, was retrieved from the Inner Lower Courtyard.

The Madonna, which stands on a pedestal, is wearing a full-length draped mantle over a gown gathered in the middle with a belt; her feet are slightly protruding. A crown is placed over a long veil which reaches to her middle. On the right side, her long curly hair is partly showing. She is holding the Child on her left arm and carries a cross in her right hand. The Child, dressed in a long robe, is wearing a halo and is holding its hands in a praying fashion.

Pipe-clay figurines in various sizes were produced as devotional objects or as childrens' toys. In medieval times the Madonna with Child was very popular. They were cheap and provided a need for the people who liked to have their favourite saint around them in their home (van Haaren 1992, 37). Travelling merchants and guild members carried a smaller size with them in their pockets (Knippenberg 1962, 54) and they were also used as merchandise and souvenirs from places of pilgrimage. The first mention of a town with its own pipe-clay industry was Cologne in the 14th century. This industry reached its height in the Netherlands, Belgium and Germany, in the second quarter of the 15th century (Baart 1977, 472-5). The origin of this figurine is not certain; it forms a big contrast in style and detail to the 15th-century pipe-clay figurines in the Rijksmuseum 'The Catharijneconvent', Utrecht. Here the Madonnas are dressed in richly draped gowns (van Bohemeen P, pers comm). Pipe-clay figurines were produced in various towns on the Continent and form an as yet unexplored field.

2   A pipe-clay fragment (illus 39), two bare legs and feet with some indication of toes on a pedestal, was retrieved from a context in the Outer Lower Courtyard which dates to the late 15th century. The fragment belongs to a larger figurine, perhaps 10-11cm high, which could have been a toy. The origin is unknown.

### CATALOGUE (illus 39)

1   Pipe-clay figurine, Madonna with Child on a pedestal, broken in half.
    Length 67mm; width 24 x 20mm; diameter of base 18 x 14mm. F104/109; Period II

2   Pipe-clay figurine fragment, two legs with feet on a pedestal.
    Length 35mm; width 20mm; diameter of base 28 x 24mm. F24; Period II

## 5.5 ENAMELLED GOLD BUTTON

Keith L Mitchell & Hugh P Dinwoodie

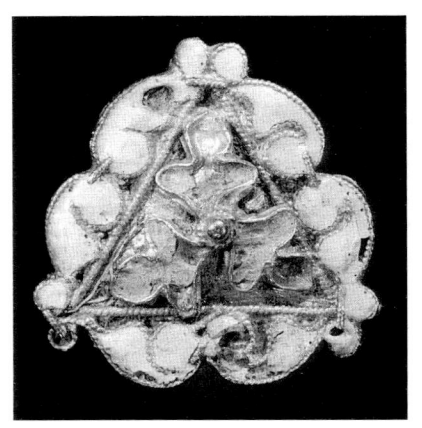

A single enamelled gold button was recovered from the Quarry pit (Illus 40, Plate IX)

The button is made of almost 22 carat gold, decorated with enamel. Essentially, the design consists of three leaves, inlaid with green enamel, radiating from a central gold ball, all within a gold wire-rope triangle. This in turn is surrounded by a three-sided, almost symmetrical, gold wire scrollwork pattern, inlaid with white enamel, inside a scalloped perimeter. The reverse of the button is undecorated but carries a small looped fastener.

This button was one of the more notable artefacts recovered during these excavations. It was discovered in an upper layer of the Quarry pit, and dates to the 16th century: on stylistic grounds, probably to the latter half.

**Illus 40**
Enamelled gold button
Scale 3:1

To date, no close parallels have been discovered, but it is likely to be of Scottish manufacture. Its owner must have been a person of some considerable substance.

The design and function of the button, its origin and dating, possible ownership and symbolism, together with notes on some contemporary Scottish jewels, are all discussed more fully in Appendix 7.1. Scientific studies of the compositional analysis of the gold, also X-ray fluorescence and scanning electron microscope studies, were kindly carried out by Paul Wilthew and Diane Mitchell respectively. Notes on their results, together with comments by Robin Murdoch on the enamel, are included.

### CATALOGUE

Enamelled gold button; obverse: Illus 40, Plate IX; reverse: illus 87. F96/206; Period III.2/IV
Dimensions: Max width 15.1mm, body thickness 1.5mm at centre, including looped fastener 6mm; wt 1.26g

## 5.6 COPPER ALLOY

Contributions by Fraser Hunter; Thea Gabra-Sanders;
Keith L Mitchell & Hugh P Dinwoodie.

Of some seventy-six copper alloy items recovered, fifty-two are included in the catalogue and the more important objects are discussed below. The assemblage is small, but of interest in its similarity, particularly with regard to pins and buckles, to finds retrieved from nearby Tantallon Castle (Caldwell 1991b). It included two residual Iron Age objects. Over half of the copper finds were found in the Quarry pit.

### IRON AGE OBJECTS

Fraser Hunter

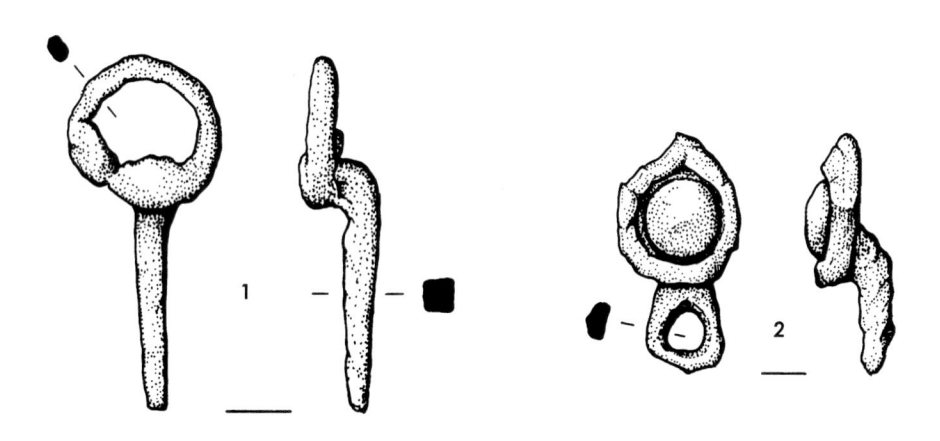

**Illus 41**
Copper Alloy: Iron Age. Scale 1:1

1 Cast projecting ring-headed pin

Projecting ring-headed pins are a long-lived tradition in Scotland, appearing first in the last few centuries BC and developing into the elaborate handpins of the 6th and 7th centuries AD. The cast variety is common from the 2nd to the 4th centuries AD, when a range of forms were made, distinguished by their head design (Stevenson 1955). The Fast Castle example does not fit easily into the existing typology, although this is not surprising given the chronological and geographical spread of such objects. Some pins with otherwise plain ring-heads exhibit slight elaboration of the shank-head junction (eg Ness, Caithness; BM Guide 1925, fig is 110), and it is to this variant the Fast Castle example probably belongs. Similar elaboration is found on some 4th-century ibex-headed pins (see references in Stevenson 1955), but although corrosion obscures the details there is no evidence that this example has the concave side-beads characteristic of such pins.

2 Button-and-loop fastener

This is an example of the most numerous class of button-and-loop fasteners. They are a Romano-British type, and were almost certainly produced in north Britain (where their distribution concentrates), although no production sites for this type are known. Finds are known from both native and Roman sites (eg native settlements - Traprain Law, East Lothian; Roman forts - Newstead, Roxburghshire; Hardknott, Cumberland). The type is discussed fully in Wild (1970), where a late 1st-2nd century date is suggested. There is considerable variety within the type, in size, dimensions of the 'boss', shape of shank, and presence of enamelling or decoration. The closest Scottish parallels for this particular example are from Traprain Law (Burley 1956, nos 222, 223 and 225). Wild argues convincingly that such fasteners were used to join straps in horse harness (cf examples in the hoard of horse harness from Middlebie, Dumfriesshire - Childe 1935, plate 15).

## CATALOGUE (illus 41)

1 Cast projecting ring-headed pin.

Extensive corrosion has destroyed or distorted much of the original surface, particularly on the head, making detailed identification difficult. The shaft-head junction is enlarged and elaborated into a flat diamond-shape which projects slightly forward from the plane of the head. The rest of the head seems to be a plain, circular-sectioned ring: there is no convincing evidence of beading. The shank broken, and tapers from a D-section at the top to a roughly circular section at the broken end.

Dimensions: overall L 46.5mm; head W 20.5mm x H 20mm; shank L 33.5mm.
Alloy type[*]: leaded bronze with some zinc. F100a; Period II.2

2 Button-and-loop fastener of Wild's class III (Wild 1970).

Sub-triangular loop and perforation, with a convex upper edge. Asymmetrical button with loop attachment point slightly displaced to one side; button and loop lie in the same plane. Air bubbles on the rear show this was a poor casting, although still functional. The surface is uneven and worn from corrosion; the button's front surface has flaked.
Dimensions: overall L 31.5mm; button L 20mm x W 16mm x D 7mm; loop L 18.5 x W 10.5 x D 9mm.
Alloy type[*]: leaded gunmetal. Layer 2 (near bedrock); Period III-IV

[*] Note
Compositions were determined non-destructively by X-ray fluorescence analysis of the surface. The results will have been affected by corrosion, and hence while the general alloy type can be stated it is not possible to provide a quantitative analysis.

**Illus 42** Thimbles

## THIMBLES

### Thea Gabra-Sanders

The concept of protecting the finger when sewing is presumably as old as the invention of the needle itself. The earliest protection of the thumb and fingers was a little shield made of wood, bone or leather (Syer Cuming 1878, 239). There are two kinds of thimbles, the open or ring type where the needle is pushed with the side of the finger for special purposes such as working with leather and canvas, whereas the closed type is intended for pushing the needle with the tip of the finger.

The two Fast Castle examples, of the latter type, date from the 16th century. The small thimble, no 4, cast with slightly tapering sides and a domed top, has hand-punched indentations or holes, which are upright in form, arranged in a continuous spiral which continues on the crown. The small indentations go with narrow straight needles such as those used for finer work and light fabrics. There is an incised straight line near the base. A similar example but with a maker's stamp is known from Sandal Castle (Goodall A R 1983, 236: fig 2, no 88).

The other thimble, no 3, also has slightly tapering sides and a domed top. This thimble has hand-punched indentation in the form of a spiral up to the crown, and has a maker's mark struck at the point where the spiral begins near the base. In the domed top was a small fragment of textile. So far as one can judge, thimbles with makers' marks normally date from 1520-1620 (Holmes 1988, 3).

### CATALOGUE (illus 42)

**3** Thimble, with maker's mark. Length 20mm; width 15-19mm; weight: 4.90g. Pit 2?; Period III

**4** Thimble. Small part missing from rim. Length 15mm; width 14-16mm; weight: 2.63g. F202; Period III-IV

## LACE TAGS

### Thea Gabra-Sanders

Nine lace tags were retrieved from various contexts within the Quarry pit, dated late 15th- or early 16th-century. Of these, two tags were found fitted to the ends of a single silk tubular lace (illus 64, 65) (Ryder & Gabra-Sanders 1992, 9).

Tags or chapes of the types listed were put on the ends of laces of leather or textiles to fasten clothing such as jerkins, hose and jackets. The tags are of copper alloy sheeting bent into tubes which vary from 15 to 21mm in length. The typology follows Margeson, Norwich (1985, 211) which is an extension from Oakley, Northampton (1979, 262-3). Type I tags correspond with those having edge-to-edge seams with the edges overlapping only at the base. There were six of these. Only one tag (no 6) is slightly tapered at the base. Tag no 10 which has one end filed has contents of possibly degraded leather. The tags, nos 11 and 12, still attached to the silk lace, are not tapered and do not overlap at the base. The tassels at each end of the lace are important, since chapes usually conceal the cut end of the lace.

One Type III tag (no 7) is cylindrical with edges overlapping along its entire length which is 15mm. Two (nos 8 and 13) are not complete and could not be grouped.

# CATALOGUE

**5** Length 21mm, dia 4mm; Type 1 (not illus); F86; Period III

**6** Length 15mm, dia 1.5mm; slightly tapered, Type I (not illus); Unstrat.

**7** Length 15mm, dia 2.0mm; Type III (not illus); Period II.2

**8** Length 18mm, dia ?; slit open. (illus 43.8) F105; Period II.1

**9** Length 17mm, dia 1.5mm; Type I. (illus 43.9) F105; Period II.1

**10** Length 20mm, dia 2.0mm; wide end broken off, other end filed; contents possibly degraded leather; Type I (not illus). F403; Period II.1

**11-12** Length 18 and 19mm, dia 2.5mm; attached to a silken lace (Textile no 26), two lace tags; no overlapping ends; Type I (illus 64, 65). F103c (104); Period II.2

**13** Length 15mm, dia 2.0mm; broken and bent (not illus). Kitchen F310; Period II

# OTHER COPPER OBJECTS

Keith L Mitchell & Hugh P Dinwoodie
with advice from David H Caldwell

# CATALOGUE
(Illus 43, except no 14)

WIRE (POSSIBLE HARP-STRING)

**14** Wire coil; see Musical Relics, Chap 5.11, illus 56. F103a; Period II.2

PINS

**15** Curved pin, with spiral/twist head. Length (approx) 51mm; thickness 1mm; width of head 3mm. F403; Period II.1

**16** Two pins, one complete (illus 43.16), with pronounced curve Lengths 49mm, 19mm. F107; Period II.1

**17-18** Two pins, one bent. Lengths 30mm, 37mm. F100a/1; Period II.2

**19** Pin. Fine point. Length 27mms. F104; Period II.2

**20** Pin, bent in middle, possibly when used originally. Head of pin is of different shape to those of other pins found. Length 30mm. Unstratified

**21-22** Two pins, one bent. Lengths 30mm, 22mm. F88; Period III.2

**23** Pin. Length 18mm, diam 2mm. Originally found inside a badly-corroded tube, 25mm long, 10mm diam, whose totally mineralised outer layer had cleaved away from central core, with little metal remaining. Centre appeared to be made of some kind of mineralised fibres. F103; Period II.2

**24** Pin in two fragments, joined (not illus). Kitchen: F303; Period IV

**25** Needle fragment?, with eye at one end. Straight, but shaft broken. Length 35mm; thickness 4mm (not illus). F101/2; Period II.2

BUCKLES

**26** Fragment of buckle, with scalloped edge. Length 17mm; thickness 1-2mm approx. Unstratified

**27** Very small D-shaped buckle, with leather adhering. 13 x 14mm (max); breadth of strap 8mm. Layer 3; Period II-III

**28** Circular buckle with centre bar. Diam 17-18mm; thickness 2mm. F86; Period III.1

**29** Buckle with twin loops and centre bar. Pin missing. Not symmetrical. Tool marks visible on most of surface. One side flat. 23 x 20mm (max); centre bar: length 13mm, thickness 2mm. F90; Period III.2

**30** Oblong shaped buckle, with two serrated edges. Bent slightly at centre. Two notches visible on rear of one edge. Breadth 18mm; length of bar 14mm. F99; Period II.2

**31** Two matching plates, 38 x 28mm and 36 x 28mm, with two pin-sized holes in corners of one end, and two larger holes in corners of opposite ends. Belt-end reinforcements; F2; Period II-III

**Illus 43**
Objects of Copper Alloy   Scale 1:1

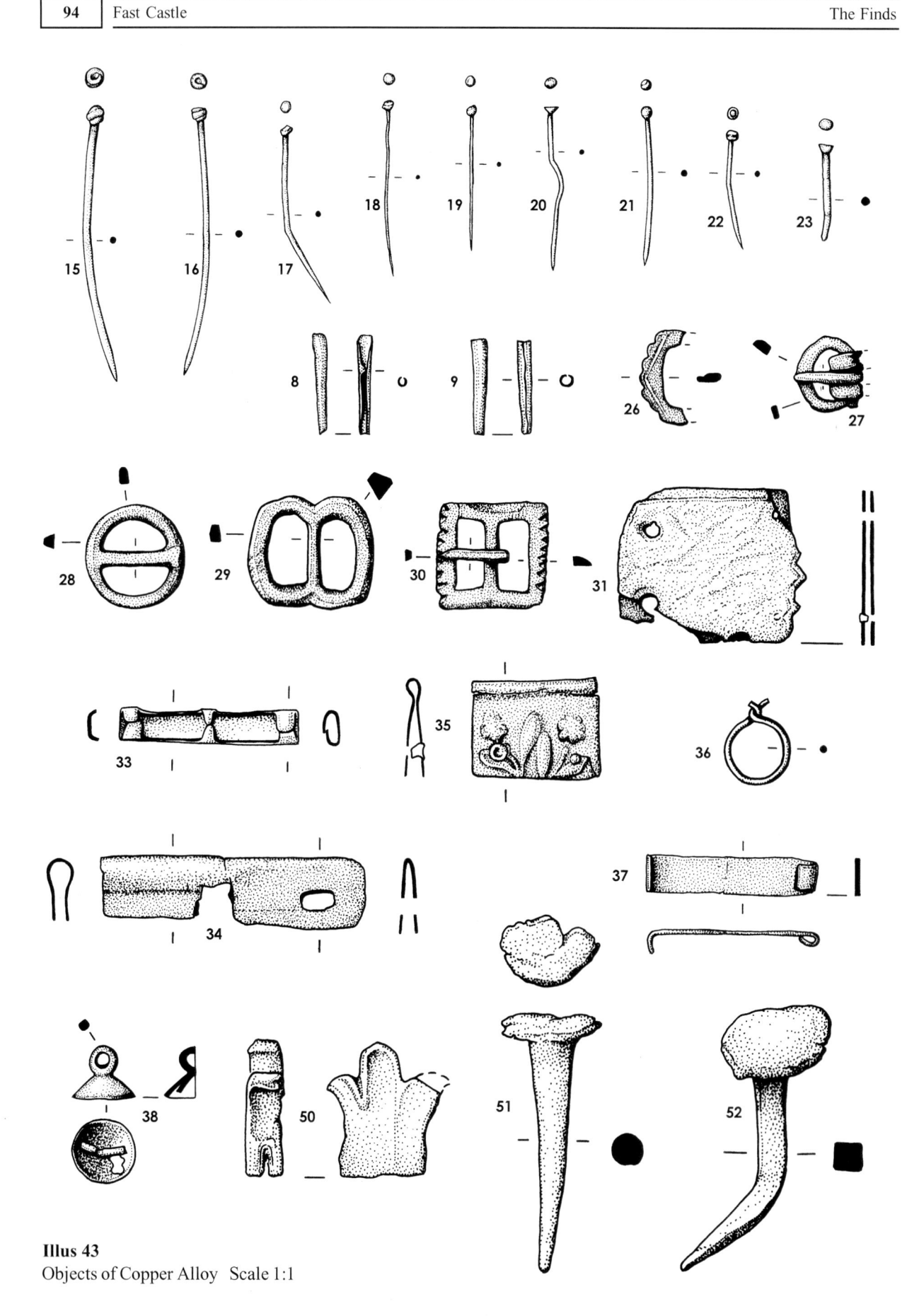

**32** Fragments of buckle. Rust and corrosion on surface. X-ray fluorescence analysis shows principally copper with smaller amounts of iron and lead, and traces of tin. 17 x 18mm approx (not illus). Unstratified

FASTENERS

**33** Mounting: use unknown. Folding clips at each end, and a narrower one in centre. 33 x 5.5mm. Layer 2; Period III-IV

**34** Clasp, broken in two parts. Hole pierced at end through both folds, presumably for a tie of some kind. Possible mount for purse. 50 x 13mm. Layer 3; Period II-III

**35** Buckle-plate or clasp. Hinge-like spine. One outer face is decorated with an embossed floral design. Appears, when closed, to have held something very thin, eg reinforcement for leather or textile; or book-clasp. 24 x 18 x 1.5-4.5mm. Layer 2; Period III-IV

**36** Circular wire loop fastener. Formed in a circle with one twist. Diam 11mm; thickness 1-2mm. Unstratified

**37** Thin strip, incomplete, folded over at either end. Use unknown. 31 x 6 x <1mm. F103b; Period II.2

**38** Button or other fastener, with loop, off-set from skirt. Diam (fastener) 12mm; (loop) 6mm. F104; Period II.2

**39** Wire loop-end fastener, formed in a circle with a twist. Diam 8mm; thickness 0.7mm (not illus). F99a; Period II.2

**40** Tag or pin fragment, split down middle (not illus). F103; Period II.2

**41** Rivet, in two parts. Used to join metal together, as known from Iron Age times to the medieval period (F Hunter, pers comm) (not illus). Unstratified

**42** Very small ring mounting or fastener; ends overlapped. Possible inlay in tool or wooden artefact. Diam 8-9.5mm thickness 1.8mm (not illus). F97a; Period II.2

VESSEL FRAGMENTS (not illus)

**43-49** Five rim and two body fragments, possibly from copper vessels or plates, were recovered from contexts of all periods. Two (nos 45, 47) were found in the Kitchen.

MISCELLANEOUS (illus 43)

**50** Fishtail-shaped pommel, from the tang of a scale tang knife, with moulded decoration of fleur de lys appearance on one face. Remains of iron blade within tang. Late 15th to early 16th century. 25 x 22 x 9mm; tang, max width 17mm. F100; Period II.2

**51** Large thick nail; hammered head. Length 50mm; head 20mm. F86; Period III.1

**52** Bent nail; hammered head. F97; Period III.2.

# 5.7 LEAD

## Keith L Mitchell & Hugh P Dinwoodie

Of the five small finds listed below, three were found in the Inner Lower Courtyard, one came from the base of the Well shaft, and one is unstratified. Aside from disc no 3, which cannot be dated with any certainty, it is likely that the remainder were deposited no later than the 16th century.

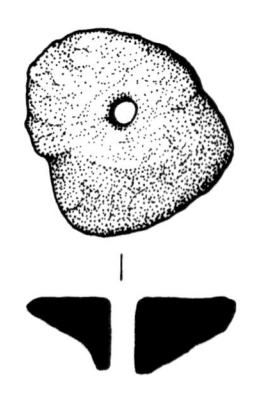

### CATALOGUE

1 Lump, probable weight, with one roughly circular flat side, and a 3mm diameter hole through the centre. Hole resembles that of no 2. Base 27 x 29mm (illus 44). Pit 2; Period III

2 Spherical object, possibly a weight, with a hole 2mm diameter drilled through the centre. At one end the hole is round, at the other, oval. It may have been modified from a piece of lead shot; diameter 19mm (not illus). F86; Period III.1

3 Plain flat disc. Dimensions: 40-45mm (not illus). Base of the Well shaft; Phase 1W-2W

4 Disc of similar dimensions to no 3, but has been bent to form a rough cylinder, open at both ends (not illus). F204; Period III-IV

5 Lead-clad iron nail. Shaft has square 5mm cross-section, the last 12mm tapering to a point. The roughly spherical head measures 32-34mm in diameter, and shows several hammer-like impressions; length 40mm (not illus). Unstratified

**Illus 44** Lead weight Scale 1:1

Other lead objects, or objects containing lead, are described elsewhere:
Lead gunshot and musket shot: see Chap 5.10 (Ordnance).
Lead core and heft of bone-handled knife: see Chap 5.16 (Worked Bone) cat no 7, illus 74.7.
Window lead: see Chap 5.3 (Glass and Window Lead, Table 3, cat nos 1-24, of which cat no 17 is shown in illus 38.19).

## Lead Waste

Of a total of 34 fragments of lead waste, 23 were recovered from the main excavation, together with 11 from preliminary work in 1969-70.

## DISCUSSION

Possible uses for nos 1 & 2 include fishing weights or plumb bobs. The nail, no 5, has a solid iron core, and an almost complete covering of lead. This coating is wafer-thin on the shaft, but more substantial on the head. Although this might be referred to as a 'lead nail', it should not be confused with 'lednayls', ie ordinary flat-headed nails used for fastening sheets of lead, as described, in an English context, by Salzman (1952, 311). The lead coating would make the nail more resistant to corrosion, and it is likely to have had some external use. This was the only example of a lead-covered nail found.

## 5.8 PEWTER

Keith L Mitchell & Hugh P Dinwoodie

PILGRIM'S BADGE

1 Pilgrim's badge. Dimensions: 50 x 29mm; illus 45. F99; Period II.2

The badge comprises three sides of an oblong frame, with a curved top. A portion of the left-hand side of the badge, with part of the inner design, is missing. The whole frame is surmounted with five 'rays', two of which are incomplete. The inner part within this frame comprises an outer section of open lattice work on both sides, separated by a pointed oval inner frame from an inner section, containing a simple face showing eyes, nose and mouth. The inner part of the badge is described as 'apparently surrounded by an almond-shaped glory' (Spencer, pers comm). On the back is part of a broken pin.

**Illus 45**
Scale 1:1

DISCUSSION

This pilgrim's badge was recovered from the Quarry pit in a context dated to the late 15th century / early 16th century. Badges such as these were purchased by pilgrims upon visiting a holy shrine, and were normally worn on the owner's hat or cape. Indeed, many pilgrims had several of these souvenirs on display to indicate the number of pilgrimages they had made. At popular shrines these badges were frequently mass-produced, and would have been commonplace. There are moulds for casting pewter pilgrims' badges in the Guildhall Museum, London (Masse 1911). Although many badges survive in England and on the Continent, they are relatively rare in Scotland.

Spencer independently dates this badge to the second half of the 15th century. His analysis suggests that the figure indicated the Assumption of the Virgin Mary. It would appear that the only popular English pilgrimage to the Assumption was to Our Lady of Eton, promoted by Henry VI after founding Eton College. However, Yeoman (1999) suggests that the shrine at Whitekirk, near Dunbar, might have been the source for the badge.

VESSEL FRAGMENTS

2 Vessel Fragments. (not illus) F108; Period II.1

This group of pewter fragments, as originally found in the Quarry pit, comprised five larger and eight smaller pieces, plus fragments. The assemblage has subsequently suffered further fragmentation. The larger pieces measured up to 100 x 40mm, and it is uncertain whether they represent one, or more, vessels. All the pieces were considerably encrusted, cracked, and extremely fragile. The shape of the larger pieces indicates they may have been part of a shallow vessel with a rim diameter of approximately 260mm, and a base ring diameter of 120mm. There is evidence of a base edge on one fragment at three points, and another shows a possible base but no clear edge. Encrustations, apparently calcareous, occur on numerous pieces, on what appears to be the 'inside' of the vessel. On one piece the encrustations appear to be on the 'outside'. It is not known if these deposits were the results of burial.

There is a series of incised lines that could be spin marks, or the remains of decorative rings, on two pieces, spaced about 3mm apart. The rings appear to be on what may have been the base of the vessel. In addition, on two pieces there is a series of lines parallel to the rim edge; on one the lines are closer together near the rim, approximately 1mm apart, the gap increasing to 2mm. On the reverse, fainter lines of a similar nature are just visible, 2mm apart. On the other, similar lines approximately 1mm apart are visible.

There are also a number of 'stress' lines visible on several pieces. These are irregular vein-like striations, generally parallel to, and between 1mm and 5mm from the edges. The presence of these lines, and the bent shape of many of the fragments, give the impression that they may have resulted from the original vessel, or vessels, having been broken up and parts being twisted off. With the passage of time these lines and cracks have spread.

## COMPOSITIONAL ANALYSIS

The fragments were submitted to Paul Wilthew and Diane Mitchell for analysis by energy-dispersive X-ray fluorescence (XRF), to establish their metallic content. The results, with the important proviso that caution should be exercised on account of corrosion, show that the fragments were all pewter. They could have derived from a single object although the analytical results do not prove this. The alloy, at least in one fragment, probably contained between two and three parts of tin to one of lead; with a small amount of copper, which would have had a hardening effect.

It is suggested that the linear markings, at least on that fragment, would have been produced by turning or carving on a lathe, and were likely to have been deliberately decorative.

Wilthew and Mitchell note that 'there are no published analyses of Scottish pewter vessels of similar date with which to compare the present results. Neither is there any legal standard for Scottish pewter of this date which states a specific composition', and they refer to two items of a slightly later date, in the NMS collections (MET 46 & MET 47).

Editor's note: The full report, with references, is available in the archive.

## DISCUSSION

These fragments, of what may have been a shallow pewter vessel of approximately 260mm diameter, were deposited in the late 15th or early 16th century. The remains are so damaged that it is difficult to be certain of its original shape: whether it was a dish, plate, or other type of vessel, such as a porringer or quaich. No pewterer's marks were evident.

The term 'pewter' covers alloys of widely varying composition and quality. Very little is known about pewter in Scotland, in the late 15th and early 16th centuries, but it is probable that articles made of this material were luxury items, affordable only by nobility and wealthy burgesses, as in England.

The pewterer's craft was included within the Edinburgh Incorporation of Hammermen in 1493; this was a century and a half after the London Company of Pewterers had been established. The manufacture of pewter at this time was almost universal in Northern Europe, though not in peripheral areas such as Spain and Scotland. The majority of vessels used in Scotland at that time were imported from France and the Low Countries (Bell 1901; Wood 1907).

Received knowledge would suggest that this vessel is a very rare example of pewter in Scotland from this period. Very little survives to help place these fragments into any meaningful context. It is almost impossible to say whether it was of local or foreign manufacture. Although probably imported, the possibility of Scottish manufacture cannot be entirely ruled out.

This scarcity lends further weight to the view that the owners of Fast Castle, particularly during the late 15th, and early 16th century, were making use of a much larger number of high status goods than otherwise might have been expected.

## 5.9 IRON

### Hugh P Dinwoodie & Keith L Mitchell

Approximately 800 iron objects were recovered, mostly from the Quarry pit. Of these, over 500 were nails or nail fragments. The assemblage also included arrowheads, horseshoes, knives, assorted implements, keys, and door accessories. A number of items were not identifiable, and due to encrustation and corrosion, many were recognisable only on X-ray. Most of the nails and nail fragments were from Periods II.2-III contexts; almost half of the remaining objects were recovered from earlier contexts, in the lower layers of Period II.

Fifteen items showed traces of copper compounds, including an arrowhead, two knives, and four nails; though some may result from contamination from objects nearby. Other items were suggestive of blacksmiths' residue (M Spearman, pers comm).

The implements recovered included chisels, wedges, and components of at least sixteen knives; also an awl, shears and a possible plane. Four chisels or wedges were recovered, the two largest from the lowest layers of the Quarry pit, Period II.1, suggesting possible use for quarrying or other stone-cutting purposes.

The majority of the knives, blades and tools date from before the mid-16th century (Period II). At least six knives (nos 10-11, and 14-17) were of the scale tang variety, with wide, flat tangs, and rivet holes for attaching the plates, or scales, to complete the handles; all the remainder are of whittle tang construction, with a straight or tapered tang for insertion into the material of the handle. One (no 5) bore a maker's mark, but details were indistinct owing to corrosion. However, it appeared to be different from all examples in the collection illustrated by Cowgill *et al* (1987, 21-3).

Two knives with unusual bone handles (nos 12-13), one a lead-weighted throwing knife, are described, and illustrated, as nos 7-8 in the Worked Bone Report (Chap 5.16). A possible dagger pommel (no 25) was also found. Apart from these, the knives are not unlike some of those found in the more domestic setting of the Perth excavations of 1979-81 (Ford 1987, 132, nos 74-82).

The small shears (no 21) resemble those illustrated by Cowgill *et al* (1987, 106-14). One blade is shorter than the other, as is the Aberdeen example (Goodall 1982, 188-9, no 84).

Ottaway (1992) distinguishes awls, with two relatively thin tapering arms of roughly equal length, from tanged punches, which either have a tang and working arm of unequal length, or are larger and thicker. Two such objects, nos 22-23, could well have been used for working leather, bone or wood.

Four small arrowheads were found, all socketed, conical, barbless and between 28 and 38mm in length. All date to Period III.1 or earlier. They have similar internal and external diameters; one (no 30) may have had a copper sheath or tip. All are of a simple pointed design, most probably for use with longbow shafts.

An English army inventory compiled in 1549 relating to the fort at Eyemouth recorded, amongst other arms, 10 bows and 40 sheaves of arrows, and noted that the equipment of Fast Castle was 'similar to that of Eyemouth' (Hist MSS Comm 1905, 193; Kennaway 1992, 86).

A single caltrop (no 32) was found. The design of this device ensured that when thrown down, it would always land with one spike pointing upwards: a simple but effective defensive weapon, used mainly against cavalry. The name is derived from the Latin 'calx' (heel) 'trappa' (snare). Caltrops are referred to as being in use at Bannockburn (Mackenzie 1913). This example dates from the time of the later 16th century occupation of the castle (Period III).

Door accessories included four keys, a latch, hinge, and an escutcheon plate (nos 33-39). Two, at least, of the keys date from the late fifteenth century (Period II); the largest key, found near the Well shaft, on the landward side of the castle promontory, probably dates from the 16th century (Period III).

One complete horseshoe with rectangular nail-holes (no 56), and several fragments were found,. It is almost certain that any horses or ponies used by the occupants of the castle would normally have been stabled to landward, or away from the castle, given the extremely restricted nature of the entrance. However, horseshoes could have been made or stored within the castle. Their size was compatible with hoof sizes of 100-110mm, corresponding with small horses or cobs, perhaps of about 13-14 hands (W Lindsay, pers comm). Horseshoes of contemporary date have been recovered from sites elsewhere, such as Perth (Ford 1987) and Edinburgh Castle (Clark 1997). Sixteen horse bones were identified amongst the faunal remains.

The large object (no 65, Plate XIV; illus 51) has disintegrated into many fragments since recovery. Made up from a number of separate components, its complexity has resulted in considerable speculation as to function. Some of the components of nos 65 and 66 are made of similar section wrought iron.

Nos 66a and 66b, a connecting bar and mount, are fixed to the remains of a large timber beam (Wood no 1), but the function of the whole remains unclear.

Three pieces of iron shot, and a small fragment of cannon, are described in the Ordnance Report (Chap 5.10); also a Jew's harp, revealed on X-ray, is discussed in the section on Musical Relics (Chap 5.11).

NAILS

In all, 561 nails, fragments and possible fragments were recovered. Of these 139 were complete, and a further 47 sufficiently complete for objective study. Of the remainder 29 survived only as heads and 23 were tentatively identified as nails. The lengths of the sample of 186 nails are noted in Table 4. The majority of broken shaft fragments were between 10 and 50mm long.

**Table 4**: Nail Length

| Length (mm) | 1-10 | 11-20 | 21-30 | 31-40 | 41-50 | 51-60 | 61-70 | 71-120 | Total |
|---|---|---|---|---|---|---|---|---|---|
| number | 0 | 10 | 21 | 54 | 45 | 33 | 13 | 10 | 186 |

## CATALOGUE

The items illustrated are shown in illus 46-51, except for nos 12-13, 27 and 66-72, which are descirbed and illustrated elsewhere, as indicated. Nos 14-17, 25, 28, 33, 44, 50, 59, 61-64, and 72-88 are tracings from X-rays and measurements are approximate. The original X-rays are held in archive and include some uncatalogued items.

**1** Cold chisel, or crowbar. One end is narrowed to a chisel-like edge (now broken). Could have had a wooden shaft or handle. Bent at the broken shaft end. Weight 700g. Overall dimensions: 250 x (20-32) x (20-27)mm. F83; Period II.1

**2** Chisel or wedge. Weight 950g. Top 10-20mm splayed out slightly obliquely, deformed by hammering. 156 x 30 x 35mm. F403; Period II.1

**3** Wedge-type implement. 69 x (10-19) x (3-5)mm. F97a; Period II.2

**4** Wedge, chisel, or bar. Possible traces of burning. Thin edge is asymmetrical, as if well used. Weight 125g approx. 60 x 35 x (7-12.5)mm (not illus). Unstratified; Period II-III

**5** Knife. Whittle tang and blade, length 310mm; tang 95mm, with square cross-section, and tapering blade, maximum width 30mm, length 215mm, with straight back. An unidentified maker's mark is present on the blade, close to the shoulder. Unstratified; Period II-III

**6** Knife blade, length 165mm. Unstratified; Period II-III

**7** Blade, incomplete: slightly bent towards point. 79 x 12 x 3mm. F86; Period III.1

**8** Knife blade tip? Length 55mm approx. Layer 2; Period III-IV

**9** Knife blade, and about 30mm of tang; rounded end. Length 102mm. Unstratified; Period II-III

**10** Small knife blade, length 83mm, in two pieces. Fragments of 6mm copper rivet, diam 2.75mm, through whole thickness; also traces of wood. Partly covered with black pitch-like substance. Tang 4-5mm wide. 83 x 15 x 4mm. Kitchen: F306; Period III

**11** Knife handle. Scale tang, within rounded and slightly tapering worked bone or horn scale plates. Length 82mm. F97a/b; Period II.2

**12** Iron tang, within lead core of bone-handled (throwing?) knife. See Worked Bone Report, Chap 5.16, no 7, illus 74.7. F109a; Period II.1

**13** Iron tang, within bone handle of knife. See Worked Bone Report, Chap 5.16, no 8, illus 74.8. Unstratified; Period II

**14** Knife handle. Scale tang. Flat, 2-4mm thick. Broken through second of two round rivet-holes 4.5mm diameter, centred 67mm apart. 86 x (18-22)mm. Unstratified; Period II-IV

**15** Knife handle, with probable fixed blade, and bone or horn sides to heft. Original length, with blade fragment, 77mm. Rounded copper band at top end; another straight copper band round the tang end of the heft, from which a broken blade (not shown on drawing) protruded about 5mm. Two small rivets (2mm diam) in middle portion of heft, two larger ones (5mm diam) at either end; that at the tang end (demonstrated on X-ray), probably secured the tang end band. 77 x (13-14) x 7mm. F100; Period II.2

**16** Knife handle, with probable fixed blade. Length 75mm. Metal band 6mm wide at end of heft. Fragmentary remains of panels survive. Two smaller rivets, 2mm diam, and two larger ones, 3-3.5mm diam: one of the latter secures the metal band. Very similar to no 15. 75 x 14 x 6mm. F103; Period II.2

**17** Knife handle. Scale tang, with rivet holes. One (47 x 15mm) of six fragments of a knife originally c275mm long. F95; Period III.2

**18** Fragments of probable knife. Length 284mm approx. Triangular in cross-section, the last 5mm tapering more or less to a point; four rivets, approx 10mm between each rivet centre (not illus). F99a; Period II.2

**19** Blade, in three pieces. 115 x 15 x 3mm (not illus). F99; Period II.2

**20** Blade, in four pieces. 85 x 11 x 1.5mm (not illus). F100; Period II.2

**21** Small shears: length 84mm. An almost circular bow, 17 x 13mm, is joined by two stems, 27mm long, to two blades: the blade tops, or shoulders, 6mm long, slope diagonally to the cutting edges, and are not recessed; the cutting blade lengths are 34mm (complete) and 27mm, (shorter, or incomplete). Both blades 11-13 wide x 2-3mm thick. Below F86; Period II

**22** Tanged punch or awl. 95 x 4 x 4mm. F202; Period III-IV

**23** Needle? No apparent eye. Diamond-shaped cross-section; tapering to point at each end. 85mm. F104; Period II.2

**24** Needle? Thin slender object: larger end flatter and has two small prongs suggestive of broken needle-eye. Shaft square or oblong in section. 85 x 8 x 8mm (not illus). Unstratified; Period II-III

**25** Dagger pommel? Circular object, with small side projection. 46 x 38 x 20mm. F85; Period III.1

**26** Spearhead-shaped object, delineated on X-ray (not illus). Shaft end broken and twisted, 118 x (45-50)mm, F99; Period II.2

**27** Plane blade (A Armstrong, pers comm). Quadrilateral piece of iron (36-45) x (22-24)mm, set into a shaped block of wood. See Wood Report, Chap 5.15, no 11, illus 72.11   F100/109; Period II

**28** Arrowhead. Length 35mm, max width 15mm.   Layer 3; Period II-III

**29** Arrowhead. Length 38mm. Int diam 9mm. Well area: Phase 2W

**30** Arrowhead. Some copper residue on tip. Length 28mm, max width 12mm, int diam 9mm. F86; Period III.1

**31** Arrowhead. Length 30mm, max width 12mm, int diam 9mm. F83; Period II.1

**32** Caltrop. Four prongs, consisting of three spikes, of square cross-section, each with a curved angle of about 110 degrees near its midpoint, and tapered to a point at each end; one end of each of the three spikes is joined together to form a fourth, thicker, spike. Spike dimensions (now): 17 x 2.5mm; 25 x 3mm; 24 x 3.5mm; conjoined spike 18 x 7mm. F207; Period III.2

**33** Key. Length 70mm. Bow: ext diam: 30mm. Bit: 25 x 16mm. F109; Period II.1

**34** Key, incomplete. Part of stem and complete bit survive. Length 56mm (of which 42mm of the stem is complete); ext diam of stem 9mm, int diam 5mm. Bit 15 x 18mm. F109a; Period II.1

**35** Key, incomplete. Part of stem and bow only remain. Length 40mm; estimated original length 60-80mm. 40 x 23 x 8mm. Layer 2; Period III-IV

**36** Key. Length 210mm. Bow: ext diam 75mm, int diam 47mm. Thickness of bow ring: 12-15mm. Bit: (50-53) x (50-53)mm. Well: Phase 2W

**37** Hinge? Possibly from door or gate. Two round nail-holes. Hook-like projection articulates with hook or ring in perpendicular plane. 173 x 28 x (3-4)mm. F83; Period II.1

**38** Latch, for door or gate. Two projections, inserted into thin rectangular bar: one the pivot (7mm long), the other a knob (13mm). 90 x (8-13) x 2mm. F99; Period II.2

**39** Rectangular door escutcheon plate, 150 x 85 x 10mm approx, with an oval key-hole, approx 55 x 20mm (cf key, no 36 above). Timber remnants attached, incorporating at least four nails. F100/109; Period II

**40** Clench bolt. Diamond-shaped rove, 35 x 26 x 8mm, fan-shaped head, 23 x 23 x 10mm. Both ends conical in cross-section. Shank: 35mm long. 8-10mm thick centrally. F107; Period II.1

**41** Buckle? (65 x 40) x (6-7)mm. F99; Period II.2

**42** Buckle, incomplete. 30 x 25mm (not illus). F206; Period III-IV

**43** Hook/bracket?, incomplete. (60+45+25) x (4-5) x (6-7)mm. F97a; Period II.2

**44** Staple. Each spike 40mm long. 55 x (45-50)mm. F104; Period II.2

**45** Staple/hook. Incomplete. 52 x 35 x 15mm approx (illus 49.45). F103b; Period II.2

**46** Staple/bracket? 3-5mm across (not illus). F104; Period II.2

**47** Hook/staple? Two straight components, 52 and 15mm long, and 3-5mm diameter, joined by incomplete ring, 17mm diameter. F202; Period III-IV

**48** Hook? 56 x 4 x 2mm. F104; Period II.2

**49** Hook. Curved end forms almost closed loop. 50 x 8mm. Kitchen, F306; Period III

**50** Hook with flat end. Broken shaft on X-ray. Hook section measures 20 x 10 x 2mm. 48 x 10 x 9mm. F86; Period III.1

**51** Hook/bracket? Possibly originally sheathed in copper. (25+7+15) x (5-7) x (2-3)mm (not illus). F103; Period II.2

**52** Hook? 41 x (2.5-4)mm (not illus). F93; Period II.1

**53** Hook/catch. Squarish section with rounded corners. (50+20) x 5 x 6mm (not illus). Unstratified; Period II-III

**54** Hook? 30 x 17 x 151mm (not illus). F206; Period III-IV

**55** Button. Three-quarters remaining, one radial rib, possible central 2mm hole. 24 x 24 x 1mm. F97a; Period II.2

**56** Horseshoe, complete. Five definite, two possible nailholes; at least three are worn through at edges. Three holes contain nailheads, one also with small part (5mm) of shank of nail. 122 x 99 x (3-5)mm. Max breadth 24mm. F86/97a; Period II.2-III.1

**57** Half-horseshoe. Two nails project, one 9mm long. Max breadth 24mm; approx 10mm at tips. 100 x (4-8)mm. F209/210; Period III.2

**58** Horseshoe, in three pieces. X-ray shows 5 rectangular nail holes (8 x 4.5mm). Approx 8mm thick. 115 x 110 x (7-15)mm; (not illus). F99; Period II.2.

**59** Ring, revealed by X-ray. Unstratified; Period II-III

**60** Unidentified iron object, with some evidence of copper. 83mm long, 18mm wide, tapering to 10mm, 5mm thick. On one face is a groove, approx 55mm long, tapering from the wide end. Trace of groove on other face, but much shorter. F206; Period III-IV

**61** Ring with two tiny adjacent loops, revealed by X-ray. F85; Period III.1

**62** Ring, with looped pin-like structure attached. F109a; Period II.1

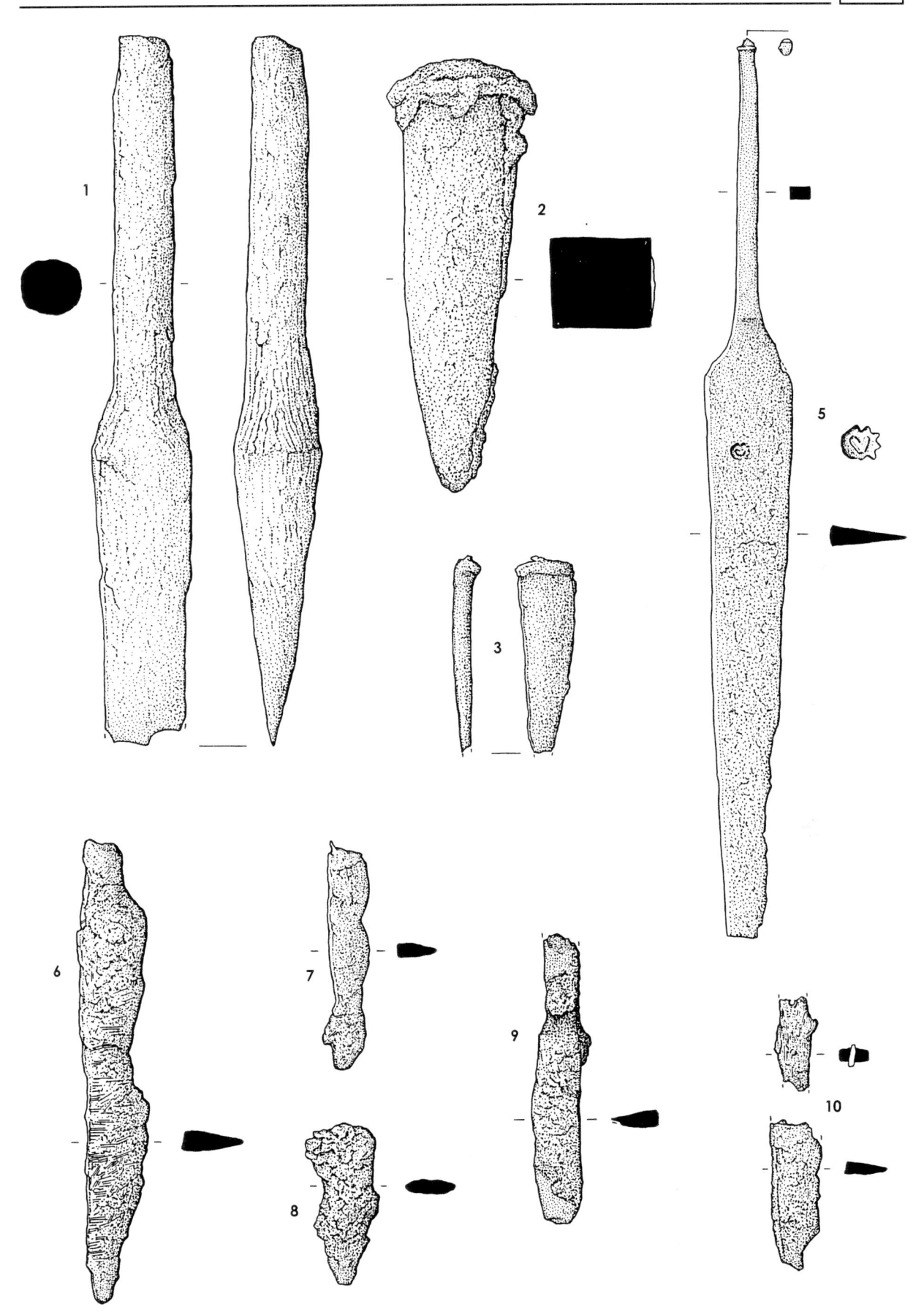

**Illus 46** Iron: Knives, blade items and chisels. Scale 1:2

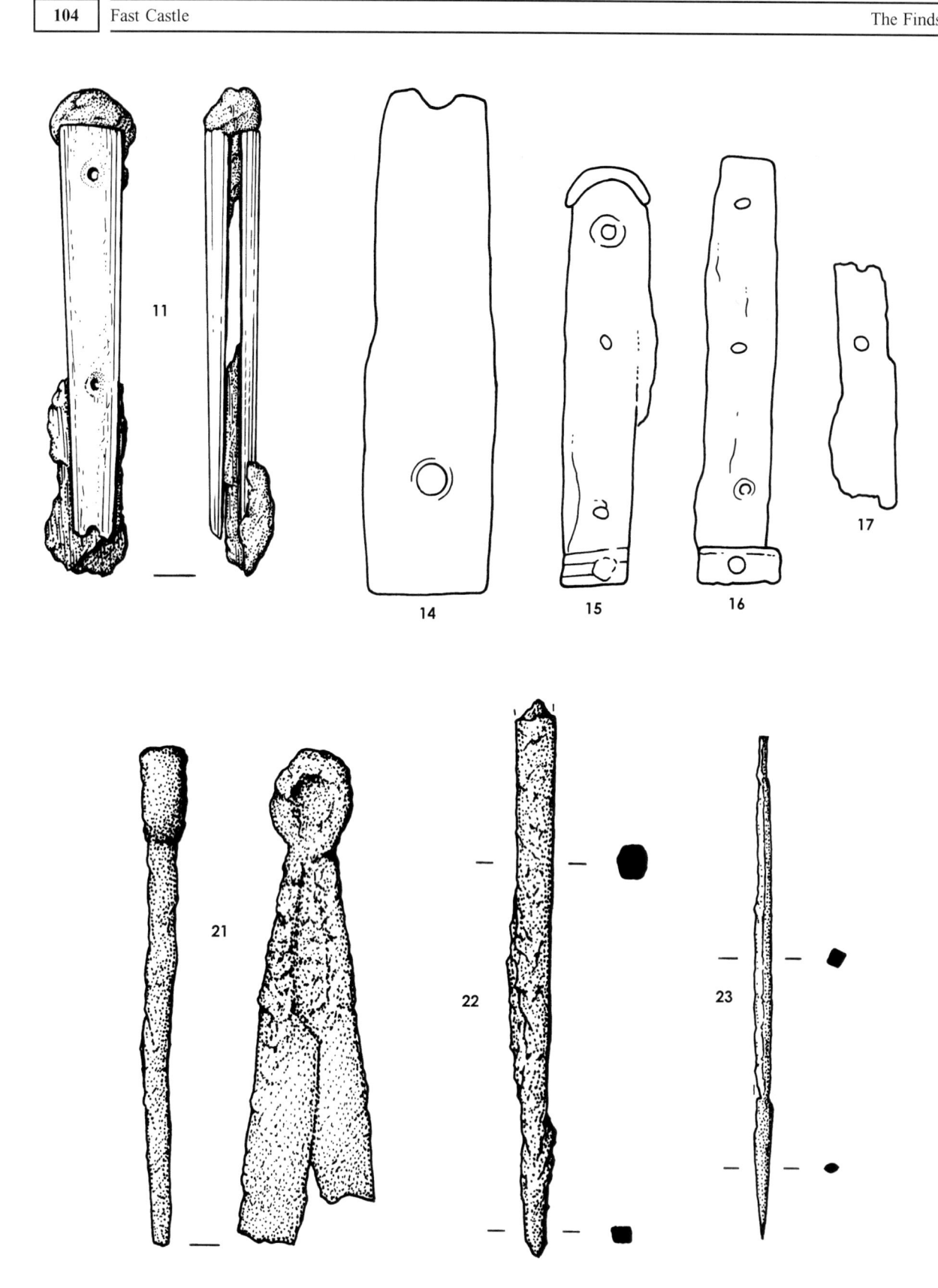

**Illus 47** Knive handles and tools. Scale 1:1

**63** Implement, with appearance similar to spanner-head, visible on X-ray. A hexagonal head, 12mm across, at one end of a flat bar, 3mm thick. 71 x 12 x 12mm. F207; Period III.2

**64** Ring, with second ring or projection at one side, and remnants of a nail or pin. F83; Period II.1

There is some similarity between objects nos 59, 62, and 64.

**65** Large unidentified complex iron object: complete when found, but now badly corroded and fragmentary. 500 x 200 x 40mm approx; Plate XIV; illus 51. F104; Period II.2

It consists of at least two main parts. A straight iron bar, originally about 400mm long, of which the largest 170mm fragment (A) is shown in the drawing. It may have articulated with a hooked component (B) at one end. The bar tapers gradually towards its other end, where it is interrupted by an abrupt upward semicircular section (C) just before that end. There were at least eight vertical components, which may possibly have been embedded in wood, along the length of the bar (A). Two of these projections are more substantial. One is the hooked component (B), which has a slender spike at one end, a semi-circular loop and a shorter spike at the other, after apparently passing through a ring at the thick end of the bar. The second is where the thinner end of the bar (C) seems to become a flattened, downward-pointing strap (D) with three rivets. It appears broken just below the lowest surviving rivet. Some of the other heavily encrusted projections may have been iron spikes or bars. Near the mid-point of the bar is an upward-projecting, broad, flat and thin curved strap (E), with a radius of at least 50mm. Its original exact spatial relationship to the bar is not clear. It has at least three nail or rivet holes, suggesting it may once have been attached to a piece of wood or metal. There are minimal traces of copper in relation to these holes.

**66** Connecting bar (no 66a), linked by mount (no 66b) to wooden beam. See Wood Report, Chap 5.15, no 1, Plates XV, XVI and illus 70. F103/103b; Period II.2.

The connecting bar (no 66a), 225mm long, is made from flat wrought bar of section 25 x 12mm; each end has been opened out to 43mm wide. Worn ovoid hole 37 x 22mm at one end; worn circular hole 21mm diameter at the other, which links it to the mount (no 66b). The mount (no 66b) approximately 250mm long has also been fabricated from flat bar, nominal section 18 x 12mm, and is U-shaped, the upper leg of the U having been passed through the wooden block and the lower leg rebated into its underside. The centre of the lower leg has been fabricated into a half loop to articulate with the connecting bar. The ends of both legs of the mount have been bent inwards flush with the face of the wooden block. Corrosion makes it difficult to assess but the mount appears to have been nailed to the wooden block for further rigidity; certainly the free end of the lower leg would have to be nailed to the block for maximum strength.

**67** U-shaped piece of iron 185mm long, max width 30mm, embedded in piece of worked wood: possible tool (eg plane). See Wood Report, Chap 5.15, no 12, illus 72. F100-103?, Period II.2

**68-70** Iron Shot (3 pieces). See Ordnance Report, Chap 5.10, nos 1-3; illus 52. Layer 2, Period III-IV; F86/97a, Period II.2-III.1; F86, Period III.1

**71** Gun fragment. See Ordnance Report, Chap 5.10, no 7; illus 53 Layer 2; Period III-IV

**72** Jew's harp. See Musical Relics, Chap 5.11, no 1; illus 55. F202; Period III-IV

**73-88** Examples of nails; illus 49.

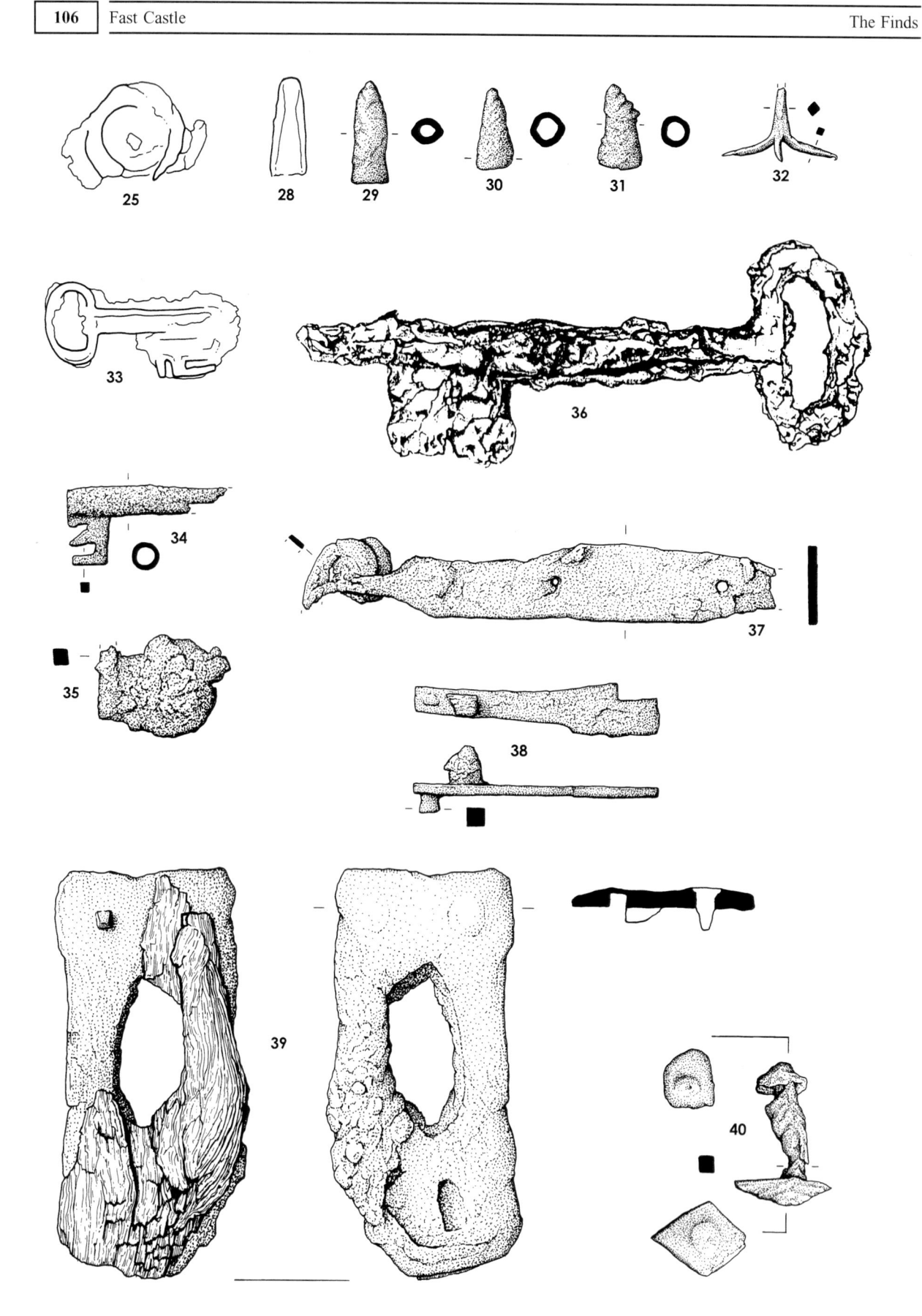

**Illus 48** Iron, arrowheads, keys etc. Scale 1:2

The Finds
Fast Castle 107

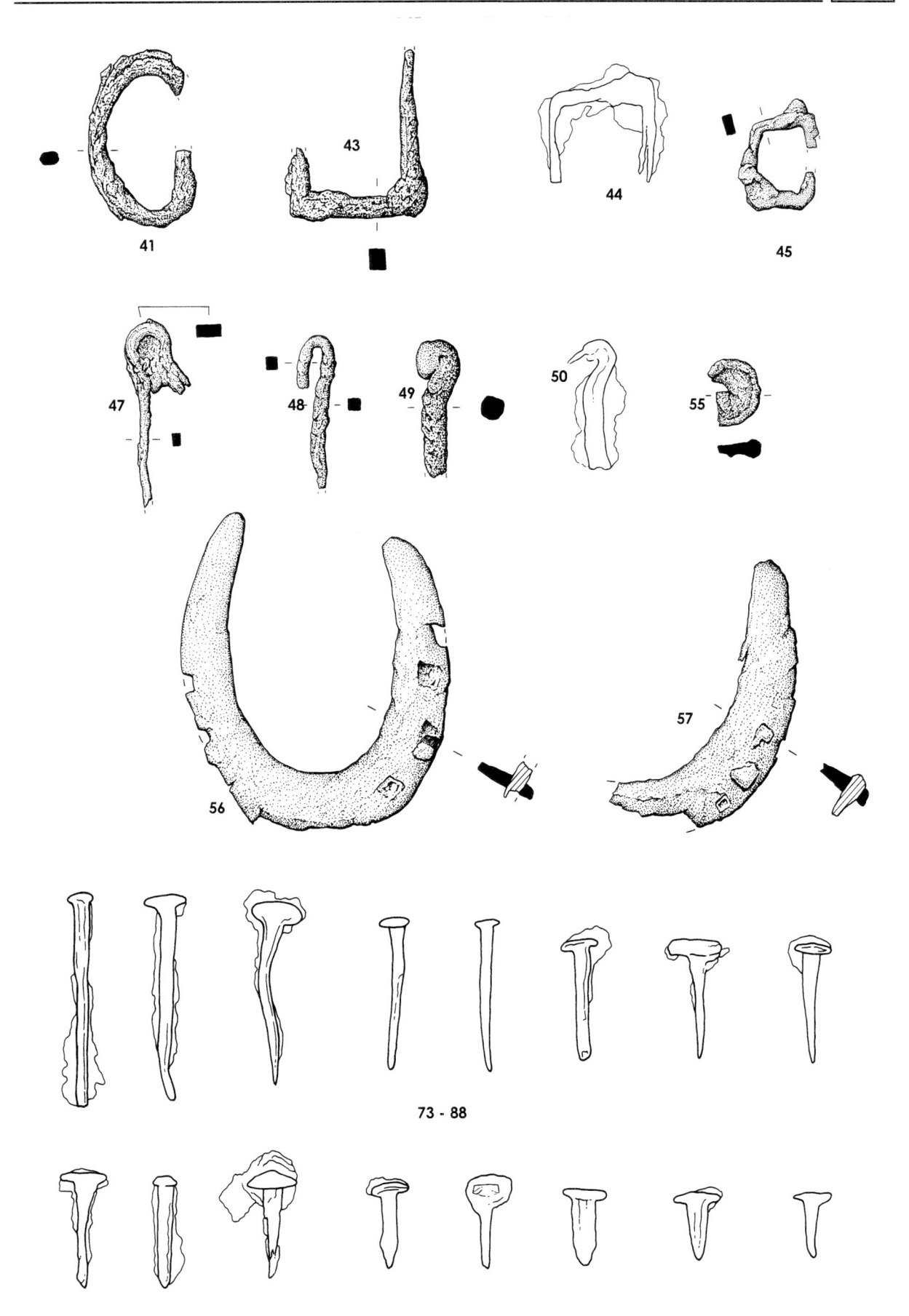

**Illus 49** Iron: Buckles, hooks, horseshoes and nails. Scale 1:2

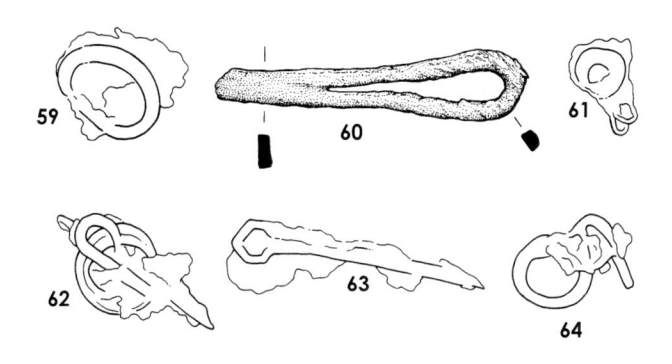

**Illus 50** Iron: Ringed objects. Scale 1:2

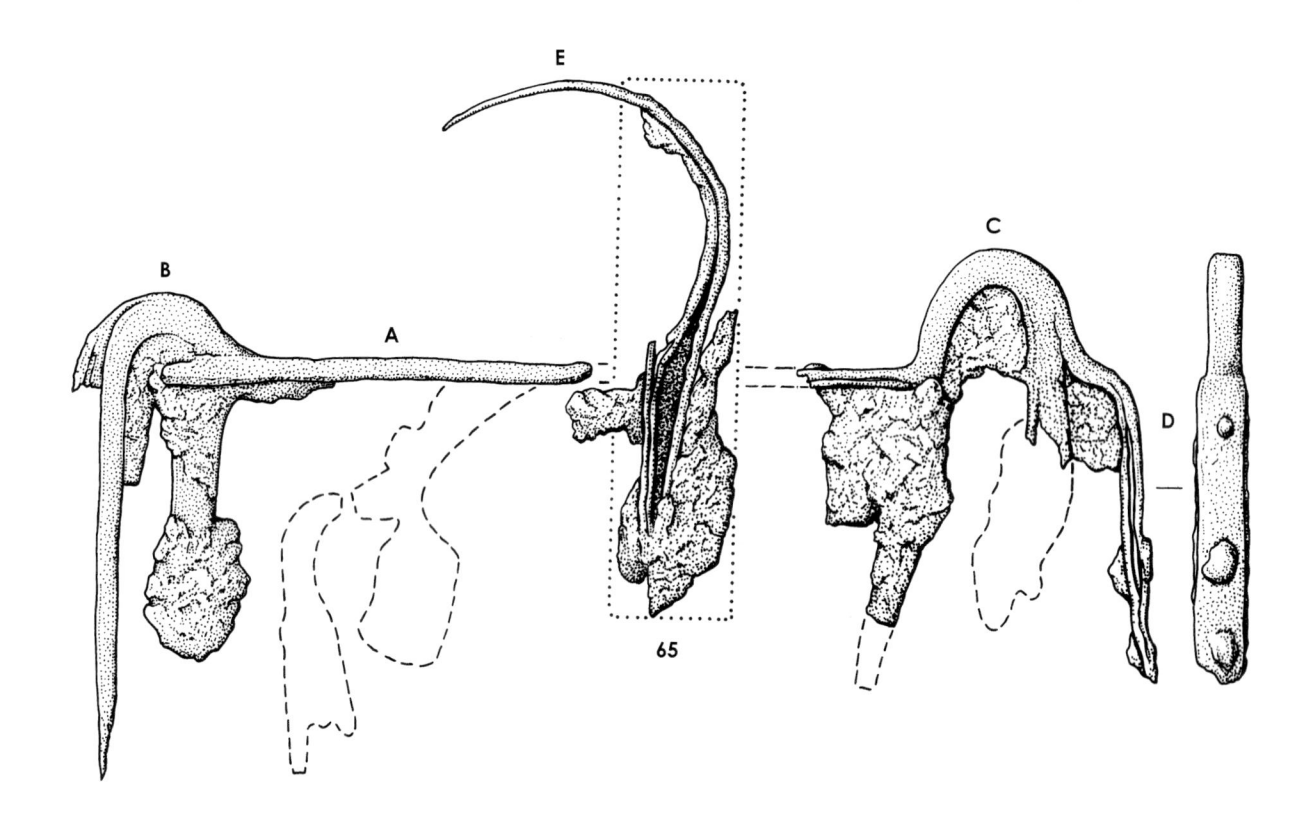

**Illus 51** Iron: unidentified object; central piece rotated through 90 degrees. Scale 1:3

## 5.10 ORDNANCE

Stuart W Allan

Bounded almost entirely by sea cliffs, Fast Castle enjoys a situation of considerable natural strength. To landward, the steep slopes which begin to rise virtually at its entrance would have provided protection against an aggressor seeking to subject the position to artillery fire. The narrow access to the promontory upon which it stands, possibly protected by a drawbridge and defended by what appears to be a splayed gun loop to the north of the entrance, would have rendered the storming of the castle a most difficult undertaking. A small garrison armed with a modest stock of weaponry could expect to hold the castle against the attack of a much larger force.

The historical record reveals that Fast Castle was frequently the scene of military activity during the fifteenth and sixteenth centuries. Along with Dunglass and Tantallon it formed a chain of strongholds guarding the eastern approach into Scotland, and was of strategic importance in border warfare between the two kingdoms and in the localised conflict which pervaded border life in this period. In 1573 the Regent Morton described Fast and Hume Castle as 'the keys of the country, and the mean whereby to contene disordered people in good rule and obedience' (Boyd 1905). Besides operating as a fortified domestic residence, Fast Castle was on several occasions garrisoned by Crown forces. Between 1410 and 1570 it was lost to English soldiers on at least three occasions (Kennaway 1992).

Finds recovered during the 1971-86 excavations reflect this activity, though not in abundance. The material examined comprised six pieces of iron or lead gunshot, a fragment of iron which was probably part of an iron-forged gun, five pieces of worked round stone which may be gunstones, and a quantity of smaller lead shot manufactured for longarms or as grape shot for field artillery. All of these, with the exception of the gun fragment and a very few pieces of lead shot, were recovered from the Quarry pit.

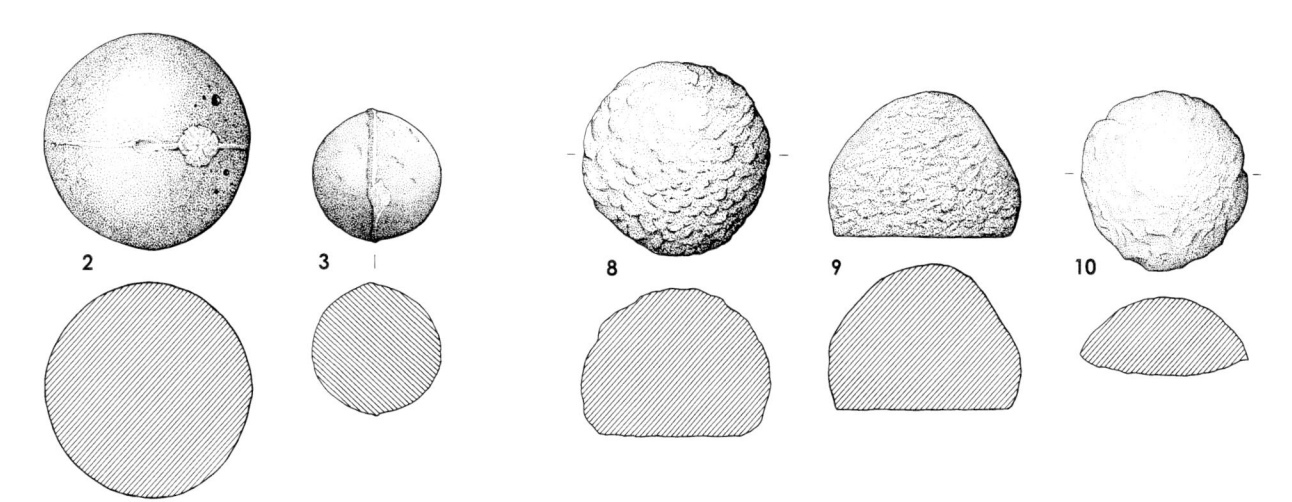

**Illus 52** Iron and stone gunshot, scale 1:3

## GUNSHOT

The three pieces of iron shot (nos 1-3) pre-date the development of iron casting in Scotland (Caldwell 1991b, 344). They may therefore be imported material, though the English forces which on occasion garrisoned Fast Castle are likely to have been more readily equipped with shot of this type. Of the three pieces of lead gunshot (nos 4-6), two (nos 4 & 5) conform to the class of muzzle loading light cannon, (as does no 3).

## NOMENCLATURE

In Table 5, an attempt has been made to relate these finds to what is known about 15th- and 16th-century artillery calibres and gun nomenclature. To concur with what can be discerned from the historical record about military activity at the site, both (a) Scottish and (b) English terminology is given. The former is drawn from comparison with data on Scottish gun nomenclature compiled by D H Caldwell (National Museums of Scotland), the latter from sixteenth century inventories of ordnance at the Tower of London (Blackmore 1976). The absence of standardisation in gunfounding in this period, meant that shot rarely fitted closely in the gun barrel. This consideration reduced the accuracy which could have been achieved by 16th-century gunners, and also limits our own capacity accurately to match individual pieces of gunshot to specific types of gun. Lack of uniformity in gun nomenclature as applied to calibre in this period further confuses matters. Nevertheless, the finds offer a serviceable guide to the class of ordnance which may have been stored at, or employed in the defence of, Fast Castle.

The larger pieces of roundshot could have been for use with defensive fortress pieces to the seaward, though the height above sea level would have impeded accuracy. To the landward, the steepness of the slope rising above the castle would have made heavy artillery unnecessary. An aggressor would have become a practicable target only when in fact close enough for small wall guns and hand firearms to be effective. Documentary evidence that field or siege pieces were stored on site is supplied by a January 1513-14 memorandum to the Lords of Council, in the wake of Flodden, 'anent the furnishing of the castell and fortalice of Fastcastell, the lordis being avisit with the captane tharof ordanis ane pece of gret artalze be send to the said castell that will brek bulwerkis, togidder with certane gun powdir for the defence and kepin of the samin' (Hannay 1932, 8). The roundshot recovered might therefore have been intended for use elsewhere.

Two surviving 16th-century documents give a further guide to the ordnance held at Fast Castle. In 1549, the Earl of Rutland drew up returns of armaments in borders fortresses held by the English. The return for Fast Castle is referred to as 'like for Eyemouth', with Eyemouth holding, 'two demi-culveryns of iron, one saker of brasse, one fawcen of brass, one fawkenet of brass, five fowlers of iron, serpentyne powder, two dimid barrell, thirty morrispikes, ten bows, forty sheaves of arrows, with shot for the respective pieces' (Hist MSS Comm 1905). When in 1573 Fast Castle was returned to the Earl of Morton by the English, ordnance from Fast which was not Crown property and which was kept back at Berwick included 'two "merlownis" of brass' and 'four falcons' (Boyd 1907). Neither of these (English) references to medium and light artillery are greatly at odds with the class of ordnance suggested by the finds recovered from the site.

**Table 5:** Gunshot

Note: Diameters are expressed in metric and imperial measure, to afford comparison with modern gun calibration.

| No | Material | Diameter mm (ins) | Weight grams (lbs) | Nomenclature Scottish | Nomenclature English |
|---|---|---|---|---|---|
| 1 | Iron | 162 (6.37) | 15.8Kg (35lb) | Cannon | Demi-cannon |
| 2 | Iron | 87 (3.42) | 2.45Kg (5lb 6oz) | Double culverin pikmoyen, saker | Saker, minnion |
| 3 | Iron | 52 (2.04) | 530g (1lb 3oz) | --- | Falconet |
| 4 | Lead | 50 (1.97) | 550g (1lb 4oz) | Small falcon, falconet | Falconet |
| 5 | Lead | 49 (1.93) | 450g (1lb) | Small falcon, falconet | Falconet |
| 6 | Lead | 30 (1.18) | 140g (5oz) | Double hagbut of crok | --- |

## GUN FRAGMENT

This piece has been built up in stages giving a stepped appearance. The method of manufacture, and the size of the fragment, strongly suggest that this is part of a small calibre, breech-loading gun of a type which was fairly common in Scotland in the 15th and 16th centuries. The inner curve of the fragment allows calculation of the bore of the gun at approximately 102mm (4.0"). This measurement need not be compared to the calibre of the recovered gunshot as guns of this type generally were not of sufficient strength to fire single lead or iron balls. Usually such guns were stone throwers or operated as anti-personnel weapons firing multiple lead shot.

These somewhat primitive guns, built up from layers of iron bound together with barrel hoops, were rather prone to bursting when fired. It is feasible that this fragment is from a gun which has exploded. One end of the fragment is a finished section, and the whole is probably part of the muzzle end of the gun. However, allowing that the gun was a composite type of breech loader, the fragment may be from the breech end of the barrel.

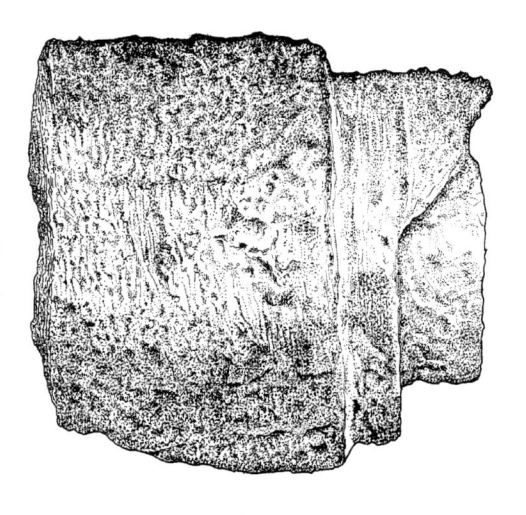

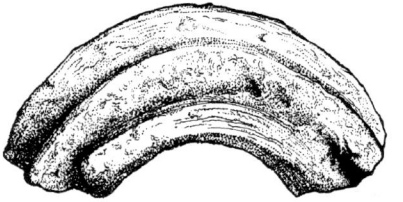

**Illus 53** Gun fragment, scale 1:3

Such guns were manufactured to a broad range of size and strength and were rather less standardised than the cast-bronze, brass and cast-iron pieces which eventually superseded them. In Scotland they were variously known as heidsteikis, slangis, bersis, and cutthroats (Caldwell 1981a, 128). The fragment is from a Period III deposit of loam found immediately on top of a wall, or wall foundation, of Period II, in the Outer Courtyard area of the site. Though cast bronze and cast iron guns, superior both in strength and accuracy, were in common use by this period, small iron-forged guns continued to be produced well into the 16th century with little change in manufacturing technique from the previous century (MacIvor 1981).

## GUNSTONES

Two manufactured stone balls and three fragments of rounded worked stone, representing a total count of four balls, were also recovered from the site. With diameters ranging from 70mm (2.73") to 85mm (3.32"), these may be gunstones and parts thereof. It is likely that a stronghold such as Fast Castle, where breech loading forged iron guns were present, would have had a store of stone shot. However, it is possible that these stone finds constitute nothing other than sling shot, weights, or gaming pieces. Two further smaller stone balls are considered to have an Iron Age origin: see Stone Report, Chap 5.21, nos 1 & 2, illus 81.

## LEAD SHOT (illus 54)

Of the forty-eight items received for examination as possible lead shot, sixteen may be discounted as being of doubtful definition, their appearance suggesting nothing more than lead waste material (possibly a by-product of shot manufacture) or an alternative function. For example, one originally described as a musket ball, has a hole drilled through its diameter and is likely to have been used as a weight (see Lead Report, no 2). Of the remaining thirty-two items, only twenty-one (65.6%) could be described as complete shot, being balls for which diameter measurements of no more than 2mm variance can be taken (for examples see illus 54). The remaining items appear to be used shot, flattened or badly deformed by impact.

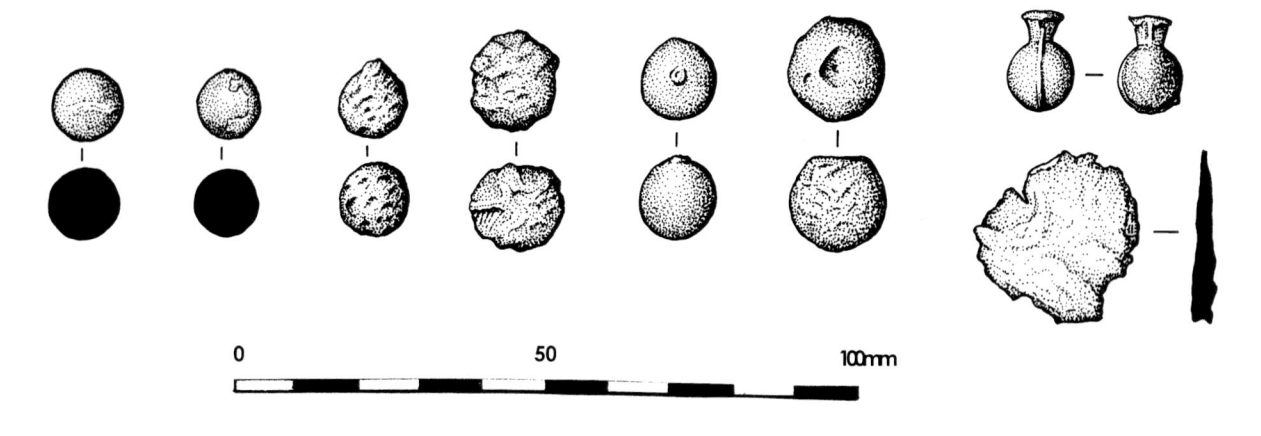

**Illus 54** Lead shot

The complete shot has been cast in two-part moulds. The seam from the mould is visible in most examples. The subtleties of this casting method are revealed in the frosted appearance of some of the shot, a consequence of the metal cast being at incorrect temperature, or of not heating the mould. There are small holes in the surface of two of the complete balls which extend into their centres. This condition also results from imperfect casting, where the use of overheated lead causes air to fill the central vacuum created when lead in the mould reservoir cools more quickly.

As observed with the larger gunshot, several of the complete balls show a slight protrusion at the point where the sprue from the mould was broken off. With the smaller shot, this finishing work has not been carried out in every example; three balls retain their sprue quite intact. The presence of an unfinished product might be taken to suggest manufacture of shot on site, which is by no means unlikely. Yet it is not the case that unfinished shot necessarily would have been useless. Such an unbalanced projectile would allow no degree of accuracy, but in this failing it would not have differed markedly from the finished article. Excessive windage resulting from a lack of standardisation in barrel manufacture necessitated heavy patching, and offered little prospect of an accurate shot. It is likely that barrels were commonly loaded with two or more projectiles to increase the chance of hitting a target. Where multiple fill in hand firearms (and canister shot in larger pieces) was employed, perfectly finished shot would not have been an absolute requirement.

Given that one need not look for standard sizes, and noting that shot would have been manufactured on the small side so as to fit the majority of gun barrels, a sufficient quantity of measurable balls was recovered from the site to give some suggestion of the sizes commonly being manufactured. With diameter measurements ranging from a minimum of 9mm (0.35") to a maximum of 20mm (0.79"), it is notable that of the twenty-one pieces of complete shot, only three were of a diameter greater than 16mm (0.63"). Nine balls gave a measurement of 11mm (0.43"), and there was a grouping between 11mm (0.43") and 15mm (0.59"), with 72.7% of the complete shot falling within this diameter range. This group corresponds with balls excavated at Threave Castle, dated to c1455-1640, which gave diameter measurements of 12-15mm (0.47"-0.59") (Caldwell 1981b).

The weight of a ball was of course an important consideration affecting the range of a weapon and the size of powder charge required. However, inconsistent casting prevented the achievement of any uniformity in weight by size. Considerable discrepancies could arise even in shot cast from the same mould, principally due to the presence of air bubbles. Thus the nine pieces of complete shot with a common diameter measurement of 11mm (0.43"), eg no 13, recorded a range of weights from 7.35g (0.26oz) to 9.81g (0.35oz). Three pieces of complete shot all of 15mm (0.59") diameter weighed 15.72g (0.55oz), 17.62g (0.62oz), and 21.09g (0.74oz) respectively. The largest piece, at 20mm (0.79") diameter, weighed 49.12g (1.73oz).

Consistent with estimates of the spread of small arms use in Scotland, the majority (68.75%) of the Fast Castle shot was Period III.2 deposit material. Five pieces (15.6%) were Period III.1 deposits. Notably, three complete balls were found at lower levels (Period II) and may be attributed to the late 15th century. With the caveat that Fast Castle was intermittently garrisoned by English forces among whom hand firearms came into common use earlier, this dating corresponds to a period held to be at the threshold of hand firearm use in Scotland. These three finds may constitute some of the earliest examples of this development (Maxwell-Irving 1971).

I am indebted to Dr D H Caldwell for his advice on Scottish gun nomenclature.

Editor's note: A single gunflint fragment is listed in the Flint section of the Stone Report (Chap 5.21).

## CATALOGUE

**1** Cast-iron gunshot. Diameter 162mm (not illus). Layer 2; Period III-IV
Visible seam from casting in two-part mould. By far the largest piece of gunshot recovered, likely to have been manufactured to serve a quite formidable piece of heavy artillery, though not quite in the class of heavy bombards. The cannon or demi-cannon, of cast bronze or brass, which fired this size of iron ball would have been likely to be found only in the siege trains of royal armies. Period III-IV deposit, but found immediately below turf level and therefore possibly of a later date.

**2** Cast-iron gunshot. Diameter 87mm; illus 52.2. F86/97a; Period II.2-III.1
Visible seam from casting in two-part mould, with considerable flashing (spillage of metal at the seam) and an indentation where the sprue from the mould evidently has been broken off. Diameter and weight conform to a medium class cast-iron field gun (double culverin, pikmoyen, saker).

**3** Cast-iron gunshot. Diameter 52mm; illus 52.3. F86; Period III.1
Visible seam from casting in two-part mould. Diameter and weight conform to the type of light cannon, probably muzzle loading and of cast bronze, likely to be present in a domestic stronghold of strategic importance, either as defensive fortress pieces or carriage mounted field guns held in store (falcon, falconet).

**4** Lead gunshot. Diameter 50mm (not illus). F209/210; Period III.2
Cracked, with some surface deterioration. May have been fired.

**5** Lead gunshot. Diameter 49mm (not illus). F209/210; Period III.2
Deeply cracked and mis-shapen, possibly as a result of firing. Found in a disturbed pit; may be re-deposit material.

**6** Lead gunshot. Diameter 30mm (not illus). F97b; Period II.2.
Visible seam from two-part mould. This find conforms to a smaller class of armament, known in Scotland as a hagbut, a heavy longarm secured for firing by means of a hook on the underside of the barrel or mounted on a small trestle.

**7** Gun fragment. Curved fragment of forged iron weighing 6.02kg (13lbs 4oz) and measuring, on average, 165mm x 150mm (6.5" x 5.88"); illus 53. F13; Period II-III

**8** Worked stone ball. Two slightly flattened surfaces; about a quarter missing. Pecked surface, rougher than the other examples because the stone is coarser. May be a gunstone. Diameter 77mm; wt 422.6g; illus 52.8. F206; Period III-IV

**9** Worked stone ball. About a quarter missing. Pecked surface, with short linear scratches from smoothing. Two flattened areas, c30mm in diameter, lie 90° apart, both towards one side of the ball. May be a gunstone, though use as a gaming piece or weight is also possible. Diameter 80mm; wt 559.3g; illus 52.9. F207; III.2

**10** Plano-convex segment of stone ball, with one relatively smooth pecked surface; some evidence of abrasion. Diameter of segment 69mm; estimated diameter of original ball c85mm; wt 158.3g; illus 52.10. F86; Period III.1

**11-12** Stone ball in two fragments. Finely worked surface perhaps too carefully manufactured to be a gunstone. The ball appears to have been shattered by impact. Dark coloured stone, not thought to be indigenous to the environs of the site. Fragment no 11 fits with no 12. Diameter c70m; wt 135.7g + 129.1g (not illus). F102 & 99; Period II.2

## 5.11 MUSICAL RELICS

### Graeme Lawson

Two finds from separate levels within the Quarry pit deposit in the Lower Courtyard are of musical interest. A small two-pronged penannular loop of iron (no 72 in iron catalogue) from Period III-IV confirms the existence on site of that most popular of our ancient traditional musical instruments, the *jew's harp* or *trump*. A coil of brass wire (no 14 in copper catalogue) from Period II.2 may be a relic of more sophisticated instrumental music-making, having a composition, gauge, length and mode of wrapping which, although not conclusive, are all at least suggestive of and consistent with identification as stringing material for a stringed instrument, perhaps a harp.

### THE JEW'S HARP

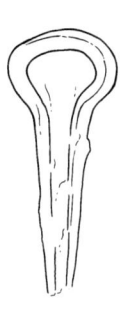

X-radiography of Fe concretion, (iron no 72), reveals the characteristic shape of the frame of a small *jew's harp* (illus 55). It is of a well attested late medieval/post-medieval form: the jaws and loop are of probably diamond cross-section, the loop medium to large and the jaws set slightly apart to accommodate the vibrating tongue or *stang*. This element would originally have been of tempered steel, less than 1mm thick, tapering in width towards the vibrating tip and held in place at its broader end by insertion into a filed notch in the centre of the loop. If it survives, its precise form and dimensions, however, are now indistinguishable within the general corrosion[1].

**Illus 55** Jew's harp, scale 1:2

The date of deposition, in the early 16th to early 17th century, lies well within the established date-range for western European examples in general and British finds in particular (Lawson 1980, 170-1, fig 8.1). Its principal significance lies rather in the Fe composition of its frame. Amongst the published finds of earlier, antiquarian investigators, such as those noted by Elliston-Erwood at Shooters Hill, Sarre, Guildown and elsewhere in Kent and Surrey (Elliston-Erwood 1943, 1947), Cu-alloy frames predominate, the only Fe component being the thin steel tongue, which is usually broken or missing. This impression may be reinforced by examination of finds in museum collections throughout the United Kingdom, in which earlier acquisitions are largely antiquarian in origin, and by stray examples from some recently excavated sites such as Winchester (Lawson 1990, 724). However, the vast majority of recent finds now suggests that in reality these may represent differential survival of only a minority group, and that those of Fe construction, previously lost through insensitive recovery and conservation, were most probably the norm. In a catalogue of published finds from Ireland, which includes examples from the environs of Dunboy and Glanworth Castles, Co Cork, and Trim Castle, Co Meath, no fewer than twenty-nine had Fe frames, while only two unprovenanced examples were of Cu alloy (Buckley 1986, 57-61).

The origins and early development of the jew's harp in Britain are not yet fully determined. Current research suggests an ultimately oriental source and the likelihood that earliest importation from Europe took place shortly after the end of the first millenium AD. Earlier dates suggested by antiquarian research (eg Elliston-Erwood 1943, 40) are difficult to substantiate (Lawson 1980, 170, notes 387 & 391). Historical sources, especially travels, provide accounts of their use in Scotland from the seventeenth to the present century (eg Martin 1698; Hawkins 1787, 473; Stoddart 1801, 179). Today, although the instrument enjoys less universal popularity than it did even fifty years ago[2], it continues to flourish within the folk music revival, and inexpensive harps of much the same form are still manufactured and readily available.

## THE CU-ALLOY WIRE COIL

A second, earlier find from the Lower Courtyard may be associated with the stringing of musical instruments: among the small finds from the Period II.2 fill within the enclosed alcove area, was a small spool comprising approximately 710mm of fine (c0.4mm gauge) Cu-alloy wire (illus 56). Neither its form nor associated finds provide absolute confirmation of musical identity, but it is now becoming increasingly clear from parallels from excavations elsewhere that such a role is quite feasible.

**Illus 56** Cu-alloy wire, scale 1:1

Spools of fine wire are known from a growing number of medieval and early post-medieval sites in Britain and on the Continent, of which at least two have already yielded further evidence of the instruments themselves. At Castle Sween, Argyll, musical identification of a coil of bronze wire is suggested by the recovery of a metal tuning-peg from a nearby context (Ewart & Triscott 1996). At the Cistercian monastery of Alvastra Kloster, in central Sweden, a recent re-investigation by the present writer, as yet unpublished, has revealed amongst numerous small bone tuning-pegs (probably from a psaltery or similar box-like instrument) remains of spooled wire of closely similar appearance and composition.

At St Aldate's, Oxford, the same interpretation was lent encouragement by the presence nearby (in Structural Phase 10, c1325-54) of two bone tuning-pegs, one finished and one unfinished, together with (in the subsequent Phase 11) further examples and bone-working waste, while by the next century there is documentary evidence that an instrument-maker may have been active on the same site (Henig 1977, 165; Durham 1977, 194; Page 1978, 60). At Fast Castle, evidence for such specialised instrument repair is absent amongst the other general workshop debris, but this need not preclude simple running repairs, such as the replacement of snapped strings, for which purpose musicians and their suppliers must have always carried such spares.

That musical relics should be recovered from fortified sites such as Fast Castle should by no means be thought improbable, for historical sources attest to the widespread importance of musical entertainment in such sites, as elsewhere in medieval and early post-medieval Britain[3]. Indeed, excavations within castles and their environs have already produced a variety of other musical instruments and their components, including stringed instruments and especially their tuning-pegs. In addition to the finds from Castle Sween there are Cu-alloy tuning-pegs from Finlaggan, Argyll (Caldwell, forthcoming), bone and metal tuning-pegs from Montgomery Castle, Powys, (Lawson, 1997), and a range of bone pipes from Castle Acre, Norfolk (Lawson, 1982) and White Castle, Gwent (Megaw, 1961). That the emphasis there seems so far to be on instruments of entertainment and not on military types (drums and trumpets are so far notable for their absence) is curious, but may be simply another example of differential survival.

Analysis of the Fast Castle wire shows it to be of brass, with a zinc content of 19% and smaller quantities of bromine (5%) and lead (1%)[4]. This contrasts with the tin-rich (bronze) alloy of the probably earlier specimen from Castle Sween, but is nevertheless consistent with possible musical use. Similar analysis of the St Aldate's, Oxford, wire proved that wire also to be of brass, cold-worked, with a zinc component of 17%[5]. Examination of finds from future excavations may help to determine whether wire manufacture for musical purposes drew upon general metal stocks or involved preparation of special alloys, with distinct chemical signatures, but so far our sample is insufficient to permit comparative study at this level.

The gauge of the wire renders it compatible with a broad range of late and post-medieval instrument types[6]. It is not at this stage possible to suggest a more specific attribution, although a range of possible candidates may be considered, from wire-strung instruments of lute type (such as the cittern) to psalteries, their key board derivatives and of course the stately harp. It is interesting to note that the surviving length of the Fast Castle wire, at just over 710mm, compares closely with the longer stringing of the overground survivals of roughly similar date: the Queen Mary and Lamont harps in Edinburgh, of which the wire required for the longest strings would have been c750-800 and 950-1000mm respectively[7], and the Trinity College, Dublin, harp which would have required a maximum of c750-800mm[8].

Notes

1 Performance on the jew's harp involves gripping the frame between the thumb and first two fingers of the player's left hand and clamping the metal jaws between the upper and lower incisors; the lips complete the pneumatic seal in such a way as to restrict passage of the player's breath solely to the narrow slit surrounding the metal tongue. The thumb of the right hand then strums the exposed (and usually everted) tip of the metal tongue in such a way as to set it in vibration, causing the air in the player's mouth, windpipe and sinuses to resonate. The vibrating tongue always sounds at the same pitch, in the manner of a drone; melody is generated by the player controlling the harmonic frequencies induced in his or her airways, using cheek and tongue muscles to alter the volume enclosed and to open and close the back of the mouth. Rhythmic control of breathing offers the opportunity to enhance the vigour of performance for eg the accompaniment of dance.

2 Before the advent of broadcast and recorded music such home entertainments were widely appreciated and (except by those sects which deprecated music and dance as works of the devil) instrumental skills were considered desirable personal accomplishments. For example, the author's own great-grandfather, John Graham, of Dipton, Co Durham (b Canonbie, Dumfriesshire, 1872) was an accomplished amateur performer on the jew's harp.

3 For the most recent account of the history and development of the harp in medieval and early post-medieval Scotland, see Sanger and Kinnaird (1993); for the harp in eastern and south-eastern Scotland see especially 93-100.

4 74% copper, 19% zinc, 5% bromine, 1% lead, trace amounts of tin, chlorine and iron; X-ray fluorescence analysis was undertaken in the Materials Laboratory, Cambridge University Department of Engineering, with thanks to Dr Claire Barlow and Mr Alan Heaver. A detailed account of methods and results of analysis of the Fast Castle and Castle Sween samples will be published separately (Lawson, in preparation).

5 Analysis undertaken in 1992 in the Cambridge University Department of Metallurgy and Materials Science, with thanks to Dr Jim Charles, identified the alloy as cold-worked brass, containing 17.3% zinc and trace amounts of less than 0.5% iron and aluminium (and no lead).

6 Compare c0.4mm gauge and length 600mm at St Aldate's, Oxford; the fragmentary wire from Castle Sween is notably heavier at c0.8mm gauge.

7 Edinburgh, National Museums of Scotland, nos LT1 and LT2; the vibrating lengths of their shortest and longest strings are 73-606mm (2.87-23.87ins) and 51-616mm (2.0-24.25ins) respectively (Sanger & Kinnaird 1993, 212: Appendix A)

8 Also previously known, erroneously, as the harp of Brian Boru. The vibrating length of its longest string, as currently restored, is c27.5ins (700mm), previously c25.75ins (650mm) (Rensch 1969, 85).

## CATALOGUE

**1** (=Iron no 72): Fe jew's harp, of common late medieval/post-medieval type. F202; Period III-IV

Surviving length 65mm; the loop is of medium size, measuring 29mm externally. The tongue is not discernible in the concretion, nor on X-ray, and may be absent. The frame appears otherwise to have been deposited in an undamaged and undistorted condition.

**2** (=Copper no 14): Cu-alloy wire, wound in coil; possibly a string for a musical instrument, perhaps a harp. F103a; Period II.2

Surviving length c710mm; gauge c0.4mm; the ends are cut, not snapped. The surface is a bright brassy colour, with little visible corrosion; traces of working are preserved.

Associated finds included remains of textiles and other organics, but no recognizable fragments of stringed musical instruments.

## 5.12 AMBER, JET, & OPAL

### AMBER

Jackie Moran

#### AMBER BEAD

During the medieval period secular bead necklaces were not considered fashionable; therefore beads such as this one, excavated from a medieval context, are likely to be from rosaries. Rosary beads were made from all sorts of materials but amber and jet were especially popular (Margeson 1993). Amber has always been treasured by man and records exist from the 15th century which tell of only one or two amber beads from rosaries being given as legacies in Britain. This is evidence that amber was obviously considered to be of great value (Fraquet 1987). It may also provide an explanation as to why only one amber bead was discovered at Fast Castle.

One very similar amber bead in shape and size was found at Rievaulx Abbey, Yorkshire, and is described as being a rosary bead. Small beads such as this were strung in groups of ten known as decades and were separated by larger beads known as gauds. The decades and gauds were not necessarily made of the same material. Two materials such as amber and ivory may have been combined, one being used to produce small beads and the other to produce larger ones (Dunning 1965).

Although amber rosary beads in various stages of manufacture have been discovered in Britain during excavations it is impossible to say for sure whether the Fast Castle bead was actually produced here or not. The amber has however been identified as being cloudy bastard amber from the Baltic Coast.

The Baltic Sea region has been the main source of amber for the world since prehistoric times. Baltic amber is the most abundant of all ambers. It is generally harder than other fossil resins and tends to take a high polish. These factors have made it extremely popular for use in jewellery and other decorative items (Rice 1980).

#### CATALOGUE

1 Amber Bead. Height: 9mm Diameter: 11mm. (illus 57.6)  F103; Period II.2

Spherical amber bead with a central perforation of 2mm in diameter running through it. The surface has a crazed effect which is an important feature to look for when examining old beads such as this one. It helps determine whether they are true amber or imitation. The bead has been chipped twice at one end near the perforation.

### JET

Fraser Hunter & Bill Russell

The five jet beads (illus 57) from Fast Castle are an interesting assemblage because of the rarity of jet on Scottish medieval sites (see Table 6). All are securely, or most likely, late-medieval: nos 2 and 4 are in good late 15th- / early 16th-century contexts, no 1 is identical to no 4, while nos 3 and 5, although unstratified, are most probably medieval, as they are unlike later jet jewellery (cf Bury 1991, 657-81; Muller 1987; Dr E Goring, pers comm).

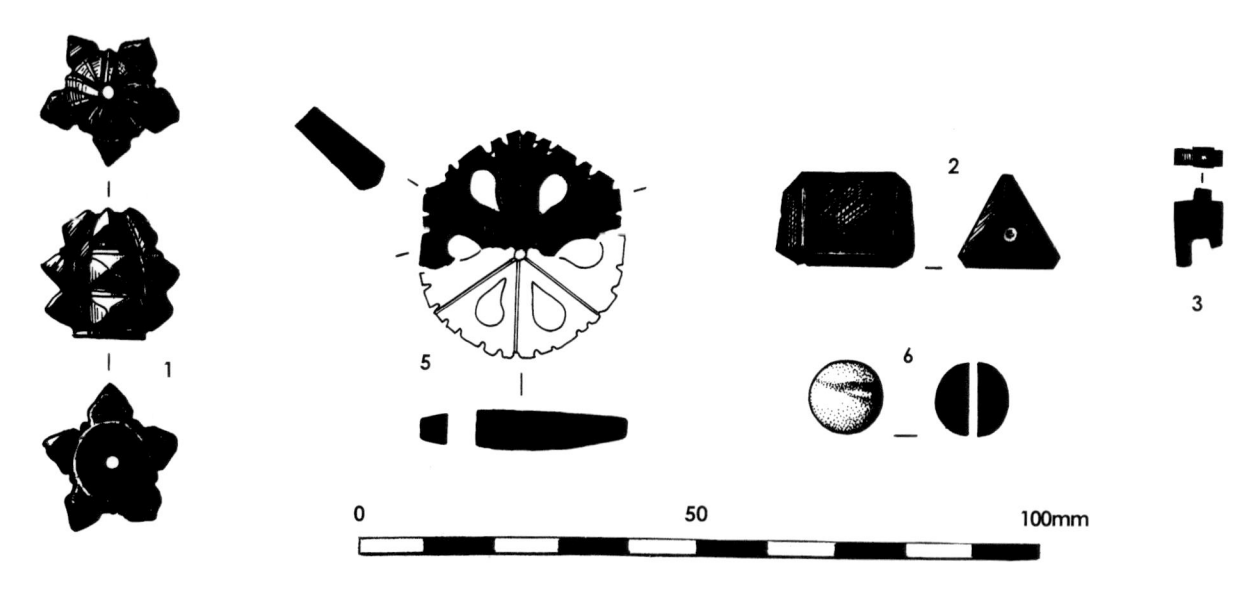

**Illus 57** Nos 1, 2, 3 and 5: Jet; no 6: Amber

Parallels for these ornate beads are hard to find. In Britain as a whole, published examples are almost exclusively simple spherical, flattened-spherical or fusiform beads (eg Dunning 1965, 61; Margeson 1993, 5; Woodhouse 1976, 34; Jarvis 1983, 73, fig 33, no 41); however, some more ornate medieval examples are known. From Kintraw, Argyll, spirally-decorated fusiform beads were recovered from a Bronze Age cairn (Simpson 1967, 57-8), but with no good Bronze Age parallels (A Sheridan, pers comm). Given the medieval buckle from the same context, they are probably medieval. Ornate beads are known among the products of the Spanish industry at Santiago (see below), although generally with symbols of St James in their decoration (eg Santiago Catalogue 1985, nos 208-9; de Osma 1916, 210-3, no 33). However, there is a parallel for nos 1 and 4 in a fragment of ribbed bead from Dissolution levels at Battle Abbey (Hare 1985, fig 44). There are also hints from literary sources that we are only seeing a fraction of the original range: for example, a record of 1483 from Siena records a paternoster of jet 'shaped as acorns' (Lightbown 1992, 348). While exact parallels are sparse, there is therefore no reason to doubt the Fast Castle examples are late medieval specimens. This very rarity makes them of particular significance.

The beads are presumably from necklaces, but whether they were secular ornaments or rosaries, perhaps even pilgrims' souvenirs, is hard to answer, particularly in the absence of specifically religious decoration. Margeson (1993, 5) notes that bead necklaces were not generally in fashion in the medieval period, and suggests there is therefore a presumption that medieval beads are from rosaries. Lay-people would habitually wear or carry rosaries at this time (Lightbown 1992, 342-50), so their presence on a secular site would occasion no surprise.

The five beads come from four different necklaces. Nos 1 and 4 are almost certainly from the same necklace, although one was unstratified; their asymmetry suggests they were terminal beads. No 2 is from a later context, and so is probably from a different necklace, while no 5 has too small a perforation to match any of these and must be from yet another. No 3 is from a delicate chain. Their ornate nature is a further pointer to the status of the site's occupants.

The postulated use of Spanish jet (see below) is consistent with these representing pilgrims' souvenirs, and there is no doubt that relics of St James from Santiago reached Scotland and northern Europe (Köster 1985, 90-1). However until we know more of medieval trade in jet, we cannot be sure: there are literary references to imports of jet beads in bulk into England (Campbell M 1991, 116). We cannot, therefore, say that the

Fast Castle beads come from pilgrim souvenirs rather than normal rosaries; even the rosary interpretation could be questioned, although it seems plausible. Other evidence of pilgrimage at Fast Castle - the unidentified pilgrim's badge and perhaps a scallop shell - is suggestive but not conclusive.

It is worth briefly reviewing the broader context of jet use. Jet has been employed for jewellery in Britain since the Neolithic. Its striking colour and electrostatic properties gave it magical qualities, and the ease with which it could be worked made it widely exploited. The early Bronze Age (Shepherd 1985) and Roman periods (Toynbee 1964, 363-8) were highpoints of craftsmanship, while related materials such as cannel coal, shale and lignite were widely used for more mundane bracelets and beads in the 1st millennium BC - 1st millennium AD. Medieval use of jet was more restricted but again displayed considerable artistry. Continuing belief in its magical qualities is seen in late medieval lapidaries (Evans & Serjeantson 1933, 32, 90-1, 130), largely derived from classical works such as Pliny (Natural History 34; quoted in Muller 1987, 21). Its black nature made it highly suitable for religious use (Hinton 1982, 13), and it became a favoured material for paternoster, and subsequently, rosary beads (Lightbown 1992, 31, 348-9). It also saw use for a range of other artefacts, both devotional and secular, including pendants, pectoral crosses, relic boxes, portable altars, crozier heads, rings, seals, amulets, dice and chess-pieces (Campbell M 1991, 116; Dalton *et al* 1925, 215; Greig & Greig 1989, 286; Dunning 1965, 61). The pinnacle of medieval jet-working was the industry based at the shrine of St James at Santiago de Compostela in north-west Spain, where a wide range of pilgrim souvenirs, many of considerable artistry, was produced (de Osma 1916; Santiago catalogue 1985, nos 208-34).

While questions remain, the value of the Fast Castle assemblage is considerable. As well as broadening our knowledge of medieval jet, and of the status and tastes of the site's occupants, it has led to the first clear demonstration that Spanish jet can be differentiated with non-destructive analytical methods from Whitby jet (see below). This is of considerable importance if we are ever to disentangle the questions of jet supply in medieval and earlier times.

## CATALOGUE (illus 57)

1 Bead; Maximum diameter 20mm; Height 18mm. Layer 2; Period III-IV

Elaborately-decorated bead, a convex-sided cone with a pentagonal arrangement of longitudinal ribs separated by plain bands. Each rib comprises three 'teeth', decreasing in height towards the point. The central cylindrical perforation is 3mm in diameter. Initial shaping done by lathe (note the basal circular 'collar' where it was detached from a larger block, surrounded by a circular channel with characteristic concentric lathe-turning marks). Toolmarks from hand-carving the decoration are visible on the teeth. Polished to a high lustre; in excellent condition.

2 Bead; Length 20mm; Width (of face) 15mm; Height 12.5mm. F86; Period III.1

Elongated triangular-sectioned bead, the three faces of equal size, with a longitudinal cylindrical perforation 2.5mm in diameter. All edges are facetted; the ends are flat, while the faces taper slightly longitudinally, from 15mm-13mm. Part of one face has split away at the narrower end in a conchoidal fracture; otherwise the bead is in very good condition.

3 Bead; Length 11mm; Width 7mm; Height 2.5mm. Layer 2; Period III-IV

Rectangular bead modified by cutting a rectangular notch from one end and carving a short rectangular extrusion at the other; the latter is not exactly central. One of the arms at the notched end is broken, but otherwise the bead is intact. Longitudinally perforated with a very thin cylindrical perforation, c0.8mm in diameter. The non-central position of the extrusion was presumably to make it lie better in a curve when attached to other similar beads. This would have been a very delicate necklace.

4 Bead; Maximum diameter 20mm; Height 15mm (not illus). Kitchen: F307/318; Period II

Elaborately-decorated bead, identical to 1 but with a less prominent collar at the base and in slightly poorer condition; one rib has two 'teeth' broken off and others are slightly chipped.

**5** Bead fragment; Length 29.5mm; Width (surviving) 17.5mm; Height 5mm. Layer 2; Period III-IV

Half of a hexagonal bead with openwork decoration, suspended by a diametrical perforation 1.5mm wide. Complete when found apart from one small break in the perimeter, but subsequently broken and half lost; a record photo gives the intact form as reconstructed in the illustration. Each segment of the hexagon is defined by radial incisions terminating in a notch on the outer circumference, and further decorated with two pairs of slanting notches; centrally each segment has an openwork lobe, pointing towards the centre, formed by drilling a hole 4.5mm in diameter and then carving a point. In the middle of the bead was a small cylindrical perforation, c1.5mm diameter, now largely lost through breakage.

**Table 6:** Medieval Jet & Related Materials in Scotland: a provisional list

| Site | Find | Date | Reference |
| --- | --- | --- | --- |
| Balfarg/Balbirnie, Fife | Mount | Early 17th c | Russell-White 1995, 1016 |
| Butchercote, Marton, Berwickshire | Gaming piece?[2] | 14th- 15th c? | PSAS 64 (1929-30), 9 |
| Cullykan, Banffshire | Die | 12th c | Greig & Greig 1989, 286 |
| Dairsie, Fife | Cross pendant | 11th- 12th c | Unpublished, NMS records |
| Elcho Nunnery, Perthshire | Bead (jet) | Mid 13th- mid 16th c | Perry et al 1988, 80 |
| Fast Castle, Berwickshire | Beads (jet) | Late 15th- early 16th c | *Infra* |
| Huntly Castle, Aberdeenshire | Bead | Late 14th- mid 17th c? | Unpublished, Huntly Museum. |
| Kindrochit Castle, Aberdeenshire | Facetted button with silver decorative loop | 14th - 16th c | PSAS 61 (1926-27), 166 |
| Kintraw, Argyll | Spirally fluted fusiform beads | ? | Simpson 1967, 57-58 |
| Lochcrutton crannog, Kirkcudbrightshire | Pendant cross fragment inscribed 'IHS' | 13th c | Callander 1924, 163 |
| Perth, Perthshire[3] | Cross, ring, bead and chess piece (jet) | Late 12th- 13th c | Unpublished, M Hall, pers comm |
| Threave Castle, Kirkcudbrightshire | Beads | Mid 15th- mid 17th c | Good & Tabraham 1981, 126, nos 202-4 |
| Whitehaugh, Peebleshire | Gaming piece? | 14th- 15th c? | Unpublished, NMS records |
| Whithorn, Wigtownshire | Bangle fragments, (cannel coal/shale)[4] | 13th c | Hunter & Nicholson 1997, nos 1.5-6 |
|  | Bead (jet) | 15th c | *Ibid* 3.3 |
|  | Whorls (shale) | 13th- 15th c | *Ibid* 4.1-2 |
|  | Perforated object (jet) | Late 15th- early 16th c | *Ibid* 5.1 |
| Woodhead, Ancrum, Roxburghshire | Gaming piece? | 14th- 15th c | PSAS 64 (1929-30), 9 |
| Woodhead, Canonbie, Dumfriesshire | 15 beads (12 fusiform, 2 facetted, 1 flattened sphere) in hoard of brooches and coins | Late 13th- early 14th c | PSAS 5 (1862-4), 216, 236-7 |

Notes

1. Only finds from Fast Castle, Perth and Whithorn have been analysed (results in brackets). It is hoped to tackle the remainder of the material in a programme of analysis.
2. We are grateful to Mark Hall for suggesting this identification.
3. We are grateful to Mark Hall for information on the Perth finds in advance of publication.
4. The bangles from Whithorn are the only ones known to us from a Medieval context. If they are indeed of this date, rather than residual, they are likely to be connected with continuing Norse period traditions. There is no other good evidence for the use of bangles continuing into the Medieval period.

**ERRATA** - Insert this slip between pp 120-121

**page 120**; Table 6: Balfarg jet should read early 13th century, not 17th

**An illustration, illus 57a,** showing XRF spectra for typical Whitby jet, Spanish jet and Fast Castle jet bead No. 2 was inadvertently omitted from this publication. Illus 57a is reproduced below.

Illus 57a should have been placed between pages 122 and 123, with consequential text changes: **Add** '& illus 57a' after 'Table 7' on page 121, para 2, last line. **Substitute** 'illus 57a' for 'Table 7' on page 122, para 1, line 1. **Page 122**, para 2, lines 3,4 and 5, 'bead No 3' should read 'bead No 4'

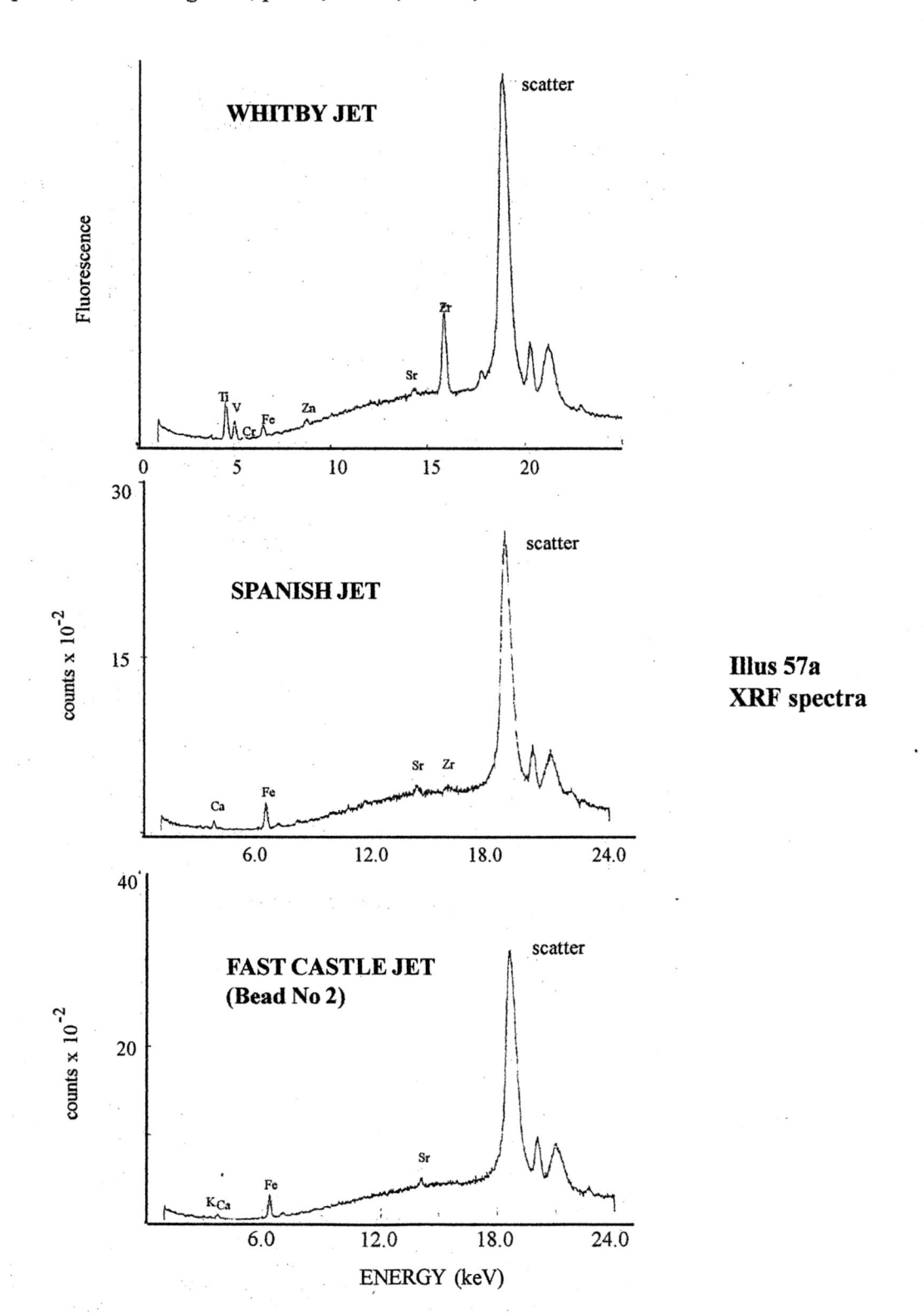

**Illus 57a
XRF spectra**

## SCIENTIFIC IDENTIFICATION OF THE RAW MATERIAL

It has been realised for some time that visual identification of jet-like materials is unsatisfactory, as there are a number of other materials (primarily lignite, cannel coal and oil shale) which are easily confused with jet. Non-destructive methods have been developed to allow the discrimination of jet from other substances (Pollard et al 1981; Hunter et al 1993), using a combination of X-ray fluorescence (XRF) and X-radiography. This methodology was applied to the Fast Castle material. Fuller details of the method and results can be found in the note on Analytical Methods and Results, below.

The results showed clearly that the Fast Castle material is indeed jet. However, the objects differed in significant details from the normal Whitby jet standards used in the NMS laboratories. It is known that, in the medieval period, jet from Santiago de Compostela in Spain and, to a lesser extent, from the Swabian Alps in southern Germany, was also used for ornaments (Muller 1987, 98-108). No samples of German jet were available, but a number of artefacts of known Spanish provenance were analysed for comparison. Allowing for contamination caused during burial of the excavated examples, the results are remarkably similar, and suggest that the Fast Castle artefacts are of Spanish jet (Table 7).

**Table 7**: Jet: elements detected in XRF analyses

Prominent peaks (higher than scatter peaks) in bold; clearly detectable peaks in normal type; trace peaks in (brackets). For KH 4, repeat analyses showed this contained a zinc-rich inclusion.

### Spanish Jet

| Sample No | Description | Elements Detected |
|---|---|---|
| KH4 | St James figurine | **Zn** Fe (K) |
| KH5 | Scallop shell | Fe Zn (K Ca Ge Sr) |
| A.1905.1158 | Mounted St James badge | Fe (Ca Sr Zr) |
| | Modern 'higa' amulet | Fe (Ge Zr) |
| | Modern 'higa' amulet | Fe (Ca Sr Zr) |

### Fast Castle Jet

| Sample No | Elements Detected |
|---|---|
| 1 | Fe (Ca Sr) |
| 2 | Fe (K Ca Sr) |
| 3 | Ca Fe Cu Br Sr (Mn Zn Zr) |
| 4 | Ca Fe Sr |
| 5 | Ca Fe Sr Zr (V Cr Mn Ge Br) |

\* Footnote:
Strontium has previously been seen as a reliable element, but as it is chemically similar to calcium, it may behave in a similar manner, which would explain in part its presence in the archaeological jet spectra.
Acknowledgements: We are grateful to David Caldwell, Marian Campbell, John Cherry, John Clark, Mary Davis, Godfrey Evans, Liz Goring and Alison Sheridan for helpful comments on parallels and references.

## ANALYTICAL METHODS AND RESULTS

### EXPERIMENTAL DETAILS

Analyses were performed on an air-path energy-dispersive XRF system, using a rhodium tube run at 46kV and 0.3mA. Spectra were detected using a Si(Li) semiconductor detector and collected for 200 live seconds into a computer with multi-channel analyser facilities. Surface preparation was minimal; artefacts were lightly swabbed with industrial methylated spirits to remove surface dirt. In addition to the artefacts and raw material samples of Whitby jet, five samples of Spanish jet were analysed, comprising two modern pendants purchased in Santiago and three medieval objects typologically of clear Spanish origin. In this trial work, no attempt was made to quantify the results; comments are based on visual comparison of peak sizes.

RESULTS

The Spanish jet samples were distinctively different from Whitby jet (table 7). While both show highly organic matrices and few elemental inclusions, the Spanish samples are significantly 'cleaner' elementally. They lack any significant traces of the typical Whitby elements of zirconium, titanium and vanadium (Pollard *et al* 1981; Hunter *et al* 1993, 77; Davis 1993). Only iron (at low levels) and sometimes zinc (generally low, but a sizeable quantity in one spectrum) are present at any level noticeably above background noise. The one high-zinc spectrum points to occasional zinc-rich inclusions, as found in Whitby jet (*ibid*). The results suggest a distinction can be made elementally between Spanish and Whitby jet, supporting the tentative conclusions drawn from Muller's limited trial work (1980).

The Fast Castle samples match the Spanish jet profiles markedly more closely than they do Whitby ones. Apart from high calcium and occasional strontium values, both likely to arise from contamination (Hunter *et al* 1993, 79), iron at low levels was generally the only significant peak present. Beads nos 1, 2, and 3 are very similar, which supports the typological arguments above that nos 1 and 3 come from the same necklace. Bead no 3 did show higher levels of iron than the others, and noticeable peaks for manganese, copper, bromine and zirconium, and its attribution to a Spanish source is less secure. However for the remainder, while our current inability to characterise other European sources prevents definitive statements, a plausible working hypothesis is that all are of Spanish origin.

These results, following the previous success in discriminating Scottish jet from Whitby jet (Davis 1993), suggest that a further programme of jet analyses could hope to discriminate all the various European sources. Weller and Wert (1993) have already reported differences in macromolecular structure between different jet sources, and elemental analysis is a promising prospect.

## OPAL

A hand worked opaline artefact of possible religious origin

Diane Mitchell

The excavations at Fast Castle have revealed several rare artefacts (some of them being of a religious nature); one of these is a small, flat object of mineralic composition (Plate XIII). It appears to have been hand worked. It was found in the lower levels of the Quarry pit (F103a; Period II.2), and was therefore deposited in the late 15th to early 16th century.

THE GEOLOGICAL EVIDENCE

The mineral is opaque, white to beige with dark brown mottling. It is banded and very fine grained, the grains having a cross-fibrous habit. The bands are on a mm scale, and vary in thickness across the piece. There is no evidence of degradational weathering on the planar surfaces, and only some on the edges.

Infra-red spectroscopy has revealed the piece to be common opal ($SiO_2.nH_2O$). Due to the mode of occurrence of opal (silica rich waters often associated with hydrothermal activity), it is very rare in Britain, restricted to only a few pockets of volcanic rocks. It is therefore probable that this particular piece was imported. Sources for common opal include the Faroe Islands, Czechoslovakia, Hungary, Romania, Austria, or Germany. Another possibility is that it may have come from as far afield as India.

Opal has a hardness of 5.5 - 6.5 (Mohs' hardness scale) and in general would therefore be equivalent to hand working agate, onyx or jasper (for examples see Hackenbroch 1979, 53-104). Other minerals of similar hardness include lapizs lazuli (5.5) and turquoise (5-6). However, opal has various morphologies and these determine the ease of hand working. For instance, nodular opal is tougher to work with, but more resistant to wear. A good analogy to this is flint which is nodular, of similar composition and only slightly harder (6-7). Others include concretionary and botryoidal forms. Although they are hemispherical, they are similar to the Fast Castle example in that they are banded. This would mean that they are more manageable, more brittle and much more susceptible to damage.

In comparison, opal is relatively soft compared to other gemstones (eg members of the quartz or corundum family). What is important here is that due to its brittleness, the piece must have been protected from hard wear. In other words, it must have been supported against a backing of some kind.

This piece was originally found whole, but unfortunately through the years has fragmented due to its friability and now lies in several pieces. Of these, most can be rejoined with varying degrees of accuracy to give an overall size of approximately 35 x 35 x 4mm (Plate.XIII). Most of the fragments have straight edges and as can be seen, they partially form three sides of a rectangle: the first evidence of hand working.

**Illus 58**  Opal, cross-section

A closer look reveals two further pieces of evidence. Firstly the edges are uniformly bevelled in a way that could certainly have been designed to be retained, probably in a copper or silver alloy in order to fix the piece to the backing (illus 58). Secondly, on one edge there is a 'scallop' measuring 11 x 4mm. Opal can suffer from brittle or conchoidal fracturing and it could be suggested that the scallop is a conchoidal fracture. This is highly unlikely, since conchoidal fracturing occurs as a ridged curve (it has best been described as resembling the inside of a shell), whereas this is a very smooth and symmetrical curve; it is the most important evidence supporting the theory of hand working.

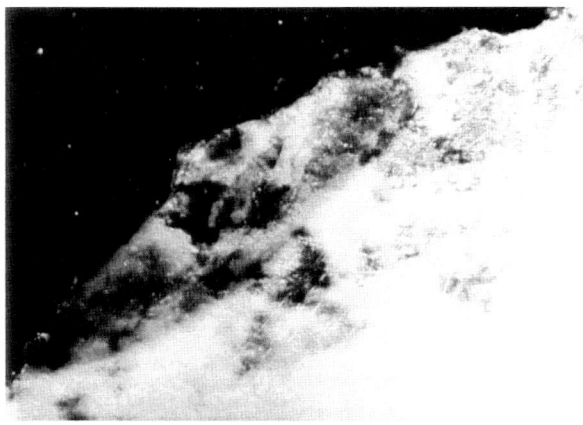

The planar surfaces have fine striations upon them which could suggest polishing of a rudimentary form (these are visible in illus 59). Further work needs to be carried out at a higher magnification, in order to assess the origin of these markings, as the surfaces also have a natural pitted effect. In other words, do they show any pattern, or are they randomly orientated? Likewise, they may be natural, as the internal planar surfaces also show similar markings, or they may post-date burial. They may also be a combination of all three. It is interesting to note that there is a curvature across the width of the piece (illus 60). Whether any importance can be attached to this cannot yet be determined.

**Illus 59**  Opal: striations, centre right

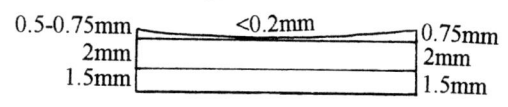

**Illus 60:** Opal, band variation

## HISTORICAL POSSIBILITIES

Precious opal was highly valued by the Romans, although examples are extremely rare, probably because of its susceptibility to decomposition. However, there are more examples of common opal (it is more resistant to weathering) being used as far back as ancient Egyptian times. Examples include a wood opal bead from ancient Egypt, and a 3rd century intaglio which now lies in the Kunsthistorisches Museum in Vienna. One example of a carved buckle has also been found dating from the Sassanian period (3rd-5th century AD).

The Fast Castle opal obviously had no practical aspect because of its fragility, and therefore must have been ornamental. Of that there is no real doubt. But what was its purpose? To date, unfortunately, no parallels have been found. Common opal, in particular this piece, is dull with no brilliant colours, pleasing pearly lustre or similar precious qualities. What then is the attractiveness of using this mineral? Precious opal often had 'mythical' connections, in that it was sometimes said to brighten when worn by those infected with the plague (now believed to be due to a change in body temperature). But common opal does not appear to have any such connections.

The most accepted suggestions are that it was either part of a book cover or religious reliquary, in which semi-precious marbles were sometimes used. The rectangular shape may support the book theory, but many reliquaries were also rectangular in shape. Despite the above examples, use for jewellery in this case is virtually out of the question. It most certainly would have fragmented due to its size and fragility. Beyond this though, no reliable information is present to substantiate these speculations.

What is intriguing, is that this piece may be related to the other religious artefacts found at Fast Castle, although there is no recorded presence of a chapel. Could this piece have been brought back from Cairo by Cuthbert Hume (Kennaway 1992, 61)? Although, as with the other pieces - such as the pilgrim's badge (Pewter Report, Chap 5.8, no 1), and the Madonna pipe-clay figurine (Pipe-clay Report, Chap 5.4, no 1) - there is a probable time gap of perhaps one or two decades, it is possible that he returned from Cairo to Scotland prior to 1509 and brought back these relics. This is of course mere speculation, but almost certainly the opal did originate abroad.

## CONCLUSION

Unfortunately there are many questions that still remain unanswered. The piece needs to be compared with other artefacts in order to find any parallels, though more in nature than mineralogy (ie flat, hand-worked, and supported against a backing). It seems most likely that it was part of a religious reliquary or book cover (religious or otherwise). Geologically, this opal most probably came from Europe, with the chances of it coming from Britain being very slim. With other religious and secular artefacts found at Fast Castle being foreign (eg Spanish, Dutch, etc), it adds additional credence to the belief that this opal also originated abroad.

Acknowledgements: Our appreciation goes to Brett Beddoe-Stephens of the British Geological Survey for an initial examination of the piece, Brian Jackson of the National Museums of Scotland for his time in helping identify the opal, and finally to John Cherry of the British Museum for giving his expert opinion in the possibilities of its use.

## 5.13 TEXTILES
### and associated objects

Thea Gabra-Sanders & Michael L Ryder
with contributions by
Frances Pritchard & Geoffrey Egan

Editor's note: The material described in this report has already been published in *Textile History* 23(1) 1992, 5-22. A grant was received from the Pasold Research Fund towards that publication. Original catalogue numbers were used therein, and are listed alongside serial numbers as used throughout this publication. It is reprinted here with minor revision.

The very interesting group of textiles, described below, results from the exceptional occurrence of those specific conditions that allow organic remains to survive.

The textiles came from the lower levels of the Quarry pit, almost all from Period II.2. They were found immediately above the floor level F109, among other organic remains, including leather and wood. Datable finds from the textile-bearing levels and above, such as Crux Pellit coins, and a Madonna and Child pipe-clay figurine, indicate a late 15th-century date for the deposition of the textiles. It was not possible to ascertain whether the textiles were residues from work in the immediate area, or were re-deposited debris from elsewhere on the site. The textiles included examples of wool and silk. The wool comprised 25 fragments of woven cloth; no complete garment was found. There were also three examples of raw wool and two locks of animal hair. The silk comprised a plaited braid and a strip of velvet, which represent luxury goods.

Finds associated with textiles or clothing included six spindle whorls, and a German cloth seal, which was from an early 16th- to early 17th-century level in the Outer Courtyard.

**Illus 61** Medium coarse wool cloth (Cat 12)

# 1 WOOL
Spinning and Weaving Features of the Wool Cloth

Thea Gabra-Sanders

The wool cloth was woven in tabby (plain weave), the most basic weave. Different qualities of cloth from medium fine to medium coarse were evident (illus 61& 62). Fabrics made of single, S-spun yarns predominated, but there was a small group with S-spun yarns in one system and Z-spun yarns in the other, and samples 2(81A) and 3(81B) had S- as well as Z-spun yarns in the same system (Table 8). A predominance of S-spun yarns was noted by Walton (1981, 193) in some 15th- and 16th-century textiles from the castle ditch, Newcastle-upon-Tyne.

Cloth fragment no 23(753C) (illus 62) had a simple selvedge reinforced by four Z-plied yarns. The same feature was noted in similar material, from medieval Perth by Bennett (1987, 159) and from Dutch sites by Vons-Comis (1982, 151-2). There was no evidence of felting in seven of the 25 fragments of cloth. Of the remainder, it was not possible to tell whether one, no 24(792), was felted or not, and eleven were felted on both sides, while six were felted on one side only. Those felted on both sides had probably been finished by fulling (pounding while wet to shrink and hence to thicken and condense the fabric), resulting in primary felting.

**Illus 62** Medium fine wool cloth with selvedge (Cat 23)

Frequent washing of (unfulled) wool cloth results in secondary felting, but that on one side of the cloth is more likely to have been the result of rubbing during wear. Nor is burial in damp conditions likely to have caused secondary felting, because the essential component, movement (usually by rubbing), was lacking, as was warmth, which assists the felting process. In any case, if felting had occurred during burial all the fragments are likely to have appeared the same. There was little evidence of sewing. Only two fragments bore traces of stitching. Cloth no 3(81B) had five stitch holes at intervals of 5mm, and cloth no 6(139B) had three stitch holes, in one of which was a 3mm length of sewing thread. Cloth no 4(108) was unusual, a short strip in which had been tied an overhand knot, and so might have been a garter (illus 63). It is very difficult to establish the use of the fabrics. Most of the fragments have cut edges, cut on the diagonal or slightly curved and some are very worn. The textiles are best interpreted as a collection of rags with tailors' waste, as well as remnants of worn-out clothing (see Fibre re-

**Illus 63** Wool strip with knot (Cat 4)

port, below). They had all been woven in tabby weave with a thread-count of 5 to 12 yarns per cm in each system. This accords with an average thread-count of 5 to 15 per cm for each system reported by Hedges (1977, 334-6) in medieval and later cloth. Weaving at home on a loom with two to four shafts is suggested by the presence of weaving faults, where a weft has been passed accidentally twice through a shed, or the warp incorrectly tied.

The general standard of the weaving is only moderate. Andrew Halyburton mentions in his account book (Innes 1867, 193) that in the 15th century bolts of cloth were being sent from east Scotland to the Low Countries to be dyed, and presumably, finished. This suggests that at the end of the 15th century textile skills in the area were poorly developed.

**Table 8:** Catalogue of wool cloth fragments; all woven in tabby weave from single ply yarn.

| Cat | Sample | Dimensions cm | Threads per cm | Spin | Fin | Colour | D | C | S | Remarks |
|---|---|---|---|---|---|---|---|---|---|---|
| 1 | 48 | 2 x 1.9 | 10 x 9 | S x S | B | Mid brown | | | | Lining of a thimble |
| 2 | 81A | 8 x 1.9 | 12 x 10 | Z + S x Z | B | Red brown | * | * | | Both spins of yarn present in one system |
| 3 | 81B | 3.6 x 3 | 11 x 11 | Z + S x Z | A | Red brown | * | * | * | Both spins of yarn present in one system |
| 4 | 108 | 15 x 0.5 | 10 x 8 | S x Z | H | Red brown | ? | * | | Strip tied in overhand knot |
| 5 | 139A | 11 x 2.3 | 10 x 10 | Z x S | B | Dk brown | * | * | | |
| 6 | 139B | 14 x 1.3 | 10 x 10 | ? | H | Dk brown | * | * | * | |
| 7 | 140 | 11 x 2.2 | 8 x 8 | S x S | | Mid brown | ? | * | | Weaving faults |
| 8 | 297A | 15.5 x 1 | ? | S x ? | H | Dk brown | ? | * | | Thick tough fabric-weave not possible to identify |
| 9 | 297B | 10.5 x 3.5 | 10 x 8 | S x S | A | Mid brown | | * | | |
| 10 | 297C | 14 x 8 | 10 x 9 | S x S | A | Mid brown | | | | Weaving faults |
| 11 | 298 | 8.1 x 2 | 10 x 8 | S x S | H | Dk brown | * | * | | One face very worn |
| 12 | 299 | 11 x 6.5 | 11 x 11 | S x S | | Mid brown | * | * | | Weaving faults |
| 13 | 302A | 14.7 x 7 | 7 x 7 | S x S | | Dk brown | | | | Weaving faults |
| 14a | 302B | 5.8 x 5.5 | 7 x 6 | S x S | | Lt brown | | | | |
| 14b | 302B | 5 x 4 | 6 x 6 | S x S | | Lt brown | | | | Three small scraps of same textile |
| 15 | 302C | 26.8 x 4.2 | 10 x 10 | S x Z | B | Red brown | * | * | | |
| 16 | 320A | 18 x 3.5 | 8 x 7 | S x S | | Mid brown | * | | | |
| 17 | 320B | 11.5 x 1 | 6 x 6 | S x S | A | Dk brown | | * | | |
| 18 | 320C | 29.5 x 1 | ? | S x ? | H | Dk brown | ? | * | | |
| 19 | 321 | 8 x 1 | 7 x 7 | S x S | A | Dk brown | * | * | | |
| 20 | 445 | 4.8 x 3.2 | 5 x 5 | S x S | | Dk brown | ? | | | |
| 21 | 753A | 10.5 x 1.9 | 8 x 7 | S x S | G | Brown | ? | * | | |
| 22 | 753B | 9 x 1.5 | 7 x 7 | S x S | A | Dk brown | | * | | |
| 23 | 753C | 14 x 1.5 - 7 | 6 x 5 | S x S | B | Lt brown | | * | | |
| | | 14 x 1.5 | 4 x 5 | Z-plied | B | Dk brown | | * | | Simple selvedge on tabby weave |
| 24 | 792 | 3.5 x 1.8 | 6 x 6 | S x S | ? | Brown | | | ? | Several layers folded together; remains of three eyelets *in situ* (one complete) |
| 25 | 293A | 8 | | S | | Brown | | | | Yarn adhering to unspun wool (292) |

Key: D = Dye; C = Cut; S = Stitching
Fin (Finish) A = Felted on one face; B = Felted on both faces;
G = Heavy felting on one face; H = Heavy felting on both faces

Note All of the above textiles came from F100a – 104 (Period II.2), except No 1, from pit 2 (Period III) and No 20, from F109 (Period II.1)

## 2 SILK TEXTILES

Frances Pritchard

**Illus 64** Tubular silk braid

**Illus 65** Tubular silk braid (detail)

26 Silk tubular braid. F103c/104; Period II.2

Tubular braid, (illus 64), length 280mm, diameter 3mm, fitted with two copper alloy tags (chapes) beyond which the free ends extend to form tassels (illus 65). The braid, which is now golden brown, had been made by hand-plaiting groups of S-plied silk thread. It was not possible to establish the sequence in which the threads were worked, but it was not the usual form of eight-strand plait.

Plaited braids were made in Europe throughout the medieval period. Eight elements, which gave a regular plait, were the most common (Hald 1980, fig 244), but other plaits similar to this example have been recorded (Crowfoot *et al* 1991, no 412, fig 110a; Ceulmans *et al* 1988, no 42, 211-2). By the early 14th century, metal chapes were being fitted to braids (Egan & Pritchard 1991). Brass chapes were usual, whereas the laces were often plaited from linen or wool, rather than silk, or made from leather (Salzman 1923, 251; Spiers 1973, 20). These laces were known as *points* or *aglets*. The frequent use of *points* for fastening armour and clothing is apparent from effigies, frescoes, and panel paintings of the 14th century and later (Wormald 1973, Pl 21; Evans 1952, 14-16). Long laces were often used to fasten the bodice of a woman's gown, either at the centre front or at the side, while shorter *points* were used to tie the sleeves of over-garments. Undergarments such as hose and linen shifts, which were worn more conspicuously during the 15th century, were also fastened with them. Short *points* were often tied with a bow and this may account for the wear marks on the braid from Fast Castle. The tassels (illus 65) are noteworthy since chapes usually concealed the cut ends of the threads. Similarly-tasselled braids can be seen in a portrait of a lady by Bartolommeo Veneto (c1502-30), in the National Gallery, London, in which she is shown wearing a series of black braids knotted to the drawstring at the neck of her white smock (NGA no 2507). This may represent a short-lived fashion.

27 Velvet. F104; Period II.2 (not illus)

The velvet has a short, solid cut pile. The warp system has three main ends to each pile end. The main warp is S-thrown with 84 to 90 ends per cm. The twist of the pile warp is not clear; it has 28 to 30 ends per cm. The weft yarn has no appreciable twist; there are three picks to each rod and 48 picks per cm. The ground weave is an irregular 3:1 twill. It is a bias-cut strip 195mm long and 17mm wide. Each long edge had been folded inwards giving a final width of 6.5mm. Stitch holes along these edges indicate that the strip had been applied as a trimming. The cloth is stained brown and the pile is very worn except under the folded edges.

This type of velvet was common throughout Europe from the late 15th to the late 16th centuries (King 1960, 10-11). The cloth that covered the coffin of Edward IV (d 1483) has a similar weave structure to the Fast Castle strip and it is of almost identical weight (Tudor-Craig 1973, no 135, 59); an analysis of that velvet by Monnas is in the Museum of London archive. By contrast, plain velvets of the 14th century often had a tabby ground weave and a Z-twisted main warp (Monnas 1986, 64). In addition, the threads were less densely packed; regulations governing the manufacture of silk fabrics in the Italian city, Lucca, in 1376 stipulated that fine velvets should have 40 or 41 main ends, and 13 or 14 pile ends per cm, a lower density being allowed for velvets that were less fine (King & King 1988, 75). An intermediate stage between these plain velvets of the 14th century and those of the late 15th century can be identified in a piece used as a relic pouch in the abbey at Saint-Maurice, Switzerland. This velvet has a S-twisted main warp, a tabby ground weave and the proportions of the main ends to pile ends was reduced from 3:1 to 2:1 (Schmedding 1978, 191-2).

How early in the 15th century the change to S-twisted warp yarn took place is uncertain. A similar change in the twist of the yarn and the spacing of the threads occurred in the production of silk cloths woven in satin some time between the late 14th century and the early 16th century, and examples of satin damask that can be dated stylistically to the 15th century use similar fine warp yarn with an S-twist. The velvet strip from Fast Castle was well worn by the time that it was discarded in the second half of the 15th century, therefore providing useful evidence that the change in the twist of the yarn had taken place earlier in the century.

### 3 TEXTILE FIBRES

#### Michael L Ryder

The material to be described is very interesting in showing the kinds of wool grown by the sheep of Scotland during the 15th century and is important in filling a gap in the archaeological record between earlier and later remains with which the Fast Castle wools are compared. In particular, these finds give the first archaeological evidence for the Old Scottish Shortwool 100 years before the first vague historical records.

## MATERIAL AND METHODS

The material came from the lower levels of the Inner Courtyard, dated from the second half of the 15th century, and comprised thirty-one wool yarns (Table 9), one silk yarn from the braid and the sewing thread from cloth no 6(139B), plus three staples of raw wool and two locks of animal hair.

The constituent fibres of each sample were separated on a glass slide to make a whole-mount preparation. A microscopic examination was made of the fibres, then the fibre diameter of 100 fibres in each sample was measured with a projection microscope using the International Standard IWTO method. The diameter distribution obtained was used to identify the fibre and, with wool, to define fleece type, which is determined from the distribution by the maximum fibre diameter, the mode (most frequent diameter) and the mean (Ryder 1983a, 47).

**Table 9:** Kinds of wool in relation to the cloth samples

| Cat | Sample | Fibre diam. distribution | Fleece type | Dye | Remarks |
|---|---|---|---|---|---|
| 1.1 | 48/1 | Skew-fine | Fine gen. med. | None seen | Prob. same wool warp and weft |
| 1.2 | 48/2 | Skew-fine | Fine gen. med | None seen | " |
| 2.1 | 81A/1 | Skew-fine | Generalised medium | Pink | Prob. same wool warp and weft |
| 2.2 | 81A/2 | Skew-fine | Generalised medium | Pink | " |
| 5.1 | 139A/1 | Symmetrical | Semi-fine (shortwool) | Yellow & blue | Prob. same wool warp and weft |
| 5.2 | 139A/2 | Symmetrical | Semi-fine (shortwool) | Yellow & blue | " |
| 9.1 | 297B/1 | Skew-fine | Fine gen. med. | None seen | Prob. same wool warp and weft |
| 9.2 | 297B/2 | Symmetrical | Fine gen. med. | None seen | " |
| 11.1 | 298/1 | Symmetrical | Semi-fine (shortwool) | Pink & blue | Prob. same wool warp and weft |
| 11.2 | 298/2 | Symmetrical | Semi-fine (shortwool) | Pink & blue | " |
| 12.1 | 299/1 | Skew-symm | Semi-fine (shortwool) | Blue | Prob. same wool warp and weft |
| 12.2 | 299/2 | Skew-symm | Semi-fine (shortwool) | Blue | " |
| 13.1 | 302A/1 | Skew-fine | Hairy medium | Natural pigment | Prob. same wool warp and weft |
| 13.2 | 302A/2 | Skew-fine | Hairy medium | Natural pigment | " |
| 14.1 | 302B/1 | Skew-fine | Generalised medium | None seen | One system coarser |
| 14.2 | 302B/2 | Skew-fine | Hairy medium | None seen | " |
| 15.1 | 302C/1 | Symmetrical | Semi-fine (shortwool) | Dark red | Prob. same wool warp and weft |
| 15.2 | 302C/2 | Symmetrical | Semi-fine (shortwool) | Dark red | " |
| 16.1 | 320A/1 | Skew-fine | Generalised medium | Blue | Prob. same wool warp and weft |
| 16.2 | 320A/2 | Skew-fine | Generalised medium | Blue | " |
| 17.1 | 320B/1 | Skew-fine | Hairy medium | None seen | Both could be Hairy medium |
| 17.2 | 320B/2 | Skew-fine | Generalised medium | None seen | " |
| 19.1 | 321/1 | Skew-fine | Hairy medium | Orange medulla | Both could be Hairy medium |
| 19.2 | 321/2 | Skew-fine | Generalised medium | Orange medulla | " |
| 21.1 | 753A/1 | Skew-fine | Generalised medium | None | Prob. same wool warp and weft |
| 21.2 | 753A/2 | Skew-fine | Generalised medium | ? Red | " |
| 23.1 | 753C/1 | Skew-fine | Hairy medium | None seen | Both could be Hairy medium |
| 23.2 | 753C/2 | Skew-fine | Generalised medium | None seen | " |
| 23.3 | 753 Selvedge | Skew-fine | Hairy medium | Natural pigment | Different yarn |
| 24.1 | 792/1 | Skew-fine | Generalised medium | None | Both could be Hairy medium |
| 24.2 | 792/2 | Skew-fine | Hairy medium | Natural pigment | " |

## RESULTS AND DISCUSSION

(a) General

The fibre diameter measurements showed that except for the single silk yarn and the sewing thread, all the cloth samples and three of the unspun samples, were wool, the other two being goat hair. There was more evidence of dye on the yarn fibres than usual in archaeological material, with not much natural coloration (ie pigment granules within the fibres: Ryder 1990). Few samples had the yellow-brown discoloration common in archaeological material; instead the fibres appeared to be white, ie completely devoid of natural pigment, dye or discoloration (Table 9). The fibre structure was in good condition with few samples showing any degradation; but at least three samples had fibres with what appeared to be moth damage, which could, however, have been caused by insect attack during burial. Fibre wear was seen as rounded fibre ends resulting from the abrasion wear similar to that seen in carpets, instead of the frayed ends of the flexing (bending) wear seen in clothing. This waste therefore could have been used as cleaning rags.

(b) The silk

The silk fibres ranged from 6 to 18 microns in diameter with a mean of 12.3 +/- 2.9 microns, and a mode of 13 microns. The yarn was not spun, but comprised twisted continuous filaments; such fineness identifies the silk as cultivated rather than wild fibre. It has not been possible to locate any other silk fibre measurements for comparison, but these are clearly much more realistic than the 15 to 25 microns quoted by Ryder and Gabra-Sanders (1985, 123-40). The source of the fibre at that time was probably the Mediterranean area, possibly Italy, and an Italian source is hinted at by Frances Pritchard in her report, although Muthesius (1982) states that many early medieval silks found in England were woven in the Near East.

(c) The sewing thread from cloth 6(139B)

The 3mm thread was tough when mounted and split into only five fibres, which when measured under the microscope ranged from 50 to 80 microns. This variation in thickness was due to a difference in the number of sub-unit 'ultimates' evident mostly at the ends of the fibres ranging from 15 to 20 microns in thickness. The fibres had the brown discoloration usual in animal (hair) fibres, but had no other features suggesting animal origin. Neither were they sufficiently regular to suggest silk. The dimensions of the ultimates were the same as those of the plant fibre flax, and flax (or similar bast fibre) seems the most likely identification, although flax is usually colourless, and has cross-striations, none of which were seen in these fibres.

(d) The unspun wool and hair (not illus)

Sample 28(293) had no staple formation (locks) nor crimp (waviness), but formed a layer of loose felt no more than 2mm thick. This appeared to be neither manufactured felt nor natural cotting of the fleece, but rather had come from the 'pilling' of clothing. The same mass of felt was obtained from the inside of some trousers of a 16th-century Basque whaler (Ryder 1989). In each case the felting process had increased the proportion of fine fibres so that the fibre diameter distribution was not typical of a fleece. Samples 29(294) and 30(300) were staples 20mm long and appeared to have come from lambs. They had close weaves and were of the same semi-fine fleece type, but not necessarily from the same fleece. There was no evidence (eg root ends) that this wool had come from skins after slaughter, so such raw wool indicates textile manufacture rather than skin working. These samples are important in indicating that the sheep with this fleece type were local since the cloth found could have been made elsewhere.

Samples 31(295) and 32(296) were goat hair 50mm and 90mm long. They had the hair diameter distribution of the summer coat (Table 10 and Chart 10) and were not necessarily going to be made into cloth, although the goat hair from medieval Perth was actually found in cloth (Table 11). They were probably from black animals and like the goat hair from Aberdeen reported (Ryder 1987a), these samples are identical to the hair of the surviving feral goats of Scotland (Ryder 1970, 335-62). The fibre diameter measurements are shown in Table 10.

**Table 10**: Fibre diameters, in microns

| Cat | Sample | Range | Mean +/- SD | Mode | % Pigment | % Medulla |
|---|---|---|---|---|---|---|
| **Goat** | | | | | | |
| 31 | 295 | 16-90 | 48.3 +/- 12.8 | 48 | 97 | obsc |
| 32 | 296 | 24-88 | 55.1 +/- 13.9 | 50 | 100 | obsc |
| **Hairy-Medium** | | | | | | |
| 28 | 293 | 14-32. 66 | 21.8 +/- 5.7 | 20 | 0 | 0 |
| 11.1 | 298/1 | 12-46, 58 | 24.6 +/- 7.8 | 20 | 0 | 1 |
| 13.1 | 302A/1 | 12-48, 56, 58, 64 | 26.5 +/- 9.8 | 20 | 65 | 1 |
| 13.2 | 302A/2 | 14-56, 62 | 28.6 +/- 9.7 | 28 | 54 | 1 |
| 14.2 | 302B/2 | 12-46, 60-110 | 30.1 +/- 18.7 | 20 | 3 | 7 |
| 17.2 | 320B/2 | 12-42, 52-78 | 26.0 +/- 9.8 | 22 | 0 | 1 |
| 19.1 | 321/1 | 14-56, 60 | 29.3 +/- 10.9 | 24 | 2 | 9 |
| 23.1 | 753C/1 | 10-46, 50, 68 | 25.0 +/- 9.1 | 20 | 3 | 0 |
| 23.3 | 753C/3 | 12-64 | 31.5 +/- 13.0 | 20 | 90 | 2 |
| 24.2 | 792/2 | 10-46, 52, 64 | 25.6 +/- 9.0 | 20 | 5 | 2 |
| **Generalised-medium** | | | | | | |
| 24.1 | 792/1 | 12-46, 50 | 24.6 +/- 7.8 | 20 | 1 | 1 |
| 2.1 | 81A/1 | 12-40, 46 | 23.2 +/- 6.9 | 22 | 7 | 0 |
| 2.2 | 81A/2 | 10-40, 48 | 22.3 +/- 6.7 | 20 | 8 | 3 |
| 14.1 | 302B/1 | 10, 14-48, 52 | 28.6 +/- 8.0 | 28 | 1 | 0 |
| 16.1 | 320A/1 | 12-44, 50 | 24.7 +/- 7.5 | (25) | ? | 0 |
| 16.2 | 320A/2 | 10-48, 54, 56 | 27.3 +/- 8.9 | (25) | 1 | 2 |
| 17.1 | 320B/1 | 14-50, 54, 56 | 28.2 +/- 9.1 | 20 | 0 | 0 |
| 19.2 | 321/2 | 14-42 | 25.4 +/- 7.5 | 20 | 1 | 1 |
| 21.1 | 753A/1 | 12-40 | 23.2 +/- 6.6 | 20 | 0 | 0 |
| 21.2 | 753A/2 | 12-38, 56 | 23.9 +/- 7.0 | (19) | 0 | 0 |
| 23.2 | 753C/2 | 14-44, 48 | 25.9 +/- 7.6 | 20 | 7 | 1 |
| **Fine Generalised-medium** | | | | | | |
| 1.1 | 48/1 | 10-38, 50, 56 | 19.3 +/- 7.3 | 14 | 21 | 3 |
| 1.2 | 48/2 | 10-38, 44 | 20.4 +/- 6.6 | 16 | 35 | 0 |
| 9.1 | 297B/1 | 10-40 | 21.5 +/- 6.2 | 20 | 0 | 0 |
| 9.2 | 297B/2 | 12-34 | 21.8 +/- 5.4 | 18 | 0 | 0 |
| **Semi-fine** | | | | | | |
| 5.1 | 139A/1 | 14-38 | 24.0 +/- 5.2 | 26 | 0 | 0 |
| 5.2 | 139A/2 | 12-42 | 25.4 +/- 6.0 | 20 | 0 | 0 |
| 29 | 294 | 14-42 | 25.6 +/- 5.6 | 26 | 10 | 0 |
| 11.2 | 298/2 | 12-38 | 23.7 +/- 5.8 | 22 | 0 | 0 |
| 12.1 | 299/1 | 12-44 | 24.4 +/- 6.6 | 20 | 0 | 0 |
| 12.2 | 299/2 | 12-40 | 23.7 +/- 5.8 | 22 | 0 | 1 |
| 30 | 300 | 16-44 | 27.6 +/- 6.1 | 28 | 1 | 0 |
| 15.1 | 302C/1 | 14-44, 50 | 25.8 +/- 6.9 | 26 | 0 | 0 |
| 15.2 | 302C/2 | 10-46 | 26.7 +/- 7.1 | 28 | 4 | 0 |

In the table, 1 micron = 0.001 mm; fibres outside the main range are listed separately; the mode is the most frequent diameter.

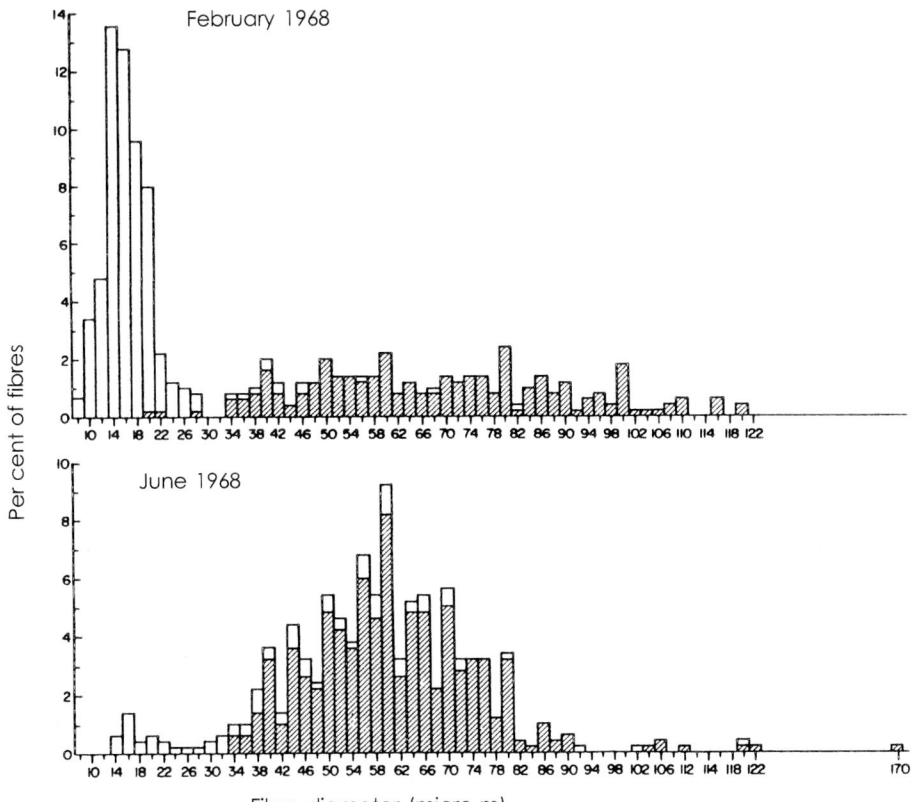

**Chart 10:**

Fibre diameter distributions from Scottish feral goats in February (top) when there is a big difference in diameter between the outer hair (right) ranging around 80 microns and the more numerous underwool fibres (left). In June (bottom) most of the underwool has been shed and the hairs, which are regrowing after the moult, range around 60 microns, being less coarse than they become in winter. The shaded parts of the bar chart indicate the proportion of hairs with a central medulla (from Ryder 1970)

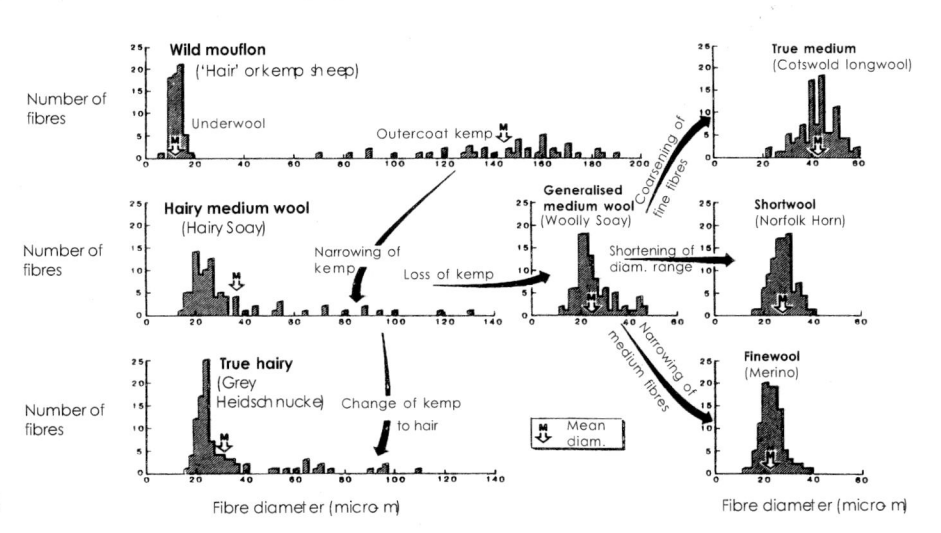

**Chart 11:**

Changes in the coat during the evolution of the fleece of domestic sheep. Each histogram represents a fibre diameter distribution defining a fleece type. The arrows indicate the changes that occurred when breeding caused one type of fleece to change into another. The main change has been a progressive narrowing of the outer coat kemp-hairs. These became finer as the coat of the Neolithic sheep (top left) changed into the first (Hairy-medium) fleece of the Bronze Age. Since this diagram was drawn, evidence has been obtained for early intermediate stages with only kemp and fine wool - the Hairy-medium fleece has fibres of medium diameter (derived from the outer coat) as well as the kemp and fine wool. The remaining finer kemps then changed into the medium fibres of the Generalized-medium fleece. Further narrowing made them into the fine fibres of the Finewool (bottom right). Other changes resulted in the Semi-fine (shortwool) and the Medium-wool (later seen in the longwool). The last three (modern) fleece types first appeared in the Iron Age and became more common during the Roman period. The Hairy type (bottom left) also appeared in the Iron Age when short kemps changed into long hairs (Ryder 1983). The breeds named are the examples used to illustrate the different fleece types.

(e) The fleece types and dyes in relation to the cloth

Although blue dye (Table 9) is usually thought to be woad and (dark) red dye to be madder, dyes cannot in fact be properly identified without chemical analysis. There were yellow and blue fibres in cloth no 5(139A) and pink and blue fibres in cloth no 11(298). It is interesting that the actual colour of the dyes was very clear. Any dyed colour has usually disappeared from buried textiles. At best, dye is seen as a diffuse grey discoloration; undyed wool usually has a yellow or brown discoloration, and the lack of this, dye, or natural pigment (distinguished by its granular nature) from cloths nos 9(297B) and 23(753C) almost certainly indicates that these were white.

The same dye in the warp and the weft does not prove that the cloth was woven from the same yarn, but rather indicates that the cloth was dyed in the piece. The same fleece type in the warp and the weft, does not necessarily mean that the wool was spun from the same fleece. Two extremes, however, are worthy of note: in cloth no 21(753A) the fibre diameter measurements of the two yarns are so close that the wool could well have come not only from the same fleece, but from the same part of the fleece; in cloth no 16(320A) the diameter values are so different that the wool must have come from different fleeces. It is common for warps to be spun from coarser wools than the wefts (eg in oriental carpets: Ryder 1987b), and so it is possible that the hairy medium fleece in cloth no 17(320B) came from the warp.

(f) Fleece types represented

All the fibre diameter distributions obtained represented recognisable fleece types, which indicates that they were spun direct from the fleece with no fibre blending (mixing). The earliest evidence for blending, which is usual in textile manufacture today, came from the clothing in the 16th-century *Mary Rose* wreck (Ryder 1984, 337-43). The fleece types found are listed in Table 10, together with their fibre measurements.

The Hairy-medium and Generalised-medium fleeces, which predominated among the Fast Castle wools, were the first to appear in the Bronze Age and were common until after the Middle Ages. They commonly had natural pigmentation, and are exemplified by the hairy and woolly types of the modern Orkney and Shetland breeds (Ryder 1983a, 531-9). Each has a skewed distribution of fibre diameter, the presence of hairy fibres greater than about 55 microns in diameter distinguishing the Hairy-medium type. Unspun sample no 28(293) was identified as mainly fine fibres from a fleece of this type, such separation being brought about by felting. The Generalised-medium type gave rise (in Iron Age and Roman times) to the three main modern types which have symmetrical fibre diameter distributions, and progressively lower means and modes: true Medium (often long), Semi-fine (often short) and Fine, which as the Merino breed is the main wool-producing sheep today (Chart 11, and Ryder 1987c, 112-19).

**Table 11**: Percentage of different fleece types found

|  | Goat | Hairy | Hairy - medium | Generalised- medium | Fine Gen- medium | Medium | Semi-fine | Fine |
|---|---|---|---|---|---|---|---|---|
| Perth | 4 | 18 | 42 | 17 | 7 | 8 | 4 | 0 |
| Aberdeen | 0 | 12.5 | 19 | 44 | 6 | 12.5 | 0 | 6 |
| Fast Castle | 5 | 2 | 27 | 30 | 11 | 0 | 25 | 0 |
| N. Scotland | 0 | 21 | 42 | 26 | 0 | 5 | 5 | 0 |

Table 11 gives a comparison with earlier and later finds. The 93 Perth and 16 Aberdeen wools of medieval date were published by Ryder (1983a, 514; 1983b, 33-41) and the 19 seventeenth-century yarns by Ryder (1988, 127-67), all of which came from the north of Scotland including Orkney and Shetland. From Table 11 it can be seen that Fast Castle had a similar range of fleece types to the other Scottish sites, except that Medium wools were lacking and, most strikingly, there was a much greater proportion of finer types, in particular a high proportion of the Semi-fine types.

The presence of raw wool of this type, which is unlikely to have been imported, suggests not only local manufacture of the cloth, but that some of the local sheep had a Semi-fine fleece. This accords with the early 16th-century description of Scottish sheep by Hector Boece as having 'such white, fine and excellent wool ...' and appears to represent what later came to be known as the Old Scottish Short-woolled sheep (Ryder 1983a, 505-509). This does not accord with a supposed worsening of the quality of Scottish wool during the 15th century owing to a deterioration of the climate (A W K Stevenson, quoted by Ryder 1983a, 509). The term quality as applied to wool means specifically fineness or fibre diameter, and a wet climate is unlikely to have reduced wool quality, ie made it coarser; but it could have reduced its value by increasing the number of faults such as cotting, which is caused by wetness. Archaeological remains have shown that the reputed fineness of medieval (particularly English) wool takes the form of Generalised-medium (woolly Shetland) fleeces, with few true Fine or Semi-fine examples. The high proportion of Semi-fine wools at Fast Castle is therefore of further interest because this fleece type later emerged in such English breeds as the Shropshire and Southdown, and it apparently died out in Scotland.

## CONCLUSIONS

The fibres were presumably preserved by damp conditions which excluded the air. That wool and silk were preserved, but no examples of bast fibres such as flax (except possibly in a short length of thread) suggests acid conditions, which favour the survival of the protein of animal fibres, but not the cellulose of plant fibres.

The presence of spun silk was confirmed by microscopic examination, the fibres being particularly fine. The unspun black goat hair was from animals killed in summer and was the same as found in a 15th-century tanning pit in Aberdeen. The Fast Castle hair was not necessarily either associated with skin working or with spinning.

The presence of the same dye in the warp and the weft indicates that the cloth was dyed 'in the piece' rather than 'in the wool'. The cloth was not necessarily made at this site, but the presence of raw wool indicates that it could have been.

A high proportion of relatively finer fleeces is in keeping with contemporary historical records of the fineness of Scottish wool and does not accord with the suggestion that Scottish wool became coarser during that period. It is interesting that the finer wools included a high proportion of the Semi-fine type, which later emerged in England in such breeds as the Shropshire and Southdown.

## 4 TEXTILE-ASSOCIATED OBJECTS

### The Spindle Whorls

Michael L Ryder & Thea Gabra-Sanders

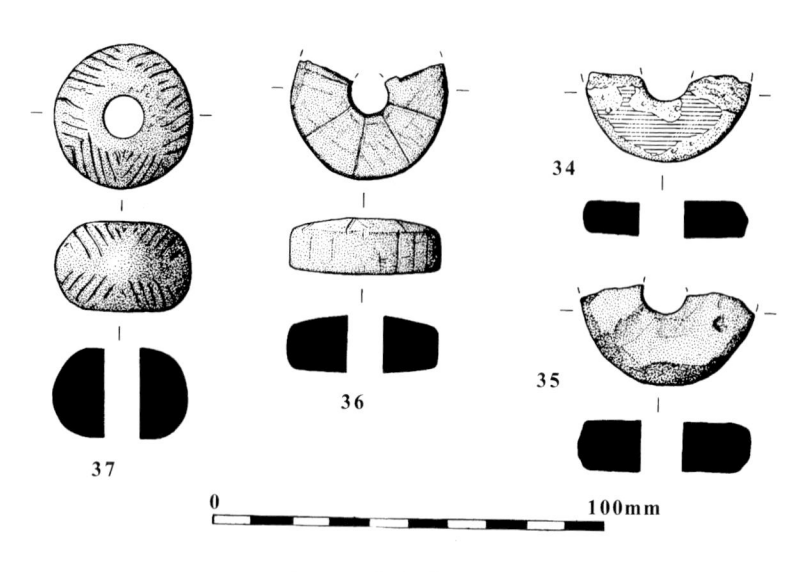

**Illus 66** Spindle whorls

The six spindle whorls found are described in Table 12. Nos 36(168) and 38(327) were found in Area 4 or 5, ie in the Quarry pit, associated with the cloth, and so dated late 15th-century; and nos 34(61) and 35(335) were dated independently as medieval. No 33(41), although dated as medieval, came from a layer of Area 8 dated as 16th-century, and no 37(62) (undated) came from a layer in Area 6. It is interesting that, when every possible kind of material has been used to make whorls, five were made from some kind of stone, and only one was of earthenware. The diameters of the whorls ranged from 33 to 45mm, ie greater than the optimum diameter of 25mm suggested by Ryder (1983a, 747). The size of the hole for the spindle was remarkably constant at about 10mm, which is in keeping with the observation of Ryder that few hand spindles are thicker than 10mm at their widest point. There was more variation in the thickness of the whorls (from 9 to 20mm), and in their weight (from an estimated 15.6g to 33.1g) than in the diameter. No whorl was as light as the 8g suggested by Ryder (1988) as being the heaviest weight of whorl that could be used to spin a woolly (Generalized-medium) Soay fleece in a free fall. But the range of weight of the Fast Castle whorls is comparable with the range of 10 to 34g recorded by MacGregor (1980) for early medieval whorls from Northampton, and the 11 to 31g recorded for medieval Perth (Bogdan 1980, pers comm).

**Table 12:** Spindle whorl catalogue with dimensions

| Cat | Period | Description | Material | Diam mm | Thkness mm | Hole diam. mm | Weight grammes |
|---|---|---|---|---|---|---|---|
| 33 | III.2 | Bun-shaped, decorated with punctuated and radial design; broken, (not illus) | Greywacke | 42 | 9 | 11 | 15.9 |
| 34 | III.1 | Broken, one half only, traces of green glaze | Earthenware | 41 | 10 | 10 | 7.8 (15.6) |
| 35 | III.1 | One half only | Stone | 45 | 11 | 10 | 12.3 (24.6) |
| 36 | II.2 | Decorated with 5 incisions on each side, about one third missing | Clay or siltstone | 39 | 12 | 10 | 20.1 (26.8) |
| 37 | II.2 | Faces and sides decorated with chevron design | Unidentified stone | 34 | 20 | 10 | 33.1 |
| 38 | II.2 | One half only, (not illus) | Stone | 33 | 14 | 7 | 11.3 (22.6) |

Notes: 1 Bracketed figures under weight are estimates for complete whorls
2 Another spindle whorl, made of sandstone, decorated with radial incised lines, has been reported in *Discovery and Excavation in Scotland* (1994), to have been found 'in a field near Fast Castle Head' (NT 862 706).
3 B Beddoe-Stephens has identified no 37(62) as 'Spindle whorl. Dark greenish-grey, fine grained (very fine sand to silt grade) clastic rock. Most probably a fine greywacke or tuffaceous silty sandstone. Colouration and hardness suggests Ordovician/Silurian affinity (eg Southern Uplands lower Palaeozoic)'.

## The Cloth Seal

Geoffrey Egan

39  Lead cloth seal.  Period II-III  (illus 67)

The incomplete two-disc lead seal is of the kind used (clamped) on textiles for quality regulation in the cloth industry from the 14th to the 19th centuries (Endrei & Egan 1982; Egan 1989). One disc has a label: 'VLM' in blackletter with three annulets above and below.  The other disc bears an incomplete stamp comprising part of a shield with: per fesse, grid in chief; V to left, L above, annulets between.  Both discs have a beaded border.

**Illus 67** Lead cloth seal

The south German city of Ulm is indicated as the source of the seal by the legends on each side, as well as by the civic arms (per fesse, sable and argent, ie black and silver or white, the grid being a conventional way of indicating black in monochrome representations of heraldry).  The seal is likely to have come from a fustian and a date in the late 16th or early 17th century is most likely from the use of blackletter together with Roman script.  Ulm was well known as a major producer of fustian (barchent) in the late medieval/early modern period (Kellenbenz 1983).  From the late 14th century there was a municipal inspection in the city, which became the centre of a wide hinterland of production of the local fustians made of cotton and linen. By the early 16th century over 100,000 pieces annually were sealed there, rising to a peak of over 430,000 in 1601.  These were mainly inexpensive black or white fabrics, most pieces being 18 yards (16.5m) long.  In the late 16th century the weaving of heavier bombazines with a hemp warp and a cotton weft began in Ulm, resulting in complaints of a decline in quality, and no fustians were inspected after 1660 (Mazzaoui 1981).  In England, Ulm textiles were known as 'holmes' from a corruption of the placename, and their import is frequently attested in late 16th- and early 17th-century documents (Wadsworth & Mann 1968).  It is therefore remarkable that apparently no Ulm seal has been recorded in England.  A similar one, with a different legend on the label, was recovered from the main drain of the Monastery at Paisley, Renfrew (PA91 109-112, acc no 260: Malden, pers comm), and a couple are known in France (Sabatier 1908).  In contrast, fustian seals from a rival manufacturer, the neighbouring city of Augsburg, are probably the most widely recorded of all categories of continental cloth seal found in Britain, having been found in over a dozen counties (Egan 1984, 1985).

## 5.14 LEATHER

### Clare Thomas

The 215 fragments of leather consist mainly of shoes but also include straps, waste material and pieces with iron studs. All were found within Period II.2 deposits of the Quarry pit, associated with textiles and wood, and date to the late 15th to very early 16th century (illus 69).

SHOES

Over half of the leather comprises shoe fragments - 31 from soles, 79 from uppers and 13 from welts and other stitching channels.

Construction

The shoes all appear to be of welted construction, where the upper is sewn, together with the welt, to the edge of an insole; the outer sole is then attached to the welt (illus 68). Eleven fragments of welt survive, each with two stitching channels. The stitch length of the inner channel, linking upper and insole, is usually 5-8.5mm, while that of the outer channel ranges from 6-11mm. Thirteen of the 31 sole fragments were identified as insoles, and four as outer soles. The insoles have edge-flesh stitching channels, similar to those on turnshoe soles, but with a longer stitch length. The use of such stitching channels is a feature of early welted shoes; later on, the upper and welt were stitched to a raised rib on the insole. The insoles were also made with the flesh side uppermost, which again is a feature of early welted construction. Later, the grain surface was placed uppermost. The insoles are all exceedingly thin, with maximum thickness of 2.5mm, compared to a turnshoe's 4-5mm. However, the grain surfaces were not exceedingly worn, indicating that they were protected by outer soles. The outer soles have grain-flesh stitching channels, with a stitch length, where it survives, of 7-7.5mm. All four examples are exceedingly worn.

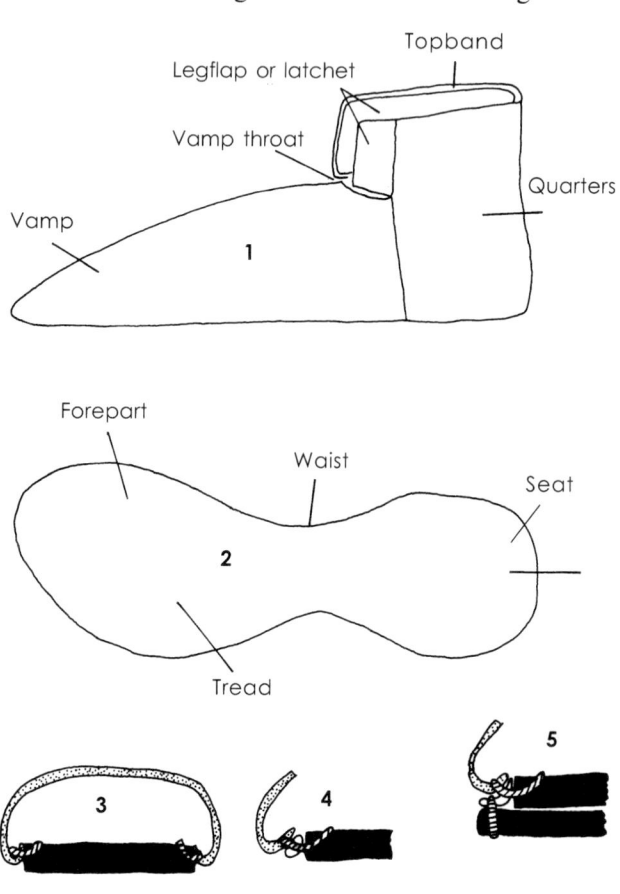

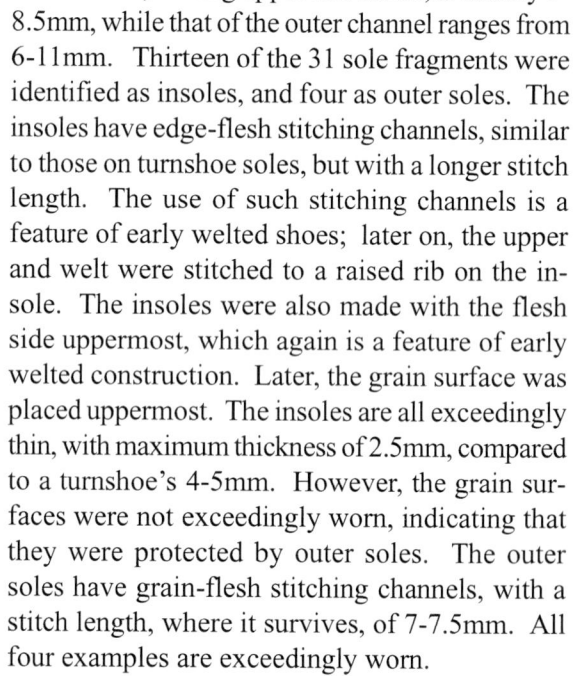

**Illus 68** Shoe construction diagram

Parts of shoe:
1 upper,
2 sole
Turnshoe construction:
3 without rand,
4 with rand,
5 with wide rand, to which extra sole has been attached
Welted construction:
6 welt stitched to underside of sole
7 welt stitched to edge of insole, using an edge-flesh stitch
8 welt stitched to upstanding rib on underside of insole

Fifty-eight fragments of upper have lasting margins with grain-flesh stitching channels, for attachment to welt and insole. Stitch lengths vary between 5 and 10mm. Five upper pieces have grain-flesh stitching channels which are not typical of lasting margins and are therefore probably for side-seams. Fragments of upper were usually joined together with butted edge-flesh stitching channels, 16 examples of which survive. Five semi-circular heel stiffeners demonstrate that the interior of the quarters of these shoes had been reinforced.

Repairs

Soles were repaired by the addition of clump soles, attached by tunnel stitching, as indicated by five surviving clumps. Repairs to insole-welt-upper seams are suggested by some examples of closely grouped stitch holes or by irregular stitch lengths. On one insole the original edge-flesh stitching channel was replaced by a grain-flesh one.

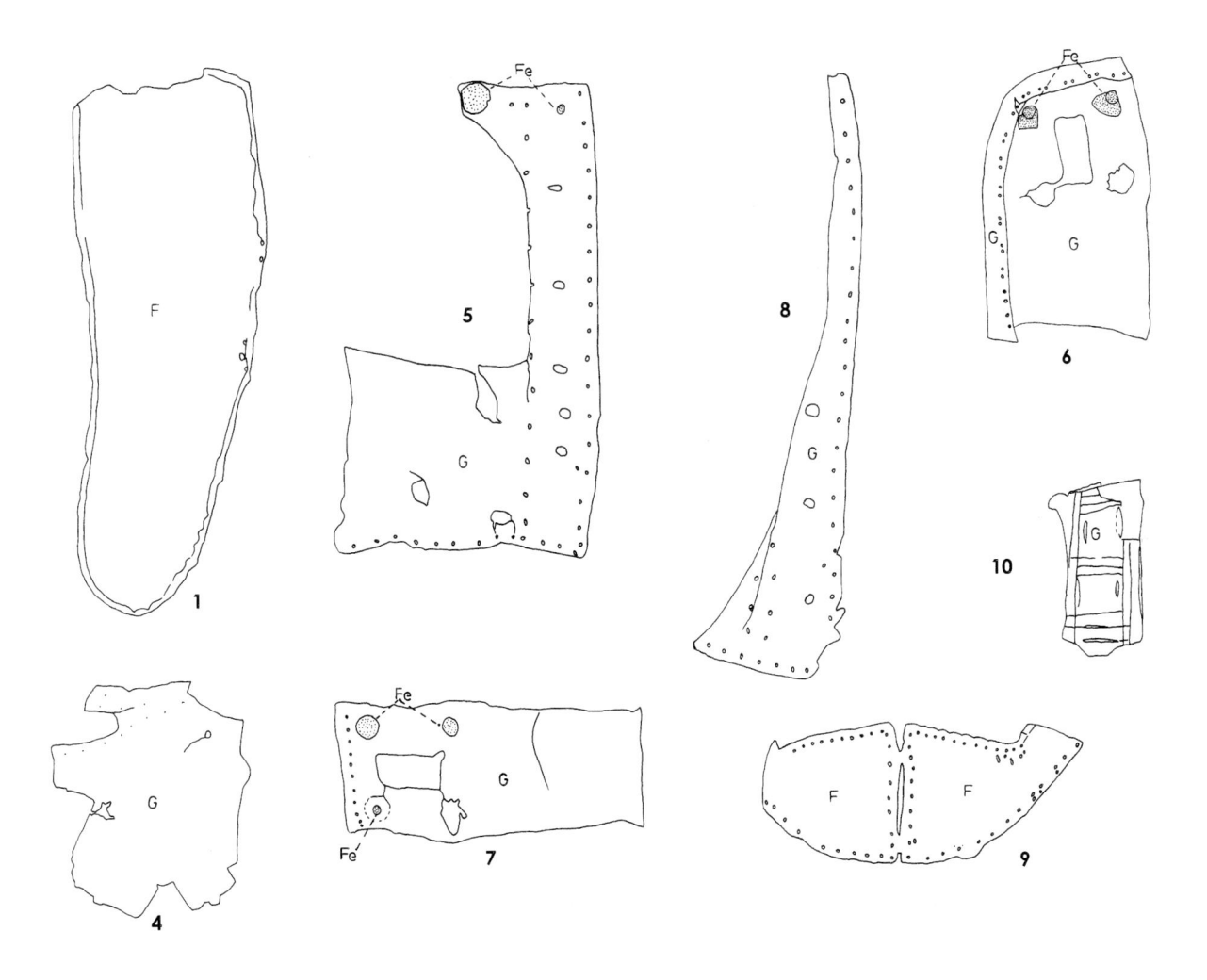

**Illus 69** Leather: Scale 1:3

1. Insole; 4. Stitched fragment; 5. Fragment with studs and stud-holes; 6. Fragment with studs, stud-holes and binding; 7. Fragment with stud-holes; 8. Fragment with lace-holes; 9 Fragment of upper with vamp throat and part of latchet; 10. Decorated fragment. F=flesh, G=grain.

STYLES

Soles

There is little evidence as to sole styles, as only one nearly complete sole (no 1) survives. This is straight-sided, with a slender seat and no narrowing at the waist. The front of the forepart is missing but appears to have ended in a blunt, square-cut toe, similar to that of another sole fragment (no 2 - not illus).

Uppers

There is a similar paucity of information as to upper styles. The few fragments of vamp and quarters suggest low cut shoes, possibly even a slight slipper (no 3 - not illus), with vamp separate from quarters and with true quarters, each shoe having two pieces joined with a backseam. The sole styles suggest the use of eared toe pieces, but none survive. Swann suggests that round and square toes date from c1490 onwards. She also dates to the same period shoes with short, square-cut vamps and low sides (Swann 1973, 21-3). An eared shoe with insole similar to no 1 found at Hall Place, St.Neots, was dated, on stylistic and contextual grounds, to the first half of the 16th century.

Fragments with Stud- or Lace-holes

Three fragments have remains of iron studs. On one example (no 5) these are set in two rows, at right angles. On the other two fragments the studs have been placed at the corners of a rectangular cut-out. Both these fragments have had at least one edge bound with a wide strip of leather, folded once (nos 6 & 7). A fourth fragment bears no trace of iron studs, but has three oval lace-holes. These fragments are possibly parts of clothing.

Bindings

Six folded strips are almost certainly bindings, stitched in position to protect a cut edge of leather. Their widths vary between 4 and 9mm. The narrower examples, c4-7mm, were probably used on shoes, while the wider one (no 11 - not illus) at 8-9mm may have been attached to an item of clothing, as, for instance, on nos 6 and 7.

Straps

This group consists of 16 straps of single thickness, three thongs and three other fastenings. Nine of the straps of single thickness have been stitched along each long edge; another two have been stitched at one end. Eight straps have central holes, oval or round, except in one case, where the holes are slits, through which a thong or something similar has once been threaded.

Waste material

The waste material comprises 24 offcuts and 18 scraps almost all of which are very worn. The offcuts consist of fourteen strips, four triangular, one annular piece, one oblong and four irregularly-shaped fragments. One triangular offcut with two concave sides resembles those resulting from sole cutting-out but is probably too thin and worn (no 12 - not illus). Otherwise there is no evidence to suggest shoe-making. The worn nature of the offcuts suggests that any leather working represented here consisted of repair and re-use. The assemblage also included seventeen miscellaneous stitched fragments. One (no 10) decorated piece might be part of a knife sheath.

## FOLLICLE ANALYSIS

Hair follicle analysis was used to determine the animal species used for the leather. This proved possible for approximately 23% of the assemblage. The only follicle pattern recognised was that characteristic of cattlehide. No trace of goatskin was found. The cattlehide pattern was found on leather of all kinds, but most notably on uppers, welts, straps and bindings. This is to be expected, as in these cases the grain surface is often at least partly protected from excessive wear, unlike for instance, that of soles. The poor survival rate of this pattern on the offcuts is attributable to their worn state. Offcuts resulting from work with new leather usually produce a very clear follicle pattern.

**Table 13**: Leather: hair follicle analysis

| Type of Artefact | Total number each type | Number identified | Percentage identified |
| --- | --- | --- | --- |
| Sole | 31 | 1 | 3% |
| Upper | 79 | 25 | 31.5% |
| Welt | 13 | 6 | 46% |
| Fragments with studs | 4 | 1 | 25% |
| Misc. stitched fragments | 17 | 3 | 17.5% |
| Straps | 22 | 7 | 32% |
| Bindings | 6 | 3 | 50% |
| Offcuts | 24 | 3 | 12.5% |
| Scraps | 19 | 1 | 5.3% |
| Total | 215 | 50 | 23% |

## CONCLUSION

Welted shoe construction is believed to be a 16th-century innovation. Unfortunately, there is little clear evidence as to its earliest use. Thornton dates its introduction to 'about AD 1500', but does not give any supporting evidence, apart from a reference to 'an early Tudor shoe' (1973a, 11). The only other known early examples from Scotland are from Skirling Castle, Peeblesshire (mid 16th-century) and from Mounthoolie Lane, Kirkwall, Orkney (16th-century) (Dunbar 1963, 244; Thomas 1982, 413-6). Accordingly, the dating of these welted shoes from Fast Castle to the late 15th/early 16th century is most significant. So this is a very important assemblage, despite its apparent lack of stylistic information.

### CATALOGUE (illus 69)

The following is a catalogue of the 12 items referred to and/or illustrated. The full catalogue (215 items) is available in the archive.

**1 Insole.** Almost complete sole, probably right foot, welted insole, missing front of forepart, which appears to end with a blunt, square cut toe. Straight-sided forepart, no narrowing for waist, narrow seat. Edge-flesh stitching channel, stitch length 8-9mm. Stitching channel worn away along parts of the outer edge, from rear of forepart to rear of seat; replaced with grain-flesh holes. Worn, especially at front and outer edge. Small hole in centre forepart, two small cracks in seat. Surface cracks on grain side, which is not, however, very worn. Slightly delaminated. Length 230mm, width of seat c57mm, width of waist c62mm, maximum width of forepart 80mm, width at front of forepart c75mm. Thickness not measured because of delamination but even edge-flesh stitching channels appear thin. Stitch length, shape, square toe, thinness, lack of wear on grain side - all these factors suggest that this is a welted insole. Possibly had eared toe-piece attached. Cattlehide.

**2 Insole fragment.** Small fragment of insole, possibly front of square-toed forepart. Edge-flesh stitching channel, stitch length 8mm. Cracked, torn, c75 x 30 x 1.5mm. (not illus)

**3 Vamp fragment?**, with throat, and inner and outer wings, but missing toe.
**(a)** Lasting margin with grain-flesh stitching channel, stitch length c9-10mm, worn, survives on both inner and outer edges;
**(b)** Edge-flesh stitching channel on vertical edges of both vamp

wings, stitch length 4mm;

**(c)** Hem stitch at vamp throat. Vamp throat is probably very low, and cut straight across, with a short V-shaped cut, 18mm long, towards toe. Edges of cut have also been oversewn;

**(d)** Top edges of vamp wings very worn, probably oversewn;

**(e)** Approximately oval slit near top corner of each vamp wing - for fastening?

Front of vamp missing; suggestion of triangular cut-out between vamp throat and toe. If vamp, very shallow slipper-height of wings, only c35mm. Thickness c2mm. Exceedingly worn and partially delaminated. (not illus)

**4** Upper fragment. Irregularly shaped fragment, with faint trace of stitching at what may be vamp throat, with beginning of latchet above. Very worn, c99 x 84 x 1mm.

**5** Fragment with studs and stud holes. Approximately oblong fragment, with part now cut out. Vertical row of six holes, three round, diameter c4mm; three oval c3.5mm; seventh hole at right angles; it and top hole contain remnants of iron studs. Other five holes bear traces of studs; this is particularly marked on flesh side of second hole from bottom. First hole is c43mm from bottom. Rest are 17, 19, 35, 40, 32, and 35mm apart. There are also three other holes, probably caused by wear. Grain-flesh stitching channel parallel to bottom edge, mostly round stitch holes diameter c1mm, stitch length 7-9mm - **not** lasting margin. Grain to flesh stitching channel on either side of stud holes, hole diameter c1mm, stitch length 11-12.5mm, probably for attachment of facing. Worn; c196 x 27-107 x 1mm. Cattlehide. Clothing? Most probably **not** upper.

**6** Fragment with studs, stud holes and binding. Approximately oblong fragment, with one rounded corner with wide binding enclosing it on two sides. Third and fourth sides roughly cut. Near rounded corner rectangular hole, c15 x 29mm. Between hole and short edge with binding, two iron studs plus concretions. At other end of rectangular hole, two round holes, diameter c12mm and 11mm. Fragment has grain-flesh stitching channel, stitch length 5mm, for attachment of binding. Binding has similar grain-flesh stitching channel on both edges; holes are very obviously in pairs. Worn. c118 x 70 x 1-2mm. Clothing?

**7** Fragment with studs, stud holes and binding. Approximately rectangular fragment with long edges irregularly cut. Grain-flesh stitching channels on both short edges, stitch length 11mm at one end, 6mm at the other end, hole diameter c1mm. At latter end, rectangular cut-out, c28 x 13mm, with remains of three iron studs, and hole for fourth, one at each corner of rectangular hole. Worn, c130 x 57 x 1.5mm. Fragment of binding now separate and opened out, with grain-flesh stitching channel, matches end of main fragment with 6mm stitch length. Worn, c53 x 22 x 0.75mm.

**8** Stitched fragment with lace-holes. Large, approximately triangular fragment, with right angle. Grain-flesh stitching channels, stitch length c10-11.5mm and 7.5mm on long and short arms of right angle respectively. Stitching channel on short arms bent inwards slightly. Three oval lace-holes, 3.5 x 5.5mm, c40mm apart, parallel to long stitched edge. Third edge cut irregularly, split at one end, which has been stitched. Repair. Right angle very worn. c250 x 10-55 x 2mm, Clothing?

**9** Stitched fragment. Approximately oval fragment, almost completely divided into two pieces.

**(a)** Curved outer edge, grain-flesh stitching channel, stitch length 6.5-8mm. Edge cut as if by thread - oversewn? or repair?

**(b)** Fairly short straight edge, oversewn;

**(c)** Short cut edge;

**(d)** Short torn edge;

**(e)** Fragment has been cut from middle of (a) to middle of (b) but is still joined together near (a) and c11mm from (b). Area between sewn with butted edge-flesh seam, stitch length 6.5mm. Worn. c135 x 22-56 x 3mm. Divided for flexibility?

**10** Decorated fragment. Folded fragment, apparently flattened tube or cylinder, no visible joins. Appears to contain folded fragment, but this is possibly a delaminated inner layer. Traces of stitching. On one side incised decoration, two parallel lines roughly parallel to each edge; within this band, three lots of roughly parallel lines, linked to the border lines. Some of these lines cut through the outer layer. Also three short lines which cut through outer layer. Lower part of knife sheath? Exceedingly worn and delaminated. Length c70mm, width c31-40mm.

**11** Two fragments of binding. Folded once, stitched with grain-flesh stitching, hole diameter c1.5mm, stitch length 6.5-8mm; c160 x 8-9 x 1mm and 490 x 8-9 x 1mm. Cattlehide. (not illus)

**12** Triangular offcut. Two concave sides. Worn; c45 x 53 x 2mm. (not illus)

## 5.15 WOOD

### Keith L Mitchell & Hugh P Dinwoodie

Over 450 pieces of wood were recovered from the Lower Courtyard, and more than 300 from the Well shaft. Almost all of the items from the Courtyard were recorded in Period II contexts in the Quarry pit. They were found in association with leather and textiles, and had survived due to the same anaerobic conditions: the wood from the Well shaft survived in completely waterlogged conditions. The species of approximately 15% of the assemblage have been identified. These include alder, birch, hazel, oak, silver birch, willow, and possibly common juniper. It is assumed that the majority represent timber which grew locally.

QUARRY PIT

Of the overall total of over 450 items, around 100 had been worked but only five complete artefacts were found. If the postulated identifications are correct, these are a wedge (no 14), two tools (nos 11 and 12) and two pegs (nos 20 and 21). The remainder includes partial artefacts, offcuts and general waste. Of particular interest are a beam (no 1) and a reputed woodworking plane (no 11), possibly for making wedge-like objects similar to no 14. The shape and quality of no 16 suggest that it may have been a panel from a small box, and at least three bucket staves (nos 8-10) were recovered.

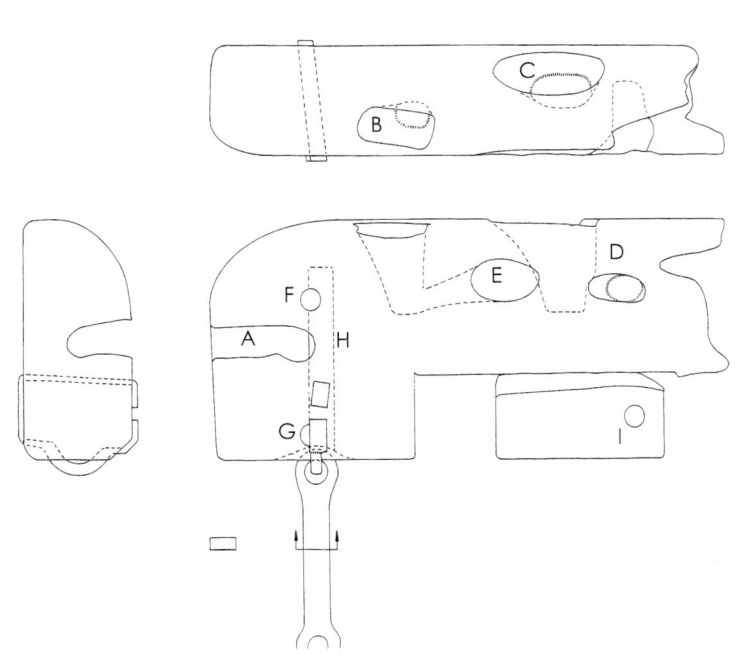

**Illus 70** Wooden beam (Cat no 1), scale 1:8

The complex beam end with iron fittings (Plates XV, XVI; illus 70) is believed to have been associated with lifting, suspension or, just possibly, haulage apparatus. Suggestions include a pawl or brake bar for a windlass, part of a gun carriage or part of a crane jib. The piece has been repaired and the number of holes may indicate re-use. Another substantial beam (no 2), with a chamfered edge and a concave depression 250mm across, has been identified as part of a barrel rack. The barrel it supported would have been quite small, approximate diameter 400mm, and may have contained gunpowder. A large, roughly trimmed, branch (no 3) may have had some crude structural function. The assemblage from the Quarry pit also included 376 pieces of branch, twig and root, and about 40 miscellaneous splinters. Of these, 240 were from Period II.2, half from a single context, F104. Forty one pieces showed evidence of charring.

WELL

Of more than 300 items from the Well shaft, only five were worked wood and one (no 7) may have been part of a ladder. The remainder were small pieces of branch, mostly between 50 and 170mm in length. This part of the assemblage consisted of 34.7% silver birch and 11.3% hawthorn; 54% unidentified. The majority had been cut or snapped. The Well operated as a catchment for hill run-off rather than deriving from a spring; consequently, it is likely to have been cleaned out on a regular basis. The material recovered from the Well shaft therefore probably dates, at the earliest, to the end of the occupation of the castle, and perhaps to considerably later.

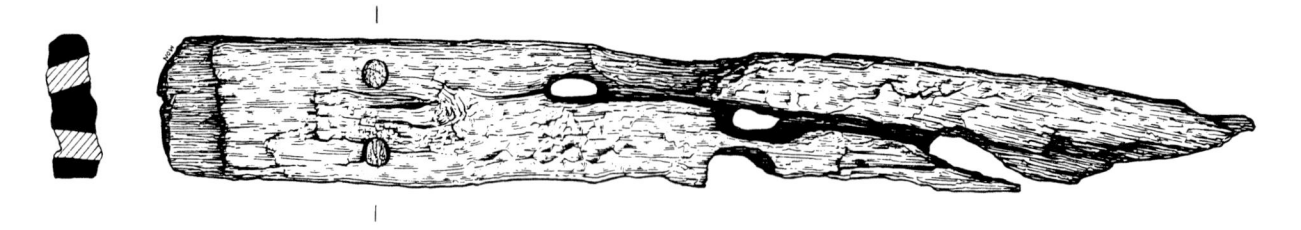

Illus 71  Barrel rack beam (Cat no 2). Scale 1:8

## CATALOGUE

**1** Oak beam fabricated from timber of maximum section 220mm x 110mm, overall surviving length 500mm (illus 70; Plates XV, XVI). Originally in one piece but block 170mm x 110mm x 80mm now detached. Deep scoring on one side of the beam appears to represent wear, and the underside of the detached block has numerous cut, saw and score marks. The slightly curved profile of one side of the beam suggests that side may be close to the sapwood and could ultimately provide a useful dendrochronological date. The beam carries a wrought iron mount which in turn articulates with a short wrought iron connecting bar, free to move in two axes (see Iron report, Chap 5.9, no 66). Four irregularly-shaped man-made holes A-D have been let into the beam; all are blind (ie they do not extend all of the way through the beam). A fifth hole, created by the popping of a knot, joins up with hole B, but whether this is deliberate or fortuitous is not known. The complex hole A appears to have been originally two holes and accommodated some form of fixing. The beam appears to have split at this point, and has been repaired by the insertion of dowel H, itself held in place by the pinning dowels F and G. It may be that the repair was augmented by the use of glue but modern fillers, to stabilise the timber during conservation, have obscured any evidence thereof. Certainly, without the use of an adhesive, the repaired beam would have considerably less mechanical strength than in its original form. A fourth dowel, I, has been let into the detached block. Dowels F, G and I are 18mm diameter and dowel H is 25mm diameter. All of the dowels are let into blind holes, and it would not have been possible to insert dowel H with the wrought iron mount in position, therefore the mount must have been fitted later. A check 80mm square has been let into what is presumed to be the underside of the beam, perhaps to allow it to rest on a cross member and the neatly cut ends of the detached block suggest that another check had been cut 170mm distant from the first. The end of the main beam is badly rotted and broken at this point. F103; Period II.2.

The Holes:

**A** - Maximum 100mm x 30mm x 65mm deep, looks to have been originally two holes c25mm diameter with centre pitch of 45mm.

**B** - Maximum 70mm x 40mm x 85mm deep, narrows to c30mm diameter at base (possible original shape of hole). Joins up with knot hole E but inner edge of junction is still quite sharp indicating little or no wear.
**C** - Maximum 110mm x 40mm x 85mm deep, narrowing to 55mm x 28mm at base, no evidence of hole originally being circular. Note: Since holes B and C are the same depth, it is suggested that they are contemporary. They are let in from opposite sides of the 'upper' face of the beam and are angled slightly inwards.
**D** - Slightly elliptical, 30mm x 25mm, but beam shows signs of shrinkage hereabouts; therefore the hole may originally have been circular.
**E** - Knot hole 65mm x 43mm at surface narrowing to c17mm diameter at junction with hole B. The hole runs obliquely at approximately 30 degrees to the finished surface of the beam.

**2** Barrel rack beam - incomplete (gunpowder barrel?) (illus 71). Part of beam, cross-section 150 x 50mm (= 6 x 2ins). Traces of burning, and decay, at one end. Features are: a half-lap check out at one end; two symmetrically placed circular dowel holes towards that end, complete with dowels (diameter 30mm) flush with surface; three elliptical holes approx 50 x 20mm. One edge planed flat, with similar rounded hole cut in it. Another edge rounded or chamfered over a length of 250mm, with signs of tool marks. May have had multiple secondary uses over time, similar to no 1. 1195 x 140mm, at broadest. F103; Period II.2

**3** Structural support? Large branch, in two pieces, bearing at least three gouge marks some 200mm apart, into which other wood or metal may have been inserted. Some charring. 1016 x (51-60) x (25-41)mm thick (not illus). F103; Period II.2

**4** Structural support? Worked on all surfaces, with traces of burning. May be part of no 5. Oak. 286 x 57 x 32mm (not illus). F100-104; Period II.2

**5** Structural support? As no 4; broadest end broken, other end pointed. Oak. 247 x 41mm, to point (not illus). F100-104; Period II.2

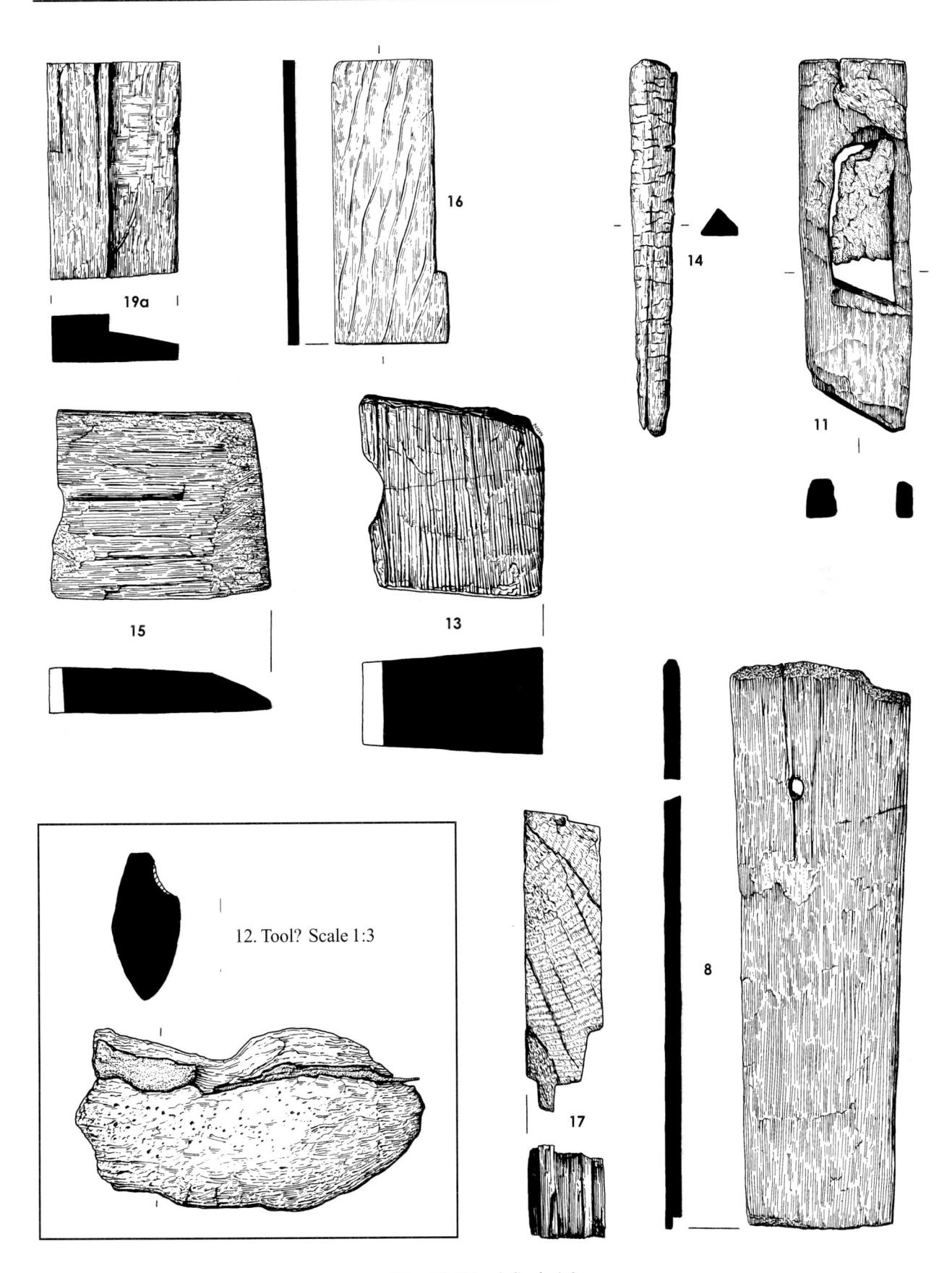

**Illus 72:** Wood: Scale 1:2.
8. Bucket stave; 11. Plane; 13. Block (three worked surfaces); 14. Wedge;
15. Barrel stave?; 16. Box panel; 17. Moulding; 19a. Moulding;

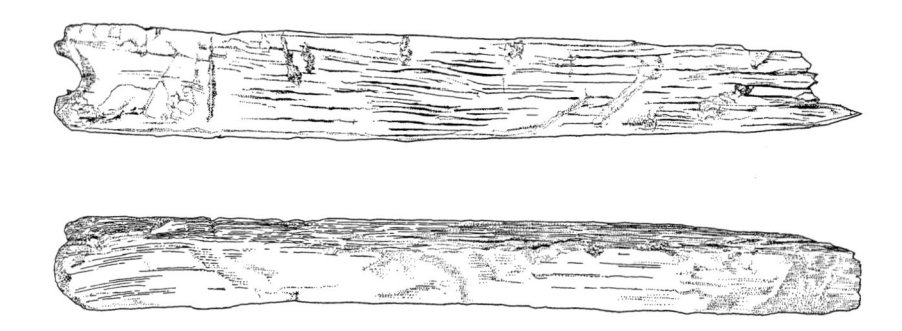

**Illus 73** Wood: Ladder fragment. Scale 1:4.

**6** Structural support? Three pieces of birch, perhaps parts of same object; 293 x 54mm; 178 x 57mm; 308 x 48mm (not illus). F104; Period II.2

**7** Ladder fragment? 432 x 51 x 38mm (illus 73). Base of Well

**8** Bucket-stave (illus 72.8). One nail or knot-hole. Resembles no 9, though thinner. 206 x 57 x 6mm. Unstratified

**9** Bucket stave fragment? Flat, oblong; two semi-circular holes scalloped out, along one edge. Resembles no 8. Probably oak. 120 x 51mm (not illus). F100-103; Period II.2

**10** Stave fragment? See also nos 8 & 9. Part of larger flat piece, one end burnt. Three chamfers at end. Two holes, one a nail hole, the other perhaps for dowel or rope. 38 x 73 x 6mm (not illus). F100a; Period II.2

**11** Plane (wedge- or peg-maker?) (illus 72.11). Oblong; one end has angled cut. Roughly oblong recess in centre, containing a corroded piece of iron as blade. See Iron report, no 27. (135-117) x 38 x (13-14)mm. Unstratified

**12** Tool? (eg plane) (illus 72.12). Roughly rounded. Embedded within upper surface is a length of iron (blade?). See Iron report, no 67. 200 x 102, x 54mm at top, x 13-19mm at bottom. F100-103?; Period II.2

**13** Block (illus 72.13). Three worked surfaces; semi-circular dent in one side, with possible remains of a dowel hole. Oak. 67 x 67 x 38mm. F100b; Period II.2

**14** Wedge or peg (illus 72.14). 140 x 13 x 19 x 6mm. F104; Period II.2

**15** Wedge (or end of large barrel stave?) (illus 72.15). Roughly oblong, slightly tapered. One end has semi-circular dent suggesting hammer-blow. Oak. 83 x 70 x 13mm. F104; Period II.2

**16** Container fragment? (illus 72.16). High quality workmanship. Smooth surfaces, all four sides cut. Rebate 78 x 3mm, cut into one side. Perhaps common juniper. 103 x 38 x 3mm. F104; Period II.2

**17** Moulding (illus 72.17). See nos 18 & 19. Soft wood. 108 x 29 x 29mm. F100b; Period II.2

**18** Moulding. (not illus) see nos 17 & 19. One end cut at angle, other broken. Oak. 127 x 32 x 13mm. F100a; Period II.2

**19** Moulding(s). Two similar offcuts, now warped. Oak. (a) 76 x 48 x 16mm (illus 72.19a); (b) 76 x 48 x 6mm (not illus). F103b; Period II.2

**20** Peg? Crudely worked; pointed; notch near top 41 x 14mm. Oak. 178 x 51mm at broadest (not illus). F104; Period II.2

**21** Peg? Roughly worked overall, knob at one end. 128 x 16 (knob), x 9 (shaft) x 6mm (not illus). F100a; Period II.2

**22** Offcut, sawn and planed. Oak. 22 x 87 x 51mm (not illus). F100-103; Period II.2

## 5.16 WORKED BONE
### (Skeletal artefacts)

Ywonne Hallén
(with an addendum by Fraser Hunter)

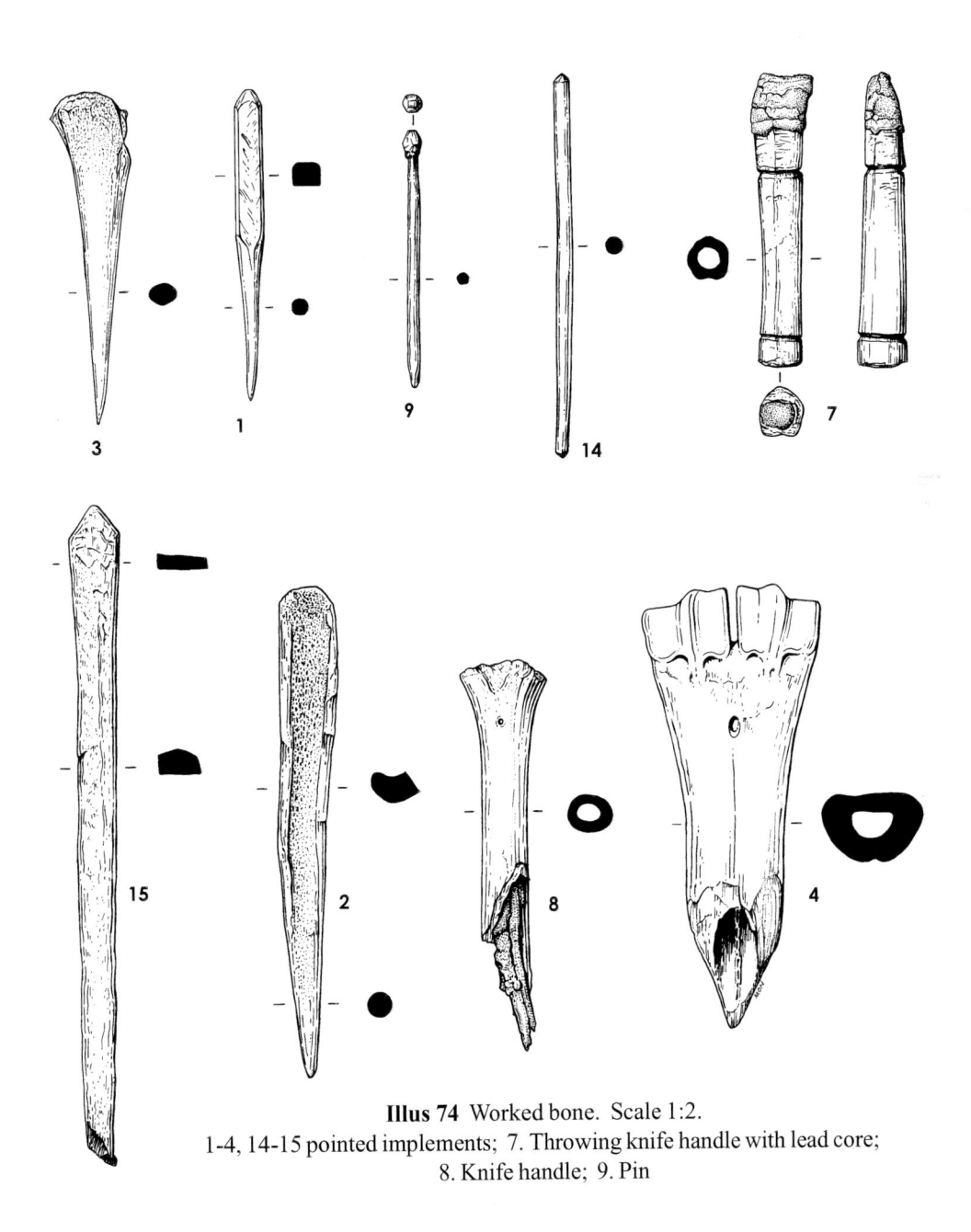

**Illus 74** Worked bone. Scale 1:2.
1-4, 14-15 pointed implements; 7. Throwing knife handle with lead core;
8. Knife handle; 9. Pin

## PIERCING IMPLEMENTS

The category of piercing implements, as here described, relates to four implements with a pointed end, worn by use. No more specific purpose can be reliably assigned from their morphology or find context. Piercing tools are common on sites from many different periods. The raw material may differ but they are generally made from splinters of longitudinally-cut long bones (as with no 2), from a slice of compact bone (no 1) or from naturally pointed bones which have had one end sharpened (no 3).

One end of no 3 is trimmed into a circular-sectioned point, with a high polish from manufacture and use extending about 40mm from the tip. No 4 is a simpler implement to make, since less of the bone is removed. It was made from a cattle metacarpal, struck almost mid-shaft in order to leave the articular end complete and to produce a length of attached diaphysis which was shaped into a blunt point, stouter than those of the other implements in this category.

ONE-PIECE DOUBLE-SIDED COMB

From the 11th century onwards, one-piece combs once more began to gain favour for everyday use over those of composite construction. Although antler continued to be used for some of them, a marked preference for skeletal bone can be detected at this time. For example cattle or horse tibiae were of sufficient size to provide the large flat plaques of bone these one-piece combs required. From later medieval contexts, examples made of ivory and box-wood are found (MacGregor 1985, 81f). It has been suggested that the horn industry rose in the medieval period, but archaeological evidence is scarce, probably because horn is prone to decay in the ground (*ibid*, 51). Horn combs are rare finds, for the same reason. However, a few such combs are recorded from Viking and medieval contexts in Britain (*ibid*, 95f). Undecorated combs with the same slender cross-section as the Fast Castle example seem to date to the late medieval period (*ibid*, 81).

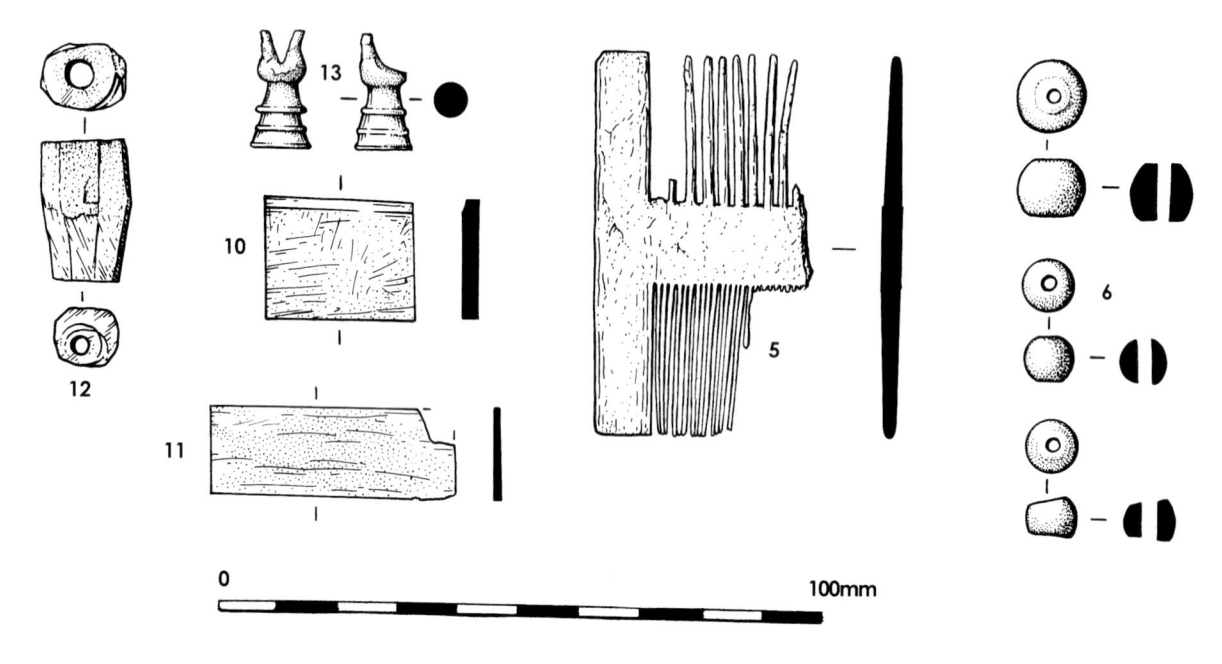

**Illus 75** Worked bone:
5. Double sided comb; 6. Beads; 10-11. Antler plates; 12. Unfinished bead(s)?; 13. playing piece.

PLAYING PIECE

No 13 may have been carved with a knife. It is unlikely that it was worn on a cord as an amulet, with a string attached around the grooves, as no smoothening from wear is visible. Rather, it is probably a playing piece, used with the plano-concave end downwards. Walrus ivory increased in popularity from the late 10th century to the 12th or 13th centuries as a raw material for working into secular and religious objects, as a result of the expanding commercial and political relations which developed with Scandinavia during this period (MacGregor 1985, 40f). Playing pieces of walrus ivory, although different from the specimen from Fast Castle, are not uncommon. (*ibid*, 135ff).

## BONE BEADS

Twenty bone beads were all found together. It is only possible with the larger beads to determine the method of manufacture. They were drilled perpendicularly from a longitudinally-cut long bone: flaking around the perforations revealed the direction of the cancellous tissue. All the beads have been lathe turned. This was a common way of making bone beads during medieval times (MacGregor 1985, 99ff; Holden 1963, 175f; Williams 1979, 318, fig 141).

Editors' note: It has been suggested that these may represent part of a rosary (Caldwell, pers comm) and they are illustrated in this way.

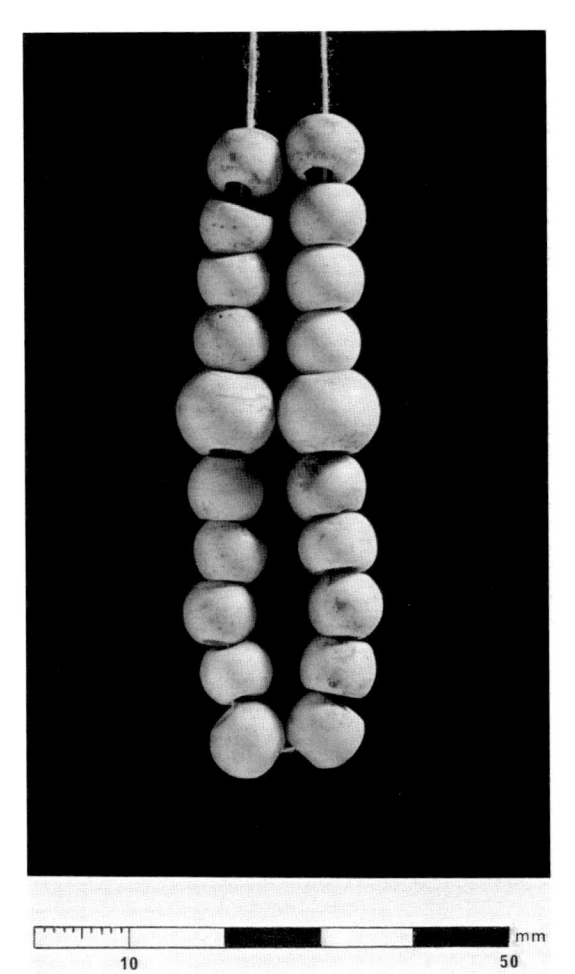

## KNIFE HANDLES

Knife handles with lead cores, as no7, appear to be rare: for example, Cowgill *et al*'s (1987) comprehensive survey of medieval knives from excavations in the City of London contains no parallels. Both knives with a tapered tang, inserted into or through the handle ('whittle-tang'), and knives with wider and flatter tangs, onto which the plates of the handle were riveted, are found from the Roman period through to medieval times (MacGregor 1985, 167ff; Cowgill *et al* 1987, 78). However, it seems unusual to have the articulation of the bone retained and untrimmed.

## BONE 'PIN'

The only parallel to the bone 'pin' (no 9) is a single atypical late Roman pin from Colchester (Crummy 1992, 146: fig 5.2, no 220). It obviously cannot be concluded from this single southern English parallel that the bone pin from Fast Castle is of Roman date. However, the general adoption of buttons rather than pins for fastening clothing in the medieval period (MacGregor 1985, 113) makes a pre-medieval date more likely.

**Illus 76** Bone beads

## PLATES

Plates similar to nos 10 and 11 are usually found amongst debris from composite comb manufacture, a comb type which survived into medieval times (see above, no 5) (MacGregor 1985, 77). The method involved in the making of sideplates and teethplates for composite combs of antler has been reconstructed on the basis of waste material (*ibid*, 70, fig 42). Initially a sawn-off tine or beam was split longitudinally. The piece was further trimmed to the preferred size and then polished. This method is likely to have been used for nos 10 and perhaps no 11 as well. Striations from polishing are visible on both plates.

## DEBRIS FROM BEAD MANUFACTURE?

The object, no 12, is stained with a red colour, concentrated around the narrower end with less at the other end. Red staining has been noted on a number of objects, for example the Lewis chessmen (Madden 1832, quoted in MacGregor 1985, 70). A socketed object from the wheelhouse at Sollas, North Uist was stained with the red pigment haematite, possibly connected with crushed haematite found in vessels from the same area (Campbell E 1991, fiche 3:B4, no 689). Numerous waste fragments from bead or button making are found from the medieval period. Finds of drilled long bones show that the holes were drilled first from one side of the bone and then the other. The implement used for drilling is believed to have been a centre-bit drill with a curving profile and an extended central point which, when it had penetrated the bone from one side, allowed the drill to be aligned on the same spot from the other (MacGregor 1985, 99ff). It is possible that this object is associated with the making of the beads, in view of the number of beads found on the site (see above, no 6). The fact that the drilled hole is off-centre may have been the reason for discarding it.

## DISCUSSION

All of the objects, apart from nos 12 and 15, were found in the lower layers of the Quarry pit. The excavators date these contexts to the late 15th to early 16th century. No 11 comes from a 16th- or early 17th-century context.

The range of artefacts from Fast Castle varies in terms of function, raw material and techniques of manufacture. The one-piece double-sided comb and the bone beads have good medieval parallels, while piercing implements, knife handles such as no 8, and plates of bone and antler are not confined to one specific archaeological period. No parallel to the knife handle with a lead core was found. A parallel to the roughly made bone 'pin' is from a late Roman context, but neither example fits well into the recognised typology of datable pins (cf MacGregor 1985, 113ff). The use of pins for fastening clothing was replaced by the general adoption of buttons during the medieval period. The Fast Castle example, and indeed the Colchester specimen, are crudely made. It is unlikely that they were used as pins in the normal sense, since these have a decorative value. These 'pins' may instead have had a different function. The date of the Fast Castle example is difficult to establish but it may be pre-medieval.

Although unparallelled at present, the possible gaming-piece is interesting in its use of walrus ivory, which increased in popularity from the late Viking to the medieval period and outlines a date range for the object.

### CATALOGUE
(illus 74-76)

**1** Pointed implement, measuring 88mm in length, made from unidentified bone. Part of the object, extending c46mm from the butt, is rectangular in cross-section, measuring c8 x 7mm, the butt itself being bluntly pointed. Several shallow and oblique cut marks are present along the surface on one side. Obliquely over these cut marks, and longitudinally on the other three sides, are striations from the use of an abrasive which has created a polished surface. The shaft is shouldered, tapering into a finely-drawn circular-sectioned point. The rectangular-sectioned part has been created to improve the grip when used as a tool, perhaps as an awl. F103; Period II.2

**2** Pointed implement, measuring 139mm in length, tapering into a finely-drawn circular-sectioned point. Made from a longitudinally-cut long bone of unidentified species. F100a/101; Period II.2

**3** Pointed implement, 94mm in length, made from the left metatarsal IV of a horse. The naturally pointed diaphysis distally has been trimmed into a sharp point. F99a/b; Period II.2

**4** Pointed implement, measuring 126mm in length. The breadth of the distal articulation (Bd) is 53mm. It was made from a cattle metacarpal with the fused, distal articulation retained. Implements worked in the same way, sometimes with the proximal articulation retained, are found on sites from many different periods, from neolithic Skara Brae, where they were described as strong piercing tools or awls (Foxon 1991, 151), to early medieval Lincoln, where they were tentatively interpreted as gouges for leather working (Mann 1982, 31). F403; Period II.1

**5** One-piece double-sided comb broken vertically in half, with one set of coarse and one set of fine teeth. It is made from horn (presumably cattle), the keratinous sheath which covers the surface of the boney horn core. As horn possesses plastic properties when heated, it could be moulded into large, flat sheets for comb manufacture (O'Connor 1987, 15). Several teeth are broken off close to the base and part of the surface is weathered. It measures 61mm in height and 3mm in thickness. The cross-section is slender. There is a milled incised line at the base of each set of teeth on one side of the comb, which provided a guideline for the depth to which the teeth were to be sawn. The space between the coarser teeth, and hence the size of the saw blade used, is c1mm: between the fine teeth it is c0.5mm. The coarser teeth have been cut out by sawing obliquely from each side, rather than by a single cut at right angles to the principal axis. However, the fine teeth are cut at right angles to the principal axis. F103b/104; Period II.2

**6** Twenty bone beads, all found together, of which two are larger, measuring c10.7mm in diameter and 8.5–9mm in height, and eighteen are smaller, c8mm in diameter and 6–7mm in height. Each bead has a drilled perforation, c3mm in diameter, and carries a high gloss. F99a; Period II.2

**7** Knife handle. Right sheep metatarsal with the proximal and distal articulations removed, used as a handle for what is believed to be a throwing knife (R M Spearman, pers comm). A tang with a broken iron blade, is inserted into the distal end of the bone and a lead core runs the length of the handle to act as a counter-balance for the throwing knife. The bone handle measures 67.5mm in length, and the protruding part at the distal end, with parts of the iron tang covered with lead, measures c16mm in length, c16mm in breadth and c7mm in thickness at the narrowest part. The implement is encircled by two grooves proximally and distally on the diaphysis, which may have been intended to improve the grip. The handle carries a high polish and cracks run along it from the blade end. F109a; Period II.1

**8** Knife handle made from a right sheep tibia, with the proximal articulation cut off and the fused distal articulation retained. At the split proximal end is the much-corroded iron tang of a broken blade. This probably originally continued to the other end of the bone. A small drilled perforation, 1.5mm in diameter, on the posterior side of the bone may have been for securing the tang with a rivet. But the perforation does not continue across to the other side of the bone, which is necessary if it was intended for a rivet to secure the tang. The perforation may therefore be unfinished or have had a different function. The object measures 111mm in length and the surface, apart from the distal articulation, carries a high polish. From lower strata of Quarry pit; Period II

**9** Roughly-made pin of unidentified bone, 73mm in length, with a crudely-shaped cuboid head and a flat top, the shank being irregular in cross-section. There is no marked swelling or hipping of the shaft. F104; Period II.2

**10** Antler plate, length 24.5mm, breadth 19mm, thickness 3mm. F103b; Period II.2

**11** Bone or antler plate (no features for identification remain due to the highly polished surface), length 40.5mm, breadth 14mm, thickness 1.5mm. F97; Period III.2

**12** Debris from bead manufacture? Object made of compact bone of unidentified species, 21.5mm in length, 14mm in breadth at the broadest end and 11mm at the narrowest end, and c10mm in thickness. It has been shaped by flaking and perforated by drilling along the long axis. The perforation, which is off centre, measures 5mm in diameter at the broadest end and 3.5mm at the other end. Each end is marked with circular grooves on the flat, cut surface. F83; Period II.1

**13** Playing piece. Finely carved object; the structure of the material is consistent with that of walrus ivory, characterized by a yellow tinged surface and, at a microscopic level, areas of marbled dentine, translucent and crystalline in appearance. It measures 19mm in length. The bulk of the object is divided into three parts, separated by ridges. It expands from about the middle of the object towards one end which is plano-concave, sub-circular in shape, highly polished, and measures 9.5 x 9.9mm. The grooves between the ridges display wear marks which probably derive from manufacture. The remaining part of the object is shouldered and then bifurcated, the ends of the points being blunt and rounded. F104; Period II.2

**14** Implement made from a slice of unidentified long bone with plain parallel sides, 109mm in length, with a circular cross-section, c5mm in diameter. It is smooth and polished all over. Each end has a simple point. Function unknown. F103b; Period II.2

**15** Slice of a longitudinally-cut unidentified long bone, 180mm in length. It has been cut off obliquely at one end, revealing the cancellous tissue. The other end is cut obliquely on both sides, forming a triangle which has been flattened out by flaking. The surfaces seem unworn. Function unknown. F303; Period IV

## ADDENDUM (illus 77)

### Fraser Hunter

**16** Length 61.5mm; width 21.5mm; thickness 7.5mm. Worked longbone fragment, surviving as one flat face with bevelled edges. Decoration comprises a saw-cut line running longitudinally along the centre of the flat face. The ends are cut square, and the cancellous tissue on the reverse appears to have been hollowed. The edges are broken: the remains of a possible rivet hole, a minimum of 4mm diameter, are centrally placed along one edge. Period II.2

Assuming the original artefact was symmetrical, the piece can be plausibly reconstructed as a hexagonal- or octagonal-sectioned artefact, carved from a hollowed-out longbone. It can be interpreted as the handgrip of a composite handle of medieval date: cf Mann 1982, 20, no 143 for a fragment from a similar but rectangular-sectioned handle.

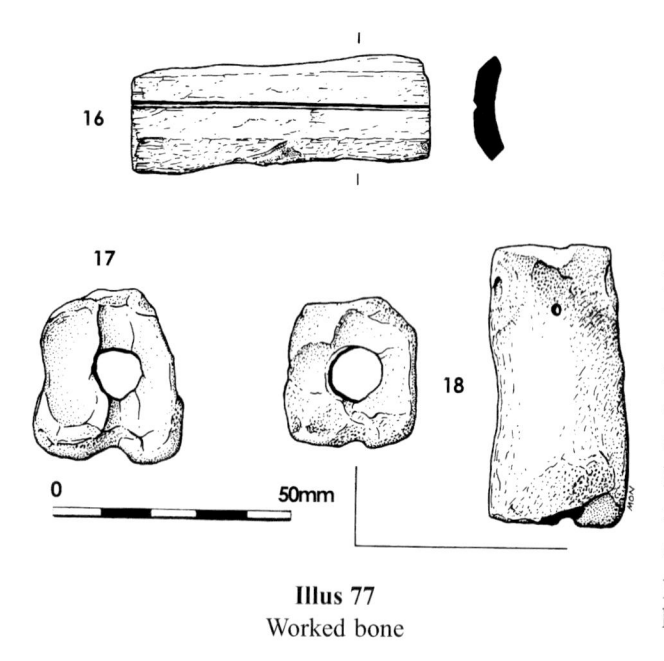

**17** Cattle phalange with cylindrical hole. Length 65mm; width 32mm; height 35mm. Period II.1

**18** Cattle phalange with cylindrical hole. Length 56mm; width 28mm; height 31mm. Period II.1

Two first phalanges of cattle, both with cylindrical holes cut longitudinally through the proximal articular surface (no 17: 10mm diameter x 44mm long; no 18: 12mm diameter x 40mm long). Their irregularity in section and surviving toolmarks show they were cut, not drilled. In addition, the distal articular processes of no 18 have been knife-trimmed, and perhaps also the proximal processes on the inferior surface, although later damage prevents certainty. The cortical bone on both artefacts shows a slight polish, perhaps from handling. The interior surface of the hole of no 18 has been burnt.

**Illus 77**
Worked bone

These enigmatic artefacts are probably handles, based on the shape of the hole, the trimming of no 18 (for ease of handling?) and the possible use-polish on both. The scorching or burning on the interior of no 18 suggests they could have been handles for a spit or something similar, with heat conducted along the spit causing the burning.

## 5.17 FAUNAL REMAINS

Lin P D Barnetson

INTRODUCTION

In the course of excavation, over 17,000 fragments of animal bone were recorded as having been recovered from the Fast Castle site. Excluding fragments in uncertain contexts or unstratified deposits, the total faunal assemblage comprised 16,194 fragments of which around 83% were identifiable to bone and species. Although belonging to several chronological phases, the assemblage accumulated in a relatively short space of time and as such provides an invaluable picture of rural economy in late 15th- to early 17th-century Scotland.

MATERIAL AND METHODS

Species representation

Of the 16,194 fragments examined (Table 14), 13,425 (83%) were identifiable to species although, as was expected, with the exception of a few deposits, notably F103, 104 and 109, fragmentation was high and there were very few intact bones of the larger species. The majority of identified fragments were of sheep (49%)

and cattle (36%). Of the other domestic species, birds (*Gallus sp.* 5% and *Anser sp.* 1.5%) were predominant but pig and horse remains were few, the former represented by only 217 fragments and the latter by a mere 19 fragments. Several features belonging to Period II rendered fragments of domestic cat; only one bone and one tooth were attributable to dog (or fox), one in F104 (the other in F202). There were, however, signs of dog tooth marks on many cattle bone fragments throughout the site. Among the non-domesticates were roe deer, rabbit and hare, fish and several bird species, including gull, pigeon, crow, lapwing, blackbird and possibly heron.

Age and sex profiles

In terms of assessing the age profile of the domesticated animals, one has to take into account the degree of erosion and damage to unfused (softer) epiphyseal ends of long bones. On relatively short-lived sites (several hundred years of occupation) with long term exposure of the assemblage to weather and later disturbance, it is not unusual to lose a high percentage of immature bones. Similarly, pigs which are generally exploited for meat before maturity, tend to be under-represented. At Fast Castle intact cattle long bones with fused epiphyses were few owing mainly to their having been chopped up during the butchery and preparation process. By contrast the sheep assemblage was in better condition, another reflection of the butchery process whereby the smaller animal skeleton is not broken up and bones chopped open to the same extent. However, the larger deposits, F103, 104 and 109, did contain evidence of both mature and immature cattle, sheep and pigs and as a reasonable number of sheep mandibles survived relatively intact, a clearer age profile for this species could be established (Tables 15-17). Age of epiphyseal fusion of long bones was based on those for modern livestock given in Silver (1971) and eruption of teeth on Silver's figures for semi-wild hill sheep and 18th-century cattle.

The same large deposits also contained substantial numbers of undamaged proximal and distal ends of long bones which could be measured to give some indication of sexual dimorphism, and for comparison with assemblages from other sites of the same period. However, there were very few intact long bones which would offer a more reliable indication of sexual dimorphism, and the presence of two possibly discrete groups of sheep (horned and hornless) may further confound the issue. Measurements were made according to Von den Driesch (1976) and are listed in the archive.

Pathology

Apart from age, sex and butchery profiles, the bones were also examined for signs of injury, disease or genetic anomaly. In this respect, the Fast Castle assemblage proved extremely interesting, with examples of cattle, sheep and bird bones exhibiting clear pathology (illus 78-79). Genetic anomalies, a reflection of inbreeding, were found only in the sheep remains, namely crania and mandibles.

## RESULTS

Owing to the nature of the site, initially it proved difficult for the excavators to separate clearly phases of occupation. For this reason, bones were examined by feature and it did appear that many deposits spanned two or more phases, or Periods, with bones from the same animals being found throughout. Measurements, therefore, are shown not by feature but by Period (see tables and archive), and it is obvious that the assemblage is relatively homogeneous. An example of this is the occurrence of both horned and hornless sheep in features associated with Periods II.1 and III.2. Although the following results are grouped by Period, the individual features are described in detail. Rabbit bones, which could be intrusive and not part of the domestic refuse, are not discussed in the text. Both young and old rabbits appeared in most deposits. In the Layer 2 horizon it seems likely that these were not associated with the features in which they were found.

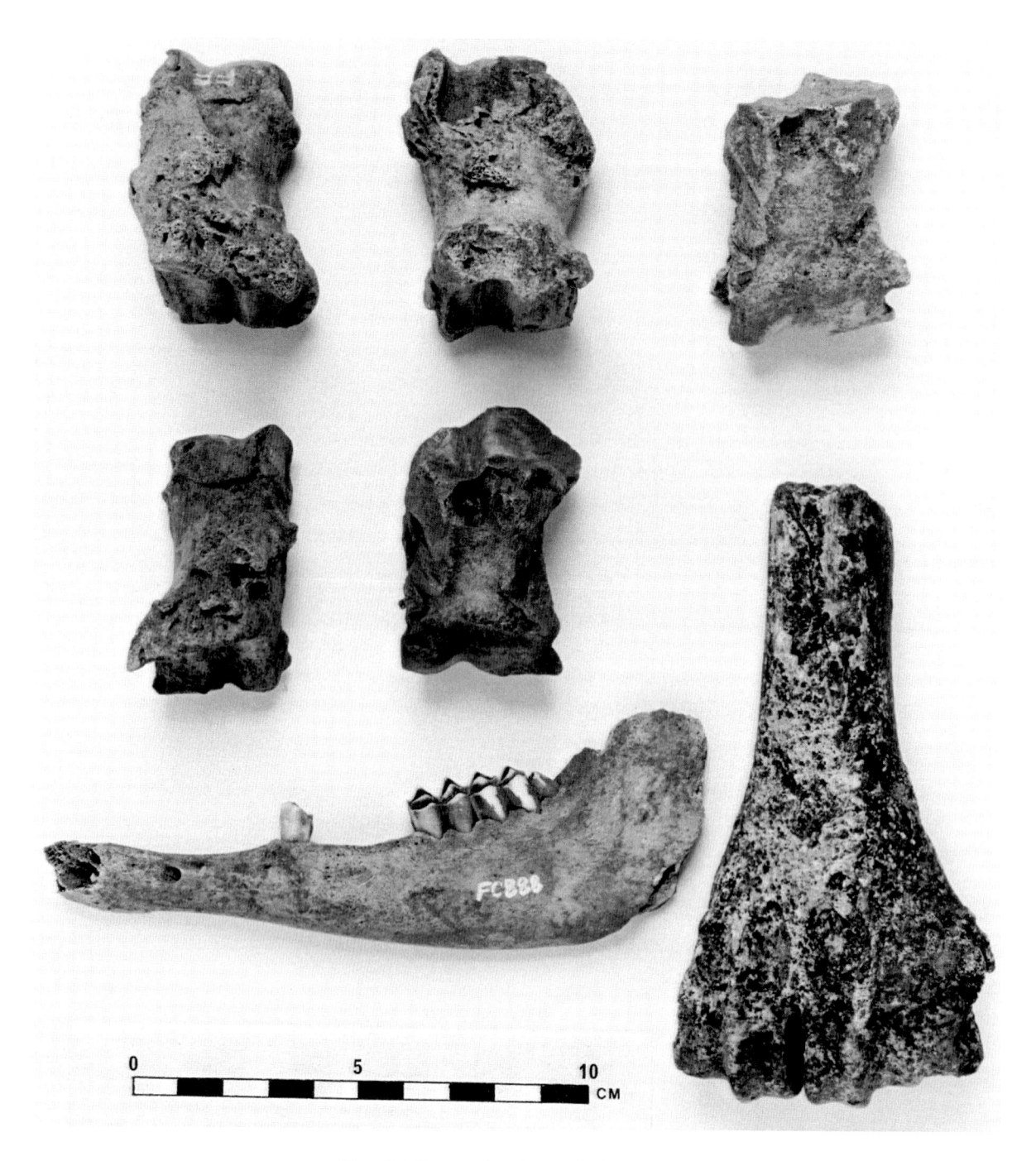

**Illus 78** Bones showing pathology

**Period II.1**: F401, 402, 403

SHEEP

Overall, this deposit, from the lowest layers in the Quarry pit, was very similar to F109 immediately above in that the bones were relatively intact with little weathering damage; the skeletal part representation was also similar, there being only one phalanx (first) and few metapodial fragments. The remainder of the sheep skeleton, long bones, crania and mandibles, ribs and vertebrae were all present. Bones of both mature and

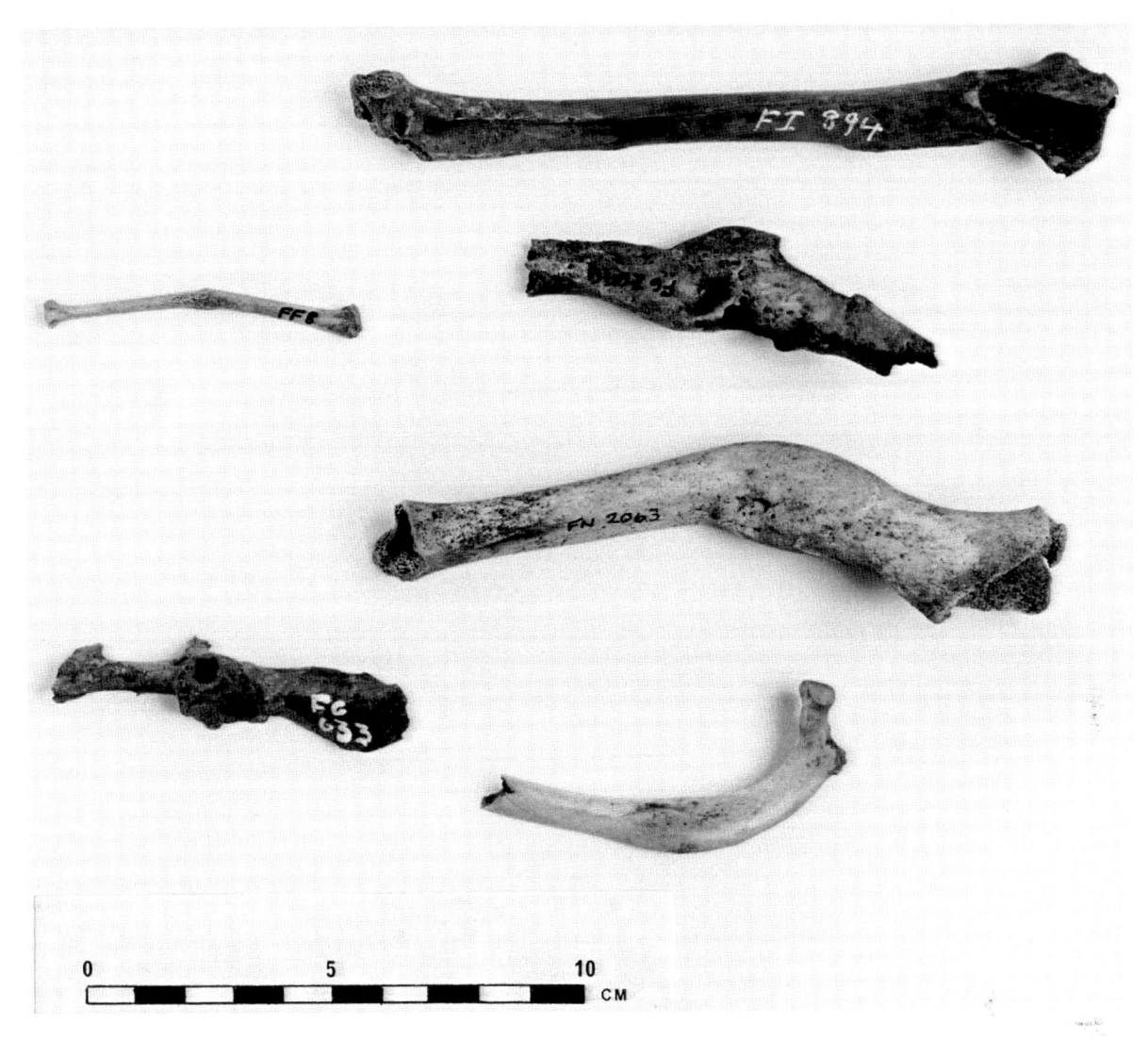

**Illus 79:** Bones exhibiting trauma

immature individuals were identifiable and of the twenty-one maxilla and mandible fragments, all but six had permanent dentition in wear. The MNI (minimum number of individuals) could not be estimated at more than 18 based on distal humerus fragments. Periodontal disease was noted on one mandible. Of interest was a single tibia diaphysis which had been broken mid-shaft and healed naturally, though out of alignment at an angle of roughly 30 degrees (illus 79). Sheep crania bearing horncores were found together with hornless cranial fragments.

CATTLE

The majority of fragments were pieces of long bone diaphyses and it was clear that these bones had been chopped up during the butchery process. Although there were few surviving epiphyseal ends, both fused and unfused epiphyses could be identified. Several phalanges showed signs of disease, one with possible osteoarthritis. Two 1st phalanges had a hole bored in the centre of the proximal surface and one of these was rubbed smooth at both proximal and distal ends though not worked in any other way. See Worked Bone, Chap 5.16, nos 17 & 18 (illus 77).

## OTHER SPECIES

There were a few bones of pig including a maxilla fragment with the permanent third molar (M3) erupted but showing little wear. The bird bones were domestic fowl and goose, and cod was identified among the few fish remains.

**Period II.1**: F109, 109a, 109b

## SHEEP

This assemblage, though extremely variable in colour, possibly reflecting periods of exposure or differing soil conditions, was generally well preserved. There were few bones of immature animals and not many fragments of the lesser meat-yielding bones of the mature skeleton, such as lower legs and feet. There was, however, a substantial quantity of crania and horncores. Careful examination of the distal scapulae failed to establish any matches between left and right bones indicating an MNI of 40. This accorded with the other main skeletal elements (humerus, radius and tibia) which showed MNIs of 39, 35 and 40.

The higher meat-yielding bones of the sheep carcass were, therefore, well represented and confirm the food residue nature of this deposit. Butchery cuts were noted particularly on innominate bones (ie pelvis) and on long bone diaphyses and vertebrae. The atlas and axis vertebrae were sliced through or bore several small, parallel cuts at the point of articulation.

Although there were 42 relatively intact mandibles (including left and right jaws), the maxillae, normally broken up and not always well represented on sites of this period, survived with *in situ* dentition in similar numbers. There were 45 of these and all except three exhibited adult dentition. Wear ranged from light to heavy but at least 17 maxillae showed heavy wear. Five of the mandibles retained deciduous teeth.

The clearest indicator of sexual dimorphism was found in the horncore sample. This included five pairs of massive cores of rams, four of which bore signs of cutting and slicing at the core base where the horn sheath had been cut off. Several smaller cores of females also bore deep cut marks. Six crania bore traces of immature cores, one of which was a young male. Among the cranial fragments were two pieces of frontal bone which were hornless.

Several long bones exhibited signs of disease in the form of exostosis or 'lipping' at the epiphyses. Periodontal disease was noted on three mandibles and one maxilla. Tooth crowding and tooth rotation associated with domestication and in-breeding were also noted. One metatarsal bone had been worked: the distal end had been removed and the remaining diaphysis and proximal end had been rubbed smooth though not polished. This may have been a rudimentary knife handle.

## CATTLE

These bones were also variable in colour and comprised mainly scraps of epiphyseal ends and pieces of long bone diaphyses. As there were very few intact bones it proved difficult to estimate the MNI. However, reasonably intact humerus distal fragments and astragali came from at least seven animals and femur fragments, though difficult to assess, belonged to ten individuals. Although the majority of epiphyseal fragments were fused, there were a few pieces of unfused epiphyses and immature long bone diaphyses. Four maxillae and four mandible fragments had *in situ* dentition, all showing permanent teeth in wear apart from one mandible where P4 was just erupting.

In contrast to the sheep assemblage, bones of the extremities were well represented, again reflecting the different method of carcass utilisation. Virtually all the bones appeared to have been chopped up and splintered but deep cuts were noted on femora, tibiae and innominates. Knife cuts were visible on ribs and vertebrae. Pathology was noted on a metatarsal distal with clear signs of osteoarthritis. There were very few cranial fragments and no evidence of horncores.

OTHER SPECIES

Pig was represented by ten bones, most of them exhibiting unfused epiphyses. There were no signs of butchery or disease. The seven bones of horse and two molar teeth belonged to a mature animal and none bore evidence of butchery or pathology. Five bones of roe deer were identified, all lower limbs and no antler fragments. A single radius, epiphyses unfused, was identified as cat. The bird bone assemblage comprised mostly domestic fowl with some geese and one fragment of duck. Although the fish bone count appears reasonably high, the majority of these pieces were vertebral (neural) spines and may represent only a small number of individuals.

**Period II.2**: F104, 104A

SHEEP

Preservation was good although there was noticeable variation in colour and some of the fragments looked water-worn. All the bones of the skeleton were present, predominantly the high meat-yielding bones. The MNI could be estimated from the long bones as follows: scapula 26, humerus 34, radius 39, femur 19 and tibia 38. Both mature and immature animals were present and of thirty-six mandibles with *in situ* dentition, twenty-one (MNI 13) had the third molar erupted and in wear. The horncore remains also indicated the presence of mature and immature animals and there were cores of at least two rams in the deposit. Although the deposit contained mainly proximal and distal ends of limb bones there were many diaphyses but little sign of chopping or cut marks. Butchery marks were confined to vertebrae, sacrum and horncores.

Pathological changes were noted on a scapula, humerus and femur which all exhibited exostosis and in the case of the former, 'lipping' around the perimeter of the glenoid cavity. Periodontal disease occurred in only one case. Tooth rotation of a lower third molar was noted, and in two mandibles with full permanent dentition, the second premolar had never erupted. One cranium fragment had traces of two horncore bases on the right side and one of these bases was itself clearly bifurcated, ie a triple-horned individual.

CATTLE

As in most other deposits, the cattle bones were highly fragmented. The MNI was estimated at no more than four animals on the basis of humerus and femur distal fragments. Both fused and unfused epiphyses of most of the principal bones were identifiable. Two maxilla fragments had permanent dentition *in situ* but there were no intact mandible fragments. Cut marks were visible on many bones, particularly innominate fragments. One distal metatarsal showed signs of osteoarthritis.

OTHER SPECIES

There were several bones of pig in these features and bones and dentition of both mature and immature animals were present. Roe deer was represented by lower limb bones and mandible fragments but there were no traces of antler. A large fragment of horse cranium was recovered but no other identifiable bones of horse were found. The bird bones comprised mainly domestic fowl, including four tarsometatarsi with spurs (cockerels) and the MNI, estimated on the basis of femur fragments, was 11. There were also substantial quantities of bones of goose with an MNI of 5. The fish remains were well preserved and were mainly cod.

**Period II.2**: F103, 103a, 103b, 103c

There was a large quantity of tiny splinters and fragments of bone less than 1 cm$^2$ in these features which were not included in the final count of unidentified fragments.

SHEEP

All the bones of the sheep skeleton were well represented and only the small foot bones, second and third phalanges, were absent. An MNI of 29 was derived from distal tibia fragments. Both mature and immature animals were present and of the twenty-five mandibles with intact dentition, seven retained deciduous teeth and in two others the permanent third molar was just erupting. Actual evidence of butchery was noted only on innominate bones. Tooth crowding was observed in two mandibles, and in one maxilla which had lost all three permanent premolars the root holes had healed over completely. Among the cranial fragments were two horncores of rams and a third fragment had the left and right bases of small (immature) horncores.

CATTLE

This assemblage was particularly fragmented and chop and cut marks were noted on many bones. The MNI was difficult to estimate but humerus and tibia distal fragments indicated the presence of at least three animals. Despite the condition of the long bones, it was clear that both immature and mature animals were present in the sample. Unfortunately, there were no mandibles or maxillae with teeth *in situ*. One first phalanx was so diseased the structure of the bone had the appearance of having 'melted'.

OTHER SPECIES

As in most other deposits, there were few pig bones and most of these belonged to immature individuals. Only one bone (innominate) bore cut marks. Roe deer was also present though probably not more than one animal. Domestic fowl again formed the main component of the bird bone assemblage and an MNI of 10 was estimated from tibiotarsus fragments. Three of the tarsometatarsi had spurs indicative of cockerels. Geese were also identified but no more than three individuals. Both cod and haddock were found among the fish remains.

**Period II.2**: F99, 99a, 99b

SHEEP

There were signs of weathering and variation in bone surface colour and condition which, combined with the high number of unidentifiable fragments in this deposit, may indicate a post depositional hiatus. The range of skeletal elements and age profile of this feature was similar to F97a-c, which lay in close proximity. An MNI of 16 was obtained from reasonably intact radius proximal fragments. There were few surviving bones of old animals but two mandibles had full permanent dentition with signs of heavy wear. There were cut marks on innominate bones and one ilium fragment had been gnawed by a dog. One distal humerus and one proximal radius showed evidence of pathology in the form of mild exostosis around the articular surface. Both horned and hornless crania were recovered.

## CATTLE

All the skeletal elements were present but highly fragmented and exhibiting many cuts and chop marks. Several limb bones were sliced through mid diaphysis. Despite the fragmentary condition, it was possible to identify both mature and immature animals in the assemblage. An MNI of 6 was obtained from scapula and tibia fragments.

## OTHER SPECIES

The remains of at least three pigs were identified and some tiny bones of piglet were also present. This was the only deposit where butchery marks were noted on a pig bone, a scapula. Although bones of deer had been found in several deposits, none yielded evidence of antler apart from F99. This was a base tine, cut off above the burr and rubbed smooth but showing little sign of having been worked. Domestic fowl again dominated the bird bone assemblage and three of the four tarsometatarsi recovered bore spurs. One goose tibiotarsus showed extreme pathology (illus 79) whereby the diaphysis appeared to have been broken, subsequently becoming infected. Among the few rabbit bones also found in F99 was the innominate of a mature animal which showed gross pathological change around the acetabulum, the rim of which was burnished with exostosis and remodelling on the surface of the ilium. The fish bones were all salt water species and the remains of plaice were identified.

**Period II.2**: F97a, 97b, 97c

## SHEEP

Preservation was good and several scapulae survived almost intact. The higher meat yielding bones of the upper limbs were present in substantial quantities but there were also several lower leg bones including metapodia and first and second phalanges. Both mature and immature animals were present and an MNI of 15 was derived from distal tibia fragments. The age profile derived from postcranial bones in this deposit was similar to that of F402-403 in that the number of bones of old animals was small. However, there were mandibles representing eight individuals where the permanent third molar was erupted and in wear, and although none showed heavy wear, at least four were from old animals.

The pattern of butchery was similar to that in prior deposits and cut marks were noted on vertebrae. One distal humerus showed signs of disease in the form of exostosis on the lateral condyle. Horned sheep were present in this deposit.

## CATTLE

In contrast to the sheep assemblage the cattle bones were extremely fragmented and the epiphyseal appeared to have been broken up into small 'chunks'. However, it was possible to note the state of epiphyseal fusion and there were several mature and immature animals in the deposit. An MNI of 5 was obtained from distal tibia fragments.

There were numerous signs of chopping and cut marks and one radius had been cleanly sliced through midshaft. Pathology was confined to the lower limb bones with one distal metatarsal showing gross distortion and exostosis on the distal shaft and both condyles. The cranial fragments were mainly frontal bones and two hyoid bone fragments had survived.

OTHER SPECIES

F97a-c, and the closely related F99, yielded the largest pig sample from the site, twenty-three and twenty-two bones respectively, not counting a few loose teeth. All told, however, these represented no more than three individuals in F97a-c, two very young and one mature adult. Only one horse bone was recovered, a distal metapodial. The bird assemblage was dominated by domestic fowl, mostly mature birds, and of four surviving tarsometatarsi, one had an intact spur normally found on cockerels. Goose was also present.

**Period III.1**: F85

This was a small deposit but contained fragments of all the domestic species with the exception of horse. All the characteristics of the larger features were found: the presence of fused and unfused epipihyses of all species, butchery cuts on principal meat-yielding bones and signs of exostosis on some sheep humeri.

**Period III.1**: F86

SHEEP

All bones of the sheep skeleton except second and third phalanges were present. F85 and 86 were counted together in estimating the MNI of 18 and 13 based on humerus and tibia distal fragments respectively. Of fourteen mandibles with intact dentition, at least five had the lower M3 in wear, three had M3 erupting and the remaining six retained deciduous premolars. There were several reasonably intact maxillae and some cranial fragments but no frontal bones and therefore no evidence of horncores.

CATTLE

The cattle bones were again noticeably chopped and cut and the MNI estimates derived from scapula and innominate fragments were 4 and 3 respectively. Bones of both mature and immature animals were present. Cut marks appeared on many bones, particularly ribs. Exostoses were noted on a distal metacarpal and three first phalanges.

OTHER SPECIES

There were remains of at least two pigs in this feature, one with deciduous dentition, the other with P4 erupted and in wear. The bird bone assemblage contained at least five domestic fowl, one of which was a cockerel, and at least one goose. Also present were some fragments of pigeon and blackbird.

**Period III.2**: F97

This deposit contained only 124 identifiable fragments among which was a sheep cranium bearing traces of spurs, the only example of this from the whole assemblage, usually indicative of polling.

**Period III-IV**: F202 - 207

SHEEP

In keeping with the earlier features, most of the bones of the sheep skeleton were present and this was one of the few deposits which contained a sheep third phalanx. The MNI was estimated from humerus distal fragments at nine individuals. There were only five mandibles with assessable dentition, all mature animals

- one with P4 in wear, three with M3 in wear and one showing M3 just erupting. Cut marks were noted on innominate and femur fragments. Among the cranial fragments was a fairly intact piece of frontal bone bearing traces of left and right horncores.

## CATTLE

The cattle bones were highly fragmented although there was clear evidence of both fused and unfused epiphyses. The MNI estimate of 4 was derived from pieces of scapula. The only evidence of cattle horncores at Fast Castle was discovered in this deposit (F206).

## OTHER SPECIES

Pig was present in this feature and two fragments of mandible came from individuals of different age. A few fragments of long bones lacking epiphyseal ends were tentatively identified as roe deer. A tibia with both epiphyses unfused could have come from either a young dog or fox. The bird assemblage contained several species, mainly domestic fowl (at least seven individuals including a cockerel), at least two geese (both young birds) and various fragments of duck, pigeon, seagull and possibly lapwing. Of particular interest was the complete radius of domestic fowl which had been broken mid-shaft and had healed extremely well without much distortion of the normally straight diaphysis (illus 79).

**Period III-IV**: Layer 2

There were signs of weathering, erosion of bone surfaces and scavenger activity in this deposit. Much of the Layer 2 horizon comprised small pockets of bone which are considered here as one assemblage.

## SHEEP

Although a small deposit, virtually all the bones of the sheep skeleton were present, including phalanges. An MNI of 12 was obtained from humerus distal fragments. Mandible fragments from four individuals had the permanent third molar in wear, with heavy wear in two cases. Cut marks were noted on vertebrae only. There were six horncores in the deposit, one of which belonged to a ram.

## CATTLE

The majority of cattle bones were small fragments of diaphyses and small pieces of epiphyseal ends. An MNI of 6 was derived from humerus distal fragments although none of these was intact. There were no cranial fragments except for one hyoid bone and two small mandible fragments. One sliver of cattle long bone showed signs of being worked. This was a rectangular fragment approximately 6cm long and 2cm wide. The cut ends had been rubbed smooth, and the surface bore a thin incised groove running the length of the piece. (See Addendum to Worked Bone Report, no 16, illus 77).

## OTHER SPECIES

Of the eleven pig bones recovered, two were mandibles belonging to a very young piglet and an older animal which still retained deciduous premolars. There was one horse phalanx. The bird bones were mainly domestic fowl and goose but very weathered and eroded tibiotarsus and carpometacarpus fragments were tentatively identified as heron. Cod was identified among the fish.

**Kitchen: Periods II-IV**: F301 to 330

SHEEP

The range of skeletal elements present in the Kitchen were similar to those in other features and several bones bore cut marks and signs of butchery. An MNI of 6 was estimated from humerus fragments. Although this area seems to be devoid of scapulae (see Tables 15-16) there were in fact four fragments recovered but none with the articulation intact. Though few in number, the other principal bones did comprise remains of both mature and immature animals and the five mandibles with dentition showed a range of ages with P4 and M3 erupted and in wear in two fragments, M3 erupting in a third fragment and deciduous premolars *in situ* in the remaining two.

CATTLE

All the skeletal elements were represented and many fragments were chopped and cut including limb bones, vertebrae and an occipital fragment. There were both fused and unfused epiphyses in the deposits and three mandible fragments had P4 erupted and in wear.

OTHER SPECIES

There were several bones of pig and some fragments of roe deer lower leg bones. The bird assemblage comprised domestic fowl, at least two birds, and one, possibly two, geese. Haddock and cod were identifiable among the fish remains.

DISCUSSION

The homogeneity of the assemblage was remarkable, and even the smallest deposits consistently showed the same range of species and similar age, butchery and pathology profiles. Surprisingly little bone was calcined or scorched; this occurred sporadically in most of the features but never in quantities indicative of hearth deposits. The dimensions recorded for both sheep and cattle accord with those from other parts of medieval Scotland - *viz* Cruggleton Castle, Phases 4-5, (Ewart 1985), Smailholm Tower (Good & Tabraham 1988) and Threave Castle (Good & Tabraham 1981); and the pattern of exploitation of both domestic and non-domestic species is similarly in keeping with other sites. Although age profiles for both sheep and cattle are indicated in the principal bones and mandibles, sexual dimorphism, in the absence of intact bones with fused epiphyses, is more difficult to assess. It appears from the shape and form of the sheep horncores that both sexes were horned. Apart from one individual in F97, the hornless sheep do not exhibit signs of polling and hence belong to a different group. Bone dimensions, therefore, are not a reliable indication of sexual dimorphism as there may be a variety of animals in the assemblage culled from various flocks. The horned group certainly shows discrete grouping of males and 'others' which would include ewes and wethers. The calcanea also separate into two groups: a large group of ewes and wethers and a small group of males. The tibiae distal breadth measurements have the same distribution in both Period II.1 and II.2 (similar range, mean and sd) suggesting some degree of homogeneity or continuity (Charts 12-17).

In terms of number of fragments, sheep formed the major part of the assemblage, although in terms of meat yield, they would not have contributed as much as cattle. Butchery marks were mainly on those parts of the skeleton which require chopping: the innominate (pelvis) and vertebrae. The mutton carcass is prepared differently from beef and entire leg joints would have been detached at the pelvis with the lower leg bones being chopped off. Fleecing and detaching of the feet may have been carried out elsewhere, and the remains within the castle reflect principally food residue. In all phases a percentage of the flock would have been kept for wool and breeding purposes, as can be seen from the number of mandibles with permanent dentition in wear. There were many fragments of crania and horn-cores throughout the site; but as the heads would have been utilised for fat, meat (such as tongue and brain) and by-products (such as horn), it is not uncommon to find these fragments within food midden deposits of this period. Signs of disease in the form of exostosis and 'lipping' around articular surfaces were noted in many features, and a few mandibles exhibited periodontal disease. These are normally regarded as evidence of a low standard of animal husbandry, associated with poor nutrition and unsuitable environmental conditions. Similar pathology is commonly observed among medieval faunal assemblages and Fast Castle is not exceptional in this sense. Most of the pathology was confined to upper limb bones but lower leg and foot bones were few in number. However, the incidence here appears to be slightly higher perhaps than one might expect, and could indicate that grazing around the site was not ideal. Possibly the area was damp or animals were being penned in damp conditions.

Genetic anomalies such as tooth crowding and double or triple horns are also not uncommon in this period. Unfortunately, the sheep cranium fragment exhibiting secondary horn bifurcation was a right side only and there is no indication as to whether the left side also bore a triple horn. Broken bones have been recorded in other assemblages and generally tend to be lower limbs and ribs. The healed tibia in F402 reveals perhaps that animals were not slaughtered if injured, or that animals were not closely monitored for injury. Fractures which healed naturally as in this case may have occurred during summer grazing and may not have been noted immediately. One sheep rib in F59 also showed signs of a minor healed injury which left a callus close to the vertebral end.

Virtually all the cattle bones were in a highly fragmented condition, a reflection of the butchery process whereby large bones were being sliced through and the epiphyseal ends chopped in the fleshing out of the carcass. Deep cuts, chopping marks, slicing and thin, superficial fleshing cuts were noted on many bones throughout the site. In contrast to the sheep skeleton, there were numerous quantities of cattle phalanges (first, second and third) and several metapodial bones. Cattle hooves may have been boiled for meat and fat and would have been discarded as part of the kitchen refuse. Although there were some cranial fragments in many features, no trace of horncores existed apart from three pieces in F206 which all belonged to the same core. It is possible the majority of animals were hornless, or that the horns were chopped off and dealt with elsewhere perhaps as part of a hornworking industry. Certainly, cattle heads were being utilised on site for meat and by-products, as virtually every feature contained cattle mandible or maxilla fragments and loose teeth. As few of these survived sufficiently intact to provide a reliable age profile, these are not tabulated. In the absence of intact, measurable long bones and crania, little can be added as regards sexual dimorphism within this population, although the few astragali (Chart 14) do indicate the presence of a few males and a small cluster of 'others', cows and bullocks. There were no obvious signs of injury on any of the cattle bones, although the high degree of fragmentation may have obscured this. However, there was a noticeably high incidence of pathology on lower limb and foot bones. Many first phalanges especially showed massive distortion and exostosis of the epiphyseal ends, and several metapodial bones were similarly affected. Not all the bones with pathology are shown in illus 78 but this does provide a representative sample. Osteoarthritis, classically diagnosed by the presence of exostosis, 'lipping' around the articular surface and grooving and burnishing on the surface, was noted on at least one metatarsal. Several other metapodials were distorted and 'melted' around the distal condyles. Given the robusticity of the cattle assemblage in general, one might assume that poor environmental conditions were the prime cause of these problems, perhaps owing to damp and marshy pasture.

Remains of pig were few and pork must have been a relatively rare item. Most of the bones appear in Periods II.2 and III-IV deposits and in the same relative proportions as on other sites. As several of the bones belonged to very immature animals, one possibly foetal, it seems likely these animals were kept within the castle itself. If young pigs were regularly culled for the table it is unlikely their soft skeletal parts would have survived and pig may be somewhat under-represented here, as in other archaeological contexts.

| Feat. | Period | Cattle | Sheep | Pig | Dr | Hs | D/F | Cat | Hr | Rabbit | Bird | Fish | N/I | Total |
|---|---|---|---|---|---|---|---|---|---|---|---|---|---|---|
| 1 | II-III | 2 | 4 | | | | | | | | | | | 6 |
| 2 | II-III | 1 | 3 | | | | | | | | | | | 4 |
| 3 | II.1 | 15 (5) | 15 (6) | | | | | | | 15 (1) | | 1 | 12 | 70 |
| 5 | II.1 | 3 | 8 | (1) | 1 | | | | | | | 1 | 5 | 19 |
| 6 | II-III | | 1 | | | | | | | 1 | 1 | | 1 | 4 |
| 7 | II.1 | 2 | | | | | | | | | | | | 2 |
| 8 | II.1 | 9 | 4 | | | | | | | | | | | 13 |
| 13 | II-III | 3 | 1 | | | | | | | | | | 2 | 6 |
| 15 | II.1 | 4 | | | | | | | | | | | | 4 |
| 24 | II.1 | 1 | 2 | | | | | | | | | | | 3 |
| 49 | III | 6 (1) | 7 | | | 1 | | | | 3 | | 1 | | 19 |
| 56 | II.1 | 2 | 1 | | | | | | | | | | | 3 |
| 59 | II.1 | 4 | 15 | | | | | | | 1 | 2 | | 3 | 25 |
| 73 | II.1 | | | | | | | | | | 2 | | | 2 |
| 81 | III-IV | 29 (4) | 43 (2) | 2 | 2 | | | | | 23 | 3 | | 11 | 119 |
| 83 | II.1 | 8 | 17 (5) | | | 1 | | | | 2 | 6 | | 6 | 45 |
| 85 | III.1 | 82 (2) | 78 (7) | 6 | 1 | | | | | 1 | 12 | | 33 | 222 |
| 86 | III.1 | 330 (13) | 276 (28) | 15 (1) | | | | | | 12 | 44 | 7 | 155 | 881 |
| 87 | III | 6 | 7 (2) | | | | | | | | 2 | | | 17 |
| 88 | III.2 | | 4 | | | | | 1 | | 8 | | | | 13 |
| 89 | III.2 | 2 | 3 | | | | | | | | | | | 5 |
| 90 | III.2 | 11 | 18 (4) | | | | | | | | | | | 33 |
| 92 | II.1 | 18 | 34 | | | | | | | | 1 | | 22 | 75 |
| 93 | II.1 | 67 | 65 (3) | | | | | | | | 6 | 2 | 31 | 174 |
| 95 | III.2 | 71 (6) | 34 | 4 | | | | | | 3 | 6 | 4 | 13 | 141 |
| 96 | III.2 | 38 (6) | 72 | 4 | | | | | | 3 | 8 | 2 | 55 | 188 |
| 97 | III.2 | 46 (2) | 57 (2) | 2 | | | | | | 2 | 13 | | | 124 |
| 97a-c | II.2 | 408 (8) | 373 (18) | 23 (1) | | 1 | | | | 5 | 71 | 14 | 358 | 1280 |
| 98 | II | 29 | 132 | 6 | | | | | | | 12 | | | 179 |
| 99 | II.2 | 394 (3) | 392 (19) | 22 (4) | | | | | | 5 | 93 | 101 | 394 | 1427 |
| 100 | II.2 | 128 (1) | 139 (8) | 5 | | | | | | 3 | 54 | 4 | 165 | 507 |
| 101-2 | II.2 | 29 | 186 (4) | 5 (1) | | | | | | 2 | 15 | 15 | 61 | 318 |
| 103 | II.2 | 443 | 878 (11) | 16 (3) | 7 | (1) | | 3 | | 25 | 160 | 45 | 460 | 2052 |
| 104 | II.2 | 523 (1) | 1073 (7) | 17 (4) | 13 | 1 | (1) | 3 | | 9 | 135 | 35 | 281 | 2103 |
| 105 | II.1 | | 10 | | | | | | | | 1 | 1 | | 12 |
| 106 | II.1 | 37 | 171 (5) | 2 (1) | | | | | | 3 | 22 | 6 | 15 | 262 |
| 107 | II.1 | 23 | 22 | | | | | | | | | | | 45 |
| 108 | II.1 | 9 | 1 | | | | | | | | | | | 10 |
| 109 | II.1 | 742 (14) | 988 (62) | 10 | 5 | 7 (2) | | 1 | 1 | 5 | 59 | 98 | 125 | 2119 |
| 122 | III.1 | 4 | 4 | | | | | | | 4 | 1 | | 12 | 25 |
| 181 | III.2 | 1 | 2 | | | | | | | | | | 1 | 4 |
| 202 | III-IV | 201 (4) | 249 (30) | 10 (2) | 4 | | 1 | | | 15 | 65 | 19 | | 600 |
| 204 | III-IV | 10 | 4 | 7 | | | | | | | 1 | | 2 | 24 |
| 206 | III-IV | 110 (5) | 90 (11) | 4 (1) | | 2 | | 1 | | 19 (1) | 42 | 5 | 156 | 447 |
| 401 | II.1 | 133 (2) | 110 (9) | 2 | | | | | | | 6 | 5 | 14 | 281 |
| 402 | II.1 | 98 | 72 | | | 1 | | | | | 3 | 2 | | 176 |
| 403 | II.1 | 150(3) | 141(9) | 3(1) | 1 | 1 | | | | | 12 | 7 | 24 | 352 |
| Lay 2 | III-IV | 205 (16) | 220 (48) | 11 (1) | | 1 | | 1 | | 73 | 27 | 8 | 219 | 830 |
| Lay 3 | II-III | 78 (2) | 89 (7) | 5 | | | | | | 29 | 17 | 3 | 63 | 293 |
| Kitch | II-IV | 135 (7) | 125 (4) | 5 (3) | 2 | | | | | 1 | 43 | 27 | 70 | 422 |
| Pit 2 | III | 52 (2) | 48 (9) | 4 | | | | | | 3 | 16 | 8 | | 142 |
| Pit 3 | IV | 25 (2) | 12 | 2 | | | | | | 3 | 15 | 2 | | 61 |
| Pit 4 | IV | 4 | 1 | (1) | | | | | | | | | | 6 |
| Totals | | 4731 (109) | 6301 (320) | 192 (25) | 36 | 16 (3) | 1 (1) | 9 | 2 | 278 (2) | 976 | 423 | 2769 | 16194 |

**Table 14:** Faunal remains: range of species, no of fragments
Key Dr = deer; Hs = horse; D/F = dog/fox; Hr = hare; N/I = not identified
Note: Figures in brackets are teeth, counted separately

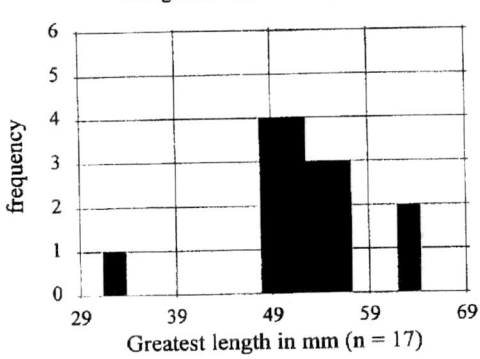

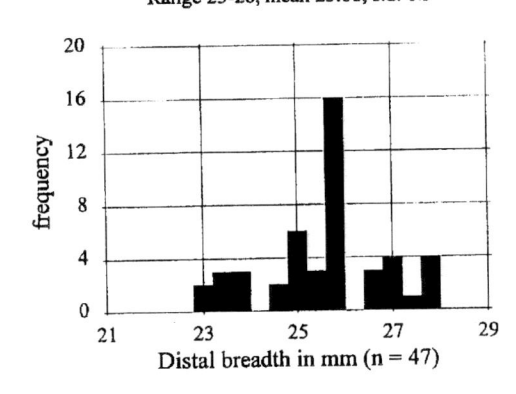

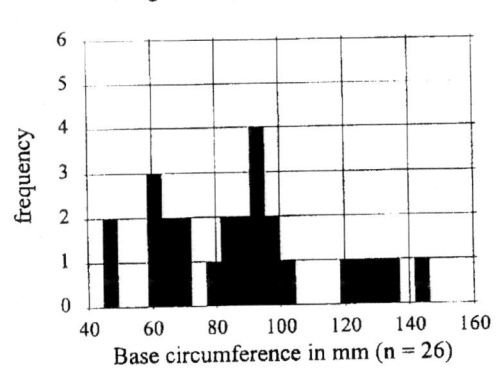

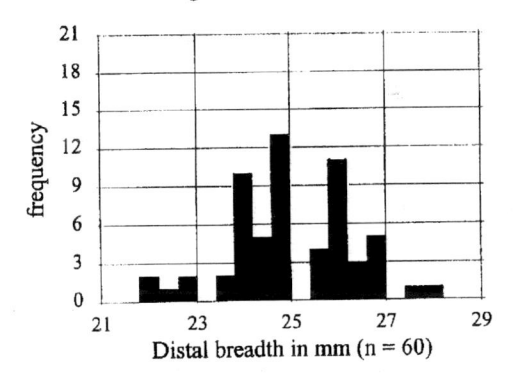

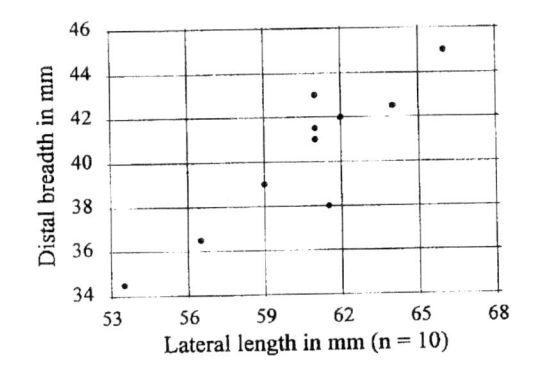

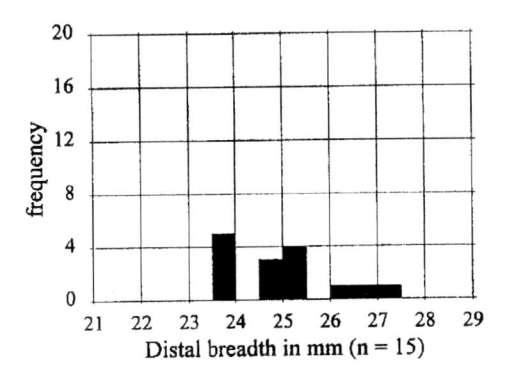

**Charts 12-17:** Frequency and range of bone measurements

Horse and deer are present but in very small quantities. Presumably the occasional piece of venison was served but could not have been a regular item.

Chickens were obviously enjoyed as part of the diet, and there were several tarsometatarsi displaying impressive spurs. These bones had survived extremely well and although the majority were legs and wings, there were many delicate sternum fragments. Crania, vertebrae and digits were not much in evidence suggesting perhaps that these parts (head, neck, feet) were discarded elsewhere when the bird was killed. Geese were also present in reasonable numbers but duck occurred twice only and may have been wild, not a domesticate. The non-domestic species are a reflection of the surrounding countryside - seagulls, heron and lapwing - all species associated with seashore, inland water and meadow.

Salt water fish also contributed to the diet as is found on other Scottish sites of this period. The fish assemblage is dominated by cod and haddock but plaice was also identified in one feature.

In conclusion, the inhabitants of Fast Castle appear to have enjoyed a diet mainly of beef supplemented with mutton, chicken and fish besides goose, pork and perhaps venison on rare occasions. Although one should not infer too much from the incidence of pathology, in percentage terms almost negligible, it would seem likely that cattle were not pastured in ideal conditions and to a lesser extent this is reflected also in the sheep assemblage.

**Table 15:** Faunal remains: Sheep, minimum number of individuals (MNI) and epiphyseal fusion.

|  | Period<br>Feature | II.1<br>402-3 | II.1<br>109-9b | II.2<br>104-4a | II.2<br>103-3c | II.2<br>99 | II.2<br>97a-c | III.1<br>85-86 | III-IV<br>202-7 | III-IV<br>Lay 2 | II-IV<br>Kitch |
|---|---|---|---|---|---|---|---|---|---|---|---|
|  | Fused by:<br>(in months) |  |  |  |  |  |  |  |  |  |  |
| Scapula p | 10 | 10 (2) | 40 (2) | 26 (5) | 13 (3) | 8 (2) | 11 (2) | 5 | 7 (1) | 1 | 0 |
| Humerus d | 10 | 18 (2) | 39 (5) | 34 (3) | 19 (4) | 10 (2) | 14 (2) | 18 (1) | 9 (3) | 12 (1) | 6 (1) |
| Radius p | 10 | 11 (1) | 35 (1) | 39 (3) | 14 (2) | 12 (2) | 8 (1) | 8 (1) | 7 | 3 | 3 (1) |
| Innomin. a | 10 | 9 (1) | 17 (1) | 16 (2) | 9 | 2 | 9 (1) | 8 | 8 | 4 | 3 |
| Tibia d | 24 | 13 (3) | 40 (5) | 38 (8) | 29 (6) | 8 (1) | 15 (3) | 13 (2) | 5 (1) | 8 (1) | 6 (3) |
| Femur p | 36 | 4 (2) | 16 (5) | 19 (11) | 6 (2) | 3 (2) | 1 | 0 | (2) | 1 | 2 (1) |
| Radius d | 36 | 6 (3) | 26 (6) | 21 (9) | 15 (8) | 6 (3) | 7 (1) | 3 (2) | 1 | 2 | 3 (1) |
| Femur d | 42 | 5 (2) | 17 (6) | 22 (12) | 18 (5) | 3 (2) | (1) | 7 (5) | (2) | 1 | 1 |
| Tibia p | 42 | 5 (4) | 25 (11) | 13 (8) | 11 (4) | 5 (4) | 2 | 2 (1) | 2 (1) | (2) | 2 (1) |

KEY: p = proximal, d = distal, a = acetabulum

Figures in brackets indicate number of unfused epiphyses within total.

**Table 16:** Faunal remains: Cattle, minimum number of individuals (MNI) and epiphyseal fusion.

|  | Period<br>Feature | II.1<br>402-3 | II.1<br>109-9b | II.2<br>104-4a | II.2<br>103-3c | II.2<br>99 | II.2<br>97a-c | III.1<br>85-86 | III-IV<br>202-7 | III-IV<br>Lay 2 | II-IV<br>Kitch |
|---|---|---|---|---|---|---|---|---|---|---|---|
|  | Fused by:<br>(in months) |  |  |  |  |  |  |  |  |  |  |
| Scapula p | 18 | 2 | 5 | 2 | 2 | 3 | 4 (1) | 4 | 0 | 3 | 0 |
| Humerus d | 18 | 1 | 5 | 4 | 6 | 5 | 2 (1) | 2 | 2 | 6 | 0 |
| Radius p | 18 | 3 (1) | 6 | 2 | 3 | 2 | 4 | 3 | 3 | 1 | 1 |
| Innominate a | 18 | 3 | 5 | 2 | 1 | 6 | 3 | 3 | 3 | 5 | 0 |
| Tibia d | 30 | 4 | 1 | 3 | 4 | 2 (1) | 5 | 3 | 1 | 2 (1) | 1 |
| Femur p | 42 | 4 | 5 (3) | 5 (2) | 4 (3) | 1 | 4 | 3 (1) | (1) | 0 | 1 |
| Humerus p | 48 | 1 | 3 (1) | 2 (1) | 3 (20) | 0 | (1) | 0 | (1) | 2 (1) | (1) |
| Radius d | 48 | 3 (2) | 4 | 1 | 4 (2) | 1 | 0 | 2 (10 | 1 | 0 | 0 |
| Femur d | 48 | 6 (1) | 10 (1) | 4 (1) | 2 | 6 | 4 | 1 | 4 | 2 (1) | 2 (1) |
| Tibia p | 48 | 4 (3) | 7 | 4 (1) | 2 | 0 | 0 | 4 (1) | (1) | 3 (1) | 2 (1) |

**Table 17**: Faunal remains: Sheep mandibles (number of individuals) with *in situ* dentition

| Period | Feature | < 6 months | 6-30 months | c. 36 months | > 36 months |
|---|---|---|---|---|---|
| II.1 | 109, 109 a-b | 2 | 1 | 4 | 14 |
| II.2 | 104, 104a | 4 | 4 | 2 | 13 |
| II.2 | 103, 103a-c | 4 | 2 | 3 | 7 |
| II.2 | 97a-c, 99 | 2 | 2 | 2 | 10 |
| III.1 | 85, 86 | 5 | 1 | 5 | 5 |

## 5.18 OTHER ORGANIC MATERIAL

### Keith L Mitchell & Hugh P Dinwoodie

A small assemblage of organic material, not covered in chapters 5.13 to 5.17, was recovered from the Quarry pit, consisting of ten samples of vegetable matter, and thirty-six faecal deposits. The vegetable items consisted of seeds from Period III, three hazelnuts from Period II.2, and a fruit stone, possibly a contaminant. Nine examples of faecal material were retrieved from the lowest levels of the Quarry pit, (Period II.1), and twenty more were recovered from Period II.2 contexts. Some organic deposits were left undisturbed at the back of the Quarry pit recess for future investigation.

## 5.19 CLAY TOBACCO PIPES

### Dennis B Gallagher

Seventeen clay pipe fragments were examined; estimating from stem bore size, eight of these may be said to be of 17th- or early 18th-century date. The most diagnostic pieces are described below in the following order: brief description; stem bore in inches (mm); possible date and source; site context.

### CATALOGUE

DUTCH BOWLS

**1** (no 11 in Table). Bowl with moulded dot rose, bottered; 6/64" (2.4mm); Dutch, probably western Netherlands, c1640-70 (cf Duco 1981, 244, no 34). Brewhouse. Layer 2; Period III-IV

**2** (no 16 in Table). Bowl, bottered; 7/64" (2.8mm); Dutch, mid-17th century. Kitchen. F303; Period IV

BOWLS OF POST-1800 DATE

**3** (nos 12-14 in Table). Adjoining fragments of front of bowl and stem of spurred pipe, light brown glaze on mouthpiece; 4/64" (1.6mm); probably Scottish, 19th century. Brewhouse. Layer 2; Period IV

**4** (no 9 in Table). Fragment of bowl of thick-walled cutty pipe, with broken spur and fragment of stamp on rear: ..(O?)N (P)IPE within an oval frame; 4/64" (1.6mm); 19th or early 20th century, possibly Scottish. F202; Period IV

DISCUSSION

Both Dutch bowls are of a poor quality, being unburnished and lacking a maker's stamp. The dot rose (no 1) is also indicative of poorer quality, a moulded form being the cheapest form of decoration (Duco 1981, 377). Lack of distinctive markings makes close dating difficult; the quality suggests a probable mid 17th-century

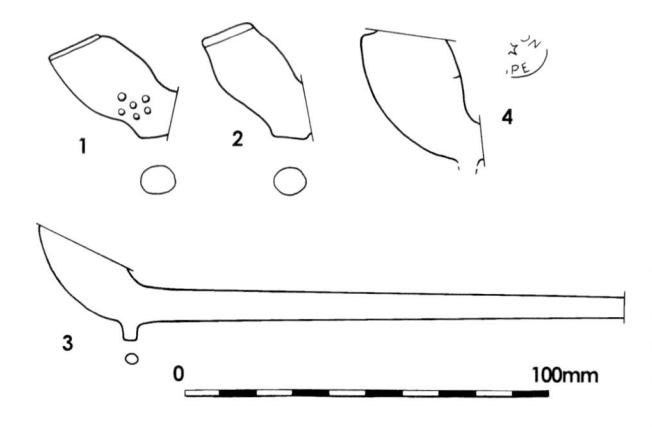

**Illus 80** Clay tobacco pipes

date for both, although the bowl forms are found earlier. Dutch pipes were common in Scotland prior to 1660, except in the immediate vicinity of Edinburgh, where home products held the market.

The stamp on the rear of bowl no 4 indicates the style of the particular pipe, rather than its maker. It probably read UNION PIPE. 'Union pipes' were produced by many Scottish pipemakers, such as Christies of Edinburgh (Gallagher and Sharp 1986, 37, no 576).

**Table 18**: Analysis of clay tobacco pipe fragments

| No | 9 | 8 | 7 | 6 | 5 | 4 | S | B | M | U | T1 | T2 | Comment |
|---|---|---|---|---|---|---|---|---|---|---|---|---|---|
| 1 | | | | | | * | | * | | | * | 1 | Spur fragment: post 1800 |
| 2 | | | | | | | | | | * | | 1 | Bowl wall fragment |
| 3 | * | | | | | | * | | | | * | 1 | 17th - early 18th century |
| 4 | | * | | | | | * | | | | * | 1 | 17th - early 18th century |
| 5 | | | | | | | | | | (*) | | 1 | Bowl fragment: ?mid 17th century |
| 6 | | | * | | | | * | | | | * | 1 | 17th - early 18th century |
| 7 | * | | | | | | * | | | | * | 1 | 17th - early 18th century |
| 8 | | | | * | | | * | | | | * | 1 | Probably post 1800 |
| 9 | | | | * | | | | * | | | * | 1 | Post 1800 |
| 10 | | | | * | | | | | * | | * | 1 | Glazed: post 1800 |
| 11 | | | * | | | | | * | | | * | 1 | Dutch: c1640-70 |
| 12 | | | | * | | | * | | | | * | 1 | Post 1800 |
| 13 | | | | * | | | | * | | | * | 1 | Same pipe as 12 |
| 14 | | | | * | | | * | | | | * | 1 | Same pipe as 12 |
| 15 | | * | | | | | * | | | | * | 1 | 17th - early 18th century |
| 16 | | | * | | | | | * | | | * | 1 | Dutch: mid 17th century |
| 17 | | | | | | * | | | * | | * | 1 | |
| Tot | 2 | 2 | 2 | 1 | | 8 | 8 | 5 | 2 | 2 | 15 | 17 | |

Note: Nos 3 and 7 are possibly part of the same pipe

Key:    9-4; stem bores expressed in sixty-fourths of an inch
        S: Stems measured      T1: Measured bores
        B: Bowls measured      T2: Total fragments
        M: Mouthpieces measured      ( ): Burnished fragments
        U: Unmeasureable fragments

## 5.20 SHELLS

Keith L Mitchell & Hugh P Dinwoodie
(with a contribution by David Heppell)

A total of 2296 shells were recovered; of these, the bulk were found in the Quarry pit, at its lower levels: at least 88% lying below F86; 1050 in Period II.1 and 971 in Period II.2. Only eighty-eight shells (3.8%) were recovered from the Outer Courtyard; and forty-one (1.8%) from the Kitchen.

Of the species represented, oysters (954 half-shells) and periwinkles (1244) were most numerous, and presumably reflect dietary habits. In many buildings of the period, shells were used as a constituent of mortar. A single sample containing a fragment of coo shell was found, with hard mortar of a type containing numerous discrete shell particles (see Mortar report, Chap 5.21.6).

A single scallop shell, from F103b, Period II.2, may or may not be local; it is complete except for a small edge fragment. Shells of this type, both perforated and unperforated, were used by pilgrims as souvenir badges after visiting the shrine of St James at Santiago de Compostela, in NW Spain. A similar, but perforated, scallop shell was found during recent excavations on the Isle of May, from a 15th-century context.

Representative samples of the different types of shell present in the assemblage were identified and commented upon by David Heppell, as follows:

| | Scientific Name | Common Name |
|---|---|---|
| 1 | *Arctica islandica* | Coo shell |
| 2 | *Buccinum undatum* | Common whelk |
| 3 | *Cepaea nemoralis* | Grove snail |
| 4 | *Helix aspersa* | Common snail |
| 5 | *Littorina littorea* | Edible periwinkle |
| 6 | *Ostrea edulis* | Native oyster |
| 7 | *Patella vulgata* | Common limpet |
| 8 | *Pecten maximus* | Scallop |

All species represented are locally common and are edible species, although the native oyster has become extinct in this area in this century. The two snails become more maritime in Scotland, being much more common along the coast. The marine species are all intertidal except the scallop, so that specimen may have been picked up from the shore as a dead shell, for use as a tool, rather than indicating the remains of a meal. It is this species that was worn as a badge of pilgrimage to Compostela. The oysters and periwinkles especially were an abundant source of food, and the oyster shells were a valuable source of lime for improving the soil and for laying down as paths or hard flooring. All these species would be expected in midden material. It is notable that the edible mussel, *Mytilus edulis*, did not feature in the assemblage, though now abundant locally; it may have been a later introduction into the area, or its somewhat fragile shells may not have survived at this site.

## 5.21 STONE

A total of six stone balls were recovered, two identified as Iron Age (see below), and the other four as probably medieval (see Ordnance report, Chap 5.10). The two Iron Age stone balls were residual, having been recovered from contexts laid down no earlier than Period III, early 16th to mid 17th century. Spindle whorls are discussed in the Textile report (Chap 5.13, p137).

# 1 IRON AGE STONE BALLS

Fraser Hunter

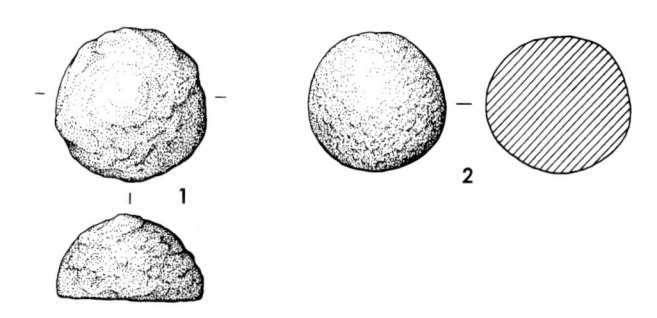

## CATALOGUE

**1** Approximately half a small stone ball, c42mm diameter. Pecked surface, slightly uneven shape. Red sandstone, wt 39.5g. Pit 2; Period III

**2** Small stone ball, diameter 36-38.5mm. Pecked surface, smoother than the stone balls listed in the Ordnance Report, Chap 5.10, apart from no 8. Sandstone, wt 73.5g. Layer 2; Period III-IV

**Illus 81** Iron Age stone balls. Scale 1:2

These two small examples, nos 1 and 2, are very similar to a well-attested series of Iron Age stone balls, the largest in the National Museum's collections (from Black Hill, Bonchester, Roxburgh) having a diameter of 66mm. A medieval origin is more likely for a further four, larger, examples (see Chap 5.10).

These two represent a well-known artefact category from Iron Age sites in south-east Scotland. The type has been studied by Cool (1982, 95-6), on whom the discussion below is based. She provides a distribution map, to which Fast Castle is a useful addition, filling out the southern range of the type. The uneven nature of no 1 suggests it is probably unfinished: such balls were made by progressive smoothing of stone cubes. These objects were long thought to be slingshots, but use as gaming pieces, perhaps in a game like boules, is more likely. They belong to Cool's Middle assemblage, which she dates to c450-250 bc (c500-200 BC in calendar years), but this is based largely on the Broxmouth evidence. A continuation up to the 1st century BC, if not later, may be suggested on other grounds. Cool rather dismisses the large number of balls from Traprain Law, East Lothian, where there is little trace of occupation in the 5th-3rd centuries BC, but abundant evidence of later activity (Jobey 1976). However, the two balls from Carronbridge, Dumfries and Galloway, a site whose main occupation spans the 2nd century BC - 5th century AD (Johnston 1994, 269, 279-80), again suggest a rather later date, certainly within the later pre-Roman Iron Age. This late dating would better fit with the other Iron Age material from Fast Castle (see Chap 6, Discussion).

# 2 FLINT

Alan Saville

Three flints were recovered (not illus). Their significance is uncertain.

## CATALOGUE

**3** A broken (distal) flake segment, from the exterior of a beach pebble. Unworked, and not certainly from a humanly struck flake. F202; Period III-IV

**4** A small, core-like fragment, heavily abraded on part of the keel. Worked, but not otherwise identifiable. F202; Period III-IV

**5** Gunflint fragment. This gunflint, which would originally have been more square in planform, appears to have broken and then probably been reused in its present shape. Turf; Period IV

## 3 ROOFING MATERIAL

K Robin Murdoch, Keith L Mitchell & Hugh P Dinwoodie

The use of thin sheets or slabs of natural stone for roof covering has a very long history. From the 17th century onwards in Scotland the great majority of the material utilised was, until this century, true geological slate: a fine-grained argillaceous metamorphic rock which cleaves easily into thin sheets. Before that time several other types of rock were also exploited, namely thinly bedded siltstones, mudstones and sandstones. Pieces of roofing material made from these latter rocks are frequently referred to generically as slates. Since none of the Fast Castle items were made from true slate, in the interests of accuracy and consistency, they are referred to as 'tiles' throughout this report. The same rule will apply to material from other sites where the precise rock type is known. Note also that the term 'tile' as used here should not be confused with ceramic composition.

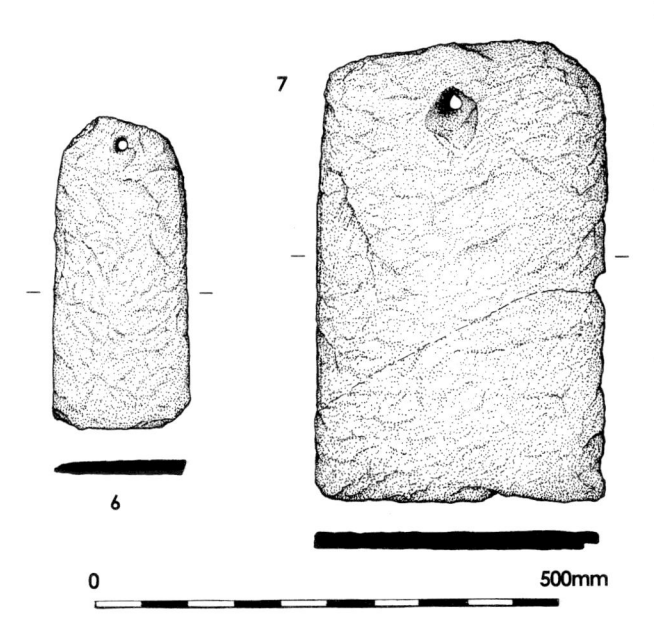

### DISCUSSION

Stone tiles were recovered from both Period II and Period III deposits. A total of 51 were selected for further examination and 10 of these were measured accurately. Thirty-six came from a deposit found lying on top of and within F86 in the Quarry pit and are believed to be associated with the Period III.1 (early 16th century) reworking/refurbishment of the castle (illus 82). Although this group of tiles was undoubtedly intended for use as roofing, their disposition when found indicated that they had probably not been used. They appeared to have been carefully laid out for selection or working; some had not been perforated with fixing holes and others may have been broken during preparation. A few tiles were recovered from the lower levels of the Quarry pit and are believed to relate to the Period II.1 building phase. Others from the upper soil layers of the courtyard are more likely to be the result of post-abandonment collapse (Period III.2).

**Illus 82** Stone roofing tiles

Numerous references, both historical and archaeological, testify to the use of roofing slates or tiles, during the 13th and 14th centuries in England (Salzman 1952, 232-5; Platt and Coleman-Smith 1975, 311-4). In Scotland, however, during the same period, historical references are less numerous and archaeological evidence is so far scant. The excavations at Fast Castle have revealed that at least part of the structure was roofed with tiles throughout Periods II and III (late 15th - early 17th century). In contemporary documents referring to similar roofing materials used elsewhere it is not easy to discriminate stone tile from true slate, although the lack of exploitation of sources of good quality slate in Scotland at that time would tend in favour of the former. Published state records of Scotland during the 15th and 16th centuries, such as the Exchequer Rolls of Scotland and Accounts of the Masters of Works, refer to materials such as 'sclaites', 'tegulis' and 'tegulis lapideis' (slate stone). This last term appears in an account of the Customars of Dundee in 1428 (Burnett 1880, 432); while 'tegulis' alone occurs in accounts of roofing tasks undertaken at Stirling Castle in 1461 (Burnett 1884, 59), Linlithgow Palace (1462-7), Edinburgh Castle (1466), Blackness Castle (1466 and 1469), Doune Castle (1467) and Falkland Palace (1469) (*ibid*, various). In 1535-36, 'Caithness sclait' was used for the roof of the new chapel at Holyrood Palace (Paton 1957, 188), but again this is not a true slate but thin-banded sedimentary flagstone.

Stone tiles have been recovered from several late and post medieval sites in Scotland. These include Threave Castle (1455-1650) (Good and Tabraham 1981, 126-7), and 15th century contexts in Perth (Holdsworth 1987, 149-50). During excavations at Finlaggan, Islay, in 1994, evidence was found of a 'slated' building which had been demolished during the 14th century. Interestingly, true slate of Easdale type, phyllite (clay-slate) and sandstone were all represented in the roofing material from this site (D Caldwell, pers comm). The Fast Castle tiles are made from fissile siltstone which occurs in several parts of the Southern Uplands, and in the past such material was included in a broader non-geological definition of slate. In a survey of slate-quarrying it is noted that 'quarries are worked in beds of the Silurian age, but for the most part cleavage is imperfect' (Davies 1878). This is because the siltstones are sedimentary rocks and many of the beds had surface ripples. In addition 'the fissility is due to the close-set nature of the original bedding planes and the siltstones, being weaker than true slates, have to be split into relatively thick, heavy slabs' (McMillan 1997). Geological examination of the Fast Castle tiles has indicated a likely quarry source within the neighbourhood of Cockburnspath (N Ruckley, pers comm).

When sources of true slate, for example Welsh or Easdale, which were stronger and lighter, became readily available, the use of other types of stone rapidly diminished. It is therefore not surprising that by the time of the Statistical Accounts of Scotland there are no references to quarrying for roofing stone in the Cockburnspath area. How many of the castle buildings were roofed with tiles is a matter for conjecture; but given the exposed nature of the site, heavy roofing would have been advantageous. David Simon has interpreted the architecture of the castle and produced putative reconstructions (Plate IV). He views the hall as having a high pitched roof and suggests that the other buildings also had sloping or lean-to roofs (Simon 1988). Sources consulted confirm that stone tiled roofs had steep pitches, and the recommended minimum for Cotswold stone is 55 degrees (Watt and Swallow 1996). The tiles from Fast Castle may fall into two distinct size groups, one group wider than the others; the first group being typically 280-320mm wide and 12-25mm thick. They weigh between 4 and 6.5kg and have a length-to-breadth ratio of less than 2:1. The second group vary from 120-270mm wide and 6-16mm thick; they weigh between 1.5 and 3kg and the length-to-breadth ratio is typically greater than 2:1. This group may, however, represent half tiles. It is not known whether the two size groups represent different building phases, or slightly different functions. The roofs backing on to the NW curtain wall would have been reasonably well sheltered and may not have needed to be as substantial as, say, the exposed roof of the hall. Stone tiles weigh much more than true slate, since they are normally at least twice as thick and frequently considerably more. They would have needed a more substantial substructure to support them. For example, assuming a pitch of 55 degrees, the hall at Fast Castle would have required in the order of 4500 tiles of the larger size found, giving an estimated roof covering weight of at least 25 tonnes. Interestingly, more than one source remarks that slates and stone tiles were often laid in diminishing courses, large at the eaves, small at the ridge. This was apparently common practice in Scotland, and McMillan (1997) cites the reason as 'fully utilising the available resource'. The size variation of the Fast Castle tiles may be related to this practice.

This, however, may be only part of the answer; in windy conditions a pitched roof will generate lift in a fashion not dissimilar to an aircraft wing. The effect is greatest just before and just after the ridge, and smaller tiles with less surface area and greater frequency of fixings would resist lift much better. Most of the Fast Castle tiles had fixing holes indicating that they had been fixed to wooden laths, probably by oak pegs (Darby 1988). The fixing holes were between 11 and 17mm in diameter, situated near the top edge of the tile, normally single but sometimes in pairs. Average fixing hole size for wooden pegs appears to be around 15mm and for nails 5mm (T Ward pers comm). Some of the 'slates', found at Finlaggan, had holes as large as 20mm diameter. Although significant numbers of ferrous nails were found at Fast Castle, it is unlikely that they were used as primary tile fixings. If wooden pegs were not used, then non ferrous pegs or nails were the preferred alternative. Using nails of any form to replace wooden pegs would pose another problem. Because of a loose fit in the fixing holes, wind could cause chatter and subsequent damage to the tiles.

Ferrous nails would have rusted quickly in the salt-laden atmosphere, but it is just possible that some were used out of simple expediency (Darby 1988). Four of the tiles, from the accurately measured group of ten, had been perforated from one side only, with resultant flaking on the other, while a further four had been perforated from both sides. The localised flaking created a natural countersink to accommodate the peg head and allowed the tile to bed down more closely (*ibid*). Although the flaking would suggest that the fixing holes were created simply by use of a pointed hammer, there was evidence of further finishing to improve circularity and fit. It is possible that a drill was used for this purpose. In 1313 'Simon de Norton, tiler, was paid 1d for a hide bought whereof to make a spyndelthoung for boring slates' (Salzman 1952, 234).

One possible wooden roof peg was found, as well as a possible manufacturing tool (see Wood report, Chap 5.15, nos 11 and 14). Two tiles from the area just N of the Quarry pit had mortar adhering to one side. Torching, the application of mortar to secure one course of tiles to another, was relatively common, especially in exposed areas (Darby 1988). Although David Simon interprets the hall as having another storey above the vault, it is equally possible that the vault itself formed the roof of that building. In that case the tiles, still required to shed water, would have been mortared onto pitched stone surfaces created directly on top of the vault. In this situation there would have been no need to perforate the tiles with fixing holes, and it is likely that the pitch would have been less.

### CATALOGUE
(Illustrated tiles)

**6** Roofing tile, complete, with one circular hole, diameter 12mm, centre 25mm from top edge. Flaking around edge of hole on one side of tile only, extending 20mm (max) from the side of the hole. Tile dimensions: 343 x 127-152 x 6-16mm; 1.47kg. F86; Period III.1

**7** Roofing tile, complete, in two parts, with one irregular hole, diameter 15mm, centre 65mm from top edge. Flaking around hole on one side of tile only, extending 62mm (max) from the side of the hole. Tile dimensions: 470-489 x 295-317 x 12mm; 4.31kg. F86; Period III.1

## 4 MISCELLANEOUS STONE ARTEFACTS

Keith L Mitchell & Hugh P Dinwoodie

Apart from gunstones, spindle whorls, and Iron Age stone balls (see the Ordnance and Textile reports, and above), nine other stone balls and pebbles, listed in archive, were examined. Some may have been used as tools, eg as pounders or scrapers. Seven came from the lowest layers of the Quarry pit, Period II. The cresset, no 8, resembles a similar object recovered from Tantallon Castle (Caldwell 1991b, 347-8).

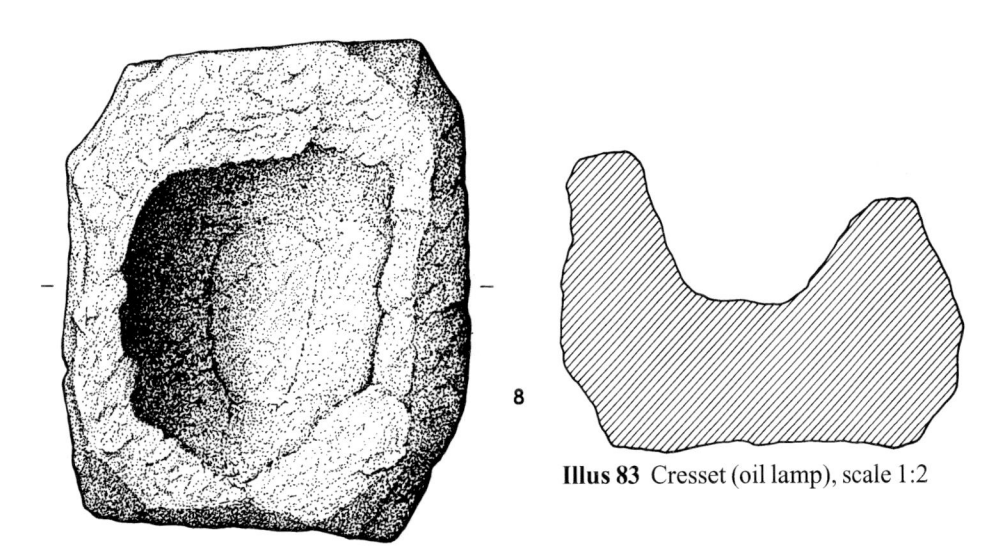

**Illus 83** Cresset (oil lamp), scale 1:2

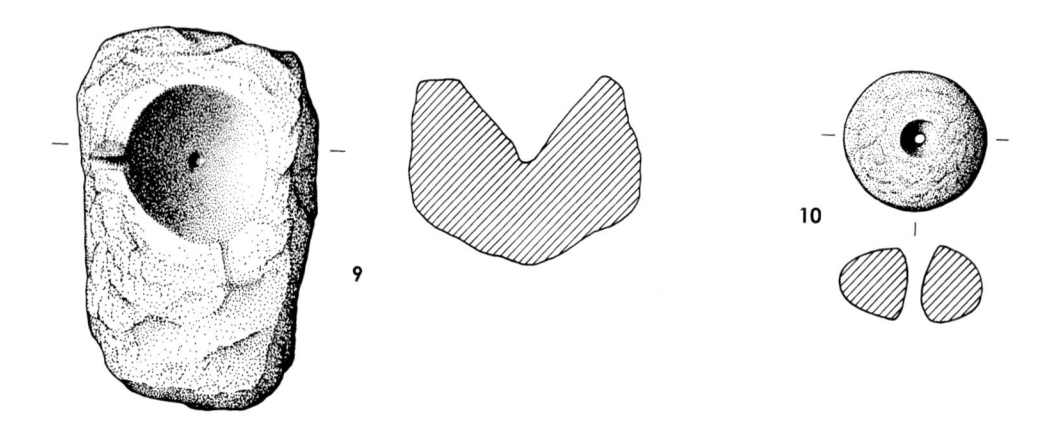

**Illus 84** 9 Pivot stone, 10 Bead or unfinished spindle whorl? Scale 1:2

## CATALOGUE

**8** Cresset (Caldwell, pers comm). Red sandstone. Roughly carved both inside and out. Traces of carbon on upper rim. 128 x 89mm, wt 1750g; (illus 83). F103/104; Period II.2

**9** Pivot-socket (Caldwell, pers comm). Red sandstone. Roughly carved, oblong shape. Smooth cone-shaped indentation carved out at one end. Three evenly-spaced narrow and shallow grooves on top of rim indentation. 102 x 56mm, wt 376g; (illus 84.9) F109/109a; Period II.1

**10** Smooth bi-convex perforated sandstone object 37mm diameter x 20mm thick; central countersunk hole, 1.5mm diameter. Bead, or unfinished spindle whorl?; (illus 84.10) F59; Period II

## 5 CHALK/LIME

Keith L Mitchell & Hugh P Dinwoodie

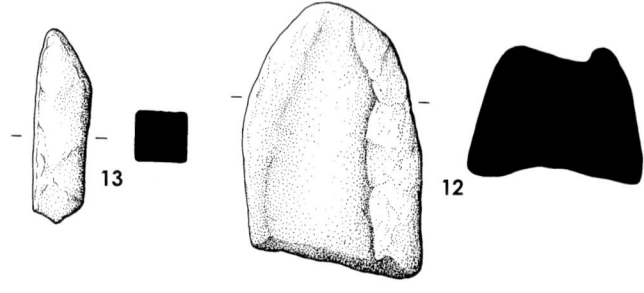

**Illus 85** Chalk, Scale 1:2

This assemblage consists of 35 small lumps of limey marl or altered limestone (Ruckley, pers comm), which are not natural to the site, nor to the immediate locality. The largest piece is c75 x 50 x 35mm. It is likely that they originated locally in other parts of Berwickshire or East Lothian, where limestone occurs in various degrees of abundance. Nearly all were recovered from the Quarry pit.

The majority of the lumps are amorphous in appearance, but generally rounded, and several show flat or flattish surfaces with edges. Half were relatively hard; the rest softer. There is evidence of possible use on some samples. This includes: worn surfaces, and cuts or line marks, such as might have been produced by masons chalking a piece of string, then striking it to mark straight lines.

The harder lumps may have been associated with the production of lime, for mortar used in the building of the Castle, or for interior decoration. The Burgh Records of Edinburgh refer in 1557 to a contract 'with the lyme men of Cousland for furnessing lyme to the wallis of the toun' (Skinner 1969, 9-10). In Fife, 'for laying in with the coal the stone (limestone) had to be broken to anything from egg-size pieces upwards, depending on the state of the fire' (*ibid*, 22).

Possible sources of limestone exist in neighbouring parishes (Statistical Account 1791-99), both on the coast and inland. It is likely that lime would have been produced in simple, fairly transient clamp kilns (Skinner 1969, 10), either where the limestone was quarried, or else on site at the castle. An example of one such kiln may have existed at Coldingham: the 'curious feature' known as the Deil's Dander (*ibid*, 13). Unlike later industrial kilns, in most cases they left few traces. Peat and wood were often used in clamp kilns (*ibid*, 22); in this connection it is perhaps worth noting the substantial quantities of ash and peat found within the Quarry pit.

One sample (no 11, not illustrated) is roughly circular and rather flat, suggesting that its whole surface had been subjected to rubbing. The contours of another (no 12) suggest that it could have been shaped by, or for, hand use; it has a very deep rubbed notch or groove. All surfaces of no 12 appear to have been worked.

## CATALOGUE (illus 85)

11  Chalk lump: roughly circular, flat, with cut edges, wt 92.16g (not illus). Pit 3; Period IV

12  Chalk lump: smooth surface. Deep notch, 60 x 45mm approx, wt 150.08g. F103a; Period II.2

13  Chalk lump: oblong shape with worked surfaces, wt 15.72g. Layer 2; Period III-IV

## 6  MORTAR & PLASTER

### Keith L Mitchell & Hugh P Dinwoodie

Examination of 57 samples indicate a variation of fabric content. These may be subdivided as follows:

1) Six specimens were lime rendering or plaster. Smooth in texture, all these samples have one flat face, presumably the external surface. They contain very fine greywacke grit tempering, measuring on average 0.5-3mm, spread evenly. The fabric very much resembles that of group 2a (below). Most of the fragments were found in Area 2, and they are interpreted as finishing for wall surfaces in Room 1, in Areas 2 and 3, constructed in the late 15th century.

2) The remainder of the samples are small pieces of wall mortar. Inspection of the fabric content demonstrates that two main sub-types are present:

> (a) Twenty-seven specimens examined. They are smooth in texture and are tempered with very fine greywacke grit, measuring on average 0.5-3mm. Some pieces appear degraded. The tempering is very even, and the fabric is very similar to that of group 1.

> (b) The remaining 21 examples are coarser. The temper here is made up of greywacke, quartzite, and sandstone grains, and tends to occur in dense clusters.

Of the total of 57 mortar specimens retrieved from identifiable contexts, 30 came from the Outer Lower Courtyard (of which 23 were found in Area 3); and 25 came from the Inner Lower Courtyard. One fragment of mortar, containing numerous pieces of tiny shells, was found. It was attached to the remains of a coo shell (see Chap 5.20). This was the only such example of mortar, with any visible shell content, besides being the only example of a coo shell found. During the medieval period, larger shells such as these, and oyster shells, were sometimes used for supportive and decorative purposes: as, for instance, at Aberdour Castle and Cramond Tower.

Examination of mortar in surviving walls within the castle corresponds with type 2b above, but shows a very even distribution of greywacke and sandstone grit. Similar mortar was found attached to greywacke stones used in an enclosure wall below Telegraph Hill. The presence of mortar, and occasional sandstone blocks, here and on neighbouring field enclosures, indicate that dykers made extensive use of the castle ruins for material, probably during the late 18th and 19th centuries (Mitchell 1988, 39-40).

## 5.22 COAL, CHARCOAL & CINDER

### Keith L Mitchell & Hugh P Dinwoodie

A total of 232 items were recovered: 136 pieces of coal, seventy-nine of charcoal, and seventeen pieces of cinder. The largest piece of coal measured 130mm and the average was c40mm. There seems to have been a fairly even spread of coal and charcoal throughout Periods II and III. Within the Quarry pit, fragments recovered were mainly from Period II to Period III.1. The charcoal items were mostly very small, the largest being 40x50x35mm. At least fourteen of the seventeen pieces of cinder originated from Period II.2, in Area 5, the same region in which most of the leather, textiles, and wood was found. Several substantial deposits of ash were found during the excavation, though artefacts within showed little evidence of burning; suggesting that most of the ash was redeposited. In the Quarry pit there were several layers composed almost entirely of ash, while others were mixed with loam or clay.

Peat would have been the normal fuel at Fast Castle, originating probably from Coldingham Moor, within a mile of the castle. The Statistical Accounts for Scotland record that it was the principal fuel used in this parish from earliest times, and express doubt as to when coal was first utilised in Scotland, prior to its first recorded use in the 12th century (1791-4, 12, 44; & 1845). Recent excavations at Port Seton recovered similar items to those above, specifically from an Iron Age context (McCullagh R, pers comm, per D H Caldwell). There is evidence that coal was used by the Romans in the North of England, on Hadrian's Wall, and just possibly also on the Antonine Wall (Robertson 1942).

By 1435, when Aeneas Sylvius Piccolomini (the future Pope Pius II), visited Scotland during the reign of James I, coal had obviously become a desirable fuel. He wrote that 'the poor, who almost in a state of nakedness begged at church doors, depart with joy in their faces on receiving stones as alms'. He further records that 'a sulphurous stone dug from the earth is used by the people as fuel' (NCB 1958, 36). This was some fifty years before Sir Patrick Home was recorded as being in possession of Fast Castle in 1488 (Kennaway 1992, 48).

Up to the beginning of the 16th century, coal-mining was a very low-key industry; mines were shallow, and worked on a part-time basis for individual or local needs only. It has been estimated that at that time, the national output of coal was probably no greater than 40,000 tons, but from the middle years of the 16th century, the expansion of coal mining in Scotland accelerated rapidly. By 1707, national production had risen to about 500,000 tons (NCB 1958, 39-42).

Between 1625 and 1677, Sir James Nicholson was laird of Cockburnspath (Rankin 1981, 10-11). His 'Diurnal' or diary contains copious information about his household and the locality, including the use of coal. It is likely that the nearest local source of coal, albeit of poor quality, was at Dunglass (*ibid*, 1-3), or Cockburnspath; while coal was also shipped from other mines around the Forth estuary, to local harbours such as Dunbar or Eyemouth. For example, Wemyss, in Fife, is known to have supplied Skateraw in the mid-17th century (*ibid*, 19-20).

## 5.23 SLAG

### Keith L Mitchell & Hugh P Dinwoodie

Over 100 assorted lumps of slag, total weight approximately 7kg, were recovered, mainly from Period II in the Quarry pit, and date to the second half of the 15th century. According to Spearman, most of the items appear consistent with small scale blacksmithing work within the castle.

Most of the Fast Castle slag seems to be divisible into two main groups, in approximately equal quantities. One group was light in weight, porous, glossy and black in appearance. The second group was heavier, though still porous, and brown, reddish-brown, or purple. At least one sample is a fragment of hearth lining, while a number of others represent dross material. Only one small sample appears to be copper slag. Another sample is clearly floor debris which has sparked off when the metal was being worked, and a number of very light fragments proved to be contaminant material. No crucible nor mould fragments were identified. Spearman comments that the available evidence suggests a small hearth size, of only about 0.45-0.6m square.

Some 90% of the assemblage had been deposited between the first working floor (F109) and the first major tip material (F104), Period II. None was found from Period III.1, and only minimal quantities in later levels. It seems clear that much of the slag probably relates to a building phase which took place no earlier than 1450 and no later than very early in the next century. However, the possibility that some of the pieces are residual Iron Age material cannot be wholly discounted. Surprisingly, very little on-site blacksmith work seems to have been carried out in the 16th century, unless the resultant slag had been tipped over the cliff-edge.

Due to the compact area of the promontory, and the probable small size of the hearth, it is likely that normally any blacksmith work there would have been on a small scale, perhaps carried out by a local man, employed there on a temporary basis as required. Some of the iron artefacts found during the excavation may have been produced by the castle blacksmith. A few small pieces contain nail fragments, so nail-making may have taken place.

The authors are grateful to Mike Spearman for his helpful advice

# 6 DISCUSSION

## Iron Age

### Fraser Hunter

The Fast Castle excavations produced a respectable scatter of diagnostic artefacts which indicate an Iron Age precursor to the medieval occupation. The evidence is summarised in Table 19, and implies activity on the headland in both the pre-Roman and Roman Iron Age, broadly in the period of the 2nd century BC - 2nd century AD, if not slightly later.

**Table 19**: Iron Age and Roman Finds from Fast Castle

| Find | Finds Section | Cat No | Area | Feature | Date |
|---|---|---|---|---|---|
| Stone ball | 5.21: Stone | 1 | 5 | 209/pit 2 | $5^{th} - 1^{st}$ century BC |
| Stone ball | 5.21: Stone | 2 | 1 | Layer 2 | $5^{th} - 1^{st}$ century BC |
| Pottery | 5.2: Pottery group A Sherds of two vessels | 1, 2 | Well | Floor N of wall | $2^{nd}$ century BC – $1^{st}$ century AD |
| Roman amphora | 5.2: Pottery group B One sherd | 1 | 4-5 | 99 | $1^{st} - 3^{rd}$ century AD |
| Button and loop fastener | 5.6: Copper | 1 | 2 | Layer 2 | $1^{st} - 2^{nd}$ century AD |
| Ring-headed pin | 5.6: Copper | 2 | 5 | 100a | $2^{nd} - 4^{th}$ century AD |
| Bone pin | 5.16: Worked bone | 9 | 5 | 104 | ?* |

\* The attribution of the bone pin to the Iron Age is not certain. Its crudity implies it was unfinished, making comparisons awkward, but pins with enlarged decorative heads are found in later Iron Age contexts, primarily post-Roman, in the Northern and Western Isles (Stevenson 1955, fig A). However, there is a dearth of local parallels due to the generally poor survival of bone, and until more comparands are published (notably the Broxburn material), this identification must remain questionable.

Few details can be discerned: all the finds are from medieval contexts, and no unequivocal Iron Age structural evidence was located during the excavations on the headland. However, the topography is typical for Iron Age promontory forts, and a rampart and ditch in the area of the medieval gateway may be envisaged. This is supported by the location of the finds. All are from the headland, except the prehistoric pottery from the Well area to the south-west. The large sherd size of this pottery assemblage implies that it was buried soon after breakage, suggesting disposal in a midden outside the settlement which may have been subsequently disturbed by the Well construction.

A promontory fort at Fast Castle would fit well into the local Iron Age settlement geography. There is a series of promontory forts along the Berwickshire coast, while the area is rich in hillforts and enclosures, most likely of Iron Age date (RCAHMS 1980, 23-4). The votive hoards of Blackburn Mill and Lamberton Moor (Piggott 1953; Anderson 1905) reflect another aspect of Iron Age life.

The sherd of Roman amphora is a useful addition to the rather sparse corpus of Roman finds from native sites in Berwickshire. Apart from items in the two hoards, these consist of a patera from Westruther, a brooch from the western promontory fort at Earn's Heugh, some pottery from Kirk Hill, St Abbs and a bead from Harelaw Moor (Robertson 1970). This suggests the occupants of Fast Castle were people of some importance, as the relative rarity of Roman goods made them status items (Macinnes 1984, 242-5). Whether the amphora came to the site with its original contents of olive oil may be debated: while such exotic commodities may have found a role in the cuisine of the status-conscious local chiefs, it has been argued in similar situations in Holland that the amphorae were reused as general containers (van der Werff 1987, 167-9). Amphorae are relatively unusual finds on native sites in Scotland (Robertson 1970), and detailed discussion must await the verdict of Fitzpatrick's broader study of their role in Roman Scotland (Fitzpatrick 1992 and in preparation).

In summary, while details are inevitably lacking, the Fast Castle evidence can now take its place as a valuable addition to our distressingly incomplete knowledge of Iron Age promontory forts.

## Medieval and later

### K Robin Murdoch and Keith L Mitchell

Because of the importance of the finds from Fast Castle, as much information as possible, within reason, including discussion, is presented in the specialist reports. The excavations are discussed in Chapter 4. Some further information is held in archive. The brief comments which follow are a summary only.

Although the excavations at Fast Castle lasted sixteen years, two points must be emphasised. Firstly, the part time and seasonal nature of the work resulted in much less actual excavation than might have been expected over such a period of time. Secondly, and more importantly, very little of the built structure of the castle was investigated. Only two rooms, the Kitchen and a small free standing building in the Outer Lower Courtyard, were excavated. The rest of the excavated area comprised the entire Lower Courtyard, as defined on the 1549 plan (illus 6).

Accordingly this report must be regarded as only a part interpretation of the site, given that over 80% of the buildings remain untouched.

From the evidence provided by the excavations, it was clear that the entire Lower Courtyard and the platform for the Kitchen had been extensively quarried in the second half of the 15th century. This quarrying was primarily to obtain building stone for 'rough' work in remodelling the castle. Historical evidence indicates that there was a castle on the site from at least the early 15th century but the quarrying appeared to relate only to the later structure. The estimated amount of stone removed from the Lower Courtyard is equivalent to what would have been required for building work at that time.

It is thought unlikely that any of the internal or external walls would have been particularly high. Corbelling, on the surviving corner of the Hall, indicates that even this building would have been only one or one and a half storeys in height. There was no need for high walling at Fast: defence lay in the height of the crag itself.

The local greywacke siltstone was used to construct most of the castle. However, it was unsuitable for items such as corbels, door and window jambs, lintels and steps. These were made from sandstone presumably obtained from Redheugh or Pease Bay, a few miles to the W, and shipped to the castle.

It is interesting to note that the major quarrying on the crag had been carried out at the E, or seaward end. This would not have compromised the defensive nature of the site while retaining the source of raw material near to the point of requirement. Examination of outcropping rock, just inside the castle entrance, suggests that alteration to the natural topography was minimal hereabouts. However, it is very likely that the chasm, W of the entrance and now spanned by a narrow, modern, concrete causeway, was itself artificially deepened for defensive purposes. Further quarrying on the landward side, particularly in the area of the Well, may have also provided some building material for the castle, although much of this stone could have been used to create the 'sponge' for the aquifer around the Well.

Finds recovered from the main fill of the Quarry pit between the upper and lower floors clearly indicate a short period of deposition, anything from a few weeks to a very few years. Interestingly, the faunal remains from the upper levels of this inter-floor fill exhibited weathering, suggesting a hiatus between completion of the fill and the laying of the new floor. However, since the new floor is believed to be associated with an early 16th century remodelling of the castle, these deposits may derive from a tidy-up elsewhere on site, thus obtaining materials to complete the fill of the pit.

Interestingly, in William Douglas's 1921 paper on Fast Castle, he comments that the Home family 'levelled' the walls of the castle in 1515 and that George, fourth Lord Home rebuilt it in 1521. Douglas obtained this information from Carr's *History of Coldingham Priory,* published in 1836. Mary Kennaway argues that it was Home castle and not Fast which was the subject of this activity (Kennaway 1992, 65-66). However, the archaeological evidence, especially from the Quarry pit, may support Carr's premise. The laying of the upper floor (F86) could easily have taken place as late as 1521 and it certainly represents a major remodelling of that particular area.

The manner of deposition of the Quarry pit contexts has revealed a snapshot of life in the late 15th to very early 16th century in a Scottish castle. The ability to cross-relate many different categories of find with dating precision is a luxury not encountered on many sites and the Fast Castle assemblage should prove to be a valuable research resource.

Fortunate circumstances prevailed which allowed preservation of organic remains. Wood, leather, cloth, silk, wool and hair were all recovered. Many thousands of food refuse bones and shells were retrieved. In these latter categories virtually everything found was kept, even to the smallest fish bones. This has allowed a reasonable picture of the diet (at least faunal) of the occupants of the castle to be established. On many sites constraints of time and expense frequently do not allow such precision with respect to food refuse.

The precise role which Fast Castle played in the wider world is open to some debate. Its remote and relatively inaccessible position suggests that it was far more suited to a strategic role than that of a permanent residence. History tells us that the occupants of the castle were responsible for the balefire on the aptly named Telegraph Hill nearby. This was one of a series of signal stations that formed an 'early warning system' against military incursions from the south.

It is perhaps worth pointing out, however, that the castle seems more remote now than it probably was during occupation, since it overlooked the main east coast sea-route. In the late medieval period most sea journeys were carried out within sight of land. In addition, the principal road to the south passed much closer to the castle than the present A1. The old road from Coldingham passed through Lumsdaine and Dowlaw, although not within sight of the castle.

During the excavation several fairly pure soil contexts were observed. Although some may have been deposited deliberately, it is more likely that the majority result from accumulation during periods of inactivity. They were particularly prevalent in the upper 16th-century levels and indicate that the castle may have been unoccupied for perhaps years at a time. Its remoteness, no doubt, contributed to its abandonment in the early 17th century, after improvement in political and military relationships between Scotland and England. Had the castle been situated more favourably it might, in common with many other primarily defensive structures of its era, have been incorporated into a later structure more suited to domestic comfort. Recovery of several finds, dating to earlier than the main group of late 15th- to early 17th-century material, is a clear indication of previous utilisation of the crag. In addition to the Iron Age artefacts already mentioned, a remnant of wall, to the SE of the Well, may actually date to that period. A small walrus ivory gaming piece is thought to be of Viking origin and the date of some of the pottery could be as early as 12th century. It seems reasonable to suggest that the defensive qualities of the site would have appealed, irrespective of era. The quality of the finds, including residual artefacts from earlier than the main post-medieval occupation, suggests that the site was of relatively high status throughout.

Excavations in the Lower Courtyard and Kitchen identified a development phase corresponding to the 1549 plan, as well as some previous structures. It is clear that at least this part of the castle was substantially remodelled towards the end of the 15th century, perhaps reflecting the importance which the site acquired about the time as a residence for Sir Patrick Home. The 1549 plan may include recent, or even intended, alterations by the temporary English occupiers.

Otherwise, however, little new light has been shed on Fast Castle's structural history, or the sequence of settlement on the promontory. In particular, no clear structural archaeological evidence has been found that the castle significantly predates the first documentary references to it in the early 15th century. This may partly result from the limited extent of the excavations, but the nature of the site must also have been an important influence. It is possible that remodelling of the castle, which entailed quarrying into the bedrock base, destroyed all trace of previous structures.

Most interest derives from the range of artefacts yielded by the Quarry pit fill (Period II, late 15th to early 16th century) and the overlying features (Period III, early 16th to early 17th century). The description and dating of the Periods is summarised on page 17 and discussed on pages 25-29. Many of the finds, quite securely dated through the coins recovered, are 'luxury' products that have rarely been recovered from late medieval Scottish sites. Exotic items recovered include silk, pewter, jet beads, some glass items, and the gold button. Some of these were imported. There is also an unusually large assemblage of imported pottery.

Several of the categories of find contain examples considered early for their use in Scotland. These include window glass, hand firearms, and certain types of leather shoe. Such material no doubt reflects the status of Fast Castle's owners, enjoying relatively good communications with the wider world by sea transport. The waterlogged organic deposits provide new information about the early development of Scottish textiles, particularly with respect to sheep breeds and shortwools, and leather working.

Speculation as to the use of the Quarry pit as an animal pen may find credence in the Faunal Remains report where Barnetson comments that bone pathology suggests that sheep were kept in 'unsuitable environmental conditions'. The Quarry pit would have been far more suited to the keeping of pigs, but these animals are poorly represented in the faunal assemblage and sheep are the likely alternative. Barnetson also comments on the remarkable 'homogeneity' of the entire faunal assemblage in terms of species, age, butchery and pathology, but notes that surprisingly little appeared to derive from hearth deposits.

An interesting feature of the 1549 plan is the depiction of a crane in the Outer Lower Courtyard, above the inlet to the great sea cave. This would have been essential for the delivery of heavy goods, particularly construction materials, and would have been invaluable in times of siege, thus enhancing the strategic value of the castle already referred to. Features uncovered during the excavations supported the premise of a crane situated in Area 1 of the Outer Courtyard (see Appendix 7.4).

Holmes comments that the 'most puzzling' numismatic finds are the group of plain copper alloy discs found in later 16th-century contexts. While acknowledging that they may have been 'gaming counters or makeshift jetons', he does not rule out their use for forgery. Given the nefarious reputation of Robert Logan, probably the last 'occupational' owner of Fast Castle, an activity of this sort would not be surprising.

A notable feature of the finds assemblage is the number of artefacts with definite or possible religious connotations. These include the pipe clay figurines, pewter pilgrim's badge, altar vase, jet, opal, amber and the single scallop shell. It is an interesting speculation that these religious, and also the exotic, imported finds might relate to the travels of Cuthbert Home in the first decade of the 16th century. After visiting France, Italy, Venice and Cairo, he returned in 1508 a wealthy man. 'The Turk rewardit him richelie for his service and send him hame to Scotland' (Kennaway 1992, 61-2). There is however no absolute confirmation of this.

Evidence for the abandonment of the castle is again mainly based on numismatic evidence but this is supported by other categories of find, such as pottery and glass. Holmes notes the 'total absence of any numismatic material minted later than 1600', but qualifies this by saying that the relative scarcity of early 17th-century coppers must introduce some doubt. However, he suggests that the absence of later issues, minted in huge numbers from 1632 onwards, is significant. Cromwell apparently took the castle in 1651, but in such dire times any defensible site would have been pressed into service. It is likely that enough of Fast Castle's structure was still upstanding to render it a formidable entity. At the time it was described as 'strong though of little importance, being not able to shelter horse' and 'the last and the least of all the garrisons which the Scots had on the South of Fife and Sterling' (*The Weekly Intelligence of the Commonwealth*, 1650).

Two Dutch clay pipe bowls of the mid 17th century were found in post-abandonment contexts in the Kitchen and adjacent Brewhouse. Excavation in the latter never progressed beyond the removal of turf. The presence of the pipe bowl, immediately under that turf, is an indication of the dilapidation of the building at the time of its deposition.

Approximate parallels to Fast Castle are numerous in Scotland with many fortified sites relying on the sea and cliffs for some, or most, of their defensive strength. Nearby Tantallon and Dunbar Castles are good examples, in principle, if not in structure. However, there does not seem to be any other castle site in Scotland where the inaccessibility, created by a combination of natural topography and innovative design, is as complete as at Fast. If any fortress lived up to the description of impregnable, it was surely this one. Indeed, it was for these reasons that as Stuart Allan reminds us, Regent Morton described Fast Castle in 1573 as one of 'the keys of the country'.

# 7 APPENDICES

## 7.1 THE ENAMELLED GOLD BUTTON

Keith L Mitchell & Hugh P Dinwoodie

With contributions by
Diane Mitchell, K Robin Murdoch & Paul Wilthew

Preparation of this section was materially assisted by many helpful communications with Charles Burnett, David Caldwell, David Chamberlain, John Cherry, George Dalgleish, Rosalind Marshall and Naomi Tarrant. Additional assistance was given by Valerie Dean, Willi & Elma Harvey, Historic Scotland, Mary Kennaway, Bert Maguire, David Mitchell, Jackie Moran, National Museums of Scotland (photographic staff), Georgina Saunders, Sheana Stephen, & Chris Tabraham. The help and advice of all is gratefully acknowledged.

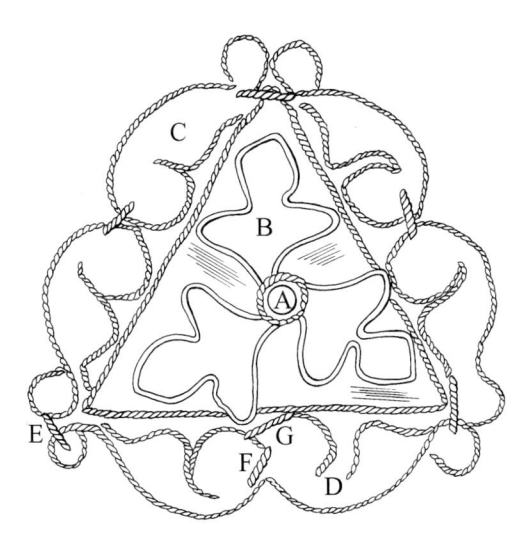

**Illus 86** Schematic diagram of button

DESCRIPTION (Plate IX, illus 86)

This delicate and finely-fashioned button is made of high quality (almost 22 carat) gold, and was originally decorated with both green and white enamel. It weighs 1.26g, and has a maximum diameter just exceeding 15mm. The body has a maximum thickness of 1.5mm at the centre; including the hoop fastener, it is 6mm.

The obverse has at its centre a single tiny gold ball (A) approx 0.8mm in diameter, perhaps representing an acorn (Chamberlain; Cherry; Dalgleish, pers comm). It is surrounded by a circle of gold wire rope. Extending from the ball, are three tri-lobed leaves in a trefoil pattern (B), which were originally inlaid with bluish-green enamel. Chamberlain thinks they represent oak leaves, but might just depict the hawthorn. The tips of two of the nine leaf-lobes overlap the triangular frame.

Outside the triangle, the scroll-type frame is made up of three similar white enamelled patterns (C), outlined in extremely fine gold wire, of diameter 0.25-0.3mm. While each of these occupies one side of the triangle, each half-side of the scroll pattern alternates with its mirror image alongside, resulting in six nearly matching profiles, one of which is slightly flawed. In the right-hand half of the scrollwork pattern, below the triangle base, at (D), there is a discontinuity in the gold wire outlining the white enamel. A gap exists between the two pieces of wire, whereas in the other five similar scroll-patterns, they are in close contact with each other. This appears to be a manufacturing error.

The curved wire shapes in these six parts are joined, at each end, to the next, by short straight links of gold wire (E), about 2mm long, and 0.4mm in diameter. Two of the vertices of the triangle are covered by one of these links, while another link is positioned near the remaining vertex, at the extremity of the scroll-work. Three links are also located at the midpoints of the sides. Two links (F) and (G), instead of one, have been required to complete the pattern at the discontinuity.

Outside the central triangle, the wire scroll design is inlaid with smooth white enamel, most of which survives, often rising above the level of the gold wire, almost obscuring it in places. The green enamel, which partially filled the trefoil with a more shallow inlay, is assumed to have originally covered the whole surface of the three leaves; about two-thirds survived burial. Most of the gold areas between the leaves show minute linear score marks, the regularity of which suggests a purposeful intention. These may have been caused by cleaning the metal surface (see K R Murdoch, below), although Burnett and Cherry have suggested that they may have been related to the filling of the areas with niello (a type of black enamel). These score marks could have acted as a key to secure niello to its gold base. Areas outwith the triangle, not enclosed by the scroll design, may also have been filled with niello, but lack score marks.

The reverse is undecorated (illus 87). It is covered with very fine scratches, which extend into the central triangular depression. This contains the central hooped fastener. The hoop itself is a plain but incomplete loop, with a diameter of 3mm (external) and 1.5mm (internal). There are several deep, roughly parallel, linear score marks, possibly needle damage during sewing; three on one side of the hoop, five or six on the other.

Surrounding the base of the hoop were minute traces of a variable red deposit. A spattering of this substance was also deposited between the hoop and one of the vertices of the depression. These deposits appear to be solder related. Two tiny pale pink coloured areas near to the hoop and spatter were raised above the gold surface (see D Mitchell, below). Both these substances were removed during recent conservation.

**Illus 87** Reverse side, scale 5:1

Apart from the flaws on the obverse already mentioned, the button appears to have been slightly damaged prior to loss. There is slight evidence of wear on the raised surface of the wire forming the triangle. At the top of the reverse, a tiny fragment of gold is missing; and the hoop is slightly bent.

## DISCUSSION

When the button was recovered in June 1975, it was apparent that a find of some significance had been made. Initial enquiries led to a suggestion by Caldwell that it might resemble buttons found in 1912 from the Cheapside Hoard, London. Until recently, little had been published on the subject of excavated medieval buttons in Britain, including those made of precious metals (Egan & Pritchard 1991, 272). Although more information is now available, the study of this subject still relies a great deal on various forms of contemporary art. Evidence from this source can be problematic, as it is often difficult to distinguish between a functional button, a decorative ornament, or even a piece of embroidery. This discussion therefore considers evidence, both direct, and of a more general and circumstantial nature.

Buttons, used as fasteners, have been found as early as the 9th century in Sweden. It appears, however, that they became generally fashionable in England and continental Europe during the early 13th century (*ibid*).

When buttons were first used in Scotland has not been established, although with high fashion decorative varieties, usage probably followed general European trends (Tarrant, pers comm).

## DATING

The Fast Castle button was discovered in a Period III deposit (F96/206, Area 5) of the Quarry Pit at a depth of about 2 metres from the top of the pre-excavation ground surface. It was deposited there during the 16th century, and on stylistic grounds, independent authorities (Cherry; Dalgleish; Marshall, pers comm) agree that the button is most likely to have been manufactured between c1550 and 1600.

Wheeler's paper (1928) on the Cheapside Hoard presents additional dating evidence of a useful but general nature. The hoard consists mainly of a large collection of rings, buttons and chains, which has been assigned a central date of c1600. But although this date corresponds very well with that of the Fast Castle button, initial comparisons so far, made between it and illustrated examples from the hoard, suggest significant differences of style and sophistication.

## PARALLELS

To date, no known parallels have been discovered. The only example of a button bearing any similarities, of which the authors are aware, is another in the Museum of London collection. It has a diameter of only 4.5mm, dates to the 15th century, and was found on the foreshore of the River Thames (Murdoch T 1991); a published illustration (*ibid*, no 199) suggests a possible distant design link between the two.

## PROVENANCE

The first question to consider is whether or not the button was made in Scotland, at one of the limited number of places where the art of the goldsmith was practised, such as Edinburgh. It was only in the 15th century that the Edinburgh goldsmiths first became part of the Incorporation of Hammermen, and then subsequently an autonomous body of their own (Finlay 1991). Scottish goldsmiths, by comparison with their English and continental counterparts, seem to have been on the whole much later in achieving a separate corporate identity.

It is perhaps worth noting that a statute of Queen Mary, in 1555, ordained that no goldsmith should produce items of gold 'under 22 carate fine', under pain of death and confiscation of goods (Acts Parl Scot 1814). The Fast Castle button is of this purity: 90.6% gold, within one per cent of this standard (see Wilthew, below).

Unfortunately, apart from the Crown Jewels of Scotland, very few examples of the work of Scottish goldsmiths from the 15th and 16th centuries survive. Even fewer can be used to compare stylistically with the Fast Castle button. These include the heart-shaped locket of Mary, Queen of Scots (1560-70); the locket of Mary, Queen of Scots and James VI (1576-9), which once formed part of the Penicuik Jewels, and the Barnhills locket (Marshall & Dalgleish 1991); also the Dunnottar gold reliquary (Barron D G 1904). Indeed, the problems of comparison are compounded by the fact that, to date, it has been impossible to compare the design and style of the Fast Castle button with any other similar Scottish contemporary example. Hackenbroch (1979, 286) has described Scotland as a poor and sparsely populated country, with 16th-century jewellery of an unsophisticated and somewhat provincial character.

While most Scottish jewellery can appear technically somewhat inferior to that produced outside Scotland, the heart-shaped setting of the Mary cameo does seem an excellent piece of craftsmanship. Evans (1953, 129) described it as having a rather heavy style, suggesting for this reason that it might be of Scottish manufacture.

The Barnhills locket (c1600) was found in 1930 near Corsewall Castle, Wigtownshire. Although damaged and lacking much of its original enamel, in several ways it bears a marked resemblance to the Penicuik Jewel. These pieces are of course much larger and more complex in design than the Fast Castle button. However, they contain similarities which include enamelling with various colours, together with the use of extremely fine gold wire. Of particular interest are the scrolls found in both the Penicuik Jewel and the Barnhills locket, which surround a central panel, as in the Fast Castle button. These examples may suggest a similar design concept of enclosure. To date, no other parallels have been found.

Another example of jewellery of probable Scottish origin from the same period, which contained gold wire and enamel, is the Dunnottar gold reliquary or locket. It is reputed to have been associated with Mary, Queen of Scots.

The use of enamel outlined by gold wire is an ancient form of decoration and has been practised in many different countries and cultures. Cherry notes that during the late Middle Ages, the use of gold wire and enamel was quite common, for example, as found on some belt fittings from Chalcis, Greece. According to Kolba & Németh (1986), this art form became a speciality of Hungarian goldsmiths, and from about the middle of the 15th century, became so popular that throughout Europe the technique became known as Hungarian enamel. Cherry, however, is of the opinion that the button is of north European manufacture.

FUNCTION

Oswald Barron (1911), an authority on early English dress, noted that buttons appeared during the time of Edward I 'as a scandalous ornament on men of low degree'. By the 14th century, they had become common, being produced both for decoration and practical purposes. He cites examples, which include a close row of buttons running from the wrist to elbow of a tight sleeve. Another, a tight-sleeved body garment known as the cote-hardie, could be fastened down the front by twelve or more rich buttons. Although by the middle of the 16th century the fashion dictates of the Middle Ages had been well and truly left behind, buttons continued to be used as before.

Was the Fast Castle button used as a functional fastener, or for decorative purposes? Was it a single item, or part of a set, and where was it worn? Was it worn by a man, woman or child, or used as an embellishment on some item other than dress, such as a book cover?

A button-like object found in medieval spoil at Billingsgate, with a diameter of 5mm, is thought to have been too small for practical use (Egan & Pritchard 1991, 280). Displayed on the sleeve of a garment as an adornment, the Fast Castle button seems visually less appropriate than perhaps on a hat, or as part of a set, although it was found to act as a fastener quite adequately. Interestingly, the score marks on the back of the button might indicate that the button had been attached to a garment on more than one occasion.

During the Tudor and early Jacobean periods, the wearing of rich jewellery, including items of gold, seems to have been largely the prerogative of royalty, the aristocracy, and persons of considerable substance. Indeed, as in previous times, both English and Scottish parliaments enacted a variety of what were known as 'sumptuary laws' dictating, at least on paper, what different classes of people should wear.

Amongst the known Scottish elite of the period, who had direct connections with Fast Castle, were Agnes Gray, her first husband Robert Logan, 6th baron of Restalrig, and her second, Alexander, 5th Lord Home (Kennaway 1992, 93). Some time after the abdication of Mary, Queen of Scots in 1567, Lady Agnes came into the possession of some of the Queen's noted collection of jewellery which had been taken from Mary and widely dispersed. In 1573, Agnes was obliged to return these items to the Regent Morton. Included were fifteen diamonds set in gold with white enamel, and a considerable number of pearls. Inventories of Queen

Mary's jewels show that she owned more than 1,100 buttons, which are described as being of gold, silver, some with diamonds, rubies, pearls, white and black and, in one case, red enamel, but none with descriptions resembling the Fast Castle button. It would be tempting to associate the button with an individual such as Lady Agnes, but there are many other possible candidates. These include other members of the Logan family and their peers who had a direct connection with the Castle. Of the latter, two examples are the Countess of Northumberland, who was given sanctuary at Fast Castle after the Northern Rising of 1569 (Kennaway 1992, 97), and John Napier of Merchiston, who in 1594 signed a contract to search for 'a soum of monie and poise' thought to be hidden there (Mitchell, 1988, 1).

How then was the button used? If, for example, it decorated a hat, then the style might have been similar to that seen in an illustration of Lord Burleigh's seventeen-year-old nephew, Edward Hoby, in 1577 (Illus 90). It has been suggested that youth was the excuse for his flamboyant headgear. Gold ornaments are set round the band, and two gold buttons and an acorn are situated at the top.(Norris 1938, 728).

**Illus 88** Prince Philip of Spain

**Illus 89** Claudia de' Medici

During the reign of Queen Elizabeth I, an Italian form of headgear became very fashionable with the ladies of England and France. This 'Bonet à l'Italienne' frequently contained, amongst other items, gold buttons set with jewels (*ibid*, 753-4). A painting of Robert Dudley, Earl of Leicester, in 1576 shows him wearing a hat, which has a set of at least six jewelled buttons (or ornaments) on it (Marshall 1986).

An example of a costume decorated with a multiple display of ornamented jewellery can be seen in a portrait of Edward VI, where there are at least forty-five emeralds in gold settings; while a further illustration shows Prince Philip of Spain in 1554 (illus 88), wearing a jerkin made up of velvet bands held together by fancy buttons (Norris 1938, Plates 20 & 22). A later example can be seen on the dress of Claudia de' Medici, c1625, (illus 89) (Evans 1953, Plate 105). As in other times, it was normal practice for many children to

**Illus 90** Sir Edward Hoby

dress in a similar fashion to their parents. For example, Lord Edward Seymour (a contender to the English throne) is shown, aged two, in a painting of 1563, wearing a bonnet of black velvet studded with gold and jewelled buttons. Similarly, James VI of Scotland at the age of eight is depicted dressed as an adult, his doublet fastened with three gold buttons (Norris 1938, 527 & 530).

The Fast Castle button may have been used for decorative purposes on something other than an item of dress. An example can be seen on the book cover held by the German girl in the painting 'Countesses Ermengard and Walburg vom Rietberg', dated 1568 (Hackenbroch 1979, 202, fig 563). At least five button-like objects are visible on the front cover. They appear identical, and were probably a set. However, the way in which they were attached to the cover is not known.

## DESIGN AND SYMBOLISM

At first glance, the obverse design of the Fast Castle button would appear to be simple decoration, without any deeper significance. This is certainly the view held by several authorities who have cogently considered the question. However, the distinctive and possibly unique pattern, including the prominent use of a triangle, raises the possibility that it might have had some symbolic significance as well as artistic value. That something of such a small size should contain any form of symbolism, is by no means unusual. For example, Egyptian scarabs, many of which are of a comparable size to the button, often contain inscriptions denoting their supposed magical properties (Bozman 1970). Other examples of symbolism include ceremonial rings and many of the designs found on Celtic jewellery.

Clearly, trefoil and triangle form the basis of the design, but do they contain any individual or linked symbolism? In one view, the triangle was designed to act purely as a partition between the trefoil and the outer scroll-work. Indeed, no other geometric figure would have been appropriate. However, its use may have had an alternative or complementary significance. The authors have so far not discovered any other example of a triangle included in the design of British or continental jewellery of that period.

From prehistoric times, the triangle has had various symbolic meanings. To the Greeks it represented the genitals, while the Pythagoreans believed it represented the principle behind the creation of the universe. Over many centuries it has also played an important part in magic rituals. During the 3rd century AD, the Manichaeans adopted it as a symbol for the Christian Trinity, but St Augustine of Hippo was so opposed to this that it was not used again as such until the 11th century (Der Grosse Brockhaus 1953). If the trefoil is indeed a representation of oak leaves, what could be its symbolic significance? The oak tree has had a place of honour in the heritage of many nations. In various historical contexts, it has been revered as both magical and sacred, and used as a symbol for strength (Buckland, undated).

Throughout the Christian era, a variety of symbols other than the triangle have been used to denote the Holy Trinity, including three interlocking circles, trefoil, or three fish (Gibson, 1996). It should also be noted that two of the principal symbols of the ternary (groups of three), are the triangle and the trefoil (Julien, 1996).

Interestingly, Burnett independently suggests that the trefoil within a triangle represents the Trinity, but thinks that the button is unlikely to have been worn by church members or clergy. A curious medieval reference to a connection between oak leaves and triangles (reported by Chamberlain) is given by Albert of Cologne (Albertus Magnus), the 13th century German philosopher and divine. He wrote that 'the (oak) leaf....can be entirely circumscribed by triangles with their bases on the leaf and their apexes outside...', but the meaning of this statement is unclear. Chamberlain reasonably comments that it is perhaps surprising this description should be influencing a design three centuries later, unless it had taken on some religious significance. Trefoil decoration is common in stained glass windows.

**Illus 91** Stylised clouds

**Illus 92** Scrollwork in stained glass, Arezzo, Italy

Chamberlain further reports a suggestion that the white motifs outside the triangle were intended to represent clouds, but disagrees; as does Burnett, who observes that the decorative elements are visually linked to create a strong feeling of enclosure. During the Middle Ages the normal stylisation of clouds was depicted as in illus 91, while the white enamel scroll-work is surrounded as in illus 86. The latter design is visually much more compressed and solid than clouds.

The manner in which these enclosing scrollwork motifs are joined by short straight links of gold wire-rope is believed to be curious and without parallel in jewellery (Cherry, pers comm). However, a similar characteristic has been noted in medieval European frescoes; also in stained glass, (illus 92) (Day 1897), and wrought iron grilles, as in Richards (1892). Further research is necessary to establish whether or not designs in such diverse materials could have influenced the design of the Fast Castle button.

Ecclesiastical architecture contains a wealth of rich and powerful symbolism which is still being incorporated into the fabric of religious buildings. One of countless modern examples is the large oak screen constructed in 1909 in the parish church of South Leith, Edinburgh (Marshall 1983). Amongst its varied decorations is a small cluster of three acorns, locally understood to represent the Trinity (J Arthur, pers comm), as well as, coincidentally, the arms of the Logans of Restalrig who, during part of the 16th century owned Fast Castle. Another striking aspect, to which it is perhaps worth drawing attention, is the number of times groups of three have been used in the design.

Several sources have reasonably questioned any possible symbolic connection, instead arguing that their existence is consequent solely upon the use of a triangle. Recently, however, a very similar observation to that of the authors was independently made by Saunders (pers comm).

CONCLUDING SUMMARY

The Fast Castle button is a piece of quality jewellery, which may be unique. It was recovered from a 16th-century south-eastern Scottish Borders context. It seems certainly of north or central European origin, and was quite likely manufactured in Scotland between c1550 and 1600. If this could be proved beyond doubt, the button would assume historical significance, as a rare example of the Scottish goldsmith's craft. Either the button's design was created both for symbolic and decorative reasons; or if decoration was the only underlying concept, then symbolism was introduced unintentionally. The former assertion seems more credible. It was almost certainly worn as decoration on a costume, perhaps more specifically on a hat. Certainly, used on the former, more than one would have been required to produce a significant effect.

## THE ENAMEL

K Robin Murdoch

The enamelling of the button was examined microscopically at magnifications up to x 40. Two colours of enamel were present, green and white. The bluish-green enamel was fairly thinly applied within the trefoil (oak leaves?), surviving surfaces being slightly concave. The green colour appeared variegated but it was difficult to establish the precise cause. Poor mixing of the metallic oxide (for colour), glass paste, and fluxing alkali or low fusing temperatures are the most likely. The enamel also appears slightly fibrous as if rather too viscous when applied. Surface cracking, probably part chrisselling and part thermal shock when the enamel was applied, had in some places resulted in mechanical instability and some loss of inlay.

The white enamel appeared in generally better condition than the green but contained larger gas bubbles, again suggesting that the enamel may have been worked at a lower than ideal temperature. This is perhaps not surprising considering the fine nature of the gold work in which it was inlaid. Chrisselling and thermal cracking were less obvious in the white enamel, and less had been physically lost than with the green. The white enamel had, however, been more thickly applied resulting in a convex surface.

Both colours of enamel had surface degradation resulting from the leaching of alkali.

Although Burnet and Cherry suggest that linear score marks, within the triangle, may relate to the application of niello, no trace was visible of this or any other inlay. However, it is just possible that the presence of small traces may have been masked by the presence of soil residues. The score marks may represent cleaning of the metal surface after the application of the trefoils themselves, perhaps as a result of removing waste flux, gold, or solder.

## COMPOSITIONAL ANALYSIS

Paul Wilthew

The gold button was submitted for compositional analysis. The results were required to try to determine the button's origin.

### METHOD

Two areas were analysed using energy dispersive X-ray fluorescence (XRF). No sample preparation was carried out prior to analysis, but the metal was visually clean. Semi-quantitative results were obtained using the fundamental parameters method calibrated with pure element standards. The results will have been affected by the uncertain geometry and finish of the areas analysed and by any difference between the surface composition and that of the original bulk metal. The effect of these sources of error cannot be accurately estimated. Although the results probably provide a reasonable indication of the original composition the possible errors should be taken into account when interpreting them. Further details of the analytical method are given below.

### RESULTS

There were no significant differences between the results from the two areas analysed. Gold, copper and silver were the only elements detected (spectra F6637B and F6638B - available in archive). The mean composition was: Gold 90.6%; Silver 7.3%; Copper 2.1%. (See discussion under 'Provenance', above).

## XRF METHOD

The analysed areas were irradiated with a primary X-ray beam produced by a rhodium target X-ray tube run at 46KV with an anode current of 0.1mA. The primary beam was collimated to give an elliptical irradiated area about 1.5mm x 1mm. Secondary X-rays were detected using a silicon (lithium) solid state detector.

The path between the sample and detector is through air which normally limits the range of detectable elements to those of atomic number 20 or above. The detection limit varies for different elements and depends on the matrix, but is typically between 0.05% and 0.2%.

The fundamental parameters program HPFUN3, based on the method described by Cowell (1977), calibrated with pure element standards for gold, silver and copper was used to quantify the results. The software assumes that the total concentration of the elements included in the analysis is 100%.

## XRF AND SEM ANALYSIS OF THE SOLDER AND ENAMEL

### Diane Mitchell

The three sections to this study cover the alloy used to solder the loop to the button, the red/brown deposits within the central depression of the back of the button, and the coloured enamels on the face. The scanning electron microscope (SEM) was used to study the alloy, whereas the enamels were studied both by the SEM's energy dispersive analytical system and by X-ray fluorescence (XRF). Through both of these techniques, sufficient data emerged that could ascertain the nature of the deposits, and help identify some of the components of the enamels.

## THE ANALYTICAL TECHNIQUES

The SEM is a high magnification imaging technique capable of magnifying up to x 100 000 (though here, the maximum magnification used was approximately x 1000). It also offers the ability to conduct compositional studies of an object. In this study, qualitative analyses were carried out on the unidentified deposits found on the back of the button (see description). However, only conductive objects can be studied in the SEM. Therefore, in order to study the enamels more accurately, X-ray fluorescence (XRF) was used. This technique gives similar compositional results, with the advantage being that it is entirely non-destructive. Again, qualitative results were obtained for this study.

## PRE- & POST-BURIAL ACTION ON A SILVER-GOLD ALLOY: Pre-Burial: Gas-Evolved Pores

While a metal or alloy is molten, gases can dissolve and bubble through the liquid. If this is viscous enough, then upon cooling the bubbles will remain as pores. Pores such as these are found on the button. Although they do resemble a casting texture, they are found concentrated in certain areas. On the face of the button they exist mainly where the decorative wire is joined to the base, in the troughs of the 'twists' of the wire (illus 93). On the back of the button they appear at the base of the loop, decreasing in abundance away from the centre, with none found outwith the central depression. As a result, they are most likely to have been formed during the soldering process.

There is doubt over how the button was manufactured. SEM image analysis of the decorative wiring and trefoil indicates that they consist of several individual pieces. When viewing the button from the back, enamel is visible (on one apex of the button) where part of the base has broken/worn away. The gold wire remains *in situ* along the edge of the enamel, which would only occur if the wire and base were not cast or moulded together. Note that also in illus 94 a faint line can be traced along the edge of the button. A shallow cavity along this line reveals an abundance of pores, but outwith this area none are found. This may suggest that the base itself consists of two separate pieces which have been soldered together with the solder joint being subsequently neatened up. In other words, much care has been taken to ensure a high-quality appearance of this button. This, in conjunction with the nature of the pores, would suggest that the button could have been worked into shape (being a high purity gold, and thus very malleable), with the loop, wire, and trefoil soldered into place. However, from a jeweller's viewpoint this is unlikely. Soldering numerous parts to the button would require the button to have been reheated on more than one occasion. As a result, whatever had been affixed first would loosen and fall away. Solders with different melting temperatures would be required to solve this problem (eg by using different ratios of silver and gold). This would be a fairly major task, although with a button of this quality, the time and skill involved would be justified. At this stage, however, further research into the properties of the solder used would be required to verify the actual method of manufacture. It could also be suggested that the pores were caused by corrosion, with only some of the alloy's constituents being dissolved out. This is not the case. As can be seen in illus 95, while still in its molten state the manufacturer has used a tool (perhaps to remove excess alloy) to scrape around the base of the loop. In doing so he has obliterated many of the pores, therefore proving their time of origin to be early. Whether or not the jeweller has used flux cannot be fully determined. Flux is used to aid the fusion of solder joints principally by excluding air (oxygen) from the immediate heated area and thereby preventing surface oxidation. This oxidisation leads to poor fusion and results in a porous 'dry' joint. Without the use of flux, the solder would not run smoothly across the button, making it almost unworkable. Therefore, although the evidence would suggest that no flux has been used, there is no logical reason as to why it should not, especially for a piece of this quality. The alloy has appeared to 'spread out' by 2-3mm from the area of application into the central depression. However, this could be due to various factors: the temperature of the molten alloy, the quantity of flux used (if at all) or the wetness/dryness of the button itself.

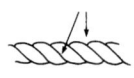

**Illus 93** Gas pore location in troughs

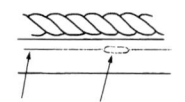

**Illus 94** Possible solder junction suggested by gas pores

POST-BURIAL: CORROSION AND CHEMICAL DEPOSITION

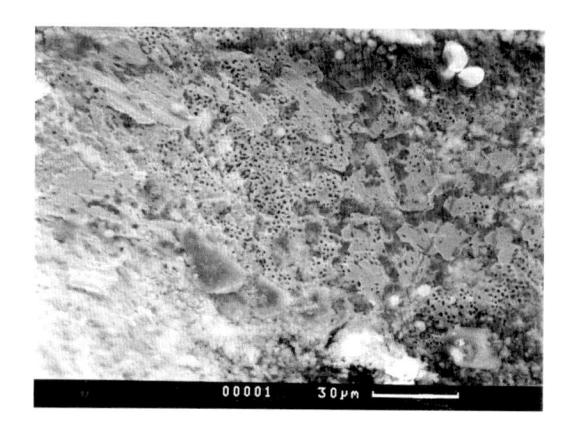

**Illus 95** SEM image of solder (note white calcareous nodules)

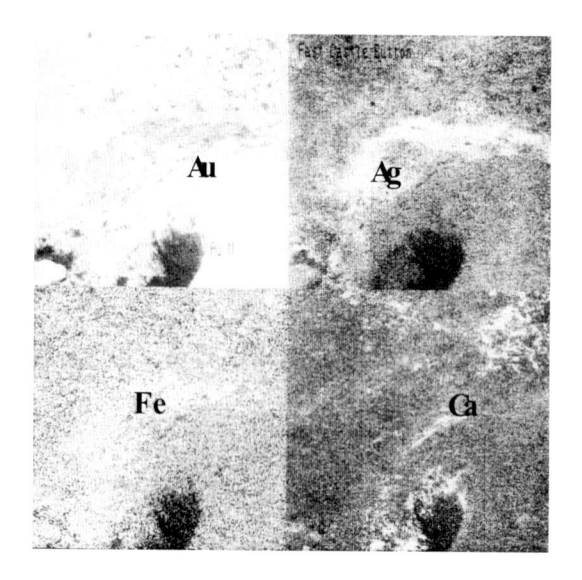

**Illus 96** Map of elements; paler areas are higher concentration

Under an optical microscope, there were three colours of deposits: pale pink, red, and dark red/black. Identifying these under the SEM was difficult due to the lack of colour in secondary electron imaging. However, there were some deposits where a positive identification could be made, and they can be grouped into two categories.

The first is the pale coloured deposits (referred to as the spatter in the description of the button). They were abundant and their shape varied from irregular to fairly spherical. They were calcareous with no measurable minor or trace elements. The cause of the pink colour is as yet unknown; possibilities include potassium (K), aluminium (Al) or manganese (Mn). They appeared only in the central depression and were randomly dispersed. It is most likely that they are post-burial, with the calcium possibly being leached out of the surrounding soil.

The second deposit was found mainly around the loop, with the darker red/black areas being much less abundant and restricted to the very base of the loop. A digital map of this area was recorded for gold, silver, iron and calcium (illus 96).

The top right hand map shows a higher concentration of silver (shown in white) around the base of the loop, ie the alloy. Of interest is the area of solder in the centre of the map lower in silver. Under an optical microscope, this was one of the red areas, whereas the area shown in white was one of the dark red/black areas. Qualitative analysis gave varying silver intensities on the red areas, although all were significantly less than the gold content. However, similar analysis of the dark red/black area gave instead a silver peak slightly higher than the gold.

Although not conclusive (as only one analysis was carried out on the darker area), this suggests that the silver was remarkably higher where the deposits are blacker in colour (silver oxide).

In addition to the silver, a very faint iron trace (bottom left hand map) was concentrated in the alloy. Again, qualitative analysis gave higher iron readings in the darker areas, but more readings would have been required to confirm this.

As only minor silver (7.3%) was detected from the base gold in a previous XRF analysis (Wilthew, above), this concludes that it must have been a silver/gold alloy that was used to solder the loop to the button. This has subsequently corroded to give the deposits seen here. No iron was detected outwith this area, suggesting that it too was a constituent of the alloy. However, the quantities recorded around the solder are too low to prove this.

## QUALITATIVE ANALYSIS OF THE ENAMELS

The SEM analyses were taken at only 25 seconds livetime (the length of time that incoming X-rays are recorded and evaluated). This compares with a livetime of 100 seconds for all other readings in this study. In addition, the deadtime (the proportion of time that the processor cannot accept a new signal, as it can only process one at a time) was very low at only 7-11%. An acceptable deadtime would roughly be between 25-50%.

The XRF analyses were both studied at 100 seconds livetime with a deadtime of 37-45%, in other words giving more accurate results. However, the gold (Au) peak derived from the button itself may have obscured peaks which might otherwise have shown up. It should be noted though that particular care was taken to avoid the green enamel when studying the white, and vice versa.

The combined data can be seen in Table 20:

**Table 20**: Gold Button: Results of the SEM and XRF studies

| Enamel type | Analysis No | XRF ||| SEM |||
|---|---|---|---|---|---|---|---|
| | | Major | Minor | Trace | Major | Minor | Trace |
| White | 1 | **Si Sn Ca** | Pb Fe | | **Si Pb** | Cu Sn | Fe |
| | 2 | **Si Pb Ca** | Sn | | | | |
| Green | 1 | **Si** | Pb Ca | Fe | | Cu | Fe |
| | 2 | **Si** | Pb Ca | Fe | | | |

The results taken at this stage sadly do not give much away. Medieval glass and enamels are reputed to be potash rich; however, potassium is an element which is readily lost during weathering. As only the surface of the enamels could be studied, it is not surprising that none was detected.

The only difference seen here is the presence of tin in the white enamel. Tin used in conjunction with lead will give a yellow colour, unless heated to over 900°C where it will turn white. As lead is found in the white enamel, this could give an indication as to temperature of formation. However, tin oxide (SnO) was also used as a white colourant. Therefore at this stage no further deductions can be made.

Under oxidising conditions, copper will dissolve in high lead enamels to give a green colour (Sayre & Smith, 1974).

CONCLUSION

Prior to this study, there were different ideas as to what the deposits on the back of the button were. These assessments were made purely on a visual basis relating to their colour and texture. The scanning electron microscope has been able to provide information which has revealed two types of deposit. Both of these are most likely to be post-burial; however the origin of the pale pink calcareous deposits is less clear. The darker deposits are most definitely corrosion products of the silver/gold alloy used for soldering. It is possibly their change in chemistry that gives the change in colour from red to red/black. However, more analyses would be required to confirm this. Unfortunately the most interesting section to this study gives the least information. From purely non-destructive methods, the data on the chemical composition of the enamels remains limited. An increase in the tin content of the white enamel is the only clear difference.

## 7.2 WATER SUPPLY TO COASTAL CASTLES

Nigel A Ruckley

FACTORS AFFECTING WATER SUPPLY

Not all precipitation ends up as groundwater; between one third and one half of the total rainfall in Britain evaporates and the remainder is further reduced either by plant uptake or as direct run off. The rest of the rain will finally pass through the subsoil into the underlying deposits until it reaches a zone of saturation where all the voids are filled. This zone of non-static water is known as groundwater and its upper surface is referred to as the water table. A well should be sunk into a zone of permanent saturation known as an aquifer. If due to geological reasons this does not happen, the well would dry up in periods of low rainfall.

The ability of rocks to store groundwater is dependent on their porosity and permeability values. Igneous and metamorphic rocks are usually poor aquifers but their permeability can be enhanced if the rock is fractured or has prominent jointing (Ruckley 1991, 18-26).

Coastal clifftop castles often had more geological difficulties to overcome before an adequate water supply could be assured, compared with their counterparts on inland hilltop sites. Both locations were often of limited area, confined by the geomorphological restraint of sheer rock faces and often the space for the provision of a contamination-free area for surface water catchment was further restricted by the siting of gun batteries. Coastal fortifications were vulnerable to the erosion of sea cliffs by wave action, the contamination of a surface water supply by salt and grit laden winds. A lower annual rainfall, when compared with inland sites, limited the rain water availability for surface water catchment (Ruckley 1990, 14-26)

METHODS OF WATER SUPPLY

The methods of obtaining a water supply that were available to the architects of coastal clifftop castles and early artillery fortifications were as follows: (a) well(s) (b) cistern(s) and/or barrels for rainwater or well water (c) combination of internal and external water supplies.

Coastal castles which used wells to reach an aquifer would usually find that the well water level would vary with the effects of tidal loading. For example, the well at *Ardrossan Castle*, NS 233 424, situated in an underground passage, was recorded by the early 17th-century historian Pont to have fluctuated with the tide (Ruckley 1991, 18). The castle, which now lies inland due to land reclamation, once stood on a 15.24m high promontory overlooking the sea. *Fast Castle*, NT 862 710, however, relied on a perched water table for its supply and did not encounter these conditions.

At clifftop sites, where the rock was suitable for constructing a well, the shaft was often of considerable depth. The conical well at *Ravenscraig Castle*, Fife, NT 291 925, was situated in the basement of the eastern tower of the gatehouse. It measured 1.82m in diameter at the top and tapered to a depth of over 12.19m into Upper Carboniferous sandstones of the Upper Limestone Group, Millstone Grit Series.

Deep wells inevitably meant an expensive lifting mechanism, coupled with a limited volume of water raised in any given period of time.

*Tantallon Castle*, NT 596 851, on cliffs over 30.48m high, had one well, 32.3m deep, within the inner defences, sunk through volcanic agglomerate belonging to the Carboniferous Calciferous Sandstone Measures. Although below the foundations of the NW walls a few metres of poorly stratified sandstone of similar age is exposed, the castle relied on the permeability of the volcanic agglomerate for its water supply (Mitchell, Walton & Grant 1960, 72-4).

## WATER SUPPLY OF FAST CASTLE

The water supply at Fast Castle demonstrates how geological problems were overcome to provide the Castle with a water supply which was not sited in the most advantageous position.

The greywackes make poor aquifers as they are not porous; their permeability and storage capacity would depend on the size of their joint planes and fracture patterns. Any well sunk in the inner ward of the Castle would have a limited water catchment area and would have to be sunk to the water table, at or below sea level. Sea water contamination could therefore be present. The cost of sinking a well, similar to the one at Tantallon, would have been considerable.

The well could conceivably have pre-dated the castle, given the proximity of nearby hill forts, eg at Dowlaw; and possibly even on the promontory itself, given the presence of the ditch on the slope above the well, and wall to the south and east of the well, both of which are not necessarily contemporaneous with the castle.

A shaft constructed in gravel deposits and rubble backfill outside the Castle in the lee of Hawks Heugh would on the other hand provide a supply from the perched aquifer formed by the glacial sands and gravels resting on top of the fissured greywackes. The Well was probably constructed by excavating a funnel-shaped depression through the glacial gravels down to bedrock, then building a dry stone shaft, the hole surrounding the shaft being backfilled with rubble. The supply would not be ideal, as it would be limited to the depth and the extent of the drift deposits. The banks to the S and NW of the Well might represent an attempt to improve the water retention of the catchment area (illus 7). Murdoch estimates that the irregular catchment area of the Well was roughly 1200 square metres and the depth varied to a maximum of 3.75m. The catchment was estimated to hold 23,000 litres with a quarter of the total capacity in the Well shaft itself (Kennaway 1992, 3). During the dry summers of 1975 and 1976 the surface of the water table was between 0.7 and 1.4m below ground level (Ward 1985, 9).

Fresh water springs have been noted at the base of the cliff near the mouth of the cave under the Castle and it is said that divers, off Fast Castle, have reported fresh water springs issuing from the seabed. As there is no proven direct access to this cave from the Castle, apart from the crane, the only two methods of water supply available to the Castle's inhabitants were either by the Well in the outer ward or by the collection of rain water from the roofs of buildings. The use of water butts or barrels might be more common than thought. Their specific use is only rarely mentioned in historical documents. Three large water barrels and seven empty wine casks were noted in the will, dated 18th May 1555, of Thomas Bertie, who lived at Hurst Castle, SZ 318 897 (James 1986, 17).

## CONCLUSIONS

Although Fast Castle was not by any means a prominent first-line fortress, it had to utilise the water sources available within the vicinity of the Castle. The costs of sinking a deep well and/or construction of stone cisterns would have been considerable, but were not necessarily beyond the means of a wealthy family such as the Homes. Nevertheless, such outlays seem not to have been thought necessary. The supply would be adequate for everyday use, assuming there were no long periods of drought. In times of siege, where the protection of buildings from fire was vital, the water supply might be fully stretched.

## SOME EXAMPLES OF WATER SUPPLY TO COASTAL CASTLES

As noted above, the methods of obtaining a water supply that were available to the architects of coastal clifftop castles and early artillery fortifications were as follows:- (a) well(s) (b) cistern(s) and/or barrels for rainwater or well water (c) combination of internal and external water supplies. Some examples of each are given below.

(a) Wells

*Ardrossan Castle, Fast Castle, Ravenscraig Castle,* and *Tantallon Castle* have already been referred to in the text.

*Dover Castle* (TR 325 418) has wells sunk through Cretaceous chalk over 106.88m (350ft) deep (Toy 1963, 100-101), and possibly as deep as 121.92m (400ft) since a nearby early 19th-century well in the citadel of Dover's Western Heights is reputed to be 134.1m (440ft) deep (Coad & Lewis 1982, 171-2). Cisterns, either for rainwater or for storage of well water, for drinking or fire fighting purposes, were present at Dover throughout most of the castle's history.

*Scarborough Castle* (TA 048 892), on a much larger site, has two wells, one in each bailey. The well within the inner bailey is 2.13m (7ft) in diameter at the well head, lined to 20.73m (68ft) and over 45.72m (150ft) deep into Jurassic oolites and grits belonging to the Corallian formation. It is probable that the lining of the well was taken down through the boulder clay and oolitic limestone until the harder grits were reached (Scarborough Castle Guide 1960).

The 'Z' plan tower house of *Ballone Castle* (NH 929 838) is situated on 20m high steep grass covered cliffs about one kilometre north of Rockfield on the south side of the Tarbat peninsula overlooking the Moray Firth. A carved stone dated 1590 confirms the late 16th-century aspect of the tower house. A small stone courtyard contains on its east wall a range of buildings, including a bakehouse. The diminutive courtyard separates the cliff face from the tower. The well of unknown depth lies within the enclosure close to the entrance of the courtyard in the east wall of the range. The well of 1.15m inside diameter is stone lined at the top to the start of the rubbish fill at 2m. The water apparently was taken from the well and transported outside the safety of the courtyard via the east gate to the kitchens near the southwest corner of the castle where a stone water inlet and outlet pipe are set in the exterior wall. The water would have been easily obtained from the fine grained light brownish grey sandstone of the Strath Rory Group Middle Old Red Sandstone age (IGS 1998, Sheet 94; also Armstrong 1977). The stone from the cliff face was utilised for the majority of the castle's fabric. At present (1998) the castle is under restoration into a private dwelling.

Where the immediate sub-surface geology consisted of impervious rocks with low water bearing potential compared with the visibly more suitable strata below, a well would often be sunk to reach this potentially enhanced water supply.

Below the dolerite of the Great Whin Sill, on which the medieval castles of *Bamburgh* (NU 183 351) and *Dunstanburgh* (NU 257 218) stand, Carboniferous sandstones provided a more suitable aquifer and were utilised (Ruckley 1990, 15; Trueman 1938, 194-7). At Bamburgh, the well 45.72m (150ft) deep, within the keep, penetrates the entire depth of the sill, 22.86m (75ft), in order to reach the sandstones below (Gunn 1900, 70 & 120).

A few kilometres south of Bamburgh, the dolerite of the Great Whin Sill forms the headland on which the early 14th-century Dunstanburgh Castle stands. Here, a cliff section reveals that the 15.24m (50ft) sill overlies at least 12.19m (40ft) of Carboniferous age sandy shale with sandstone partings (Carruthers *et al* 1930, 76). Today, the uncleared well within the inner ward is 16.3m (53.48ft) deep. When first dug it would have just penetrated the sedimentary rocks which provided a more adequate water supply than a well relying solely on fissure flow through joints within the dolerite sill.

A well could prove troublesome during a siege, especially if the water supply was from a perched aquifer which relied on water being retained within the internal fissures of a low porosity rock. For example, a dolerite or basalt sill could contain water only in fissures that either were open to the collection of surface water or from the ground water table, if it was able to penetrate the joints and fissures from below the sill. A perched water table within an igneous sill, that was unconnected to the natural ground water table, could be vulnerable to changes to the fracture pattern brought about by the effects of gunfire (Ruckley 1991, 21).

*Mingary Castle* (NM 502 631) sits on top of a Tertiary sill. The location and depth of the well is unrecorded. Its water level dropped during a siege of the castle in 1644 and ale was substituted in an attempt to extinguish a fire near the castle's gate (Inventory of Argyll 1980, 209-17; Ruckley 1991, 21).

(b) Cisterns

Cistern(s) and/or barrels for rainwater or well water: some castles were situated on strategic sites of restricted area where the potential for an underground water supply was low, and the garrisons had to rely either on cisterns or a mixture of internal and external water supplies.

A felsite intrusion of possibly Ordovician age forms a prominent 30.4m (100ft) coastal headland on which *Criccieth Castle* (SH 500 377) now stands, but the rock failed to provide an adequate underground water supply (Neaverson 1947, 38-9). The original supply envisaged by the builders of the mid 13th-century castle is not known. During construction of the gatehouse a small seepage was discovered and utilised by the construction of a shallow cistern within the entrance passage. Apparently, this proved inadequate, as an additional rain water cistern was constructed at the opposite end of the inner ward probably during the rebuilding of the castle in the late 13th century (Ruckley 1990, 21; O'Neil 1944, 1-51; Avent 1989).

(c) Combination of internal and external water supplies

Sometimes there are local legends of an external piped water supply into a clifftop coastal fortification. Occasionally some documentary evidence survives but archaeological evidence for a supply is very rare.

*Dundarg Castle* (NJ 895 649), situated on a narrow peninsula of Middle Old Red Sandstone, high above the Moray Firth is not unlike Fast Castle. Both sites have a very narrow neck of land separating the inner portion of the castle from its outer defences. No archaeological evidence for a piped water supply was recorded by Fojut and Love (1983, 449-56) from their limited excavation at Dundarg but documentary evidence suggests the possibility of a piped supply (Old Statistical Account 1794, 578-9). Beveridge (1914, 184-91) identified two circular structures, one in each ward, as wells.

Where the internal water supply was limited due to geological problems an external supply, although vulnerable during times of siege, was considered a viable proposition. Recent archaeological investigations at *Dunure Castle* (NS 253 158), under Thomas Addyman, has revealed indications of an external supply that might have supplanted the use of the earlier well situated in the c14/15th-century forebuilding. This cliff top castle overlooking the southern approach to the Firth of Clyde sits on an irregular outcrop aligned roughly NW/SE, comprised of volcanic conglomerate of Old Red Sandstone age (Eyles *et al* 1980, 40). The present structure has its long axis parallel to the outcrop and is divided into three components. The remains of the 13th-century shell keep with subsequent alterations occupies the higher northern end. Adjacent to the keep and extending to the south east at a lower elevation lies the c14/15th-century forebuilding that was extended to the south east in the c16th century by the addition of a kitchen range. Excavations have exposed a square stone lined shaft in the south east corner of the forebuilding. This has been interpreted as a well and is considered to be one of the earlier features on the site and appears to have been infilled at the time of the construction of the c16th-century kitchen range. Within the later kitchen range recent excavation has uncovered evidence of stone lined water channels that serviced the building. One possible source for the water is a series of springs that lie to the east-south-east of the kitchen range (T Addyman, pers comm).

Sometimes, natural fissures or gullies could provide a defensive barrier and a water supply. At *Conway Castle* (SH 784 775), the inner ward does not have a well. The castle ridge of Silurian grits with impervious Ordovician shales below contained a natural fissure that was used to delimit the boundary between the inner and outer wards. Here, the fissure was artificially deepened to form a covered well-cum-cistern, 27.7m (91ft) deep and fed by a spring as well as percolation of surface water. Originally covered, a drawbridge crossed this pit into the inner ward (Taylor 1986). Local tradition implies that there was an external piped supply into the castle from a spring above Ty Gwyn (Neaverson 1947, 43-6).

The external, separate, and reputedly principal medieval water supply of *Dunnottar Castle* (NO 882 839) was via a wooden pipe from the 'Barrel Well' on the mainland. It was not connected to the large cistern constructed within the castle (McGibbon & Ross 1980, 562-73; Simpson 1976, 52). Dunnottar was built on a 48.77m (160ft) high promontory of Lower Old Red Sandstone (LORS) conglomerate. The Dunnottar Group conglomerate lies stratigraphically above the Stonehaven Group, the oldest rocks of the LORS series and contains rounded boulders, up to 1m across, mainly of quartzites, schistose grit, fine grained igneous rocks and Cambro-Ordovician lavas (Craig 1991, 304). Possibly the fabric of the rock precluded the sinking of a well and a cistern was constructed to utilise surface water percolating through the weathered upper surface of the rock. The bonnet-shaped cistern is 9.44m (31ft) in diameter at ground level, is 7.62m (25ft) deep, stone lined for the top 3.96m (13ft) and apparently partially clay lined for the remainder of its depth. The base diameter of the cistern was only 1.52m (5ft). The cistern was originally covered by a funnel-shaped top that mirrored its underground structure (Simpson 1976).

The castle of *Dunivaig*, Islay (NR 405 454) lying on the south shore of Islay four and a half kilometres east of Port Ellen is another example of a coastal clifftop castle with a poor water supply augmented by later external piped water. Historic records indicate how vulnerable such a supply was when the castle was under siege by traitors from one's own side. The castle is situated at the seaward end of a prominent NE/SW ridge of metabasite (epidiorite), dissected by the sea into an irregular series of commanding rocky outcrops with seaward facing cliffs. To the south west the sea has cut through this hard ridge into the softer

Laphroaig quartzites to form a shallow bay formerly known as Surnaig Bay. Today, the bay takes its name from the prominent Lagavulin distillery that occupies part of the bay's foreshore. Dunivaig comprises an irregular polygonal outer courtyard or barmkin facing landwards, once partially flanked by later artillery platforms. A sea gate gave the garrison access to Lagavulin Bay on the south west side of the castle. A small triangular inner courtyard allowed access from the outer courtyard to the 14m high steep sided irregular outcrop containing a rectangular 16th-century building with late 16th-century additions (Inventory of Argyll, 1984, 268-75).

The layout of the castle reflects the underlying geology. The core of the castle lies almost entirely on an intrusion of Dalriadan metabasite (epidiorite) intruded into Dalriadan flaggy quartzites belonging to the earlier Laphroaig Quartzite Formation. The junction between the two can be seen below the former drawbridge that gave access to the summit of the castle when viewed from the shore outside the outer courtyard's sea gate. The lower defences occupy an area of marsh and raised beach deposits of very limited thickness resting on weathered outcrops of fissile quartzites (BGS 1998, Sheet 19). Water via fissure flow in the quartzites and surface run off would provide a limited supply. The hardness of metabasite intrusion would mean that it would be virtually impossible to construct a deep well shaft and water within the intrusion would be limited to fissure flow through very limited fractures. Two wells are reputed to have been constructed. A rectangular shaft in the north east corner of the outer courtyard is thought to be the remains of a well. Another well is thought to lie within the inner courtyard. Sir Oliver Lambert in his report on his successful siege and capture of the castle in 1615 reported that the 'inner bawn and the well were chockt upp' by his bombardment. Later accounts give no mention of this well (Inventory of Argyll 1984, 272). Both wells lying so close to the high tide level would be vulnerable to water fluctuation and ingress of salt water.

Historical records indicate that a piped supply, presumably of 17th-century date, led from a small river, possibly in the vicinity of the former manse on the west side of Lagavulin Bay, under the waters of the shallow bay to its eastern shore at the sea gate of the castle (Old Statistical Account of Scotland 1794, 289-90). The wooden pipes (lead, not wood, according to the New Statistical Account of Scotland 1845, 663) were reputed to have been damaged by a traitor during the last recorded siege of the castle by Sir David Leslie in 1647. His successful capture of the castle brought about the close of the castle's military role (Site Note 4747, Dunivaig Castle, Historic Scotland)

Fragments of stonework and ditches mark the remains of *Dunaverty Castle* (NR 688 074), near Southend on the Mull of Kintyre. The castle stands on a prominent headland of Lower Old Red Sandstone conglomerate. A small rock cut depression, about 12m north and below the inner defences has tentatively been described as a well (Inventory of Argyll 1971, 157-9). The capture of the castle is attributed to the failure of its water supply during the siege of the castle during June and July 1644. The garrison of around 300 depended on the well and an external piped water supply from a spring outside the castle. The besieging forces discovered the course of the pipes around the 10th July and severed them, forcing the garrison to risk their lives collecting water from a nearby stream as the well was unable to supply all the needs of the garrison. Not long afterwards the continuing dry summer weather forced the large garrison to surrender when all available water sources failed (New Statistical Account 1845, 422-6).

The introduction of a mains piped water supply, to either complement or replace the internal water supply, was a common occurrence to coastal fortifications that still provided a military function in the late 19th and early 20th century.

At *Dumbarton* (NS 400 745), the 73.15m (240ft) high twin-peaked plug of Lower Carboniferous age basalt formed a natural defensive feature which was utilised from pre-historic times until the middle of the 20th century (MacPhail 1979). Permeability of the rock depends on fissure flow and basaltic volcanic plugs are not a good source of underground water. The castle originally relied on a natural loch, 4.27m (14ft) deep lying between the twin peaks for its original water supply. Sometimes it failed and the drying up of the loch in 870 after a four-month siege, significantly contributed to the capture of the fortress. The water quality varied. In the late 17th century it was described as being 'rotten sometimes'. The loch became a covered well sometime after the late 17th century and was the garrison's principal water supply. Water continued to be pumped from it until about 1874 when the fortress was connected to the town's water main (MacPhail 1979, 6, 134). Another and lower well shown on the 17th-century plans lay at the top of the stairs beyond the portcullis arch (Slezer 1696). Mair, in MacPhail (1979, 185-6, note 125) recorded a well located a short distance above and to the right of the path leading from the present Duke of Argyll's Battery to the summit of the eastern peak. This well was reputed to have dried up in 1884 following the excavation of a dock belonging to the Leven shipyard.

Although not strictly a clifftop fortress, the water supply to the fortifications on the island of *Inchkeith* (NT 293 828) evolved from wells outside the 16th-century fort, to a complex water system in the 20th century, of wells, water catchment areas, static water tanks and during World War Two the use of a water lighter (Ruckley 1984, 67-82).

Information updating the known water supply to coastal castles continues to be unearthed. Recent excavations at *Carrick Castle* (NS 194 945) and site investigation undertaken at *Castle Tioram* (NM 663 725) have revealed information regarding their water supply. Both castles occupy rocky islets in Scottish lochs where the local geology indicates that the water flow would be limited to surface run off and fissure flow through any joints in the metamorphic schists.

The 14th-century castle walls with its later 16th-century tower house makes *Castle Tioram* a very formidable structure on its tidal island (MacGibbon & Ross 1990). A well was known to have existed within the castle under the inner wall of a later building occupying the south east corner of the castle. Recent site investigation by GUARD (Glasgow University Archaeological Research Division) has brought to light a depression situated to the east and outside the castle that might be a well. Roughly 4m diameter and open to a depth of 1m with no evidence of a lining. Local tradition does indicate the possibility of it being a retting pond. It is hoped that further work will shed more light on the structure (Alan Rutherford, GUARD, pers comm).

*Carrick Castle* occupies a small island close to the western shore at the seaward end of Loch Goil. Over a ten year period the castle has undergone a series of archaeological excavations. The final one in the early summer of 1996 by Kirkdale Archaeology shed light on the early water supply to the site (Ewart & Baker, 1998). The present castle comprises a rectangular tower that can be dated to the late 14th to early 15th century. The barmkin wall on its eastern side is not original and there is evidence for two previous defensive walls. Today a 17th-century rectangular building defines its northern side. The 3m high castle rock with sheer sides is composed of Dalriadan psammitic grits belonging to the Beinn Bheula Schist Formation (BGS 1990, Sheet 37E).

Archaeological excavations have indicated the presence of a timber hall with dry stone outer wall that pre-dates the present late 14th-century stone hall house. A roughly circular rock cut pit over 3m deep was discovered underneath the present 17th-century vaulted prison within the earlier hall house. The pit's location within a natural depression of the rock was clearly sited in order to exploit a natural fault in the bedrock which allowed the stone to be prised away from a natural face rather than being more actively quarried. (The rectangular section of the Forewell of *Edinburgh Castle* is another example where the natural jointing in the rock was exploited in the sinking of the shaft - see Driscoll & Yeoman 1997, 19-21). Chisel or pick-axe marks were clearly visible on the remaining sides giving added strength to this method of construction. The plan of the pit shows a relatively straight upper south side before the outline of the pit becomes curved in plan. The sides of the pit are not vertical, as the pit widened gradually towards the base. Formerly a grill had been attached over the mouth of the pit.

Rough hewn pits are uncommon within keeps and a good example can be seen at *Dundrum Castle*, Co. Down (Waterman 1964, 136-9). Water would have been obtained only by fissure flow and there would be the ever present threat of contamination by salt water and sewage. Perhaps because of these two factors the function of the pit changed in the mid 16th to early 17th century with the construction within the keep of a vaulted prison. Waste material, including human faecal deposits, were found in the fill of the pit belonging to this period. If the pit ceased to act as a water supply for the castle cum prison in the early 17th century, the new source of water supply to the castle awaits discovery.

## 7.3 THE CAVES

### Hugh P Dinwoodie, Keith L Mitchell & K Robin Murdoch

The promontory, on which Fast Castle stands, contains two caves on its seaward aspect, running beneath the castle. It is hardly surprising that a tradition exists of a passage leading from a cave to the castle ruins above. William Douglas (1920) quotes three 19th-century references to such a legend (Carr, 1836; Fraser-Tytler, 1864; McGibbon and Ross, 1889); however, Mitchell (1988) comments that the latter two appear to stem from the first, Carr's *History of Coldingham Priory*, which reads:

> 'According to tradition, there was a communication between the castle and a large cavern at its base, by means of a stair constructed through its heart, which if it existed, must have contributed greatly to the security of the castle during a siege.'

Records of at least four 20th-century cave explorations exist - those of 1920, 1933, 1969, and 1976. None of these confirmed the existence of any communicating passage.

In 1920, Sang and Raeburn, (Douglas W, 1920), estimated the length of the cave to be 80 yards, terminating in a little tunnel with slimy bits of broken wreckage. In 1933, Ian Campbell and his brother explored both caves, but made no reliable measurements (Campbell, 1935).

In 1969, divers from Eyemouth Subaqua Club, and members of the Grampian Speleological Groups, made an unspecified number of visits to the caves (Douglas F, 1971). On early visits, they noticed a large rock basin scooped out by tide action, directly under the castle's back court, and the supposed site of its crane. The divers briefly explored the 'great cave' and reported that once they were two-thirds of the way in, the floor of the cave was well beyond the tide. Seabirds escaped from the cave, indicating dry ledges inside. They thought that the direction of the cave suggested it might link up with the vicinity of the Well, in a grassy hollow on the far side of the cliff top site. However, the way was choked with rotting driftwood and flotsam and apparently they proceeded no further. On later visits, however, it was claimed that there was a 'rift' about a third of the way in to the cave. A current of fresh air was said to come through the rift, but it was too narrow to enter at floor level. Access was gained by means of a ladder near roof level enabling further progress towards a dead end, although it seemed there was still a draught, hinting at a chamber beyond.

**Illus 97** Cave mouth, (note rope suspended from postulated site of crane)

During the EAFS excavations at the castle, an arrangement was made with a small team of Army volunteers, from 16th Battalion RAOC, Bicester, to explore and survey the caves. This took place during ten days in June 1976. The major part of their findings and conclusions, extracted from the account which was written within a few days of its completion, by the officer in charge, the late Lieut Adrian Ashby-Smith, has already been posthumously published in Mitchell 1988, Appendix 8. Ashby-Smith completed this preliminary report before leaving shortly afterwards on an expedition to Ecuador, during which, tragically, he was accidentally killed.

The notes, measurements, drawings and photographs, obtained at the time, are believed to be no longer extant. The bones recovered by Ashby-Smith, described below, are also not available for examination. His report (1976a) revealed that:

> 'Tide-swept boulders had been packed to the back of the cave (to) roof level, conjectural vertical height: 18ft (5.5m), ... a distance of 260ft (79.24m) from the cave mouth. Removal of flotsam revealed a passage over the bank of spoil. This was originally too narrow for exploration, although its visible length was 20ft (6.1m). This was dug out to a depth of 3ft (0.9m) and extended physically to a length of 25ft (7.6m). At the conclusion of the project, a number of animal bones had been located in the soil at the furthest reach of the passage, and a further air passage - giving another 10ft (3m) visibility, had been located. Time prevented exploitation of what could prove to be an exciting extension to the passage.'

A further, more personalised, account (Ashby-Smith 1976b) is in the archive, and included a little additional information. It described moving equipment and even bedding into the cave at that time. Efforts concentrated on digging as far as the bedrock would permit, but the job was left unfinished. The end of the cave had not been reached despite removing several tons of flotsam, rock, and clay spoil.

## DISCUSSION

The first two explorations left few details; the second two were more serious attempts to determine the contours of the cave, and were of some duration.

In 1969, it was thought that the direction of the cave suggested that it terminated near to the area of the Well. In 1976, while bearings were taken, the only surviving record of them is a diagram, which suggests that the end of the larger cave lies directly underneath another ground depression, around 15m N of the Well (illus 7); and that the smaller cave lies just to the N of the range of rooms NW of the Lower Courtyard. Figures for the bearings are given on the diagram as 4380m (milliradians) for the former, 4320m for the latter (ie 251 and 248 degrees, respectively: approximately WSW). However, the diagram is schematic only, and there is no indication whether these were true or magnetic bearings.

Ashby-Smith's reports do not specifically identify the 'rift about a third of the way into the cave', noted in 1969. However, it is stated that there was 'no evidence to substantiate the existence of passages or tunnels connecting Cave no 2 (the main cave) to the SE face of the promontory, and that observations made prior to the digging-out of the main cave passage gave no indication of air movement within the cave' (Mitchell 1988, 103). This 'rift', if it indeed lay one-third of the way into the cave, would lie directly below the S part of the Quarry pit, the Brewhouse, or the E end of the main Hall of the castle. His team's efforts seem to have been concentrated mainly on the far end of the cave, beyond. Ashby-Smith also considered the possibility of a man-made horizontal passage, across the rock strata, from the vicinity of the Well to the cave, but found no evidence to support this.

## CONCLUSION

The main cave is between 79m and 90m long, running in a WSW direction, at or just above sea-level throughout its length. There is no evidence to indicate that any connection between the Castle and cave ever existed. The depth of the Quarry pit, the rudimentary steps hewn in the rock to it, and the recess behind the Enclosure wall, may have given rise to the tradition of a passage from Castle to Cave referred to above. The channel leading to the cave would have provided a secure supply route for use by small boats in calm weather.

## 7.4 THE CRANE

### Hugh P Dinwoodie, Keith L Mitchell, & K Robin Murdoch

Fast Castle sits on its promontory surrounded on three sides by sheer sea cliffs, between 30m and 50m in height. The ground to the SW of the castle, its only landward access, rises steeply to a height of 130m above sea level. Throughout its occupation, the surrounding countryside was almost devoid of proper roads.

Therefore the supply of heavy goods, by an overland route, would have been very difficult; much easier by sea. It is likely that food provisions, acquired locally, comprised the great majority of deliveries to the castle by land. Indeed, the only historical reference to overland delivery of goods records an enterprising use of this practice for military purposes. It recounts an incident which took place during the winter of 1549-1550, when the English garrison commander ordered local farmers to supply provisions to the castle; after crossing the drawbridge, 'sum gentilmen' in 'husband menis claithes', on the pretext of bringing in stores, slew the gatekeepers, and recaptured the castle for the Scots (Kennaway, 1992, 86).

The 1549 plan (illus 6), presumably drawn up shortly before this incident, depicts a crane in the Outer Lower Courtyard above the inlet to the great sea cave. The crane has been drawn obliquely and is almost certainly merely an indication of the presence and position of the device rather than an accurate representation of its structure. For instance, no winding gear is shown, and this, probably in the form of a windlass, would have been essential for the 40m lift from the base of the crag.

The lifting rope from the jib is connected to a bucket, a type of container commonly used with hoists or cranes since they were strongly built and could accommodate a diverse range of goods. There is a suggestion that a bucket may have been used to obtain brine, or even fresh water, which apparently issues from the base of the crag in copious quantities just about sea-level (T Dykes, pers comm), although sea-water contamination would probably have been a problem in the latter case.

Information on medieval or post-medieval cranes in the locality is scant: a crane bastion existed outside the walls of Tantallon Castle, while Slezer illustrated a crane on the Bass Rock in 1693 (Cavers, 1993, 71). Notwithstanding this, many castles would, for simple reasons of expediency, have been fitted with lifting devices, and all would have required them during construction phases.

The main question regarding the crane at Fast is: was it a permanent fixture? It would have been essential during building phases, and given the continuing extreme difficulty in supplying heavy goods other than by sea, it is reasonable to assume that it was. However, slight doubt may be cast by the circumstances under which the 1549 plan was drawn up, that is, under temporary English occupation. Supply by sea may have been their only option.

At the base of the crag, immediately to the N of the sea inlet and cave mouth, there is a rock ledge which may once have been part of a landing stage. This ledge, just above average high water mark, is about 2-3m wide and extends at least 15m E from the cave in two sections. It is remarkably level and, although no trace of construction remains, probably attained its profile by artificial means.

The sea inlet is approximately 6m wide and its S edge actually lies 1.5m outwith the line of the vertical from the S edge of the Courtyard above. Because of the sloping nature of the rock strata, a considerable offset exists between the roof and base of the cave. This offset, combined with the 40m height to the Courtyard, would have made it difficult and hazardous to raise heavy loads directly from the deck of a boat. The vagaries of sea condition would also be important in such activities. It seems much more likely that cargoes were normally offloaded to the landing stage before being raised to the courtyard.

Many hundreds, if not thousands, of sandstone blocks had to be imported for the finer work in the construction of the castle and it is very likely that some form of landing stage would have been essential for this purpose.

Several archaeological features, thought to be associated with the crane, were excavated in the SE corner of the Outer Courtyard. Several bedrock outcrops were left projecting upwards from an otherwise fairly level quarried surface and some of these, in particular F19 and F21, may have had some function related to the stabilisation of the base of the device. The flagstones, F12, may have constituted a handling area. The disposition of these features is better aligned with the rock ledge than the sea inlet (illus 97).

The 1549 plan depicts the crane as being situated in a small alcove projecting outwards beyond the line of the rest of the Courtyard rampart. There are two basic alternatives to consider as to the mode of operation of the crane: a fixed or a movable jib. The former would have been simpler to build, easier to maintain and inherently stronger but would probably have required some form of projecting platform for unloading; this may be what is implied on the 1549 plan. Conversely, if a system with a movable jib was used, goods could have been swung directly onto the Courtyard after hoisting. However, jib and winding gear would both have required to rotate, resulting in a far more complex device. One advantage of a swinging jib would have been the ability to lift directly from the deck of a boat when loads were relatively light and sea condtions favourable.

In the SE corner of the Courtyard, the lower part of the outer rampart comprised natural bedrock and a gap had been created, possibly to give access to the putative unloading platform or, alternatively, to allow loads to be swung in. The presence of the rock outcrop, F19, however, effectively blocking the centre of the gap only 1.2m in from the crag edge, is enigmatic; and the gap had also been further blocked by the construction of F9.

A large piece of timber, with ironwork attached (Chap 5.15, no 1; Plates XV, XVI; illus 70), recovered from the Quarry pit, has tentatively been suggested, among other possibilities, as part of a windlass pawl, an anti-runback device (A Armstrong, pers comm).

**Illus 98** 'The last shovelful', summer 1986 (Keith Mitchell and Robin Murdoch)

# 8 GLOSSARY

**GLASS**

BROAD GLASS: Window glass made by cylinder process.
CAME: Lead surround to hold glass pane in place.
CHRISSELLING (Crizzeling, etc): Network of fine cracks.
CROWN GLASS: Window glass made by spun disc process, characterised by bulls-eye centre.
FIREBRIGHT: Surface as made.
GROZED: Clipped edges.
KICK: Indent in base.
KNOPPED STEM: Series of knops (generally rounded blobs).
LATTIMO: White (milk) glass.
MARVERED: Rolled on flat slab.
OGEE: Double curve, first one way, then the other.
PATINA: Surface degradation.
PEDESTAL STEM: Hollow pillar-like stem.
PLUMOSE: Feather-like.
PONTIL: Solid rod to which a vessel/bottle is attached for finishing.
QUARRY: Small pane.
RIBBEKER: Ribbed beaker.
VERRE DE FOUGERE: Fern-glass.

**LEATHER** (see illus 68 for shoe construction)

BINDING: A folded strip of leather which is used to bind or enclose the edge of another piece of leather.
CLUMP SOLE: A half sole added to a shoe, usually as a repair (Thornton 1973b, 45).
EARED TOE-PIECE: In the sixteenth century, following a long period of pointed shoes, toes became very square and wide; for a short time, 1535-55, the corners of the toe were extended sideways resembling ears (*ibid*, 45).
EDGE-FLESH STITCHING CHANNEL: The stitching holes are pierced from the edge of the section (usually the sole) to the flesh side; commonly used in the majority of medieval shoes (*ibid*, 45). Also used to link fragments of uppers.
FOLLICLE PATTERN: The distinctive pattern left on the grain side of the leather by the animal's hairs.
FOREPART: The front of the sole or insole.
GRAIN-FLESH STITCHING CHANNEL: The stitching holes are pierced from the grain side to the flesh side.
GRAIN SURFACE: The outer surface of a piece of leather originally bearing the hair, fur, wool etc. Each animal has a characteristic grain pattern and the surface is usually smooth. Soles usually have the grain side downwards resting on the ground; insoles usually have the grain side upwards so that the foot rests on it. Uppers normally have the grain side outwards except for suedes (*ibid*, 45).
HEEL: A component added to the rear (or seat) end of the sole, originally for utility but then as fashion. It may consist of separate 'lifts' ('built heel') or be a block of wood covered with leather or other material. In either case the bottom section which rests on the ground is called the 'top-piece' (*ibid*, 45).
HEEL-STIFFENER or STIFFENER: A reinforcement placed inside the back of the quarters. In early shoes the top edge is often stitched to the quarters by a type of hem-stitch (or oversewn or whipped seam) which produces a scalloped effect along this edge; the bottom edge is lasted in with the upper (*ibid*, 47).
INSOLE: The inside bottom part of a shoe on which the foot rests, sometimes referred to as 'the foundation of the shoe'. In a turnshoe (qv) there is no separate insole, the foot resting on the inner surface of the sole which also acts as an insole (*ibid*, 45).
LASTING MARGIN: The lower edge of the shoe upper which is turned under and fixed to the insole (or sole) during lasting (*ibid*, 46).
OFFCUT: A fragment with at least one cut edge, and no stitched edges, which represents waste material, either from original cutting-out of leather, or from re-use.
OUTER SOLE: The part of the shoe which is in contact with the ground. If the shoe has a separate heel (qv) the bottom section of this next to the ground is called the 'top-piece'.

QUARTERS: The sides of a shoe upper joining on to the vamp at the front and meeting each other at the back of the heel. If there is a seam here it is called a 'backseam'. The name 'quarters' is derived from the fact that if there is a join at the back, then a pair of shoes has four of them. Medieval shoes do not usually have a backseam, as the inside and outside quarters from a continuous section (*ibid*, 46).

RAND: A long narrow strip of leather of roughly triangular cross-section included in an upper/bottom seam, or elsewhere, to make it more waterproof or decorative. Some early turnshoes have such a rand and if this is wide enough, an additional sole, possibly a repair one, can be stitched to it (*ibid*, 46).

SCRAP: A fragment with neither cut nor sewn edges.

SEAT: The rear end of the insole or sole on which the heel of the foot rests (*ibid*, 46).

SOLE: The part of a shoe which is in contact with the ground (ibid, 47).

STITCHING CHANNEL: a row of stitch holes, sometimes set in a groove.

STITCH LENGTH: The distance between the centres of the stitches or stitch holes in a row (*ibid*, 47).

TUNNEL STITCHING: A seam used in repairing to attach a new piece of leather, eg a clump sole (qv) on top of an old one. The holes enter the surface of each piece, pass for a short distance through the substance (between grain and flesh) and then reappear on the same side. Sometimes called a 'caterpillar stitch' (*ibid*, 47). Also used to describe the stitches used to attach facings and top edges of quarters to the flesh side of the shoe, without perforating the leather.

TURNSHOE CONSTRUCTION: The shoe is made inside out, normally with the flesh side outwards, by sewing a lasting margin (qv) of the upper to the edge of a single sole, which also acts as an insole. The shoe is then turned the right way round so that the grain side of the leather is on the outside of the shoe and the upper/sole seam is now inside. It was apparently introduced to this country by the Saxons (*ibid*, 47).

UPPER: Parts of a shoe covering the upper foot and consisting of vamp, quarters and, possibly, inserts or side-pieces. Usually of finer leather than the sole, and made with the grain side upwards. Joined to the sole at the lasting margin (Grew & de Neergaard 1988, 125).

VAMP: The front section of a shoe upper covering the toes and part of the instep (Thornton 1973b, 48).

WAIST: The narrow part of a shoe sole or insole under the arch of the foot (also called the waist) (*ibid*, 48).

WELT: A narrow strip of leather sewn round the lasting margin (qv) of the upper and joining it either to the insole edge or to a 'rib' raised on the flesh side of the insole near the edge. The sole is attached to this welt by a second seam. It appears to have been developed from the rand (qv) and the two words are sometimes confused with each other (*ibid*, 48).

WELTED CONSTRUCTION: A method of shoe construction introduced to this country circa A.D.1500 and still used, although mechanised. It takes place in three stages:

(1) The upper is lasted and held in position by nails or bracing thread.

(2) The lasted upper is sewn together with a welt (qv) to the edge of the insole; early examples use the actual edge itself with an edge-flesh seam (qv), but later ones used an upstanding rib set in a short distance from the edge.

(3) The sole is then stitched to this welt (*ibid*, 48).

**BONE**

ACETABULUM, -a: The socket(s) for the thigh bone(s) in the pelvis.
ANSER: Goose.
ASTRAGALUS, -i: Ball(s) of ankle joint(s).
BURR: Part of antler.
CALCANEUM, -a: Heel bone(s).
CARPOMETACARPUS, -i: (Avian) bone(s) formed by fusion of carpal and metacarpal bones.
CONDYLE: Rounded process at end of bone, for articulating with another bone.
CORTICAL: Pertaining to the outer part of an organ (eg the thicker, outer part of bone shaft).
DENTITION: The characteristic arrangement of teeth in an animal.
DIAPHYSIS, -es: The shaft of a bone, or bones.
DIMORPHISM: Exhibiting two distinct forms.
DISTAL: Away from the centre; the end of a bone furthest from the centre of the body.
EPIPHYSIS, -es: The end(s) of a bone.
EPIPHYSEAL: Pertaining to the end(s) of a bone.
EXOSTOSIS, -es: Bony outgrowth(s).
FEMUR, -ora: Thigh bone(s).
GALLUS: Chicken.

GLENOID (cavity): The hollow in the shoulder-blade, in which the humerus rotates.
HUMERUS, -i: The upper bone(s) of forelimb(s).
HYOID: A small bone around the front of the throat.
ILIUM: The hip-bone.
INNOMINATE bone: The (three) bones of one half of the pelvis (ilium, ischium, pubis).
KERATINOUS: Rough or horny, in relation to skin.
MANDIBLE: Lower jaw-bone.
MAXILLA, -ae: Upper jaw-bone(s).
METAPODIAL: Pertaining to metatarsus and/or metacarpus, taken together.
OCCIPITAL: Of the back of the head, skull, or brain.
OSTEOARTHRITIS: Degenerative wear and tear of joints.
PERIODONTAL: Around the teeth.
PHALANX, -ges: Bone(s) beyond metacarpal and metatarsal bones.
POLLING: Cutting off horns.
POSTCRANIAL: Behind the brain.
PROXIMAL: Towards the centre; the end of a bone nearest the centre of a body.
SACRUM: The lowest, fused, bones of the spine which articulate with the pelvis.
SCAPULA, -ae: The shoulder-blade(s).
SCUR: Small roughened areas on the cranium where horns would have grown.
TARSOMETATARSUS, -i: (Avian) bone(s) formed by fusion of tarsal and metatarsal bones.
TIBIOTARSUS, -i: Large (avian) bone(s) formed by fusion of tibia and tarsal bones.

**MISCELLANEOUS:**

BOMBAZINE: Twilled material of worsted with silk, with cotton, or alone.
BOTTERED: Smoothing of the rim.
BOTRYOIDAL: Like a bunch of grapes.
CONCHOIDAL: Shell-like.
COTTING: Compacting of wool: matted or felted together.
CRESSET: Oil lamp.
ESKER: Elongated, often flat-topped, mounds or ridges of postglacial gravels.
FUSTIAN: Coarse thick twilled short-napped cotton-cloth, usually dyed dark.
GREYWACKE: A Lower Palaeozoic rock deposited in sedimentary environments; essentially an impure sandstone of variable coarseness and usually dark colour.
JETON: A counting token.
PATERA: A round flat dish for receiving a sacrificial libation.
PENECONTEMPORANEOUS: Almost at the same time as.
PILLING: 'balling' of wool: the gathering of fibres into small balls of fluff on the surface of a fabric.
ROVE: Metal plate for rivet to be passed through and be clenched over.
SPRUE: One of the passages leading to a mould, also the metal which solidifies in it.


With acknowledgements to the Oxford English Dictionary, 2nd edition; Concise Oxford Dictionary; Black's Veterinary Dictionary (ed West); The Geological History of the British Isles (Bennison & Wright); Practical Archaeology (Webster); also to Clare Thomas (leather) Robin Murdoch (glass), and Denis Gallagher (clay pipes).

# 9 REFERENCES

Abbreviations: BAR = British Archaeological Report; NMS = National Museums of Scotland; RCAHMS = Royal Commission on the Ancient and Historical Monuments of Scotland.

Acts Parl Scot 1814 *The Acts of the Parliaments of Scotland, (1424-1567)*, 2, 499.
Adair, J 1703 *A True and Exact Hydrographical Description of the Sea Coasts and Islands of Scotland*. Edinburgh.
Anderson, J 1905 'Notes on a Romano-British Hoard of Bronze Vessels', *Proc Soc Antiq Scot,* 39 (1904-5), 367-76.
Armstrong, M 1977 'The Old Red Sandstone of Easter Ross and the Black Isle', *in* Gill, G (ed) *1977 The Moray Firth Area: Geological Studies.* Inverness Field Club.
Ashby-Smith, A 1976a *Exercise Jock-Trap, 6-16 June 1976.* Edinburgh Archaeological Field Society archive.
Ashby-Smith, A 1976b *Report on Exercise Jock-Trap - A 16 Battalion Adventurous Training Project.* Edinburgh Archaeological Field Society archive.
Avent, R 1989 *Criccieth Castle.* C A D W Guidebook.
Baart, J 1977 *Opgravingen in Amsterdam, 20 jaar stadskern onderzoek*, 472-5.
Barnard, F P 1917 *The Casting-Counter and the Counting Board.* Oxford (repr Castle Cary 1981).
Barron, D G 1904 'Donations to the Museum and Library', *Proc Soc Antiq Scot,* 38 (1904), 413-5.
Barron, O 1911 in *Encyclopaedia Britannica,* 11th ed, 7 (1911), 238. London: Cambridge University Press.
Bell, M 1901 *Old Pewter,* 63-4 & 72. London.
Bennett, H 1987 'Textiles', *in* Holdsworth 1987, 159-174.
Beveridge, W 1914 'Notes on excavations at Dundargue Castle, Aberdeenshire, and a stone circle and grave at New Deer, Aberdeenshire', *Proc Soc Antiq Scot,* 48 (1913-14), 184-91.
BGS 1990 Lochgoilhead, Scotland, Sheet 37E. Solid Geology, 1:50,000 Ser. Keyworth, Nottingham: British Geological Survey.
BGS 1998 South Islay, Scotland, Sheet 19. Solid and Drift Geology, 1:50,000 Prov Ser. Keyworth, Nottingham: British Geological Survey.
Blackmore, H L 1976 *The Armouries of the Tower of London, 1, The Ordnance.* London: HMSO.
Blanchard, L M 1983 'An excavation at 45 Canal St, Perth 1978-9.' *Proc Soc Antiq Scot,* 113 (1983).
BM Guide 1925 *Guide to Early Iron Age Antiquities,* 2nd ed. London: British Museum.
Bown, L 1985 'The Pottery', *in* O'Sullivan, D M, 'An excavation in Holy Island village, 1977', *Archaeol Aeliana,* 5th ser, 13 (1985), 47-80.
Boyd, W K (ed) 1905 *Calendar of State Papers relating to Scotland and Mary Queen of Scots, 4 (1571-1574)*, no 726. Edinburgh: HM General Register House.
Boyd, W K (ed) 1907 *Calendar of State Papers relating to Scotland and Mary Queen of Scots, 5 (1574-1581)*, no 164. Edinburgh: HM General Register House.
Bozman, (ed) 1970 *Everyman's Encyclopedia,* 11 (1970), 34-5.
Brooks, C M 1981 'Medieval Pottery from the kiln site at Colstoun, E Lothian', *Proc Soc Antiq Scot,* 110 (1978-80), 364-403.
Bruijn, A 1979 *Pottersvuren langs de Vecht: Aardewerk rond 1400 uit Utrecht.* Rotterdam Papers 3.
Buckland, A R (ed) undated. *The Universal Bible Dictionary,* 343. London: The Religious Tract Society.
Buckley, A I 1986 'Jew's harps in Irish archaeology', 49-71 *in* Lund, C S (ed), *Second Conference of the ICTM Study Group on Music Archaeology, 1: General Studies.* Stockholm.
Burley, E 1956 'A catalogue and survey of the metal-work from Traprain Law', *Proc Soc Antiq Scot,* 89 (1955-56), 118-226.
Burnett, G (ed) 1880 *Exchequer Rolls of Scotland, 4 (1406-1436)*, 432. Edinburgh: HM General Register House.
Burnett, G (ed) 1884 *Exchequer Rolls of Scotland, 7 (1460-1469)*, 59; 154, 404 & 506; 427; 403, 525 & 628; 488; & 654. Edinburgh: HM General Register House.
Burns, E 1887 *The Coinage of Scotland.* Edinburgh.
Bury, S 1991 *Jewellery 1789-1910.* Woodbridge: Antique Collectors' Club.
Caldwell, D H 1981a 'Metalwork artefacts', *in* Good & Tabraham 1981, 128.
Caldwell, D H 1991a 'The Pottery', 348-53 *in* Caldwell, D H, 1991b.
Caldwell, D H 1991b 'Tantallon Castle, East Lothian: a catalogue of the finds', *Proc Soc Antiq Scot,* 121 (1991), 335-57.
Caldwell, D H (ed) 1981b *Scottish Weapons and Fortifications 1100-1800.* Edinburgh: John Donald.
Caldwell, D H (forthcoming) *Finlaggan* (Monograph)

# References

Caldwell, D H & Dean, V E 1992 'The pottery industry at Throsk, Stirlingshire, in the 17th and early 18th century', *Post-Medieval Archaeol*, 26 (1992), 1-46.

Caldwell, D H & Ewart, G 1997 'Excavations at Eyemouth, Berwickshire, in a mid 16th-century *trace italliene* fort' *Post-Medieval Archaeology* 31 (1997), 61-119.

Callander, J G 1924 'Fourteenth-century brooches and other ornaments in the National Museum of Antiquities of Scotland', *Proc Soc Antiq Scot*, 58 (1923-24), 160-84.

Campbell, E 1991 'Excavation of a wheelhouse and other Iron Age structures at Sollas, North Uist, by R J C Atkinson in 1957', *Proc Soc Antiq Scot*, 121 (1991), 117-73.

Campbell, I 1935 *Scottish Mountaineering Club Journal*, 20 (1933-35), 102-5.

Campbell, M 1991 'Gold, Silver and Precious Stones', *in* Blair J & Ramsay N (eds), *English Medieval Industries*, 107-66. London: Hambledon.

Cardonnel, A de 1786 *Numismatica Scotiae*. Edinburgh.

Carr, A 1836 *A History of Coldingham Priory*. Edinburgh.

Carruthers, R G, Burnett, G A & Anderson W 1930 'The geology of the Alnmouth District', (Explanation of Sheet 6). Memoir of the Geological Survey of England and Wales. London: HMSO.

Cavers, K 1993 *A Vision of Scotland - The Nation Observed by John Slezer, 1671-1717*. Edinburgh.

Ceulmans, C, Deconinck, E & Helsen, J (eds) 1988 *Tongeren Basiliek van O.-L.-Vrouw geboorte I. Textiel*, (1988), No 42, 211-2. Louvain.

Cheer, P 1990 'Scottish Medieval Pottery: a Review', *Medieval Ceramics* 14, 19-22.

Cheer, P 1991 'Pottery imported into medieval Perth', *Medieval Ceramics*, 15, 50-1.

Cheer, P 1995 'Ceramic Use Zones in Medieval Scotland', *Medieval Ceramics*, 18 (1994), 83-6.

Childe, V G 1935 *The prehistory of Scotland*. London: Kegan Paul.

Childe, V G & Forde, C D 1932 'Excavations in two Iron Age forts at Earn's Heugh, near Coldingham', *Proc Soc Antiq Scot*, 66 (1931-32), 152-83.

Clark, J 1997 'Medieval Ironwork' *in* Driscoll & Yeoman 1997, 154-63.

Close-Brooks, J 1986 'Excavations at Clatchard Craig, Fife', *Proc Soc Antiq Scot*, 116 (1986), 117-84.

Coad, J G & Lewis, P N 1982 'Fortifications at Dover', *Post Medieval Archaeology*, 16, 141-200.

Cool, H E M 1982 'The artefact record: some possibilities', *in* Harding 1982, 92-100.

Cowell, M 1977 'Energy Dispersive X-ray Fluorescence Analysis of Ancient Gold Coins', *PACT (=Journal of the European Study Group on Physical, Chemical, Biological and Mathematical Techniques applied to Archaeology)*, 1, 76-85.

Cowgill, J, de Neergaard, M & Griffiths, N 1987 *Medieval finds from excavations in London: 1. Knives and Scabbards*. Museum of London. London: HMSO.

Cox, E, Haggarty, G & Hurst, J G 1985 'Ceramic material', *in* Tabraham, C J, 'Excavations at Kelso Abbey', *Proc Soc Antiq Scot*, 114 (1984), 381-98.

Craig, G Y (ed) 1991 *Geology of Scotland*, (3rd ed), 304. London: Geological Society.

Craw, J H 1924 'Fast Castle', *History of the Berwickshire Naturalists' Club*, 25 (1924).

Crowdy, A 1986 'The Pottery', *in* Dixon, P, *Excavations in the Fishing Town of Eyemouth, 1982-4*, 38-55.

Crowfoot, E, Pritchard, F & Staniland, K 1991 *Medieval Finds from Excavations in London: 4. Textiles and Clothing*, (1991), No 412, Fig 110A. London.

Cruden, S 1951 'Glenluce Abbey: Finds recovered during excavations. Part 1', *Trans Dumfriesshire Galloway Natur Hist Antiq Soc*, 3rd ser, 29 (1950-1), 177-94.

Cruden, S 1954 'Scottish Mediaeval Pottery: the Bothwell Castle collection', *Proc Soc Antiq Scot*, 86 (1951-2), 140-70.

Cruden, S 1955 'Scottish Mediaeval Pottery: the Melrose Abbey collection', *Proc Soc Antiq Scot*, 87 (1952-3), 161-74.

Cruden, S 1958 'Scottish Medieval Pottery', *Proc Soc Antiq Scot*, 89 (1955-6), 67-82.

Crummy, P 1992 *Excavations at Culver Street, the Gilberd School, and other sites in Colchester 1971-85*. Colchester Archaeological Report 6.

Curle, A O 1915 'Account of excavations on Traprain Law in the parish of Prestonkirk, County of Haddington, in 1914', *Proc Soc Antiq Scot*, 49 (1914-15), 139-202.

Dalton, O M, Mitchell, H P & Couchman, J E 1925 'The Warden Abbey and Chichester croziers', *Archaeologia*, 75, 211-5.

Darby, K 1988 *Church Roofing*, 9-12. London: Church House Publishing.

Davies, D C 1878 *Slate and Slate Quarrying*. London.

Davis, M 1993 'The identification of various jet and jet-like materials used in the Early Bronze Age in Scotland', *The Conservator*, 17, 11-18.
Day, L F 1897 *Windows - a book about stained and painted glass*, 70, Fig 41. London: Batsford.
Dean, V E 1997 'The Pottery Vessel', *in* Holmes, N M McQ, 'The Ednam, Roxburghshire, hoard, 1995', *British Numismatic Journal*, 66 (1996), 43.
Dean, V E (forthcoming) 'The Medieval Pottery', *in* Cramp, R, '*The Hirsel, Coldstream*'.
Dean, V E (unpublished) Report and pottery from Hyndford House: held by Biggar Museum Trust.
de Osma, G J 1916 *Catálogo de Azabaches Compostelanos*. Madrid.
*Der Grosse Brockhaus* 1953 3, 350. Wiesbaden: Eberhard Brockhaus.
*Discovery and Excavation in Scotland* 1994 (Batey, C E & King, M, eds), 5. NMS Daybook no DB 1993/73 Edinburgh: Council for Scottish Archaeology.
Douglas, F 1971 *Gold at Wolf's Crag?* Edinburgh: Oliver & Boyd.
Douglas, W 1920 *Scottish Mountaineering Club Journal*, 15 (1918-20), 305.
Douglas, W 1921 'Fast Castle and its owners', *Proc Soc Antiq Scot*, 55 (1920-21), 56-83.
Driscoll, S T & Yeoman, P A 1997 *Excavations within Edinburgh Castle*, 19-21. (=Soc Antiq Scot Monogr Ser, 12) Edinburgh.
Duco, D H 1981 'De Kleipijp in de Zeventiende Eeuwse Nederlanden', *in* Davey, P, *The Archaeology of the Clay Tobacco Pipe*, 5, 111-468 (=BAR International Series, 106 (2). Oxford.
Dunbar, J G 1963 'Excavations at Skirling Castle, Peeblesshire, and at James Fort, Stirling', *Proc Soc Antiq Scot*, 96 (1962-63), 244-5.
Dunning, G C 1965 'Heraldic and decorated metalwork and other finds from Rievaulx Abbey, Yorkshire', *Antiquaries J*, 45, 53-63.
Durham, B 1977 'Archaeological investigations in St Aldates, Oxford', *Oxoniensia*, 42 (1977), 83-203.
Edwards, B J N 1967 'Medieval pottery', *in* Jobey, G, 'Excavations at Tynemouth Priory and Castle', *Archaeol Aeliana*, 4th ser, 45 (1967), 70-83.
Egan, G 1984 'Leaden Cloth Seals', *in* Thompson, A, Grew, F & Schofield, J, 'Excavations at Aldgate 1974', *Post Medieval Archaeology*, 18 (1984), 125-6, no 121.
Egan, G 1985 'Leaden Seals for Augsburg Fustians', *in* Lambrick, G, 'Further Excavations of the Dominican Priory, Oxford', *Oxoniensia*, 50 (1985), 169-70.
Egan, G 1989 'Leaden Seals for Textiles - some archaeological evidence relating to fabrics and trade', *Costume*, 23 (1989), 39-53.
Egan, G 1994 *Lead Cloth Seals & Related Items in the British Museum*, British Museum Occasional Paper 93 (1994). London.
Egan, G & Pritchard, F 1991 *Medieval finds from excavations in London: 3. Dress Accessories c1150-c1450*. Museum of London. London: HMSO.
Elliston-Erwood, F 1943 'Notes on bronze objects from Shooters Hill, Kent, and elsewhere, and on the antiquity of jew's harps', *Archaeologia Cantiana*, 56 (1943), 34-40.
Elliston-Erwood, F 1947 'Further notes of jew's harps', *Archaeologia Cantiana*, 60 (1947), 107-8.
Endrei, W & Egan, G 1982 'The Sealing of Cloth in Europe, with special reference to the English evidence', *Textile History*, 13 (1982), 47-75.
Evans, D H 1985 'The Pottery' *in* Evans, D H & Carter, A, 'Excavations on 31-51 Pottergate', *E Anglian Archaeol*, 26, 27-49.
Evans, J 1952 *Dress in Medieval France*, 14-16. Oxford.
Evans, J 1953 *A History of Jewellery 1100-1870*. London: Faber and Faber.
Evans, J & Serjeantson, M S 1933 *English Mediaeval Lapidaries*. London: Early English Text Society.
Ewart, G 1985 *Cruggleton Castle; Report on the Excavations 1978-81*. Dumfries and Galloway Nat Hist and Antiq Soc.
Ewart, G & Baker, F 1998 'Carrick Castle: Symbol and source of Campbell power in South Argyll from 14th to the 17th century'. *Proc Soc Antiq Scot* 128 (1998), 937-1016.
Ewart, G & Triscott, J 1996 'Archaeological excavation at Castle Sweem, Knapdale, Argyll & Bute, 1989-90', *Proc Soc Antiq Scot*, 126 (1996), 517-57
*Exchequer Rolls of Scotland* Burnett G (ed), 1877-1908. Edinburgh: HM General Register House.
Eyles, V A, Simpson, J B & MacGregor A G 1980 *The Geology of Central Ayrshire*, 2nd ed 1949, repr 1980. Natural Environment Research Council. Edinburgh: HMSO.

Finlay, I (ed Fotheringham, H) 1991 *Scottish Gold & Silver Work*, 34-7. Stevenage: Strong Oak Press.
Fitzpatrick, A P 1992 'La place des amphores dans l'approvisionnement militaire de l'Ecosse romaine' *in* Laubenheimer F (ed) *Les Amphores en Gaule: Production et Circulation*. Paris: Centre de Recherches d'Histoire Ancienne, vol 116.
Fitzpatrick, A P (in preparation) 'Amphorae in Roman Scotland'.
Fojut, N & Love, P 1983 'The defences of Dundarg Castle, Aberdeenshire', *Proc Soc Antiq Scot*, 113 (1983), 449-56.
Ford, B 1987 'Iron objects', *in* Holdsworth 1987, 130-41.
Fotheringham, H (ed) 1991 *Scottish Gold & Silver Work*, 34-7. Stevenage: The Strong Oak Press.
Foxon, A D 1991 *Bone, antler, tooth and horn technology and utilisation in prehistoric Scotland*. Unpublished PhD thesis, University of Glasgow.
Franklin, J A (forthcoming) Report on pottery from excavations at Dundonald Castle, Ayrshire.
Franklin, J A 1998 'Pottery' *in* Caldwell, D H & Ewart, G, 'Excavations at Eyemouth, Berwickshire, in a mid 16th-century *Trace Italienne* Fort', *Post-Medieval Archaeol*, 31 (1997), 96-103.
Fraquet, H 1987 *Amber*, 32-7. Kent: Butterworths.
Fraser-Tytler, P 1864 *History of Scotland*, 4, 286.
Gaimster, D 1987 'The supply of Rhenish stoneware to London 1350-1600', *London Archaeol*, 5(13), 339-47.
Gallagher, D B & Sharp, A 1986 *Pypes of Tabaca*. Edinburgh.
Gibson, C 1996 *Signs and Symbols*, 36. London: Grange Books.
Good, G L 1987 'The Pottery', *in* Good, G L 'The Excavation of two docks at Narrow Quay, Bristol, 1978-9', *Post-Medieval Archaeol*, 21 (1987), 34-100.
Good, G L & Tabraham, C J 1981 'Excavations at Threave Castle, Galloway, 1974-78', *Medieval Archaeology*, 25 (1981), 90-140.
Good, G L and Tabraham, C J 1988 'Excavations at Smailholm Tower, Roxburghshire', *Proc Soc Antiq Scot*, 118 (1988).
Goodall, A R 1983 'The Finds', *in* Mayes & Butler, 1983, 231-239.
Goodall, I H 1982 'Iron objects', *in* Murray, J C (ed), 1982, 188-9.
Goodall, I H 1983 'Iron objects', *in* Mayes & Butler, 1983, 240-52.
Gooder, E 1984 'The finds from the cellar of the old hall, Temple Balsall, Warwickshire', *Post Medieval Archaeology*, 18 (1984), 229.
Greig, D C (ed) 1988 *Geology of the Eyemouth District*: Memoir for 1:50,000 geological sheet 34, (Scotland). British Geological Survey. London: HMSO.
Greig, M K & Greig, C 1989 'Remains of a 12th-century structure and other medieval features on the Knoll of Castle Point, Troup (Cullykhan), Banff and Buchan', *Proc Soc Antiq Scot*, 119 (1989), 279-96.
Grew, F & de Neergaard, M 1988 *Shoes and patterns*, 125. Museum of London. London: HMSO.
Gunn, W 1900 'Geology of Belford, Holy Island and the Farne Islands, Northumberland'. (Explanation of quarter-sheet 110 SE, New Series, Sheet 4 =Memoir of the Geological Survey of England & Wales), 70 & 120.
Hackenbroch, Y 1979 *Renaissance Jewellery*. London: Sotheby Parke Bernet.
Haggarty, G & Jennings, S 1994 'The Imported Pottery from Fast Castle, near Dunbar, Scotland', *Medieval Ceramics*, 16 (1992), 45-54.
Haggarty, G & Will, R 1995 'Ceramic Material', *in* Lewis, J & Ewart, G, *Jedburgh Abbey*, 98-105 (=Soc Antiq Scot Monogr Ser, 10).
Hald, M 1980 *Ancient Danish Textiles from Bogs and Burials*, Fig 244. Copenhagen.
Hall, D 1982 'The Pottery', *in* Wordsworth, J & Garden, A R, 'Lesmahagow Priory', *Glasgow Archaeol J*, 9 (1982), fiche.
Hannay, R K (ed) 1932 *Acts of the Lords of Council in Public Affairs, 1501-1554*, 8. Edinburgh: HM General Register House.
Harding D W (ed) 1982 *Later Prehistoric Settlement in South-East Scotland* (= Univ Edinburgh Dept Archaeol Occas Pap 8). Edinburgh.
Hare, J N 1985 *Battle Abbey: the eastern range and the excavations of 1978-80*, (=Historic Buildings & Monuments Commission Archaeological Report, 2). London.
Harvey, J H 1975 '*Mediaeval Craftsmen*'. London & Sydney: Batsford.
Hawkins, J 1787 *The Life of Dr Samuel Johnson*, 1. London.
Hedges, J W 1977 'Medieval and post-medieval finds from Exeter, 1971-1980', *in* Allen, J P (ed), *Exeter Archaeological Reports*, 3 (1977), 334-6.

Henig, M 1977 'Objects of bone, antler, and shell', 160-6 ('Bone instrument pegs', 163-6), *in* Durham, B, 1977.
Henkes, H E 1994 *Glas zonder Glans*. Rotterdam Papers 9.
Hinton, D 1982 *Medieval jewellery from the eleventh to the fifteenth century*. Aylesbury: Shire.
Hist MSS Comm 1905 *Manuscripts of His Grace the Duke of Rutland preserved at Belvoir Castle*, 4. London: Historical Manuscripts Commission.
Holden, E W 1963 'Excavations at the deserted medieval village of Hangleton', part 1, *Sussex Archaeological Collections*, 101, 54-181.
Holdsworth, P (ed) 1987 *Excavations in the Medieval Burgh of Perth, 1979-1981* (=Soc Antiq Scot Monogr Ser, 5). Edinburgh.
Holmes, E F 1988 'Sewing Thimbles', Finds Research Group 700 - 1700 (1988), Datasheet 3, 3.
Hume, I N 1972 *Artifacts of Colonial America*, 219-20.. New York: Knopf.
Hunter, F J, McDonnell, J G, Pollard, A M, Morris, C R & Rowlands, C C 1993 'The scientific identification of archaeological jet-like artefacts', *Archaeometry*, 35, 69-89.
Hunter, F & Nicholson 1997 'The Jet, Shale and Cannel Coal', *in* Hill, P, *Whithorn and St Ninian: The Excavation of a Monastic Town, 1984-91*. Stroud: Whithorn Trust / Alan Sutton, 441-3.
Hurst, J G 1971 'Sixteenth-century Beauvais drinking jugs', *Groupe de Recherches et d'Etudes sur la Ceramique du Beauvaisis*, Bull No 3, 6-15.
Hurst, J G, Neal, D S & Van Beuningen, H J E 1986 *Pottery produced and traded in North-West Europe 1350-1650*. Rotterdam Papers 6.
IGS 1998 Cromarty: Scotland Sheet 94, Solid Geology, 1:63,360 Ser. Edinburgh: Institute of Geological Sciences. (see also Armstrong, M 1977).
Innes, C (ed) 1867 *The Ledger of Andrew Halyburton, 1492-1503*, 193. Edinburgh.
*Inventory of Argyll* 1971 *Argyll: An Inventory of the Ancient Monuments: Kintyre*, (1) 1971, 157-9. Edinburgh, RCAHMS.
*Inventory of Argyll* 1980 *Argyll: An Inventory of the Monuments: Mull, Tiree, Coll & Northern Argyll*, (3) 1980, 209-17. Edinburgh, RCAHMS.
*Inventory of Argyll* 1984 *Argyll: An Inventory of the Monuments: Islay, Jura, Colonsay & Oronsay*, (5) 1984, 268-75. Edinburgh, RCAHMS.
James, J 1986 *Hurst Castle; an illustrated history*. Stanbridge: The Dovecote Press.
Jarvis, K S 1983 *Excavations in Christchurch 1969-1980*. Dorset Natural History & Archaeological Society.
Jennings, S 1981 *Eighteen centuries of pottery from Norwich* (=East Anglian Archaeology Ser, 13.
Jobey, G 1976 'Traprain Law', 191-204, *in* Harding D W (ed), 1976, *Hillforts*. London: Academic Press.
Johnston, D A 1994 'Carronbridge, Dumfries & Galloway: the excavation of Bronze Age cremations, Iron Age settlements and a Roman camp', *Proc Soc Antiq Scot*, 124, 233-91.
Julien, N 1996 *The Mammoth Dictionary of Symbols*, 452. London.
Kellenbenz, H 1983 'The Fustian Industry of the Ulm Region in the 15th & early 16th centuries', *in* Harte, N B & Ponting, K G, *Cloth & Clothing in Medieval Europe - Essays in Memory of Professor E M Carus Wilson*. Pasold Studies in Textile History 2 (1983), 259-76. London.
Kennaway, M 1992 *Fast Castle: The Early Years*. Edinburgh Archaeological Field Society, Edinburgh.
Kenyon, G H 1967 *The Glass Industry of the Sussex Weald*. Leicester.
King, D 1960 'Les Velours Renaissance sont-ils espagnols ou italiens?', *Bulletin de Liaison du C.I.E.T.A.*, 12 (1960), 10-11.
King, D & King, M 1988 'Silk weaves of Lucca in 1376', *in* Estham, I & Nockert, M (eds), *Opera Textilia Variorum Temporum*, Museum of National Antiquities, Stockholm Studies, 8 (1988), 75.
Klein, D & Lloyd, W 1991 *The History of Glass*. London: MacMillan.
Knippenberg, W H Th 1962 'Pijpaarden beeldjes', *Brabants Heem*, 14, 54-57. Budapest.
Kolba, J H & Németh, A T 1986 *Treasures of Hungary - Gold & Silver from the 9th to the 19th century*, 7-8. Corvina.
Köster, K 1985 'Les coquilles et enseignes de pèlerinage de Saint-Jacques de Compostelle et des routes de Saint-Jacques en Occident', *in* Santiago catalogue, 1985, 85-95.
Laidlay, J W 1870 'Notice of an ancient structure and remains from a "kitchen midden" on an isolated rock near Seacliff, East Lothian', *Proc Soc Antiq Scot*, 8 (1868-70), 372-7.
Laing, L R 1971 'The Pottery', *in* 'Medieval and other material in Linlithgow Palace Museum', *Proc Soc Antiq Scot*, 101 (1968-9), 137-45.

# References

Laing, L R 1974 'Medieval Pottery from Coldingham Priory, Berwickshire', *Proc Soc Antiq Scot*, 104 (1971-2), 242-7.

Laing, L R & Robertson, W N 1973 'Notes on Scottish Medieval Pottery', *Proc Soc Antiq Scot*, 102 (1969-70), 146 54.

Lang, A 1902 *James VI and the Gowrie Mystery*. London.

Lawson, G 1980 *Stringed Musical Instruments, Artefacts in the Archaeology of Western Europe, 500 BC to AD 1200*. Unpublished PhD dissertation, Cambridge.

Lawson, G 1982 'Musical Instruments', 252 in Coad, J & Streeten, A, 'Excavations at Castle Acre Castle, Norfolk, 1972-77: country house and castle of the Norman Earls of Surrey'. *The Archaeological Journal*, 139 (1982).

Lawson, G 1985 'Musical instrument pegs', 151-4 in Hare, J N, *Battle Abbey: the eastern range and the excavations of 1978-80*. Historic Buildings & Monuments Commission Archaeological Report, 2, London.

Lawson, G 1990 'Jew's harp', 721-5, in Biddle, M, *Object and Economy in Medieval Winchester*, Winchester Studies Volume 7: Artefacts from Medieval Winchester, Part 2 (1990). Oxford.

Lawson, G 1997, 'Musical instrument remains', 196-203, in Knight, J K, 'Excavations at Montgomery Castle, Part 3: The finds other than metalwork', *Archaeologia Cambrensis*, 143 (1993) 1997, 139-203.

Lawson, G (in preparation), 'Report on a SEM study of coils of copper-alloy wire from Fast Castle (Berwickshire), Castle Sween (Argyll) and related finds' (for submission to *Archaeometry*).

Lewis J (forthcoming) 'Excavations at Spynie Palace'.

Lightbown, R W 1992 *Medieval European Jewellery*. London: Victoria & Albert Museum.

McAdam, A D, Clarkson, E K N, and Stone, P (eds) 1992 *Scottish Borders Geology: An Excursion Guide*, 23-30. Edinburgh: Scottish Academic Press.

MacAskill, N L 1983 'The Pottery', in Wordsworth, J, 'Excavation of the settlement at 13-21 Castle Street, Inverness, 1979', *Proc Soc Antiq Scot*, 112 (1982), 355-68.

MacAskill, N L 1987 'The Pottery', in Holdsworth 1987, 89-120.

McCarthy, M R & Brooks, C M 1988 *Medieval Pottery in Britain AD 900-1600*.

McGibbon, D & Ross, T 1889 *Castellated and Domestic Architecture of Scotland from the twelfth to the eighteenth century*, 3, 224. Edinburgh: David Douglas.

McGibbon, D & Ross, T 1990 *The Castellated and Domestic Architecture of Scotland from the twelfth to the eighteenth century*, 1, 562-73. Edinburgh: (reprinted by) James Thin, Mercat Press.

MacGregor, A G 1980 *Skeletal materials: their structure, technology and utilisation c AD 400-1200*. MPhil thesis, University of Durham.

MacGregor, A 1985 *Bone, antler, ivory and horn*. London: Croom Helm.

Macinnes, L 1984 'Brochs and the Roman occupation of lowland Scotland', *Proc Soc Antiq Scot*, 114 (1984), 235-49.

MacIvor, I 1981 'Artillery and major places of strength in the Lothians and the East Border, 1513-1542', in Caldwell, D H (ed), 1981b.

Mackenzie, W M 1913 *The battle of Bannockburn - a study in medieval warfare*, 108. Glasgow: James MacLehose & Sons.

MacMillan, 1997 *Quarries of Scotland*. TAN 12 (=Technical Advice Note 12). Edinburgh: Historic Scotland.

MacPhail, I M M 1979 *Dumbarton Castle*. Edinburgh: John Donald.

Mann, J E 1982 'Early Medieval Finds from Flaxengate 1: Objects of antler, bone, stone, horn, ivory, amber, and jet', *The Archaeology of Lincoln*, 14(1). London: Lincoln Archaeological Trust.

Margeson, S 1985 'The Small Finds', in Atkin, M, Carter, A & Evans, D H (eds), 'Excavations in Norwich 1971-1978' (2), *East Anglian Archaeology*, 26, 201-13.

Margeson, S 1993 'Norwich Households: The Medieval and Post-Medieval finds from Norwich Survey Excavations 1971-1978', *East Anglian Archaeology*, 4-5.

Marshall, J S 1983 *The Church in the Midst*, 194-5. Edinburgh: Edina Press.

Marshall, R K 1986 *Queen of Scots*, 80. Edinburgh: HMSO.

Marshall, R K & Dalgleish, G R (eds) 1991 *The Art of Jewellery in Scotland*, 19. Scottish National Portrait Gallery. Edinburgh: HMSO.

Martin, M 1698 *A Voyage to St. Kilda* (see Hawkins 1787, 473).

Masse, H J L J 1911 *Chats on Old Pewter*, 107-13 & 121. London.

Maxwell-Irving, A M T 'Early firearms and their influence on the military and domestic architecture of the Borders', *Proc Soc Antiq Scot*, 103 (1970-71), 193-224.

Mayes, P & Butler, L A S 1983 *Sandal Castle Excavations 1964-1973*. Wakefield: Wakefield Historical Publications.

Mazzaoui, M F 1981 *The Italian Cotton Industry in the Later Middle Ages*, 140-5, 157 & 190-1 note 39. Cambridge.

Megaw, J V S 1961 'An end-blown flute or flageolet from White Castle', *Medieval Archaeology*, 5 (1961), 176-80.

Megaw, J V S 1968 'Problems and non-problems in palaeo-organology: a medical miscellany', 333-58 *in* Coles, J M & Simpson, D D A (eds), *Studies in Ancient Europe: essays presented to Stuart Piggott*. Leicester.

Metcalf, D M (ed) 1977 *Coinage in Medieval Scotland (1100-1600)* (= Brit Archaeol Rep 45). Oxford.

Mitchell, G H, Walton, E K & Grant, D 1960 *Edinburgh Geology: An excursion guide*. Edinburgh Geolog Soc. Edinburgh: Oliver and Boyd.

Mitchell, K L 1988 *Fast Castle - A History from 1602*. Edinburgh Archaeological Field Society, Edinburgh.

Mitchiner, M 1988 *Jetons, Medalets & Tokens: The Medieval Period and Nuremberg*. London.

Monnas, L 1986 'Developments in figured velvet weaving in Italy during the 14th century', *Bulletin de Liaison du C I E T A*, 63/64, (1986), 64.

Moorhouse, S 1982 'The Pottery', *in* Hunter, J R, 'Medieval Berwick-upon-Tweed', *Archaeol Aeliana*, 5th ser, 10 (1982), 99-124.

Muller, H 1980 'A note on the composition of jet', *J Gemmology*, 17, 10-18.

Muller, H 1987 *Jet*. London: Butterworths.

Murdoch, K R 1989 *in* Mitchell, K L, 'Fast Castle Post-Excavation Report', Edinburgh Archaeological Field Society Annual Report, 1989.

Murdoch, K R 1997 'Glass', *in* Proudfoot, E & Kelly, C A, 'Excavations at Niddry Castle, West Lothian 1986-90', *Proc Soc Antiq Scot*, 127 (1997), 783-842.

Murdoch, T (ed) 1991 *Treasures and Trinkets*, 198, no 199.

Murray, J C 1982 'The Pottery', 116-76, *in* Murray J C (ed), 1982.

Murray, J C (ed) 1982 *Excavations in the Medieval Burgh of Aberdeen 1973-81*, (=Soc Antiq Scot Monogr Ser, 2). Edinburgh.

Murray, J E L 1977 'The Black Money of James III' *in* Metcalf, D M (ed), 115-30.

Muthesius, A 1982 'Anglo-Scandinavian finds from Lloyds Bank, Pavement', *in* MacGregor, A (ed), *The Archaeology of York: the small finds*, 17 (1982). Council for British Archaeology.

NCB 1958 *A short history of the Scottish coal-mining industry*. Edinburgh: National Coal Board (Scottish Division).

Neaverson, E 1947 *Medieval Castles in North Wales: a study of sites, water supply and building stones*. London.

*New Statistical Account of Scotland* 1845 Edinburgh: Blackwood & Sons.

Nicholson, R 1974 *Scotland. The Later Middle Ages*. The Edinburgh History of Scotland, vol 2. Edinburgh.

Nicolas, H (ed) 1843 *Proceedings and Ordinances of the Privy Council of England*, vol 1 (1843), 237.

NMS Catalogue = National Museums of Scotland Catalogue.

Norris, H 1938 *Costume & Fashion, The Tudors, 1547-1603*, 3(2). London: J M Dent & Sons.

North, J J 1975 *English Hammered Coinage*, vol 2. London.

Norton, C 1994 'Medieval Floor Tiles in Scotland', *in* Higgitt J (ed) *Medieval Art and Architecture in the Diocese of St.Andrews*, Brit Arch Assoc Conf Transact, 151 & 171-2.

Oakley, G E 1979 'The Copper Alloy Objects', *in* Williams 1979, 248-64.

O'Connor, S 1987 'The identification of osseous and keratinaceous material at York', *in* Starling K & Watkinson D (eds), *Archaeological Bone, Antler and Ivory*. United Kingdom Institute for Conservation of Historic and Artistic Works: Occasional Papers 5.

*Old Statistical Account of Scotland* 1794: See *Statistical Account of Scotland*, 1791-1799.

O'Neil 1944 *Criccieth Castle, Carnarvonshire*, 98 (1), 1-51.

Orton, C, Tyers, P & Vince, A 1993 *Pottery in Archaeology*. Cambridge.

Ottaway, P 1992 *Anglo-Scandinavian Ironwork from 16-22 Coppergate*. Archaeology of York, 17: The Small Finds. Council for British Archaeology, London.

Page, C 1978 'Stringed instrument-making in medieval England, and some Oxford harp-makers 1380-1466', *Galpin Society Journal*, 31 (1978), 44-67.

Paterson, J C 1958 *Scottish Glass, a Collector's Notes*, Edinburgh City Museums Occasional Publications, 1. Edinburgh.

Paton, H M (ed) 1957 *Accounts of the Masters of Works for building and repairing Royal Palaces and Castles, vol 1, 1529-1615*. Edinburgh: HMSO.

Perry, D R, Reid, A G & Lye, D M 1988 'Pitmiddle Village & Elcho Nunnery'. Perth: Perthshire Society of Natural Science.

Piggott, S 1953 'Three metal-work hoards of the Roman period from southern Scotland', *Proc Soc Antiq Scot*, 87 (1952-3), 1-50.

Piggott, S 1958 'Excavations at Braidwood Fort, Midlothian and Craig's Quarry, Dirleton, East Lothian', *Proc Soc Antiq Scot*, 91 (1957-58), 61-77.

Piggott, S & Piggott, C M 1952 'Excavations at Castle Law, Glencorse, and at Craig's Quarry, Dirleton, 948-9', *Proc Soc Antiq Scot*, 86 (1951-52), 191-6.

Platt, C & Coleman-Smith, R 1975 *Excavations in Medieval Southampton, 1953-1969* (2). Leicester University Press.

Pollard, A M, Bussell, G D & Baird, D C 1981 'The analytical investigation of Early Bronze Age jet and jet-like material from the Devizes Museum', *Archaeometry*, 23, 139-67.

Rankin, E 1981 *Cockburnspath - A documentary social history of a border parish*, (ed) Bulloch, J. Edinburgh: T & T Clark.

RCAHMS, 1980 *The Archaeological Sites and Monuments of Berwickshire District, Borders Region*. Edinburgh: Royal Commission on the Ancient and Historical Monuments of Scotland.

Remnant, M 1978 *Music Instruments of the West*. London.

Rensch, R 1969 *The Harp*. London.

Rice, P C 1980 *Amber - The Golden Gem of the Ages*, 3-23. Toronto: Van Nostrand Reinhold Company.

Robertson, A 1970 'Roman finds from non-Roman sites in Scotland', *Britannia*, 1, 198-226.

Robertson, A S 1942 'A Roman Oven at Mumrills, Falkirk', *Proc Soc Antiq Scot*, 76 (1941-42), 119-27.

Ruckley, N A 1984 'Inchkeith: the water supply of an island fortress', *Fortress*, (12), 67-82.

Ruckley, N A 1990 'Water Supply of Medieval Castles in the United Kingdom', *Fortress*, 7 (1990), 14-26.

Ruckley, N A 1991 'Geological and Geomorphological factors influencing the form and development of Edinburgh Castle', *The Edinburgh Geologist*, 26 (1991), 18-26.

Rule, M 1982 *The Mary Rose - The Excavation and Raising of Henry VIII's Flagship*, 168-83. London: Conway Maritime Press.

Russell, J 1938 'Fast Castle: its Romantic Story', *Trans East Lothian Antiq and Field Naturalists' Soc*, 3 (1934-8), 40-8.

Russell-White, C J 1995 'Medieval features and finds from Balfarg / Balbirnie', *Proc Soc Antiq Scot*, 125 (1995), 1001-1021.

Ryder, M L 1968 'The origin of spinning', *Textile History* 1, 73-82.

Ryder, M L 1970 'Structure and seasonal change of the coat in Scottish wild goats', *J Zoology*, 161 (1970), 335-62.

Ryder, M L 1983a *Sheep and Man*. London: Duckworth.

Ryder, M L 1983b 'The hair and wool from the Perth High Street excavations', *in* Proudfoot, B (ed), 'Site, Environment and Economy', Symposia of the Association for Environmental Archaeology (3), BAR International Series 173 (1983), 33-41.

Ryder, M L, 1984 'Wools from textiles in the *Mary Rose*, a sixteenth-century English Warship', *J Archaeol Sci*, 11 (1984), 337-43.

Ryder, M L 1987a 'Report on hair from fifteenth-century tanning pit in Gallowgate, Aberdeen' (submitted).

Ryder, M L 1987b 'The measurement of wool fibres in yarns as an aid to defining carpet type', *Oriental Carpet & Textile Studies*, 3 (1987), 134-52.

Ryder, M L 1987c 'Evolution of the fleece', *Scientific American*, 255 (1), (1987), 112-9.

Ryder, M L 1988 'The evolution of Scottish breeds of sheep', *Scottish Studies*, 12 (1988), 127-67.

Ryder, M L 1989 'Report on wool from clothing of sixteenth century basque whalers in Canada' (submitted).

Ryder, M L 1990 'The Natural Pigmentation of Animal Textile Fibres', *Textile History*, 20 (1990), 135-48.

Ryder, M L & Gabra-Sanders, T 1985 'The Application of Microscopy to Textile History', *Textile History*, 16 (1985), 123-40.

Ryder, M L & Gabra-Sanders, T 1992 'Textiles from Fast Castle, Berwickshire, Scotland', *Textile History*, 23(1) 1992, 5-22.

Sabatier, A 1908 'Etude Revisionelle des Sceaux de Plomb Fiscaux et Commerciaux', *Bull Soc des Sciences et Arts du Beaujolais*, 9 (1908), 5-30, 111-47, nos 49, 50.

Salzman, L F 1923 *Medieval English Industries*. Oxford.

Salzman, L F 1952 *Building in England*. Oxford: Clarendon Press.

Sanger, K & Kinnaird, A 1993 *Tree of Strings (Crann nan Teud): a History of the Harp in Scotland*. Temple, Midlothian (1992): Kinmor Music.

Santiago catalogue, 1985 *Santiago de Compostela: 1000 ans de Pèlerinage Européen*. Gand: Centrum voor Kunst en Cultuur.

Sayre, E V & Smith, R W 1974 'Analytical Studies of Ancient Egyptian Glass', *in* Bishay, A (ed), 1974, *Recent Advances in Science and Technology of Materials*, 3, 47-70. Plenum Press.

*Scarborough Castle Guide* 1960 London: HMSO.

Schmedding, B 1978 *Mittelalterliche Textilien in Kirchen und Kloster der Schweiz*, (1978), No 162, 191-2. Bern.

Scott, C & Blanchard, L 1984 'The Pottery', *in* Blanchard, L (ed), 1983, 503-10.

Scott, W 1819 *The Bride of Lammermoor*. Edinburgh

Shepherd, I A G 1985 'Jet and Amber', *in* Clarke, D V *et al*, *Symbols of Power at the Time of Stonehenge*, 204-16. Edinburgh: NMAS / HMSO.

Silver, I A 1971 'The ageing of domestic animals', *in* Brothwell, D & Higgs, E (eds), *Science in Archaeology*.

Simon, D 1988 'A Conjectural Illustration of Fast Castle', 76-80, and Cover, *in* Mitchell, K L, 1988.

Simpson, D D A 1967 'Excavations at Kintraw, Argyll', *Proc Soc Antiq Scot*, 99 (1966-67), 54-9.

Simpson, W D 1976 *Dunnottar Castle, historical and descriptive*. Dunnottar Castle Guide (13th ed). Aberdeen: Milne and Wyllies.

Sinclair, J (ed) 1791-1799 see *Statistical Account of Scotland*.

Skinner, B C 1969 *The Lime Industry in the Lothians*. EUEA Studies in Local History, University of Edinburgh.

Slezer, J 1696 *Plan of Dumbarton Castle*. Public Record Office, MPF 244.

Spearman, R M 1983 'Metalworking debris', *in* Blanchard, L M (ed), 1983, 514.

Spearman, R M 1987 *in* Holdsworth, P, 1987, 157.

Spiers, C H 1973 'Deer-skin leathers and their use for costume', *Costume*, 7 (1973), 20.

*Statistical Account of Scotland* 1791-1799 Sinclair, J (ed). Edinburgh: William Creech.

*Statistical Account of Scotland* 1845: See *New Statistical Account of Scotland*

Stevenson, R B K 1955 'Pins and the Chronology of Brochs', *Proc Prehistory Soc*, 21, 282-94.

Stewart, I H 1967 *The Scottish Coinage*, revised edition. London.

Stoddart, J 1801 *Remarks on Local Scenery and Manners in Scotland, 2.* London.

Swann, J 1973 'Shoe Fashions to 1600', *Trans Mus Assistants Group*, 12 (1973), 14-24.

Syer Cuming, H 1879 'On Thimbles', *J Brit Archaeol Assoc*, 35, 238-42.

Thomas, M C 1982 413-6 *in* McGavin, N, 'Excavations in Kirkwall, 1978', *Proc Soc Antiq Scot*, 112 (1982), 392-436.

Thoms, L M 1978 'Coarse pottery', *in* Schofield, J, 'Excavations south of Edinburgh High Street, 1973-4', *Proc Soc Antiq Scot*, 107 (1975-6), 190-206.

Thoms, L M 1983 'Preliminary list of North European pottery in Scotland', *in* Davey, P & Hodges, R (eds), *Ceramics and Trade: The production and distribution of later medieval pottery in north west Europe*, 254-5. Sheffield.

Thornton, J H 1973a 'Excavated Shoes to 1600', *Trans Mus Assistants Group*, 12 (1973), 2-13.

Thornton, J H 1973b 'A Glossary of shoe terms', *Trans Mus Assistants Group*, 12 (1973), 45-48.

Toy, S 1963 *The Castles of Great Britain*, 3rd ed, 100-1. London: Heinemann.

Toynbee, J M C 1964 *Art in Britain under the Romans*. Oxford: Clarendon Press.

Trueman, A E, 1938 *The scenery of England and Wales*, 194-7.

Tudor-Craig, P 1973 *Richard III*. National Portrait Gallery, London, (1973), no 135, 59.

van der Werff, J H 1987 'Roman Amphoras at "De Horden" (Wijk bij Duurstede)', *Berichten van de Rijksdienst voor het Oudheidkundig Bodemonderzoek*, 37, 153-72.

van Haaren, H 1992 'Zwarte Archeologie', *Scarebee*, Okt/Nov 1992, 37.

Vince, A G 1985 'The Saxon and medieval pottery of London: a review', *Medieval Archaeol*, 24, 25-93.

von den Driesch, A 1976 *A guide to the measurement of animal bones from archaeological sites*. Peabody Museum Bulletin, 1976.

Vons-Comis, S Y 1982 'Medieval textile finds from the Netherlands', *in* Jorgensen, L B & Tidow, K (eds), *Textilsymposium Neumünster*, (1982), 151-2.

Wadsworth, A P & Mann, J de L 1968 *The Cotton Trade and Industrial Lancashire*. New York reprint, (1968), 18-9.

Walton, P 1981 'An excavation in the castle ditch, Newcastle-upon-Tyne, 1974-76', *in* Harbottle, B & Ellison, M (eds), *Archaeologia Aeliana*, 5th ser, 9 (1981), 193.

Ward, J 1985 *Excavations at Fast Castle: The Well*. Edinburgh Archaeological Field Society. Edinburgh.

Waterman, D M 1964 'The Water Supply of Dundrum Castle, Co Down', *Ulster Journal of Archaeology*, 3rd Ser, 27, 136-9.